Sanctity and Self-Inflicted Violence in Chinese Religions, 1500–1700

Sanctity and Self-Inflicted Violence in Chinese Religions, 1500–1700

JIMMY YU

OXFORD
UNIVERSITY PRESS

OXFORD
UNIVERSITY PRESS

Oxford University Press, Inc., publishes works that further
Oxford University's objective of excellence
in research, scholarship, and education.

Oxford New York
Auckland Cape Town Dar es Salaam Hong Kong Karachi
Kuala Lumpur Madrid Melbourne Mexico City Nairobi
New Delhi Shanghai Taipei Toronto

With offices in
Argentina Austria Brazil Chile Czech Republic France Greece
Guatemala Hungary Italy Japan Poland Portugal Singapore
South Korea Switzerland Thailand Turkey Ukraine Vietnam

Published by Oxford University Press, Inc.
198 Madison Avenue, New York, New York 10016

www.oup.com

Library of Congress Cataloging-in-Publication Data
Yu, Jimmy Yung Fung, 1968–
Sanctity and self-inflicted violence in Chinese religions, 1500–1700 / Jimmy Yu.
p. cm.
Includes bibliographical references (p.) and index.
ISBN 978–0–19–984488–3 (hardcover)
ISBN 978–0–19–984490–6 (pbk.)
ISBN 978–0–19–984489–0 (ebook)
1. Self-mutilation—Religious aspects—History—16th century.
2. Rites and ceremonies—China—History—16th century.
3. Violence—Religious aspects—History—16th century.
4. Self-mutilation—Religious aspects—History—17th century.
5. Rites and ceremonies—China—History—17th century.
6. Violence—Religious aspects—History—17th century.
7. China–Religious life and customs. I. Title.
BL1812.R57Y85 2012
299.5′11342—dc23
2011035537

Dedicated to the memory of my teacher
Venerable Sheng Yen (1930–2009)
and my father, Pin Yu (1928–2011)

Contents

List of Illustrations

Acknowledgments

MANY PEOPLE HAVE made this project's evolution from dissertation to book possible, and I am grateful to them all. Though it would be impossible to mention all of them, I single out the most important ones. I would first like to express my deepest gratitude to the late Venerable Sheng Yen, whose life and scholarship inspired my interest in the study of religion and of China in the sixteenth and seventeenth centuries. It would not be an exaggeration to say that, without his heartfelt concern for my progress as a student and as a person, I would not be where I am today. I am immensely grateful to my mentors and teachers at Princeton University, who, over the years of my graduate study and the writing of this book, shaped my historical instincts and habits in numerous ways. Stephen F. Teiser, Susan Naquin, and Jacqueline Stone have generously offered their time and wisdom. Their uncanny abilities to see my point, even when it was lost to me, have deeply influenced the progress of this book. I am particularly grateful to Stephen Teiser, whose kindness, intellectual energy, and keen eye for the unanswered questions served as a source of inspiration and confidence when my imagination was failing me. My research and study at Princeton have permitted me to learn from scholars such as Ben Elman and Willard Peterson, who brought to bear the rigor and thoughtfulness of our readings of sixteenth-century texts. Many thanks also go to my colleagues at the Center for the Study of Religion at Princeton.

Several scholars have commented on parts of this book at various stages over the years. The first is Daniel Stevenson, who has been generous with his time as an informal teacher, supporter, and critic since the time I first studied under him at the University of Kansas. James Benn, Barend ter Haar, Lynn Struve, and Miaw-fen Lü have also helped me greatly by providing suggestions and sources. My research and writing would not have been nearly as enjoyable without the companionship of colleagues and friends: Asuka Sango, Stuart Young, Jessey Choo, Hsueh-Yi Lin, Paul Copp, Mark Meulenbeld, Ian Chapmen, Mark Rowe, Bryan and Michiru Lowe, Levi McLaughlin,

Ethan Lindsay, Sarah Irving, and Bryan Cuevas. They have provided stimulation and advice, critical suggestions, encouragement, and friendship. I also want to thank Harry Miller for his numerous editorial suggestions. I am grateful to Cynthia Read and the anonymous reviewers for their support and suggestions in developing this book.

Finally, whatever in the long run I have accomplished in writing this book, as elsewhere, I am indebted to my wife, Chiho Nishida, for her love and emotional support for all my endeavors over the years.

Tallahassee, FL
June 2011

A Note on Dynasties and Reigns

Major Chinese Dynasties

Zhou (ca. 1045–256 B.C.E.)
Qin (221–206 B.C.E.)
Han (202 BCE–220 C.E.)
Jin (265–420)
Southern and Northern Dynasties (420–588)
Sui (581–617)
Tang (618–907)
Song (960–1279)
Yuan (1279–1368)
Ming (1368–1644)
Qing (1644–1911)

Reigns of Ming Emperors

Hongwu Taizu 洪武太祖 (1369–1398)
Jianwen Huidi 建文惠帝 (1399–1402)
Yongle Chengzu 永樂成祖 (1403–1424)
Hongxi Renzong 洪熙仁宗 (1425–1425)
Xuande Xuanzong 宣德宣宗 (1426–1435)
Zhentong Yingzong 正統英宗 (1436–1457)
Jingtai Daizong 景泰代宗 (1450–1456)
Tianshun Yingzong 天順英宗 91457–1464)
Chenghua Xianzong 成化憲宗 (1465–1487)
Hongzhi Xiaozong 弘治孝宗 (1488–1505)
Zhengde Wuzong 正德武宗 (1506–1521)
Jiajing Shizong 嘉靖世宗 (1522–1566)
Longqing Muzong 隆慶穆宗 (1567–1572)
Wanli Shenzong 萬曆神宗 (1573–1619)

Taichang Guangzong 泰昌光宗 (1620–1620)
Tianqi Xizong 天啟熹宗 (1621–1627)
Chongzhen Sizong 崇禎思宗 (1628–1644)

Reigns of Early Qing Emperors

Shunzhi Shizu 順治世祖 (1644–1661)
Kangxi Shengzu 康熙聖祖 (1662–1772)
Yongzheng Shizong 雍正世宗 (1723–1735)
Qianlong Gaozong 乾隆高宗 (1736–1795)

Sanctity and Self-Inflicted Violence in Chinese Religions, 1500–1700

Introduction

IN 1532 A twelve-year-old boy named Feng Xingke 馮行可 cut open his body and used his own blood to write a letter to the emperor, begging to substitute his own life for that of his father, a minister who had been imprisoned for criticizing an influential eunuch. The emperor was originally offended by the father's criticism but was so moved by the boy's filial piety (*xiao* 孝) that he pardoned the father. Some years later, the subsequent emperor rewarded both the father and the son with imperial positions for their acts of righteousness and for the son's filial piety. Modern scholars associate the practice of blood writing with Chinese Buddhism. However, by the sixteenth and seventeenth centuries, it had become a socially sanctioned and widely recognized expression of sincerity. In this context Feng Xingke demonstrated his filiality through blood writing in an effort to negotiate his father's fate. His act not only challenged the first emperor's authority but also eventually won him and his father political positions.

In the mid-seventeenth century the Buddhist esoteric cleric Zhoufu 周福, also known as "Zhou the Transcendent (Zhouxian 周仙)" by local villagers, immolated himself (*zifen* 自焚). Before his act, he said to his disciples and the villagers that "If there is ever a drought in the future, call my name, and rain will fall heavily!" After his passing, the villagers' prayer to Zhoufu to end a drought would always be rewarded with rain, along with sounds of the wooden fish and the chanting of spells. His self-immolation transformed him into a rain-bestowing god. Modern scholars may explain the rain-making ritual of self-immolation as the workings of the sympathetic universe, in which a practitioner's virtue stimulates the benevolent response of heaven. Yet the distinctive feature and rhetorical marker used in primary sources for this sort of practice by Buddhist clerics, local shamans, and community magistrates is not "virtue" but *ling* 靈, or "numinous efficacy."[1] Moreover, even though he was a Buddhist cleric, Zhoufu exhibited thaumaturgical powers, not infrequently (and perhaps mistakenly) associated with Daoism, which complicates our idea of what a

"Buddhist" is. For example, his story is included in a Buddhist hagiography, but contemporary villagers called him a "transcendent," a loaded term reserved for seekers of everlasting life. The story may appear to be a straightforward hagiography of a local holy man, but upon close inspection, it forces us to recognize that Zhoufu's act cannot be tied to any specific religious tradition or cultural *topoi*, as defined by either premodern writers or scholarly taxonomy. Despite his ambiguous identity, what stands out in his act is the performance of thaumaturgy, which cuts across social and religious boundaries.

These two vignettes, which are discussed in chapters 2 and 5, respectively, are windows into a wide range of self-inflicted, violent bodily practices in sixteenth- and seventeenth-century China. Thousands of men and women during this time exercised the instrumentality of their bodies to accomplish different goals. Buddhists and non-Buddhists alike sliced open their tongues and fingers to copy scriptures with their blood; emperors and magistrates exposed their naked bodies to bring rain; sons and daughters secretly sliced off a piece of their own flesh to feed their parents to demonstrate their filial piety; young, chaste widows cut off their noses to permanently diminish their eligibility when forced to remarry. During this time nearly every gazetteer in China devoted sections to pious children and chaste widows who engaged in such extreme practices ("extreme" only according to our modern sensibilities). Graphic illustrations of self-inflicted violence are also found in religious tracts, illustrated books, popular literature, fiction, and poetry during this period. In some sources, performers are eulogized and revered as exemplars to be emulated. In others, they are scorned, and their acts are questioned. Yet, whether revered and scorned, these practices were an inextricable part of the mores of sixteenth- and seventeenth-century China.

The abundance of documentation of self-inflicted violence during this period raises many questions: What were the agendas of the different performers and authors who narrated their stories of self-inflicted violence? What were the material conditions that fostered these practices? What did these practices conceal and reveal? What ends did they serve? How do these practices reinforce or challenge cultural values? Most important, why should people who are interested in Chinese religions find this phenomenon both intriguing and significant?

The Significance of This Study

Sinologists have long recognized the syncretic nature of the "three religions" of Confucianism (Rujia 儒家), Buddhism (Fojiao 佛教), and Daoism (Daojiao

道教) in later China.[2] Yet the rhetoric of what scholars would consider syncretism is never so simple; many of the sources that scholars rely on have the hidden agenda of privileging discursive Confucian perspectives.[3] Moreover, when we historicize these traditions as discrete "isms" with a discrete text-based system of beliefs and doctrines—in other words, symbolic forms—that somehow govern bodily action and ritual, we fail to appreciate the rich, variegated forms of Chinese religious life.[4] Both tendencies of historicizing Chinese religions from the Sinological vantage point of Confucianism and seeing all three "religions" as a system of symbols are, of course, inextricably linked. In this book, I approach "syncretism" from another perspective.

I do not replace existing scholarly narratives about syncretism by painting another grand picture of Chinese religions. I want to shift our gaze to very specific cases of extreme bodily practices carried out by Buddhist clerics, educated writers, Daoist practitioners, local village shamans, chaste widows, scholar-officials, and children. Their stories reveal the central thesis of this book: self-inflicted violence in the form of socially sanctioned and routinized bodily mutilations was a widespread and highly visible part of the sixteenth- and seventeenth-century cultural life that transcended religious boundaries. It was the most effective way people negotiated their subjectivity and sanctity. Performers engaged in self-inflicted violence to exercise power and to affect people, events, and the environment. It enabled them to graphically and viscerally demonstrate moral values, reinstitute order, forge new social relations, and secure boundaries against the threat of moral ambiguity. Their acts were often systematic, ritualized, and replete with meaning for both the performers and their audiences.

The prevalence of these practices can be attributed to the economic prosperity, the increase in literacy, the production of numerous works that explored human passion and subjectivity, and the repercussion of progressive and changing intellectual and moral discourses that began in the fifteenth century and peaked in the sixteenth and seventeenth centuries. These changes reconfigured the way people related to their own bodies and cultural values; they cannot be pinpointed to one particular cultural sphere, religious tradition, or textual source but can be appreciated only after a comprehensive examination of all forms of evidence, including official history, local gazetteers, morality books, religious hagiographies, popular novels, and illustrated books for popular consumption. It is in these works that one recognizes the extent to which self-inflicted violence figures prominently in the culture.

It is important to look beyond emic categories and rhetorical tropes presented in primary sources. The pattern of self-inflicted violence cannot be topologically objectified by any single category or tradition. It was often woven into the larger cultural milieu through cultural markers such as "blood writing," "ritual exposure," or "thigh slicing." These markers signal highly structured, even ritualized, regimens of action that were distinct from other acts. They were recognized and intelligible to nearly everyone in society, from adults (both men and women) to children. Yet, because they were often veiled by emic discourses such as loyalty, filial piety, female chastity, and religious orthodoxy, all of which legitimated the state, secured the family, and established interpersonal and cosmic relations, it is difficult for scholars to recognize their relationship to one another. Understanding the significance of these markers and their relationships would allow us to appreciate a much more vibrant and dynamic side of Chinese religiosity that was centered on bodily performances, which scholarship has tended to ignore.

Self-inflicted violence in the sixteenth and seventeenth centuries was a constituent and sanctioned aspect of cultural life. Yet, sometimes it was in tension with the prescriptive and ideological teachings of established religious traditions. Hence it was subject to suspicion and criticism even as it was praised. For example, certain influential writers at the time criticized the practice of filial slicing by citing the *Classic of Filial Piety* (*Xiaojing* 孝經) to justify not harming one's body. Yet, the descriptive reality was that performers who engaged in self-inflicted violence were regularly eulogized by other influential writers and even rewarded by the imperial state. People engaged in self-inflicted violence for many reasons. For example, Buddhist clerics such as Ouyi Zhixu 蕅益智旭 (1599–1655) regularly engaged in self-mutilation and also encouraged others to follow suit even though his own mentor vehemently condemned the practices.[5]

I use this category of "self-inflicted violence" heuristically to refer to culturally sanctioned expressions of sanctity that involve self-mutilation and transfiguration. I have found this category quite productive in answering questions about the pattern of these sorts of behavior in premodern China. This category is historically attentive to native concepts in premodern China and is theoretically applicable to broaden certain scholarly discussions. It operates within and at the same time complicates prescriptive and normative discourses on filial piety, loyalty, female chastity, and religious austerity by concentrating on how performers engaged in various extreme practices to achieve many social and personal goals. It also challenges Western categories of violence and asceticism by showing that subjects who engaged in such acts held assumptions that differed greatly from our modern sensibilities and ideas, which stem from the Judeo-Christian tradition.

This book examines a range of practices, including blood writing, filial body-slicing, chastity mutilation and suicide, and ritual exposure and self-immolation, which were common during the sixteenth and seventeenth centuries. Blood writing, or *xieshu* 血書, refers to the practice of using one's own blood to copy a particular scripture or even write out a memorial to the emperor. Performers usually sliced their tongue or finger tips to draw blood. Sometimes the particular text they copied was quite long, consisting of thousands of characters, and so the ritual of cutting and drawing blood would occur every few days. Because the winter months would make the blood congeal, blood writers usually stopped the practice during that season. Therefore, depending on the climate, the practice could have lasted for many years. There was also a structured technology for drawing and storing blood so it would not congeal.

The second practice of filial body slicing is my rendering of the term *gegu* 割股, which literally means "slicing a piece of flesh from one's thigh." However, the term in the sixteenth century came to refer to slicing flesh from any part of the body. Some scholars define it as a "Confucian" practice, but its genesis and etymology are quite complex. The purported aim of this practice was for filial sons and daughters to use their own flesh as nourishment to feed ailing parents in order to repay them in a condensed form for what they had received while still in the womb and throughout childhood. However, performers engaged in filial slicing for many purposes, and, as I explain in chapter 3, sometimes children were coerced into the practice by their parents.

The third ritual—chastity mutilation and suicide—was practiced by young girls and widows who, out of their "pure moral fidelity," or *zhenjie* 貞節, in order to resist forced remarriage and rape (*shoujie* 守節). They de-eroticized themselves by cutting off their noses (*gebi* 割鼻) or other parts of their bodies. The state regularly rewarded women who showed their wifely fidelity because it resembled political loyalty through self-sacrifice. Shrines were built for widows who killed themselves to resist rape or forced remarriage. However, what lurks behind these imperial recognitions may have been a general fear of the deceased widows' vengeful ghosts. In premodern China, those who died wrongly, prematurely, or violently were particularly feared. The notion that a person unjustly killed could return as a vengeful ghost was quite pervasive in Chinese culture. Also, the writings of the educated elite, which aimed to use the stories of chastity mutilation as moral lessons, complicate the boundaries of morality and entertainment.

Practices of ritual exposure (*baoshen* 暴身) and self-immolation (*zifen* 自焚) were rain-making techniques in times of extreme drought. Performers of rain-making rituals included the emperor, local magistrates, Buddhist and Daoist clerics, and community shamans (both male and female). People argued about which kind of religious specialist was more effective in bringing rain, but they never questioned the body's ability, particularly the naked body, to intervene in the workings of the cosmos. This power was corporeal and thaumaturgical. Writers have articulated ritual exposure and self-immolation differently, but the performers shared a common understanding of the awesome power that bodies could produce.

One of the problems in delineating and historicizing these practices is that they are usually accompanied by rich repertoires of exemplary trope and narrative, which are inextricably tied to how modern scholarship categorizes and compartmentalizes "Chinese religions." For example, current scholarship still reproduces the same prescriptive tropes that filial children should not harm the body because of the Confucian axiom that the body is a gift from one's parents.[6] Yet, as I show in this book, performers demonstrated their filial devotion to parents through self-sacrifice, self-mutilation, and self-maiming—the very practices that were supposedly condemned. The historical realities of filial piety and other cultural ideals were much more complicated than prescriptive, philosophical ideals.

As a distinctive refrain, these practices cut across and run through multiple options, in effect blurring their presumed boundaries. For example, narratives of chaste widows who took their own lives in order to come back as ghosts to haunt those who had wronged them often presume a popular understanding of karmic retribution and rebirth. They may have prayed to Guanyin 觀音, or the Bodhisattva of Compassion, or Tudi gong 土地公, the Earth God, before they took their own lives. Yet, I have never come across cases in which women explicitly categorize their "beliefs" or "prayers" into separate spheres of "Buddhism," "Daoism," or "Confucianism." Even a clear boundary between their secular lives and their religious beliefs does not seem to exist. There is little support for circumscribing any particular practice in this book as Confucius, Buddhist, Daoist, or anything else. Similarly in the case of Zhoufu, whom I describe at the beginning of the introduction and discuss in chapter 5, his supposed vocation was a Buddhist monk, but he was known by local villagers as a *xian* 仙, or "transcendent" or "immortal."[7] If we are to attend to the ways in which people of the sixteenth and seventeenth centuries lived their lives, experienced their worlds, and embodied moral values, we must take seriously the dynamic ways in which different traditions, customs, and values wove together seamlessly in people's experiences.

Self-inflicted violence as a category allows us to see our own biases, which tend to marginalize certain phenomena in Chinese culture while highlighting others. For example, certain ideas inform us that Confucianism is humanistic and rational and that Daoism favors naturalness or that Buddhism teaches a philosophy of the middle way, free from the extremes of hedonism or asceticism. There is also a strong bias in scholarship that privileges text-based belief and ideology over bodily action. Self-inflicted violence challenges these caricatures and brings to light larger and more systemic preconceived ideas that accompany our basic analytic categories of religion, culture, and ritual.

Emic Categories and Exegetical Apparatuses

Even though the word "religions" appears in the title of this book, the category is not a native phenomenon and does not signify a known, invariable, and discrete class of objects and events in the Chinese landscape. As soon as we engage with the specific historicity of and mechanism behind any supposed religious practice, we are confronted with a whole range of political and cultural issues. Conversely, behind every secular practice were particular assumptions of the cosmos or the invisible world of gods, ghosts, and demons that shaped people's lives. I also do not see religion as "solely the creation of the scholar's study... created for the scholar's... imaginative act of comparison and generalization."[8] Such a narcissistic, self-referential claim not only divorces scholars from their subject of study but also is inattentive to the meaningfulness of people's lives. It reduces everything to mere cultural category. People of the sixteenth and seventeenth centuries recognized different ways to heal an illness, fulfill filial duties, or bring about a change in the weather. Descriptions of their self-mutilation are often imbued with a sympathetic understanding between the human world and cosmic agencies. People expected gods (or heaven) to intercede when they were in trouble and performed extreme forms of self-sacrifice to appeal for help. Miracles are documented even in the earliest historical documents in China, and they have appeared persistently since then in numerous genres of texts—including non-hagiographical works—right up to the modern time.

These were the real conditions in which people lived. Indeed, they demonstrate that what we would consider "religion" and "secularism" in premodern China were not ontologically distinct. However, they also expose the reductive tendency, especially among the social sciences, to read all (especially ritual) action as socially constructive and "expressive" rather than instrumental and transformative of people's lives—the idea that everything one does is simply meant to have strategic public impact in the bottom-line interest of social power and capital. Hence everything boils down to social, economic, and political "power," and nothing more. This is "social functionalism," pure and simple. To my thinking this is a huge methodological problem—one that fundamentally and mistakenly places all other cultures at the disposal of an analytic project and a set of categories that are culturally and historically specific to the post-Enlightenment (and Protestant Reformation) West. Can the culture of bodily austerities (which could well destroy the very body and mind that one seeks to empower) conceptually challenge or talk back to these models? To the performers, self-inflicted violence as a ritual was not simply a "signifying behavior"—a type of activity to be classified separately from practical, effective behavior. Rather, it was an embodied practice, a "developable means" for achieving a range of physiological, social, and spiritual human objectives, including maintaining the purity of one's body, negotiating one's marital status, and attaining ecstatic states of transcendence. This way of understanding self-inflicted violence seems to avoid the Cartesian dualism of mind and body.[9]

Those who engaged in self-inflicted violence could be understood as performers, not in the sense of actors on stage but in the sense of the term that captures the interpersonal and public nature of their practices. Even when some of these acts were carried out alone, they were often scripted, thereby signaling certain sets of cultural expectations, and highly intelligible to both the person doing the act and those who argued about them. For example, those who wrote about and commented on self-inflicted violence sometimes cast the performers in a repertoire of behavioral patterns to advance their own agenda. At other times they would criticize those who harmed their bodies. Yet, the value, whether denied or granted, of using one's own body to demonstrate certain truths was never questioned. Moreover, the significance of the performers' acts sometimes hinged on the way they controlled their circumstances in order to manage the way they were perceived.[10]

It is important to pay attention to how performers and those who wrote about them described these practices. Emic categories should be part of the analytic process, but they need not always translate to scholarly taxonomies. One may argue that it is not justifiable to read certain practices discussed in this book as "self-inflicted violence." Even though this category is not a term that our premodern authors provide overtly to describe such actions, it nevertheless offers important insights into the multivalent experiences of our subjects. Beneath the veil of normative discourses and categories, we would gain new insights into premodern China that would not be available if we operated only according to traditional Chinese ideas.

The category of self-inflicted violence aims to bring more nuances to contemporary studies of "violence" in religions, which generally focus on the ways in which it has "served religion" or is "constitutive of religion." Most scholars define violence as acts of *external* aggression, disruption, terrorism, murder, and armed conflict.[11] Others have nuanced these negative views and argued that violence in societies is much more "meaningful" and productive than we are led to believe.[12] Still, many explanations tend to see violence as stemming from external sources, which is not necessarily helpful when individuals inflict violence on themselves. They cannot explain a son's filial act of feeding his ailing parent with his own flesh or a young widow's practice of body mutilation, both of which are not acts of aggression, disruption, or assault. Instead, these acts were methods of cementing family relationships and order. When do filial acts of body slicing become a form of negative violence? When do practices of female chastity, where women resisted remarriage or rape by cutting off their noses and ears or committing suicide, become performances of virtue? At the same time, how can the so-called Confucian prescription of "not harming the body" reconcile with a son's act of filial piety by using his own blood to write an appeal to the emperor? The category of self-inflicted violence has the potential to bring to the forefront the productive and nuanced dimensions of violence in premodern China.

Self-inflicted violence also indirectly raises questions about its relationship to asceticism. I have chosen to avoid using the term "asceticism" because of its overly broad usage and its connections to Western religious traditions. Geoffrey Galt Harpham, in *The Ascetic Imperative in Culture and Criticism*, argues for a generalized understanding of the interconnection between ethics and asceticism by elevating asceticism to a level of abstraction: He states that "all cultures are ethical cultures" and that every culture "impose[s] on their members the essential ascetic discipline of self-denial."[13] This argument of the ascetic imperative is useful for theoretical reflections because it opens up new implications for cross-cultural comparison. However, if we use this definition and apply it to specific historical contexts, we run the risk of ending up with the impression that virtually everything is ascetic; thus the term loses its analytical potential.[14] Scholars of East Asian religions also use the term without sufficiently problematizing its baggage, which is carried over from studies of Judeo-Christian traditions.

Historians working in Western medieval Christianity have already made great strides in bringing nuance to our understanding of asceticism. They have rejected an earlier view of sexual restraint and austere fasting as dualistic, masochistic, or irrational and instead view these practices as an integral aspect of piety and religious expression. Peter Brown, for example, argues that ascetic practices are not necessarily the world-renouncing, self-hating, decadent responses of a society wracked by plague, famine, heresy, war, and ecclesiastical corruption.[15] Caroline Bynum claims that late-medieval asceticism for women was an effort to "plumb and realize" all the possibilities of the flesh; it was a way of manipulating and controlling the self and one's environment by ideologically fusing with and emulating a Christ, whose suffering saved the world.[16] In short, scholars have attempted to remove the negative associations of asceticism and assign positive aspects to self-inflicted violent practices situated within their cultural contexts.[17]

In their effort to complicate our understanding of asceticism and the body, these scholars have naturally tied their work to the cultural constructions found in medieval European sources. Yet, if we closely examine the emic categories in those sources, we find an excess of textual evidence provided by medieval ascetics themselves that accentuates the suppression of sexual passions and bodily pleasures. As Brown himself pointed out, the Christian Desert Fathers of Egypt saw their ascetic practices as an alternative to civilization and city life; their rejection of the "world" was signified by their move to the desert. In his own words, "[the desert] was the deep grave in which he [i.e., the ascetic] lay 'dead' to the world, in the desert,"[18] and "The ascetics thought of themselves as men and women who had gained a precious freedom to mourn for their sins and to suffer in this life so that they might regain a future glory for their bodies."[19] Bynum has also noted that "women's food practices [of fasting] were in some sense a rejection of family."[20] Essentially, the body was perceived as a "burden" pulling the spirit and the soul away from God.[21] These men's and women's practices of leaving the world and enduring self-inflicted suffering were essentially aimed at enjoyment in the kingdom of heaven.

The key difference between Western asceticism and premodern Chinese practices of self-inflicted violence is the renunciation of the world by practitioners of the former, who moved to the desert; their suffering in the present life so as to enjoy a better future life; and their giving up of food as a rejection of domesticity. These characterizations of asceticism are absent in the cases I study, and I would argue that they are not very relevant in premodern Chinese acts of self-inflicted violence in general. Yet, East Asian scholars continue to historicize Chinese religions through the lens of Judeo-Christian traditions. For example, John Kieschnick uses the term "asceticism" in his descriptions of Buddhist "painful austerities," or *kuxing* 苦行, without ever problematizing its Christian baggage. The section of his book on ascetics is thematically framed in terms of "sexual abstinence," "dietary restraints," "poverty," all of which follow the same scholarly trajectory in the study of medieval Christian ascetic.[22] These issues, I would argue, have little relevance to the circumstances and purpose of austere practices by Chinese Buddhists. Numerous Buddhist clerics who engaged in austere practices never moved away from hustle and bustle of city life; some may have engaged in them to enjoy a future life, say rebirth in the Pure Land (*jingtu* 淨土), but they did not necessarily rejected their bodies; they may have cut them open to use their own blood to copy Buddhist scriptures and in preparing to do so may have followed a special diet, but they did not see their bodies as a symbol for "civilization," which must be rejected. I avoid reading Chinese bodily practices through the lens of premodern Western asceticism, which assumed a religious outlook that was very different from Chinese understandings of the body. Buddhist austere practices engaged with the body were productive. I discuss this in detail in chapter 2.

Self-inflicted violence was productive to performers for making themselves subjects of sanctity. The notion of the performer as a "subject" has two meanings: Performers were "subject to someone else by control and dependence," but that person also acted as an agent in developing a self-identity in relation to these mechanisms of power by means of "conscience or self-knowledge."[23] This "someone else" was not any particular person but was rather the cultural values placed on the discourses or rules of political loyalty, filial piety, female chastity, and religious orthodoxy legitimated by the state, the family, and religious institutions. Their subjectivity was both "the way in which the individual establishe[d] his [and her] relationship to these rules" and "the basis of their identity through conscious self-knowledge."[24] Sixteenth- and seventeenth-century performers negotiated their positions in society within larger cultural discourses. By subordinating themselves to these mechanisms of power and becoming exemplars in this system with their extreme acts, performers became subjects of sanctity.

Sanctity is inextricably tied to patterns of power, but I do not reduce my study to notions of power in the Western poststructuralist sense. However, I do recognize that many of these practices exhibit a circulatory system of "force relations" that were always in "ceaseless struggles and confrontations"[25] and that these relations were never top-down and stable. In this system no one person or constituency "holds the power," and there is no one way to read cases of self-inflicted violence. Interpretations and acquisitions of power were constantly being negotiated and defended by performers and different writers. I use the term "sanctity" to describe practices that assert moral suasion and blur the boundaries between the seen and the unseen worlds. Performers of self-inflicted violence may have disagreed about the source of power, whether it was from heaven, spirits, demons, or buddhas, but the spiritual potency of certain individuals to influence the natural world was never denied.

Specifically, sanctity, as it is used in this study, is intimately connected to a cluster of discursive markers in traditional Chinese literature such as sagehood (*sheng* 聖), numinous efficacy (*ling* 靈), and effective power (*de* 德). These terms cannot be ascribed to one religious tradition or even one text. They were not understood by everyone to the same degree. The terms elicited different meanings for different people even when those people shared the same educational background or linguistic competence. For these reasons they cannot be defined straightforwardly. Rather, they must be understood contextually, more as patterns of and powers within a "sympathetically responsive" (*ganying* 感應) cosmos.[26]

In this sympathetic world *sheng* usually refers to people and to the embodiment of cosmic order. Scholars may assert that *sheng* is most notably tied to Confucianism as its ideal state of being. However, I am using this category as one aspect of the general model of sanctity. It was applied to people of Daoist or Buddhist persuasion or some other tradition and who wielded special occult powers or exemplified moral virtues—no matter what they sought to become: a sage, a righteous official, or a bodhisattva.

Connected to these people of spiritual import were *ling*, or numinous efficacy, and *de*, or effective power, both of which were most often described in the sources as a material force that could be channeled through ritual.[27] For example, effective power was graphically and semantically connected to the homophone "to get" or "to obtain" *de* 得,[28] suggesting that one who possessed it could obtain power over others and even over forces of nature. One could also become a sage or *sheng* by aligning oneself to the will of the cosmic order because one's actions would then resonate with the will of heaven. Effective power (*de*) or numinous efficacy (*ling*) could also accrue to and reside within an individual who had acted favorably toward ancestral spirits, heaven, or the workings of the cosmos. Such sanctity was an attribute of the ideal ruler, which enabled him to "obtain" the authority from the ancestral spirits, who acted as intercessors with the Lord on High (*shangdi* 上帝) or heaven (*tian* 天).[29] Aside from rulers, this was also an attribute of shamans.

Modern scholarship often portrays these two concepts of effective power and numinous efficacy as opposite pairs similar to "official" versus "popular" or "state" versus "local."[30] I argue that the polarity of these two concepts is misleading because the performers themselves seldom distinguished efficacious power from numinous efficacy. Also, these two categories of value (or structures of power) differ in some respects in the way they were used in different contexts, but they can nonetheless be contingently reconciled. The only difference between these two categories lies in how editors or redactors of the sources described this cosmic pattern. Both rest on a moral and sympathetic universe, where the actions of human beings have an effect on the cosmos, which responds to the inner moral development of human beings. This was the way the Chinese people ordered and conceived of their world, with its political and socioeconomic institutions and cultural forms, until the latter part of the Qing dynasty, when it faced the challenges of Western hegemony.[31] This pattern informs all Chinese institutions, whether they are of high culture or folk belief, and cannot be uniquely ascribed to social classes. It governed the way people thought about their world and guided their bodily practices. Self-inflicted violent practices made sense in this context of the need to exercise one's sanctity by emulating sages, winning the favor of heaven, or negotiating the boundaries of orthodoxy.

A dynamic reciprocity exists between the inner cultivation and the outer verification of sanctity. In the sixteenth and seventeenth centuries, notions of sanctity came to mean something that could be cultivated, something that anyone could either forfeit or earn through one's moral and religious obligation and prowess. In effect, it became a source of legitimacy for not only rulers but also for literati officials, religious professionals, and commoners. They all had their own understanding of what "sagehood" constituted. So powerful was this discourse that the moral power of sons to move heaven to heal their ailing parents has been interpreted by premodern Chinese historians and authors as the success or failure of the inner moral cultivation of the individual's effective power. As the subsequent chapters explain, the discourses of sanctity suffused different types of literature of the sixteenth and seventeenth centuries, including official state documents, religious literature, and novels. In these texts external phenomena (such as healed parents, absence of calamity, good harvests, or peace) were a litmus test for the actions and inner cultivations of sages, emperors, officials, literati, religious professionals, and commoners alike.[32]

Self-inflicted violence was understood as a concrete assertion of sanctity. For example, in the sixteenth and seventeenth centuries conservative men of the literati eulogized chaste widowhood and extreme practices of self-maiming in the lives of those women who remained faithful to their husbands. However, young women who refused to marry by engaging in these practices actually challenged the custom of arranged marriage and filial obedience.

Sometime they also committed suicide in order to avoid forced marriage or rape. In some of the stories I examine, they return as a ghost to haunt those who have betrayed them. In this sense, the literati's eulogies and state-sponsored building of shrines dedicated to these women may be interpreted as a way to appease the vengeful female spirits.

Similarly, in late imperial rain-making rituals, emperors, officials, and Buddhist clerics would publically expose their bodies to the blazing sun for days or weeks or even self-immolate in order to end a drought. The success of their attempts was invariably interpreted as the triumph of their inner effective power to influence the cosmos. Yet, such power was always politicized. When the Ming emperor Taizu and subsequent officials who emulated him successfully relieved drought through their sacrificial acts, they were represented in the *Ming History* in a language that alluded to the sage kings of ancient times. Not surprisingly, when attempts to end droughts failed in particular regions (particularly in areas outside the imperial capital, where the emperors resided), the official sources typically described these natural disasters as the "moral failure" or the dissipation of the local magistrates' effective power. Meteorological disasters verified their lack of self-cultivation.

Not only was the sympathetic cosmos politicized, but the expectations of and pressures on the officials were often enough to push them to engage in public acts of penance in the form of self-inflicted violence or austere practices, either willingly or unwillingly. The discourses on physical practices and effective power were used by various people to construct sanctity and legitimacy for different ends. All of these men and women demonstrate that practices of self-inflicted violence were sites of transformation and contestation, both for the performers and for others who witnessed or narrated their stories.

The sanctity embodied in these practices is distinct from other bodily rituals in the sixteenth and seventeenth centuries that might appear to be acts of self-denial or austerity but were not demonstrative of sanctity. I have therefore not included them in this study. Foot binding is one example. In this practice, mothers bound their young daughters' feet to keep them from growing because men considered small feet sexually appealing. Having small feet would place these young girls well in the marriage economy. This practice was painful and invariably caused deformity of the feet, so it may be perceived as a way that mothers used the young girls' bodies to negotiate their daughters' marriage and social status. However, as Dorothy Ko shows, the practice of foot binding was more of a custom, intimately "bound" to social prestige and eroticism, male fantasies and female desires.[33] It had little to do with sanctity as I understand the term. Nor was it a form of self-assertion because it was forced on girls at a young age by their mothers.

My focus in this book is on the practice of self-inflicted violence and not necessarily "bodies" per se. However, in presenting these practices I do discuss various "technologies of the body"[34] as sites of transformation and contestation. While I follow the now well-established lines of scholarship in literary studies, history, and anthropology, I show the complexity of an individual performer's life and circumstances and how one's practices might have been meaningful and transformative. Mary Douglas has argued that the human body is a "symbol of society" and that "the powers and dangers credited to social structure" are "reproduced in small on the human body."[35] Similarly, Pierre Bourdieu explains that the body is a mnemonic device upon and within which the habitus is inscribed.[36] I use these scholarly approaches to analyze the performances of bodily practices in order to show their relationship to larger premodern Chinese cultural concerns about group identities and social systems. However, I also recognize the limitations of these approaches. For example, drawing on Marcel Mauss,[37] Douglas has shown how the body was socially invested, but her own commitment to "symbolic analysis" has prevented her from appreciating the dynamic constitution and instrumentality of embodied practices. In this sense I differ with her reading of the body, which I see as an assemblage of embodied aptitudes—teachable and learnable—not only as systems of symbolic meaning.[38]

Bodily practices were a visceral and an elemental way for performers to negotiate social relations and family crises. Scholars have noted that at particular moments during a crisis of belief—that is, when certain central ideas cease to elicit conviction either because they have been shown to be manifestly fictitious or because they have been challenged or divested of meaning—the sheer materiality or physicality of the human body might lend that cultural construct an aura of "authenticity" and "certainty."[39] This makes sense in the contexts of the sixteenth and seventeenth centuries because the general sense of moral values was being reinterpreted and challenged, and people's social boundaries were being transgressed.[40] Both the performers of self-inflicted violence and those who argued about them acknowledged the instrumentality of the human body to substantiate important cultural and religious values in times of change. Yet, I show that practices such as blood writing, filial body slicing, chastity mutilation, and ritual exposure were not negations of the body. Instead, these technologies of the body were instrumental and in themselves epistemologically productive; they fashioned the body "with a much 'higher' aim"[41] in order to produce a particular kind of social subject and participant in society—one that was sanctified and revered.

The Chinese term *shen* 身 (the closest classical approximation to our English word "body") sometimes referred not only to the corporeal form of human beings but also to the "self" as a sentient being with a living history and subjective consciousness. It often blurred the mind-body dualism that makes our English-language "body" the object of our own gaze. *Shen* privileges process, function, and performance over anatomical structures. Working with the Chinese notion of the body/self, I draw on Judith Butler's contention that the human body is itself a social process and that no universal, essential norm of the human body exists—even the "materiality" of the body is socially informed through the ritualized, repetitive performance of social norms.[42] In this sense I show that the "bodies" or "selves" of children, adults, males, and females—people of different social and political status—were productive and constitutive of social, political, cultural, and religious values through their practices. Yet, their bodies were not, as the social constructionist perspective would have us believe, a passive surface on which culture leaves its imprint. For example, there were different representations of the same bodily practices and more than one understanding of the body, which presented the performers in all their richness and variability. In other words, their bodies were defined and reified by active performances.

Another important but implicit idea that informs the ways in which I historicize performers of self-inflicted violence is the notion of "discourse." Discourse is never innocent of power relations between authors and readers, where they are formed and upon whom they have an impact. I use discourse to simultaneously include both action and discussion of action. For example, during the sixteenth and seventeenth centuries conservative literati produced staunch morality books (*shanshu* 善書) and authored ledgers of merit and demerit (*gongguoge* 功過格)[43] that show how human actions could positively affect cosmic processes. They were cognizant of the potential hazard of widely circulated romantic novels, seditious books (*yinshu* 淫書), or sex handbooks that celebrated immoral impulses.[44] However, they nevertheless increasingly subsumed ever more risqué fictional output under the rubric of "ethically" edifying texts in order to rectify society. They often resorted to making their works "entertaining" and appealing to their readers. The literature on female chastity, which details how women mutilated or killed themselves to avoid rape or forced remarriage, was supposed to be nothing more than unambiguous stories of virtue that promoted mainstream ideology. Yet, because of readers' demands and the publishers' commercial interest, these stories highlighted dramatic illustrations and entertaining motifs that often undermined their original moral intent. Historicizing these phenomena through theories of discourse allows me to reveal a more nuanced understanding of how self-inflicted violence operated in narratives and illustrations.

Methodological Approach

Scholars of various academic disciplines may question my bringing together different kinds of body practices and genres of texts into a single study. How were these different practices related? How can the specific sociohistorical contexts be reconciled? Buddhist scholars may question my juxtaposition of Buddhist scriptures and the literati's memorials, both of which were written in blood. Sinologists may question the study of female chastity suicides from the perspective of religious studies. Yet, one of the things that readers will quickly realize is that routinized and sanctioned self-inflicted violent practices were intelligible to observers and performers, for it was only by such identifiability and intelligibility that people transmitted, copied, replicated, and repeatedly talked about them (positively or negatively) as cultural *topoi.* It is this plausibility, intelligibility, and appeal (or revulsion) that I believe justifies us in studying them together in a systematic way. I contend that the complexity of these practices will evade any scholar who examines them through the lens of a single academic discipline or by concentrating on only one genre of primary materials. My methodological approach is a combination of ritual studies and discourse analysis of different genres of texts, including miracle tales, official history, popular novels, literary essays, local gazetteers, and exemplary narrative. These texts are closely related historically, as are their production and circulation. I see them as active agents that reveal the dynamics of cultural value, not as ahistorical static entities but as practice.

An examination of different sorts of texts provides us with a better understanding of how they actively affected people's lives, specifically their practice of self-inflicted violence. I use various sources to examine the subject of my study from different angles. Each kind of text is generative of certain sensibilities that contribute to larger cultural discourses through which people think about their actions, bodies, environment, and events in their lives. In a sense, texts are mediums that orchestrate, encode, aestheticize, provide parameters for discursively mapping and strategizing people's actions, and create a plot around these actions. They are ways of "disciplining the senses." In this sense, it is very difficult to see texts as separate from action; they inhibit it.[45]

Examining self-inflicted violent practices within the cultural nexus of social relations is not to conveniently replace religion with the concept of culture, which is most commonly thought of as the domain of values, meanings, symbols, and other ideal entities that require some form of material support: bodily practices, communities, institutions, and texts. Such a concept would falsely assume that people act on ideological valuations and that somehow underlying people's various experiences are convictions, values, and conceptual frameworks within which their world is defined in relation to the moral and ethical truths to which they adhere. Rather, I explore the cultural nexus of social relations through an interdisciplinary approach that remains attentive to the incidence of the production of materials, individual circumstances, and social realities of contestations and accommodations that bring to bear a more textured history of both the performers' lives and their practices.

Sources and Their Agency and Limitations

My refusal to limit myself to one religious tradition in the study of self-inflicted violence also correlates with my use of primary sources. Even though thousands of performers have mutilated their bodies, their cases have been told by different writers for many reasons in an array of textual genres. This has led scholars to frame some of the practices I discuss in this book as discrete phenomena, unrelated to each other, within the boundary of one academic discipline, religious tradition, or genre of texts.[46] Such a narrow approach to studying self-inflicted violence cannot appreciate the fact that historical records do not exist simply as neutral documents (merely passive sources of details of historical events) but as *strategic agents* in ongoing cultural and social practice. Writers argued about self-inflicted violent practices; performers read them and emulated the practices, which in turn generated more discussions and cultural values. Nor can the narrow approach recognize similar patterns of sanctity between, for example, the blood memorial of a son and the blood scriptures of a Buddhist monk. These practices of body mutilation demand an inclusive approach and reflection in order to appreciate their larger cultural significance. To date, no book has systematically analyzed several forms of self-inflicted violence in premodern China under a single cover.

It is, of course, tempting to construct a history of self-inflicted violence from beginning to end, but the available evidence only leads us to construct a simple chronology that would tell us mostly about the limitation of my sources. Therefore, I have chosen to adopt a thematic and episodic presentation that focuses on specific self-inflicted violent practices during a specific period of Chinese history. This approach allows me to examine a wide array of primary sources and to cross modern disciplinary boundaries of Chinese religions, Buddhist studies, and Chinese social and literary histories. It also allows me to group together the similarities among various types of self-sacrifice and self-mutilation under one rubric of self-inflicted violence. An episodic and detailed history indeed has its shortcomings and merits. One main shortcoming is that I cannot provide a continuous narrative voice. I have cobbled together a history from partial perspectives, disparate comments, biased views, graphic illustrations, and sometimes people who were anything but influential. Some of these sources are richly descriptive of the violent performance; others mention these practices only in passing. Yet, the merit of an episodic history is that by homing in on specific events and sources, I can illustrate the rich nuances and conflicting meanings that violent body practices had for people during the sixteenth and seventeenth centuries. I can also demonstrate the extent to which these practices were embedded in the cultural, political, religious, and poetic life of late imperial China by using different genres of literature and show why self-inflicted violence as a cultural construct has remained resistant to scholarly attention for so long.

The important point is that the "episodes" I analyze and present actually illustrate larger patterns of bodily discourse. That is to say, they participate in and affect larger fields of bodily action and communication that are at once socially recognizable, sanctioned, and intelligible. Elements of "exegesis" naturally lurk therein since the people who engaged in these practices and the writers who debated them do so under the assumption that they were meaningful (even when regarded with disapproval by others) and transformative in people's lives.

Whenever possible, I draw out the unstated structures and significations regarding body, performance, and discourses about the cosmos that give these practices moral suasion, sanctity, and meaning in premodern Chinese culture. I start with notions such as numinous efficacy, effective power, and sympathetic response. However, these "systems" also reveal considerable fluidity, disparity, and innovation such that they cannot be explained by a single systematic statement. Thus intelligibility need not mean ideological systematicity. For example, the calculability of karmic retribution was something new in the sixteenth and seventeenth centuries. The Buddhist textbook explanation of karma is insufficient in its understanding of how people may have conceived of their actions. Likewise, with the rise of medical literature in late imperial times and under the aegis of cosmic reward, the practice of filial slicing took on a new valence very different from, say, cannibalism.

I have chosen to focus on the sixteenth and seventeenth centuries because they represent a critical phase of unprecedented changes in Chinese history. Textual sources on self-inflicted violent practices appear to be particularly abundant during this time. The sixteenth and seventeenth centuries correspond encompassed the final decades of the Ming dynasty (1368–1644) and the early decades of the Qing (1644–1911). The historical context of this period is discussed in greater detail in chapter 1. However, it is worthwhile to point out that, aside from the violent, tragic ending of the Ming dynasty in 1644, the decades before the fall, which scholars typically call the "late Ming,"[47] constituted a period of accelerating change characterized by enormous socioeconomic dynamics, irrepressible intellectual daring, and cultural upheaval. It was a unique age of exceptional tolerance of widely different social, intellectual, and religious practices, different attitudes toward life, and an economy rich in resources. This tolerance existed particularly in the central and southern parts of China, in the cities to the south of the Yangtze River, the geographical focus of this study. The period also witnessed an unprecedented change in traditional values. In civil matters, the imperial state had difficulties governing its people and exerting strong control over its territories. On the economic front, commercialization generated prosperity, which led to the abundant production of art, literature, and entertainment, as well as moral profligacy.[48] Moral values were being reinterpreted and focus on concretely demonstrating these values were being praised in popular literature. Self-inflicted violent practices, as an ultimate expression of sanctity, came to fruition during this period.

The numerous primary sources from which I extrapolate the phenomenon of self-inflicted violence include both official histories, such as dynastic histories (*zhengshi* 正史) and local gazetteers (*fangzhi* 方志), and nonofficial writings, such as hagiography (*chuanji* 傳記), miracle tales (*yanji* 驗記; *ganying chuan* 感應傳), popular fiction (*xiaoshuo* 小說), poetry (*shi* 詩), miscellaneous jottings (*biji* 筆記), and illustrations (*huitu* 繪圖). I believe these sources are complementary to one another in reconstructing the rich historical contexts of self-inflicted violence in China in the sixteenth and seventeenth centuries. Examining the layers of discourse in these sources is fruitful in showing that everything has a history, even histories of disfiguration. Of course, official sixteenth- and seventeenth-century histories generally express the official ideal. Yet, sometimes details of material life and family activities mentioned therein, which are incidental to the main purpose of the records, are quite useful. For example, in the numerous official accounts of chastity suicides, the state's efforts to convert altars dedicated to vengeful ghosts into shrines for deceased widows can be read as a concerted effort to appease vengeful female ghosts. The veneration displayed at shrines dedicated to deceased widows and eulogies written about them can also be read this way. Thus, when using official histories, one should employ them for purposes other than those their compilers intended. As scholars have attested, it is possible to re-read official histories in new ways, especially when they are supplemented with other kinds of sources.

Many scholars have found that using hagiography, popular fiction, poetry, and miscellaneous jottings can open up new possibilities for a richer historical understanding of people's everyday experiences at various points in history. However, the use of such supplemental research tools requires consideration of several issues. For example, the people that I study were a varied group divided by socioeconomic stratification, occupational cultures, and gender. Moreover, many self-mutilators were documented and written about by educated men. Thus, it would be problematic for me to treat these writings as nothing more than mirrors of their world, objective report of events. Therefore, I have contextualized the authors' agendas (e.g., promoting certain moral ideals, advancing the efficacy of a particular scripture, critiquing existing social norms) and acknowledged the possibility that some or whole segments of these writings may be made up or exaggerated. Knowing the intended audience of these writings, to the extent that this is possible, has also helped me to situate them in their historical contexts.

While it is important to address the agendas and assumptions under which records of miraculous healing from self-inflicted violence were produced and received, it is imperative to recognize that they deserve to be included to the same extent as what Sinologists normally consider historical writing. This is because, in most circumstances, such writing tells us what would be familiar to and thereby accepted by the readers. Robert Campany argues that:

> Precisely because hagiography intends to inspire belief, veneration, and perhaps emulation, its depictions of the contexts of religious life must be, for the most part, realistic, which is to say, recognizable and familiar to readers... because it announces itself as an account of the lives of real persona, hagiography must meet readers on that familiar landscape before attempting to move them to the horizon... it must give a recognizable model of life as readers know it, and cannot content itself only with giving models for the ideal religious life.[49]

Other scholars who are studying the history of medieval Christian saints have made this point quite clearly.[50] We need to recognize that, even though the tropes and themes in these cases may appear fantastic and can take on a life of their own, they may nonetheless derive from social reality and may come, in turn, to influence social practice. The same can be said for novels and illustrations.[51] Andrew Plaks has also argued that sometimes novels achieve a "cinematographic" realism with special reference to problems of rhetoric, realism, and its relation to trends in sociointellectual history.[52]

Works of fiction can be of value to us in reconstructing the everyday details of the authors' lives and observations, especially if they are trying to write realistic narratives. This is because narratives reveal the mental stereotypes of people and their likely reactions to the circumstances in which the authors place them. Even the most extreme fictional stereotype can take on a life of its own as a literary discourse and influence social practice. Thus, when novels depict a protagonist engaging in filial slicing to help an ailing parent and go on to describe the cosmic responses to or miracles surrounding such an act, they actually provide us with a window into the expectations and understandings of those who have actually engaged in this practice in real life.

The body practices I study are a site (to use Catherine Bell's phraseology) that permits us to appreciate the extremely rich and complex religious lives of different sixteenth- and seventeenth-century performers and the ways they were perceived by their writers. These practices reveal to us the impact texts had on practices and how practices both produced and resisted cultural values.[53] It is my hope that this book creatively and accurately presents the multivalent, divergent, and yet surprisingly persistent practice of self-inflicted violence in China in the sixteenth and seventeenth centuries.

I

A Culture in Flux

Historical Background

THE SIXTEENTH AND seventeenth centuries were a unique time of exceptional tolerance of widely different social, intellectual, and religious practices and of different attitudes toward life and an economy rich in resources. This tolerance was true particularly in the central and southern parts of China, in the cities to the south of the Yangtze River, the geographical focus of this study. The period witnessed an unprecedented change in traditional values and met with radical ideas.[1] The Ming began with the impressive achievements of the founding generation, whose political and military successes were accompanied by cultural and literary accomplishments of the first order and were followed by a period of retrenchment during much of the fifteenth century. Then the pace began to pick up again in the final decades of that century, resulting in a period of remarkable economic prosperity, new ideals of morality, and an ethos that stressed a corporeal demonstration of moral sanctity. It was during this last phase that the number of cases of self-inflicted violence seems to have grown. The change in religious and moral outlooks was intimately connected to the increase in accounts of self-inflicted violence, which can be attested by the several hundred Ming local gazetteers, didactic works, and popular literature produced during this time. While I would not attribute this increase to a political and moral "decline" of the period,[2] I do see several factors that determined these changes.

It is difficult to explicate the exact relationship between social and economic transformations and the changes in religious practices and moral outlooks in sixteenth- and seventeenth-century China. Modern scholarship has not sufficiently investigated this relationship to enable me to summarize it here. Yet, the fact that changes took place is quite clear. The social instability, economic growth, and diversification of traditional values were the backdrop of many cases I have studied. In the following chapters, which detail the practices of self-inflicted violence, I show that none of them are entirely new inventions of this era but that each had a complex discursive history that can be found in different source materials, antecedent narratives, and myths that were particularly prevalent during the late imperial times. I do not deny the importance of these practices in earlier periods and developments. However, it is the sixteenth- and seventeenth-century sources we have that represent the most significant phase of the processes of change that these practices became accepted by the mainstream culture. I believe that the new bottles, in this case the sixteenth and seventeenth centuries, may be more significant than the old wine.

This chapter places self-inflicted violence in a broader context by speculating as much as possible about the reasons these bodily practices attained a high degree of influence at this moment in history. In the subsequent pages I show that the sixteenth and seventeenth centuries happened to take in marked developments in a wide variety of fields. I suggest that these economic, cultural, intellectual, and political developments had a direct impact on the four practices discussed in this book. Many of the important historical figures mentioned in this chapter were involved in the practice of self-inflicted violence, which I discuss in later chapters. Thus, what follows is a useful historical context in to understand the subsequent chapters. I claim no original contribution in providing this context. I synthesize the state of the field in order to show the remarkable contributions, problems, and radical transformations of the sixteenth and seventeenth centuries, which may have fed the development of self-inflicted violence.

Dramatic Economic Prosperity

The sixteenth and seventeenth centuries enjoyed great economic prosperity, which led to the abundant production of art, literature, and entertainment, as well as anxiety about social disorder. Scholars generally note the tremendous material growth and monetization of the economy over the course of the Ming dynasty and how these were damaging the moral fabric of the society, such that the goal of maintaining proper social order was much harder to accomplish. They cite writers who were especially bitter about the disorder in politics, society, family, and people's livelihoods.[3] Yet, premodern Chinese people of every dynastic period tended to see their own day as a time of moral profligacy. So from another angle, one could argue that this was a period of considerable vitality and diversity in Chinese economic, intellectual, and religious life.[4] This period produced a number of creative thinkers who explored areas of life that had previously been ignored; it also yielded many broad-minded syncretists who blurred the boundaries of institutionalized religious traditions. Far from our received idea of religious decline, this could be understood as a period of great efflorescence of Chinese religions stimulated by the economic, social, intellectual, and cultural fronts.

The economic prosperity of this period is reflected in the commercialization of the countryside, proliferation of periodic markets and small towns, crop specialization, development of handicrafts, and interregional trade. Stimulating these economic changes were improvements in agriculture. The introduction of new, rapidly maturing strains of rice, the intensified use of fertilizer, and the improvement of irrigation and flood control made possible, according to one estimate, an increase in grain yields of more than 40 percent between 1400 and 1770.[5]

The importation of large quantities of silver to supplement the limited yields from China's own mines further stimulated economic development. During the 1530s silver began trickling into China from Japan, where rich deposits had just been uncovered. After 1571, with the Spanish establishment of an administrative center in Manila, silver from Mexico and South America poured into China through trade with the Philippines.[6] It is uncertain how much silver circulated in China during the last decades of the Ming, but silver clearly had an enormous impact on the Chinese economy and society and eventually led to well-documented, catastrophic inflation. The penetration of ample amounts of silver even into remote rural areas made possible, for example, a tax-reform method called the single whip (*yitiao bian fa* 一條鞭法), which was adopted on a national scale in 1581.[7] Introduced experimentally in the 1530s, taxes were collected in silver rather than grain, the tax base was changed from households to land, and payments for land taxes and labor services were unified. By thus simplifying taxation, officials eliminated many tax dodges that the wealthy and powerful had exploited to avoid paying their fair share. Though the levy of one payment in silver to cover the many miscellaneous labor services—such as the courier service and the militia—the government could hire people efficiently and fairly to perform these tasks. The increasing commercialization during this period was qualitatively and quantitatively different from the earlier Yuan and Song periods. Due to its incorporation in the world trade system and the ensuing influx of large quantities of silver, the sixteenth and seventeenth centuries became far more monetized, at least from the southeast coast up to the entire Lower Yangtze region.[8]

The use of silver stimulated the economy and made beneficial tax reforms possible, but the fluctuating supply created much anxiety. One official noted that silver had become the main medium of exchange and also commented on the difficulties caused by the popular preference for silver over copper. As people abandoned the use of copper, the price of silver became highly inflated, and the conversion from tax payments in produce to payments in silver consequently became increasingly complex.[9] Peasants and craftsmen, vulnerable to fluctuations in both the supply of silver and the market demand for specialized products, gave vent to their frustrations throughout the sixteenth and seventeenth centuries. Bandits roamed the countryside, weavers rioted, and members of various sectarian movements were particularly active because of these changes.[10]

The increased production of cotton also stimulated the economic change. In part, the trend derived from the policies of the early Ming emperors, who ordered the imperial government to make payments in cotton rather than in grain. By the sixteenth century, according to one estimate, the imperial government needed not less than five or six million bolts of cotton just for the annual salaries of military personnel.[11] One scholar has called the late imperial period "a cotton revolution."[12] Realizing how lucrative the new textile industry had become, local officials occasionally encouraged the general public to take up the weaving of cotton.[13]

The remarkable convergence of these factors occurred within the space of a hundred years, when the population of China increased two- to threefold,[14] which may have been the cause or the effect of these economic shifts. Peasants who found opportunities to weave for middlemen or to sell surplus crops to the towns often yielded to the temptation to specialize and consequently became entangled in and dependent on large interregional economic networks. To facilitate the exchange of resources between the major urban areas and the rural villages, periodic markets and small towns proliferated.[15]

Economic changes naturally affected social relations. As towns grew more attractive, landowners turned absentee, and the paternalistic ties between them and their tenants gave way to impersonal businesslike relationships. Some educated elite noted that market towns were cheating the villages by using inaccurate scales, bullying the uneducated villagers during transactions, and levying excess taxes.[16] Commoners sometimes rose up and challenged the local elite, whose wealth, prestige, and pedigree provided them not only with exemptions from the service levy but also with the prerogative of exercising official influence.[17]

If some rural areas consequently prospered, signs that the commercialization might lead to a new, creative, yet ominous view of moral values also surfaced. The introduction of money, many literati feared, had tainted the traditional ideals. Lü Kun 吕坤 (1536–1618), one of the most articulate Ming writers and social commentators, observed that financial disagreements turned brothers into enemies. Another rural lecturer also noted that children's filial allegiance ceased as soon as they got their hands on money.[18] Others grumbled that everyone had grown competitive, greedy, and selfish. Economic prosperity blurred social distinctions. Sumptuary regulations withered away as wealthy townspeople began sporting the caps formerly worn only by budding scholars and men who dressed effeminately. The prosperity caused sixteenth-century literati to worry that peasants were extravagantly indulging in meat or wine, gambling in the market towns, and, worst of all, contributing their savings to potentially rebellious millenarian groups.[19]

Political Intrigues at the Court

The prosperity and perceived social ills must be understood in conjunction with the growing alienation between the literati-officials on the one hand and the autocratic and sometimes irresponsible late Ming emperors on the other. The imperial state had difficulties governing its people and exerting strong control over its territories. From the mid-fifteenth century on, the relation between the Ming emperors and the officials was distant; emperors could afford to oppress, demean, and dismiss their officials because the spread of education had expanded the valuable pool of scholars; emperors who reigned during this time often showed little ability or even interest in performing their duties; bureaucratic functions were frequently hijacked by palace eunuchs; and fights between the eunuchs and the bureaucracy and among the officials themselves were fierce. All of this turned the late Ming into an age of tremendous dynamism and action, leaving to history a string of names, both evil and heroic. Many barely escaped death for their forthright criticisms of the Jiajing and Wanli emperors. Officials were painfully aware that speaking carelessly in court frequently led to disaster.

There were powerful upright ministers, such as Zhang Juzheng 張居正 (1525–82), but when they died, order at court rapidly disintegrated. Shaken by the moral relativism and the heightened sense of crisis, a number of upright scholars—including many who had been dismissed from government service—banded together, first in 1604 and then more determinedly in the 1620s, at Donglin 東林 Academy to clarify their moral standards and to root out the evil influences at court. Yet, even as they criticized in the inner court, the Donglin members also blamed their own peers for the loosening of morals and the resulting confusion. Specifically, they singled out the numerous heterodox thinkers who had drifted away from Confucian teachings to iconoclastic, selfish, and individualistic views.

Two of the most detested eunuchs during the sixteenth century and the rivals of many bureaucrats were Liu Jin 劉瑾 (1452—1510) and Wei Zhongxian 魏忠賢 (1568–1627), both of whom used the secret police force and the imperial prison to frighten their opponents. The secret police force and the imperial prison were independent of the official administration organ, the board of justice. They were originally established to enhance the emperor's personal control, but in the hands of these two eunuchs, who were favored by their emperors, these two wings became agencies of terror. The extent of their power was able to virtually disable official government agencies. Everyone who opposed them was removed from their posts, put in prison, tortured, or murdered. For example, in the next chapter I discuss the case of Yang Lian 楊漣 (1572–1625), who met a heroic death fighting Wei Zhongxian. When he was taken to Beijing by Wei's secret guards, tens of thousands of literati and commoners supposedly demonstrated along the roadsides, trying to stop the guards from taking Yang Lian away. The villagers burned incense and held sacrifices to pray for Yang Lian's safe return. Of course, Yang never returned; he was tortured to death. However, before he died Yang wrote a testimonial in his own blood.[20] His blood writing, which affirmed his innocence, was subsequently publicized in various writings that circulated rapidly throughout the empire and helped to shape popular opinions of moral sanctity.

Yang Lian's political action was part and parcel of the intellectual and cultural climate of a society in flux. If we are to understand the significance of this event, we cannot isolate it from the rest of the society, which emphasized a corporeal embodiment of sanctity through self-inflicted violence. Below I explain how such an embodied value of morality came about through multiple factors.

Widespread Literacy and New Ideas of Morality

The late imperial times placed an inordinately high value on education and literacy, which significantly affected the intellectual and cultural life of the people. In the context of literary outpourings and pluralism, intellectuals and social commentators also challenged traditional moral values. The founding emperor of the Ming, Taizu—who had risen to power from peasant origins and who consequently both envied and distrusted the urbane literati in his bureaucracy—wanted education to be available to all and monopolized by none. He therefore ordered community schools to be established in every prefecture and county.[21] Although his program met with only limited success in general, sixteenth-century officials in charge of local administrations and wealthy local merchants did try to set up community schools.[22]

The community schools provided students with functional literacy. In one year, boys could master roughly two thousand characters and three classical primers, and in two to three years they would be able to learn the Four Books and the Five Classics by heart.[23] A Korean monk visiting China in the 1480s reported that in one prosperous area "even village children, ferrymen and sailors could read,"[24] and estimations in the Qing dynasty suggest that 30 to 45 percent of the male population and 2 to 10 percent of the female population enjoyed functional literacy. Literary historians have also brought to light a voluminous body of poetry and other writings by women of this period, demonstrating the high level of classical education attained by some elite women and the opportunities it afforded them as teachers and, to a limited extent, participants in literary discourse.[25]

By the seventeenth century, new genres of literature had emerged to cater to the new reading class. These works not only focused on the concerns of the common people but also engendered intellectual debates about traditional moral values. Several important thinkers, novelists, and poets explored the subjects of human desire, efficacy, and action. To attract such semiliterate readers, publishers and authors lavishly illustrated their books, wrote in the informal vernacular style, and often added explanations and keys to the pronunciations of difficult characters. Thus, alongside the classics and other serious works, numerous unscholarly genres—easy, practical, and entertaining—suited the impatient and those with limited education and now competed for the reader's attention. For example, didactic texts on female chastity circulated widely during this time, inculcating women with the value of demonstrating their fidelity through extreme acts of self-sacrifice and self-mutilation. The content of these texts suggests that they were not written simply to educate women; they were written in response to problems that arose as a result of educating women.[26] At the same time, these tracts were also attractive and entertaining. As I show in chapter 4, even staunch literati sought ways to make these didactic works attractive to the general population at the expense of diluting the moral message.

Many kinds of literature were produced. Practical household handbooks informed the common people on everyday matters such as how to care for their cats, blend fragrances for soaps, and even calculate one's karmic actions and measure one's virtue. Vernacular fiction, which flourished greatly during the sixteenth and seventeenth centuries, commented on religious salvation and heroic adventures of the Robin Hood types portrayed in *Shuihu chuan* or *The Water Margin*.[27] Other popular works were manuals for interpreting dreams and omens or tales of crime and passion, satisfying diverse popular interests. Idle, housebound women found escape in the erotic love stories, just barely disguised as didactic literature. Abridged, simplified versions of the classics helped less than diligent students to prepare for the civil service examinations.

These literary outpourings were intimately connected with the wider literary, cultural, and philosophical movement to reinterpret traditional values. One of the most prominent and radical types of literature that characterized this period was produced by the cult of "sentiment" or "passion" (*qing* 情), which challenged traditional values. This movement formulated a new morality based on powerful, impulsive, natural, and primal feelings.[28] These thinkers pursued the significance of emotions in religion, philosophy, literature, social life, and the political domain.[29] Many culturally important works were produced during this period, and scholars have noted that they were fueled by this new morality and "revalorization of desire."[30] The effect of this valorization was extremely widespread, beyond anything else in this culture of pluralism. Scholars have also noted that never before in Chinese history had people been so openly fascinated with desire, so eager to experience it in different forms, and so enthusiastic about discussing these experiences. At the same time, people were acutely aware of the complex implications of desire and how it actually played out in their lives.[31]

Influential writers increasingly blurred the lines between "moral" and "immoral" texts. Among the early sixteenth-century reformers, Li Zhi 李贄 (1527–1602) was one of the first to assimilate what had hitherto been considered "immoral fictional texts" to newly defined categories of morality.[32] In many ways the cult of passion provided a backdrop for the production of all kinds of vernacular literature, including slanderous fiction, romantic novels, seditious works, or sex handbooks that celebrated immoral impulses. One of the most notable literary critics at this time even argued that these types of works displayed genuineness of emotion (*zhenqing* 真情).[33] The seventeenth-century thinker Chen Que 陳確 (1604–1677), even though he recognized that sages do not indulge in desire, nevertheless states, "All desires for food and sex originate from righteousness and principle, whereas longings for examination success, fame, wealth, and rank are motivated by one's moral virtue. As I said before, originally there was no heavenly principle in one's mind; heavenly principle is perceivable only through human desires... Desires are the intent arising from one's mind. They are the origins of all virtue."[34]

Many literati were interested in exploring emotions and desires partly because of their literary interests, which were connected to how many found themselves "disenfranchised." The low quotas for successful candidates in the examination system and the few bureaucratic positions in relation to the growing cadre of qualified educated men left many without access to that traditional means of acquiring elite status. Even when the elect few were able to succeed to officialdom, they did not succeed because they were morally upright. Benjamin Elman notes that rote learning of the classics for the civil examinations "tended to cut against the grain of moral cultivation because the examinations had no means to measure morality directly or determine whether the memorization of the Daoxue doctrine brought with it increased intellectual awakening."[35] Some literati also chose the path of monkhood as an alternative to officialdom. Several actually became prominent monks and continued their close network ties with the educated literati.[36] Many celebrated novelists during this time had frustrating scholarly careers. Feng Menglong 馮夢龍 (1574–1646), a famous novelist and an advocate of the cultivation of genuine passions, received his licentiate degree (*xiucai* 秀才) in his twenties, but it was not until he was fifty-six that he became a stipendiary student (*gongsheng* 貢生) and was offered a very minor position as assistant county instructor. Four years later he was appointed magistrate in a remote county, an official position of the seventh grade (*qipin* 七品).[37] It was not uncommon for those who were frustrated in their careers to seek solace in writing popular literature. One writer observes, "A famous courtesan forced into prostitution is no different from a romantic scholar who suffers many career frustrations. Both have failed to fulfill their lifelong ambitions."[38] Feng Menglong must have found the alternative of a career as a writer an appealing way to compensate for his unrecognized talents. However, he was not alone in what seems to have been a pattern for many writers and thinkers during this period.[39] As the subsequent chapters explain, he commented on the practice of self-inflicted violence as the utmost demonstration of genuine passion, the fulfillment and foundation of all moral sanctity.

An Age of Sages?

The literary outpourings fueled by an exploration of passion reinterpreted cultural ideals and moral values placed on filial piety, female chastity, loyalty, and self-cultivation. As literacy spread, the assumption that achieving sagehood or moral sanctity was difficult gave way to the belief that learning should be widespread, pleasurable, and easy. Literacy, one gazetteer declared, was as essential to life as breathing. Sages, who in former times had appeared only once every few centuries, now filled the streets. Students were reassured that "wine, women, wealth, and passion do not block the road to enlightenment."[40] Everyone, including commoners, could demonstrate moral fortitude.

New interpretations of moral relativism and paradoxical behavior, although characteristic of the time and complex in their causes, can be traced back to the groundbreaking ideas of Wang Shouren 王守仁 (1472–1529), more familiarly known as Wang Yangming 王陽明. In reaction to an earlier view of the Song philosopher Zhu Xi 朱熹 (1130–1200), that principle (*li* 理) inheres in all things and can be perceived through the investigation of the external world (*gewu* 格物), Wang Yangming maintained that principle could be found within one's own mind through introspection.[41] He elaborated on the concept of "innate knowledge" (*liangzhi* 良知) and believed that through the extension of innate knowledge (*zhi liangzhi* 至良知) each person could achieve moral perfection, regardless of social standing. Moral perfection could be attained by the illiterate and the educated alike. He insisted that knowledge and practice cannot be separated (*zhixing heyi* 知行合一). All of these ideas eventually evolved and paved the way for moral relativism and individualism in the sixteenth and seventeenth centuries. His ideas were interpreted in many different ways—one scholar identifies an existentialist left wing, a quietist right wing, and an orthodox center[42]—and disseminated like wildfire by his students and followers to a wide audience of commoners. One of the latter was Wang Gen 王艮 (1483–1541) and his Taizhou School by way of popular lectures (*jiangxue* 講學). Wang Gen was a commoner who wandered throughout the countryside to teach artisans and peasants. His lectures attracted hundreds and thousands of people. Through him, the impact of Wang Yangming's thoughts on all strata of society was felt.

Wang Gen was a son of an uneducated salt merchant. He attended one of the village schools that the emperor Taizu had promoted for only five years. He also never took the civil service examinations. Nonetheless, he harbored grand ambitions to save the world. He once dreamed that when a crowd of thousands was screaming in terror because the sky was falling, he alone shouldered the sky and won everyone's praise and gratitude. His dream intimated that in real life the commoners were so eager for education that even he, albeit poorly educated, could gain prominence without an official position. Fueled by a sense of mission, Wang Gen wandered throughout the countryside to educate the artisans and peasants. As in his dream, so in real life he attracted enormous audiences, and on his death he left behind devoted disciples who energetically carried on his work.

He Xinyin 何心隱 (1517–1579) also followed in the wake of Wang Yangming.[43] He was initially somewhat more conventional than Wang Gen and took the district examinations in 1546. However, when persuaded by one of Wang Gen's followers that an official career would not be forthcoming, he took no further examinations and found other ways to serve his society. He organized his family members to work as a cooperative and encouraged them to follow egalitarian principles. He established a boarding school with the aim of removing children from parental influence and instructing them in his new principles. He even went so far as to convince his relatives to protest the local bureaucracy's excessive taxation. For his last act, he barely escaped punishment. For the rest of his life he wandered about lecturing and sometimes forming alliances with dubious fringe social groups. He was consequently arrested for theft and died in prison. While some, like Wang Gen, rushed to the countryside to educate the artisans and peasants, others attracted large followings to their academies in the bustling urban centers. Each disciple and each academy founder inspired by Wang Yangming's view that morals rested within one's own mind developed a personal philosophy and hence fostered an atmosphere of intellectual and moral relativism.

It would be facile to say that, by insisting on the concrete realization of abstract truths, Wang Yangming and his followers, who attempted to bring sagehood to the common people, were responsible for the subsequent blossoming of the cult of passion and the cultural manifestation of self-inflicted violence. However, on a more subtle level, the new exploration of the substance of genuine passion and the reappraisal of the significance of moral action in a changing culture, for example, have a very special relevance to the intellectual and religious underpinnings of a culture that encouraged a bodily performance and demonstration of moral values.

Moral teachings from different traditions, texts, and authors shared the notion that sanctity is to be realized in action. Scholars often characterize the religious landscape of the late imperial times as a "unification of the three teachings" (*sanjiao heyi* 三教合一) of Confucianism, Buddhism, and Daoism, an emic concept that was forged by the Chinese themselves. In outlining the history of this period, scholars generally treat this as a passing fashion, sometimes even as a hodgepodge of unsophisticated popular notions.[44] To be sure, mutual appropriation, competition, codification, imperial sponsorship, and attempts to find common grounds among these teachings have always been part of this continuing process of syncretism, as least early as the Six Dynasties period.[45] Yet, it was during the sixteenth and seventeenth centuries that the syncretism of the three teachings began to provide the basic language of discourse across the entire spectrum of writings and from common knowledge on up to serious philosophical inquiry.[46] Joint worship of representatives from the three teachings was common in popular religious rituals throughout China during this time. Buddhist monasteries housed non-Buddhist deities, and the same was true for state-cult and Daoist sites.[47] Popular writings also blended the three teachings, but they exhibited a certain degree of careful intellectual pursuit; there were still hidden suggestions of the superiority of one tradition over others.[48]

Moral action, of course, was a topic of great interest and discussion during this time. The emergence of new genres such as "morality books" (*shanshu* 善書), the "ledgers of merit and demerit" (*gongguoge* 功過格), and tracts on repentance were only some of the concrete manifestations of a performance-based morality.[49] These works closed the gaps between different religious traditions and different social classes in the sense that the content of many of these didactic works varied little, and they all addressed the concerns of people in different sectors of the society. The morality books also strengthened the age-old notion that heaven, bodhisattvas, or other sources of power in the cosmos (depending on one's point of view) responded to human actions by exhorting people to perform concrete deeds that accorded with cosmic intent. They accomplished these goals by invoking graphic ideas of karma retribution (*yebao* 業報) and the efficacious power of the universe. The morality books were written with the intention of redressing moral profligacy by, for example, assigning an exceedingly high number of "demerits" (conceived of in minus points) to certain actions and a high number of "merits" for concrete actions that upheld virtues.[50] The practices espoused in these works were taken quite literally to the point where—at the end of the day—one could have a precise numerical tally of one's moral progress.[51] Moral ideals had to be concretely demonstrated. Sometimes people were even coerced to demonstrate extreme acts of filial piety in competition with others.[52] Novels and popular writings also transmitted ideas of causality.[53]

These works reflect the bedrock conceptions of moral action during this time. Influential didactic texts and generations of exemplars therein emphasized to the general populace the importance of a corporeal demonstration of virtue. Children grew up reciting didactic stories of people sacrificing their lives to save their parents, and as adults they emulated them. Consider the *Poems on the Twenty-Four Filial Exemplars*, a popular didactic text detailing numerous ways that children can repay their parents' kindness,[54] and other novels that focus on passion by praising acts of extreme self-expression, not to mention the morality books and ledgers that promoted an embodied form of moral calculation. Many of them included graphic illustrations of self-mutilation and self-sacrifice. They were very popular among commoners and the educated elite alike, which paved the way for a milieu that favored extreme acts of sanctity. These stories were not only read but also, as the subsequent chapters explain, enacted in real life and historically documented in local gazetteers. Moreover, performers of self-inflicted violence who demonstrated cultural ideals were regularly reward by the local government and the imperial state during this time.

The heightened sense of commitment to the rigorous evaluation of individual moral behavior perhaps lent urgency to the dilemma of these few generations of intellectuals, who were imbued with the state value of noble service. It also imparted an edge to the defensiveness that characterized the heated polemics and debates of the period, in which the participants often seemed to be struggling just to put their names on the intellectual map.[55] Even when these people lived promiscuous lives, they were compelled to write about morality and self-cultivation. Numerous famous thinkers who wrote about self-cultivation were deeply troubled by their own sexual desires. Tu Long 屠龍 (1543–1605), for example, wrote extensively on didactic work advising people against sexual pleasures. His essay "On Awakening from Delusions" (*Xingmi lun* 醒迷論) focused on karmic retribution for those who committed sins caused by greed. In his essay titled "Ten Delusions" (*Shimi* 十迷) he meticulously listed different desires and their respective delusory natures. He was extremely aware of the dangers of desire. But Tu Long's life was full of contradictions. He was notorious for indulging in various sensual pleasures. In fact, his liberal views on sex and his own uninhibited behavior contributed directly to the abrupt end of his otherwise promising career. In 1583 Tu Long was accused of sexual misconduct and was put on trial just a year after he had been promoted to the position of secretary in the Ministry of Rites in Beijing.[56] In chapter 5 we will read about his failed attempt to end drought by ritually exposing himself in the blazing sun.

Many others also led a contradictory life. Historians have often quoted the famous "five true happinesses" (*zhenle* 真樂) of devout Buddhist Yuan Hongdao 袁宏道 (1568–1610), who was also a member of the literati, as an example of the typical seventeenth-century hedonism. First on the list is sensual pleasure.[57] The paradox is that those who were enthusiastic about and articulate in promoting desire were often the same people who were the most conscious of and the most vocal about their fear of the inevitable perils of desire. Prescriptively, their writings celebrated the importance of moral sanctity. Descriptively, their lives reflected a much more complicated picture. A symbiotic relationship existed between dramatic acts of sanctity and moral profligacy.

In the background against which the practice of self-inflicted violence thrived stood economic and commercial growth, intellectual innovations, new moral outlooks, and political changes, all of which unleashed a great anxiety in what has been described as "confusions of pleasure."[58] These changes led to the perceived decadence and moral decline of society in the eyes of many sixteenth- and seventeenth-century thinkers and writers. Tremendous material growth and monetization of the economy over the course of the Ming changed the moral fabric of the society. New religious outlooks were undoubtedly connected with these changes. During this period, acts of self-inflicted violence flourished. One may argue that the economic prosperity led to moral profligacy, which mobilized writers and social commentators to criticize the social behaviors they disapproved of. In this sense, they used extreme acts of self-inflicted violence as ideological weapons in their fight to secure the stability of the world. Yet, from another perspective, the same perceived moral corruption also produced genuine subjectivity in the heroes and heroines who engaged in extreme acts of sanctity. The reality is always more complex.

In the next several chapters we will read about men, women, and children who inflicted violence on their bodies to passionately demonstrate their virtue and to negotiate new social relations. There is no simple link between sixteenth- and seventeenth-century socio-intellectual changes and the practice of self-inflicted violence except that changes in the economic, moral, and intellectual milieu, along with the perennial religious idea of self-cultivation, would have fostered a focus on concrete moral action. The prosperities and problems during this period did not engender a more "ethical" society, but they did affect people's behaviors and perceptions of morality. During this period of change, prosperity, and confusion, self-inflicted violence took on new significance. Performers engaged in self-inflicted violence for many reasons. Nothing shows this more clearly than the sheer number of cases in local gazetteers, hagiographies, scholarly jottings, and novels that I discuss in detail in subsequent chapters.

2

Embodying the Text through Blood Writing

I, a follower of the bodhisattva precepts, Zhixu, vow to prick my tongue to copy Mahāyāna scriptures and *vinaya* in my blood. First, I will, in front of the Three Jewels, burn my arm with twelve sticks of incense and make twelve vows. May my deceased father [of this lifetime], and my loving fathers of countless lifetimes, sever self-attachment from time without beginning, ascend to the Land of Bliss, and receive the prediction [of buddhahood] by the Buddha.[1]

—Ouyi Zhixu 蕅益智旭 (1599–1655)

BLOOD WRITING (*xieshu* 血書), the practice of copying or writing texts with blood from one's own body was one of the most potent rituals for conveying one's message and authenticating one's sanctity. Those who engaged in this practice used it to accomplish many things, including negotiating a pardon by the emperor, transferring religious merit to one's deceased parents, curing illness, and securing or challenging existing religious or political order. By means of this ritual, performers constructed their subjectivity and produced, reproduced, and reconfigured a particular vision of the world, society, or community. Even though scholars commonly connect blood writing with Buddhist monks copying Buddhist scriptures in blood,[2] this ritual simultaneously elicited many associations. It had complex origins in blood covenant, sacrifice, and the production of apotropaic talismans. It is in this larger cultural context and through these associations that the practice was intelligible and meaningful to both the performers and their audience. Little has been done to show the widespread popularity of blood writing beyond this specific Buddhist context, and the logic and the broader significance of this act remain unexplored. In this chapter I discuss several cases of blood writing and show how different people, both lay Buddhists and Confucian officials, constructed sanctity and personal meaning and defended certain boundaries through this practice. I also examine the practice in relation to its symbolic associations with bodily sacrifice.

Blood Writing as Filial Devotion

One of the most common themes associated with the practice of blood writing was filial sacrifice. Devotion to one's parents was the paradigmatic virtue for the Chinese. Yet, sometimes such devotion took extreme measures that crossed the boundaries of what was expected of children. Some scholars claim that harming the body was explicitly discouraged in texts on filial piety.[3] However, such a claim favors prescriptive truths over descriptive realities. What better way to demonstrate one's filiality than by using one's own flesh and blood, which come from one's parents? As we will read below, pious children had little problem with cutting open the tips of their fingers or tongues for blood in order to copy long scriptures and dedicating the merit from this act to their parents. The threat of losing their lives in the process of performing blood writing dramatized and intensified their filial piety and was for many performers the pinnacle of moral cultivation. In the text-centered culture of premodern China, writing itself was a public testimonial—an act of authentication and legitimization in concrete material terms—of filial devotion.[4] Blood writing was a textualization of this cultural ideal.

Traditional scholarship typically cites the following injunction from the *Classic of Filial Piety* and claims that the Chinese avoided "harming the body" because they viewed it positively as a precious gift from one's parents:

> Now, filial piety is the root of virtue from which grow [all moral] teachings . . . Our bodies—to every hair and bit of skin—are received by us from our parents, and we must not injure or wound them: this is the beginning of filial piety. Establishing our character by the practice of the [filial] way, so as to make our name famous in future ages, and thereby glorify our parents: this is the end of filial piety. Filial piety commences with the service of parents; it proceeds to the service of the ruler; it is completed by the establishment of the character.[5]

If the *Classic of Filial Piety* seems to proscribe any damaging of the body, then how can we interpret the actions of many pious children who inflicted violence on their bodies to fulfill their filial duties? How can we explain the case of a literatus who copied the *Classic of Filial Piety* in his own blood? And why did educated contemporaries—sometimes even the emperor—eulogize and reward such actions, which were supposedly unfilial? The answer is that it was precisely the harming of their bodies that "established the character" (*lishen* 立身) and "made their parents' name famous" (*yangming* 揚名) for posterity. Although at a rudimentary level the text proscribes "injuring the body" (*huishang* 毀傷), this was precisely what pious children had to do to demonstrate their filial devotion. Influential late Ming moralists asserted that one's duty to heaven and to one's parents, who give one life, was to nourish, preserve, and reproduce that life in its most fundamental biological form.[6] Moreover, the long history of self-sacrifice as part and parcel of moral cultivation would have encouraged sons and daughters to interpret the passage in the *Classic of Filial Piety* to "glorify parents" (*yixian fumu* 以顯父母) as giving up something as precious as one's own body to one's parents, the source of one's own life.

The *Classic of Filial Piety* actually stipulates spiritual and cosmic benefits for those who with the utmost dedication devote themselves to their parents. Willingness to engage in self-inflicted violence for the sake of moral virtues was believed to result in heaven's sympathy and support. The *Classic of Filial Piety* asserts that, "When in the ancestral temple one conveys respect, spirits and deities manifest themselves. When filial piety and brotherliness reach their pinnacle, one communicates with the heavenly spirits, shines throughout the four seas, and travels everywhere."[7]

The social realities behind filial sacrifice are, of course, very complex. There is evidence that many people on the lower rungs of the social ladder engaged in extravagant gestures of filial piety because they might have either been coerced into doing it or had no other means of aiding their parents. For example, I came across a sixteenth-century case where a father was jealous of the neighbor's son, who had used his own flesh as medicine to cure his father's illness. As a result, the jealous father encouraged his own son to do the same.[8] There were also poor children who voluntarily jumped off cliffs, hoping to touch the sympathy of the gods so they would cure their parents' illness because either the children had no means of paying for a doctor or the medicines were ineffectual. Alternatively, they believed that sacrificing their own lives would extend those of their parents.[9] Their only hope rested on divine intervention. Such phenomena are beyond the purview of prescriptive texts and the control of the literati-officials who documented them in their prescriptive "Confucian" moral claims.

During the sixteenth and seventeenth centuries, numerous apocryphal Buddhist scriptures detailed the importance of children repaying their parents' kindness. Their circulation must also have been a factor in the spread of blood writing. These scriptures include the *Scripture on the Difficulty of Repaying the Kindness of Parents*, the *Scripture on the Profound Kindness of Parents*, and the *Scripture on the Difficulty of Repaying the Profound Kindness of Parents*.[10] What these scriptures share is the notion that serving one's parents to the utmost (which may involve self-maiming and austerities) and relieving them of suffering are considered superior to making offerings to all the Buddhist sages and buddhas.

These esteemed cultural values shaped the way Chinese Buddhists engaged in extreme practices. Numerous clerics in the sixteenth and seventeenth centuries produced "blood scriptures" (*xiejing* 血經). Prominent monks, such as Hanshan Deqing 憨山德清 (1546–1623) and Ouyi Zhixu 蕅益智旭 (1599–1655), not only engaged in blood writing but also encouraged their lay followers to do so.[11] Their passion for the dharma translated into blood writings, which signaled particular "structures of feeling" that were understood during the sixteenth and seventeenth centuries as a corporeal demonstration of genuineness. As discussed in chapter 1, it was during this period that many of the cultural values prized in earlier times, such as filial piety, loyalty, humaneness, justice, and female chastity, took on a new level of understanding that demanded concrete demonstration.[12]

Evidence suggests that even common people perceived blood writing as a dangerous, extraordinary act. Consider the case of Wu Junping 吳君平 (fl. Wanli era), a scholar-official who resided in Tongxiang 桐鄉 County in Zhejiang province. He was orphaned in his youth. Every time he thought about his parents, he was moved to tears. One day someone told him that he could copy a Buddhist scripture in his own blood to repay his gratitude to his deceased parents. Upon hearing this, Wu took up a light vegetarian diet for forty-nine days and, at the end of the fast, sliced his own chest—at the point closest to his heart—eleven times to draw enough blood to copy the *Diamond Sūtra* (*Jingang jing* 金剛經). The night he finished copying the scripture he dreamed that his father and mother were standing on clouds saying that, due to his pious act, they had been reborn in the Pure Land of Amitābha Buddha.[13] This story is included in a Buddhist collection of miracle tales associated with the *Diamond Sūtra*.[14]

Wu Junping's blood scripture was concrete, visible, and public. Upon its completion, monastics and laity living in his vicinity supposedly flocked to see his blood scripture and wanted to verify his scars. After seeing the marks on his chest, they all reverently praised him for the sincerity of his austere, painful act (*chengxin kuxing* 誠心苦行).[15] The difficult process by which the scripture was produced and the scars displayed for the public to witness generated awe in the spectators. The medium of blood sanctified and animated Wu Junping's message in a powerful and visceral way. His blood scripture was not meant for publication or mass production. It was not a mere artifact, inert and complete unto itself; its physical existence or thingness was in a constant state of interaction between him as its producer and these spectators as his witnesses. His scripture communicated a message through the medium of blood. The interaction of message and medium enabled him to create merit and allowed his viewers to gaze upon him with awe.

Indeed, the Mahāyāna scriptures served as a strong internal motivation for Buddhists to engage in blood writing. Some of these scriptures were germane to the development of Chinese Buddhism as a whole. In them the ideals of self-sacrifice as a means of perpetuating the Buddhadharma are valorized.[16] Not surprisingly, the scriptures that promote self-sacrifice are those that Buddhists most commonly copied in blood. They include the *Lotus Scripture*, the *Brahma Net Scripture*, and the *Flower Ornament Scripture*, as well as the genre of the *Perfection of Wisdom* literature, which would include the *Diamond Sūtra*, which Wu Junping copied.[17]

These texts extol the propagation not just of Buddhist teachings but also of Buddhist books that contain them. Many Mahāyāna scriptures make an implicit connection between the preciousness of Buddhist teaching in the world for posterity and its material form as books, encouraging Buddhists to physically produce and uphold them.[18] Of course, one can explain the practice of hand-copying texts as the result of the scanty circulation of manuscripts, but this cannot possibly explain its persistence even after the printing boom in the sixteenth and seventeenth centuries. One would have to conclude that the very practice of copying a text reveals what a text is to those who copied scriptures in their own blood.

For example, the *Diamond Sūtra*, the text that Wu Junping and many other Buddhists copied in their own blood, advocated not only the teaching of emptiness (Skt. *śunyatā*) but also the notion that the material presence of the scripture is the location of the Buddha. We do not have the exact copy of Wu Junping's blood scripture of the *Diamond Sūtra*, but we do have below a copy of the *Diamond Sūtra* in blood that supports this view (figure 2.1).

The passage in Figure 2.1, beginning with the third line from the right, reads as follows: "Subhuti, the spot of earth where this *sūtra* exists, that spot will be worthy of worship by the whole world with its gods, men, and *asuras*,

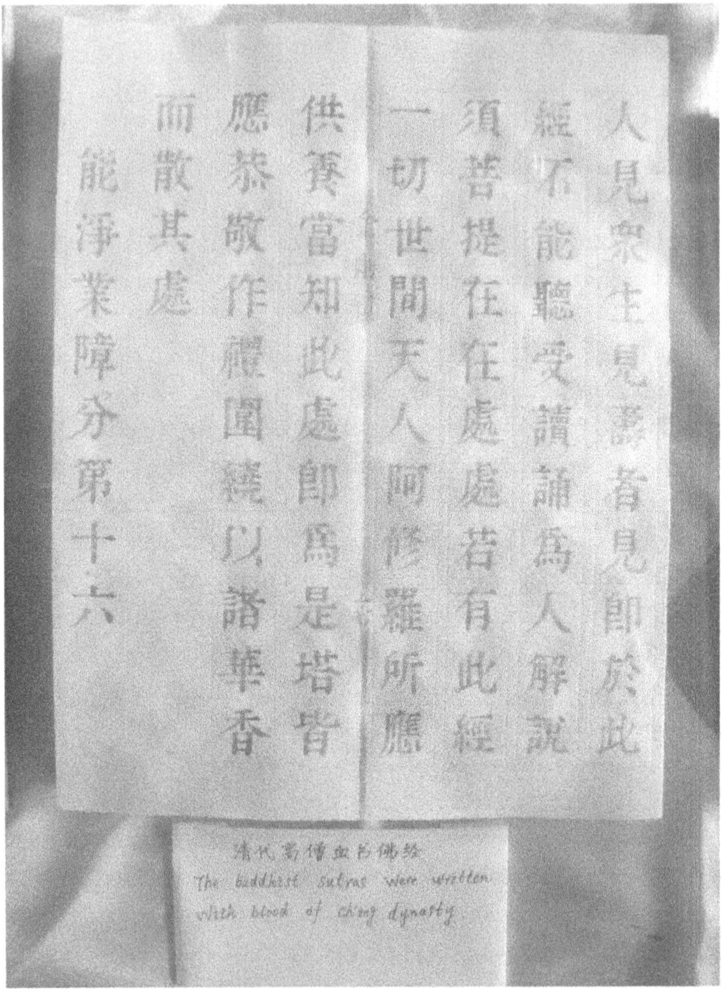

FIGURE 2.1 The *Diamond Sūtra* copied in blood by a Qing Dynasty Buddhist cleric. The two-page spread measures 8 × 13 inches. The text is on public display under a glass case at the Tripiṭaka Hall of Yongquan Monastery 湧泉寺 on Mount Gu 鼓山 in Fujian province. Photograph © by the author.

that spot of earth will be worthy of being saluted respectfully, worthy of being honored by circumambulation—like a *stūpa* will be that spot of earth."[19] A *stūpa* is a reliquary for the Buddha's remains (Skt. *śarīras*). It is an object of worship, around which Buddhists practiced circumambulation. The preceding passage states that where the *sūtra* or scripture is, there the Buddha is also. The veneration of this scripture, which elaborates on the wisdom of emptiness, or *prajñā*, is equivalent to the worshipping of the Buddha's remains or the Buddha himself. Elsewhere in the *Perfection of Wisdom* literature, the practice of hand-copying scriptures, a practice that materially produces the dharma, is valued even above ordinary worship.[20] Scholars have noted that the Mahāyāna scripture itself is often equated with the body of the Tathāgata or Buddha and is considered an object of veneration in its own right.[21]

This complex interdependence of medium and message—a hand-copied blood scripture and its contents promoting self-sacrifice—helps not only to open up new understandings of what a scripture was to the premodern Chinese but also to explain why they chose certain texts to copy in blood. The forty-fascicle version of the *Flower Ornament Scripture* (i.e., the *Avataṃsaka sūtra*), which advocates the importance of embodying the Buddhist scripture, states the following:

> Since the inception of his career as a bodhisattva, Vairocana Buddha has been extremely diligent in practice and has offered his own bodies [lifetime after lifetime] in inconceivable ways. He peeled off his skin and used it as paper, broke off his bone and used it as a pen, and pricked himself to draw blood as ink; the scriptures he copied in this manner accumulated as high as Mount Sumeru. He did so out of great reverence for the Dharma.[22]

Mount Sumeru in Indian Buddhist mythology is said to be so tall that it holds up the cosmos.[23] To copy enough blood scriptures to stack up as high as Mount Sumeru is to offer millions and millions of lifetimes of bodies and blood. What is important in this passage is that the bodhisattva embodies the dharma literally. Not only are his body parts used to produce the scriptures, but the scriptures are also his bodies. The veneration of the dharma is celebrated by acts of self-sacrifice and blood writing. Whereas ordinary people hold dear their own bodies, Vairocana sacrificed his for the continuance of the dharma, implying that those who aspire to be true bodhisattvas should emulate him.[24] The *Flower Ornament Scripture* was also one of the favorite scriptures chosen to be copied in blood by Buddhists, clerical or lay, in the history of Chinese Buddhism, particularly in late imperial times.[25]

The impact and significance of using one's own body to produce a text goes well beyond Buddhist monastic circles. In another case of filial blood writing discussed later, Feng Xingke 馮行可 (1521–ca. 1609) used his blood to negotiate his father's fate. His blood writing served as a vehicle to assert his claim to moral power in order to manipulate his social circumstances. In 1532 Feng Xingke wrote a memorial to the emperor in his own blood to save the life of his father, Feng En 馮恩 (1491–1571).[26] His father was supposedly a virtuous censor of note and one of the last disciples of Wang Yangming. As noted in chapter 1, as arguably one the most influential thinkers of the sixteenth century, he paved the way for a morality that privileged physical action over mere knowledge.[27]

Feng En's ordeal began when the imperial court observed the comet that appeared in September of 1532. The comet supposedly lingered in the sky for 115 days, just a year after the one later known as Halley's Comet. Emperor Shizong interpreted this as a bad omen signifying the existence of disloyal ministers at court. The principle of heaven was understood as operating in symbiotic resonance with earthly phenomena. The logic of this resonance is that if the imperial court is immoral or the court ministers are corrupt, heaven will mimic that imbalance and rain down disasters on humankind. Emperor Shizong solicited criticism from his ministers in an effort to dispel this bad omen. It was then that Feng En submitted a memorial to the emperor that reviewed twenty high officials. He criticized ten of the emperor's favorite ministers for their flaws. As a result, he was jailed, tortured, and sentenced to death. His elder son, Feng Xingke, who was only twelve years old at the time, wrote a memorial with his own blood and offered his own life to save that of his father (*daifu si* 代父死). He stated that if his father were to die, his grandmother, who was already more than eighty years old, would surely die of grief, and this would inevitably make his father impious. Begging for mercy, Feng Xingke submitted his memorial to the emperor through sympathetic officials, who recommended that the sentence be reduced. The son then wrote the following:

> Ever since my official father [Feng En] lost his own father in his youth, my grandmother Madame Wu remained chaste to educate him until he reached adulthood and became a censor. Our whole family receives his emolument.... Now that he has fallen under the emperor, and my grandmother is over eighty, the pain of her sadness is deep, and she has only a few breaths left. If my official father were to die today, grandmother Wu would also surely die today.... I beg your majesty to have pity, revoke the sentence placed [on my father], release him, and extend the lives of the mother and son [i.e., my grandmother and father].... I sincerely extend my neck and wait for your naked sword.[28]

Feng En's sentence was indeed reduced as a result of his son's pious act. He was banished to Leizhou, in Guangzhou province. Later in 1567, when Emperor Muzong ascended the throne, he recalled to service many officials who had been exiled. As a result, Feng En was given the title of vice minister of the Grand Court of Revision and, because of his age, was granted the right to live in retirement. Furthermore, his eldest son, Feng Xingke, was given an imperial citation for his filial piety and was then made head of a bureau in the Court of Imperial Entertainment.[29]

Feng Xingke's blood memorial invoked the power of virtue, honor, and self-sacrifice. He drew on the virtues of his grandmother's chastity, his father's filial piety toward her, and his own filial devotion to his father. He negotiated his father's sentence and gave witness to his resolve by offering to sacrifice his own life, which was demonstrated by his blood memorial. It was important to restore his father's good name by publicly announcing his father's virtue (and that of his entire family). Feng Xingke's blood writing won not only a pardon from the emperor but also a higher social status for his father and for Feng himself. The elaborately constructed synthesis of passion, morality, bodily violence, self-sacrifice, and political intrigue demonstrates the power of the practice of blood writing.

Consider also the case of Ouyi Zhixu, who regularly engaged in blood writing throughout his monastic career. On receiving the bodhisattva precepts in 1629, he wrote the following votive testimonial (*yuanwen* 願文) in his own blood. It is the full translation of the text (an excerpt of which appears as an epigraph at the beginning of this chapter):

> I, a follower of the bodhisattva precepts, Zhixu, vow to prick my tongue to copy Mahāyāna scriptures and *vinaya* in my blood. First, I will, in front of the Three Jewels, burn my arms with twelve sticks of incense and make twelve vows. May my deceased father [of this lifetime], and my loving fathers of countless lifetimes, sever self-attachment from time without beginning, ascend to the Land of Bliss, and receive the prediction [of buddhahood] by the Buddha. May my deceased mother, and my compassionate mothers of countless lifetimes, sever the fundamental afflictions, be reborn in lotuses, and receive the prediction [of buddhahood] by the Buddha. May my fellow practitioners of this lifetime, and all the past true virtuous friends, perfect and fulfill Bodhi before me. May sentient beings of the dharma realms universally destroy the two attachments, sever the various sufferings, attain the adamantine body, purify the three collective precepts, complete all the correct *samādhis*, realize genuine wisdom, give rise to Bodhi-mind, acquire non-retrogression, and return to the unsurpassable awakening [of a buddha]. I dedicate the causes and conditions of the benevolent power from

> the vows and bestow them universally on the dharma realms, [so that sentient beings therein may] together attain the nonduality of the unborn, the nonattainment of the uncreated, and permanently separate themselves from delusion and realize permanent happiness.[30]

Here we see the same motif of acquiring moral power through blood writing and other practices to benefit one's parents. Ouyi specifies the kinds of benefit he would like to bring to his parents: the severance of attachments and afflictions, rebirth in the Land of Bliss, and attainment of buddhahood.

His vows accord rather well with stock Mahāyāna teachings on the two hindrances (*erzhang* 二障), which can be found in many scriptures. Ouyi first wishes that his parents would sever their "self-attachment" (*wozhi* 我執) and "fundamental affliction" (*genben fannao* 根本煩惱), which correspond to the first of the two hindrances: the afflictive hindrances (*fannao zhang* 煩惱障; Skt. *kleśa-āvaraṇa*). Then he states that he wishes his parents, along with all beings, could "give rise to the Bodhi-mind" (*fa putixin* 發菩提心), or the bodhisattva's altruistic intention of saving all beings. The Bodhi-mind is the main factor that leads to the severance of the second hindrance: the subtle cognitive hindrances (*suozhi zhang* 所知障; Skt. *jñeya-āvaraṇa*).

These two broad hindrances articulate what Mahāyāna Buddhists take to be the kinds of attachments that prevent the attainment of buddhahood. The first afflictive hindrance corresponds to self-attachment. The second corresponds to the attachment to phenomenal reality, or *dharmas* (*fazhi* 法執), as having true existence. According to his Buddhism, sentient beings suffer from a wide range of afflictive, emotive attachments, such as greed, anger, ignorance, pride, and suspicion, which ultimately stem from the continuous misapprehension of the senses of self as having autonomous, separate, and permanent existence. Ouyi saw this self-attachment as rooted in the perception of the body, or *shenjian* 身見 (Skt. *satkāya-dṛṣṭi*).[31]

The cognitive hindrances, the fundamental error of attachment to phenomenal reality as separate from the self, are subtler attachments that the bodhisattva strives to let go of before attaining full buddhahood. This involves generating the Bodhi-mind. Buddhism teaches that to truly benefit others is to perceive the nonduality of self and others, which would free one from all constraints imposed by phenomenal reality. Ouyi's perception of all beings as none other than his own fathers and mothers of "countless lifetimes" may be interpreted as the interconnectedness of all beings, a form of nonduality.

If my interpretation is accepted, then the logic of this ritualized program becomes clear. Ouyi would overcome the two hindrances by first inflicting violence on his body by copying Buddhist scriptures in his own blood and burning his arms with twelve sticks of incense. These two practices demonstrate his detachment from the self, which is the core of afflictive hindrances. He makes vows to the bodhisattva in wishing that his parents, along with all sentient beings as his past and future parents, may attain happiness by "destroying the two attachments." Perceiving sentient beings as intimately connected to one another would free him from perceiving the world in dualistic terms and thus overcome the second cognitive hindrance. Inflicting violence to his own body would result in "attaining the adamantine body" of the Buddha, and benefiting all beings by generating the Bodhi-mind would result in "realizing genuine wisdom."

With his blood writing, Ouyi was making a clear statement with and about his body, which must be relinquished in order to realize wisdom, or *prajñā*. We may also understand blood writing as a way to secure a sense of religious authority in situations when sanctity was threatened or challenged.

Self-Sacrifice and Negotiating Boundaries

Blood writing was a form of self-sacrifice and a means of negotiating the boundaries between religious ideologies, social relations, and political loyalty. The conflation of blood writings, sacrifice, and boundaries is evident in the writings of the performers themselves, who used blood writing as a vehicle to establish their own subjectivity as moral agents and as defenders of the faith or to challenge political authority. Their bodies instantiated and thus conferred facticity on abstract ideals and values that were otherwise difficult to demonstrate to the public.

For dedicated Buddhists, the intent to protect the true dharma from benighted practices in a degenerate age demanded they take drastic measures. They believed that only genuine spiritual practices would be able to save Buddhism from corruption. The best way to do this was to personally engage in self-inflicted violence. Consider the case of Deqing, one of the most illustrious clerics of the late Ming. In 1581 Deqing finished a task he had begun in 1577; he copied the *Flower Ornament Scripture*—one of the longest scriptures in the Chinese Buddhist canon, consisting of eighty long scrolls and close to six million characters—in his own blood mixed with gold powder:

> In the spring of my thirty-second *sui*, I returned from Yanmen [Wild Goose Pass, situated in the modern northwest corner of Dai County, Shanxi province]. Recalling the benevolence of my [deceased] parents

> and the care they had given me, I thought of the numerous obstacles that stood between me and the Dharma. On reading the votive text of the great master [Hui]si of Nanyue,[32] I vowed to prick [my arm for] blood [and copy the entire text of the *Flower Ornament Sūtra*] by mixing my own blood with gold [powder] to make it into a paste. Above, this [act] would serve as a superior causal condition to realize *prajñā*, and below it would repay the enormous debt [to my parents] for their kindness.[33]

Like his peers, Deqing believed that copying Buddhist scriptures in his own blood could generate a great amount of merit. The positive karmic reward could be transferred to his parents as an offering and also enable him to gain effective power and overcome obstacles in realizing wisdom, or *prajñā*. However, a distinctive connection must be pointed out—the connection between the decline of the dharma, self-inflicted violence, and blood writing. Deqing's blood writing was inspired by Nanyue Huisi's 南岳慧思 (515–577) vow, in which he promised to engage in endless austerities and self-sacrificial practices. Huisi stated explicitly that for fifty-six million years, in all of his future rebirths, he would engage in painful austerities so that dharma would never decline. His vows drew a connection between the inherent power in austerities and the continuance of Buddhadharma in the world.

Scholars have noted that Huisi was the first Chinese Buddhist cleric to have systematically periodized Śākyamuni Buddha's teaching into the "true dharma" (*zhengfa* 正法), the "semblance dharma" (*xiangfa* 像法), and the "degeneration or the decline of dharma" (*mofa* 末法).[34] His exaltation of austerities in a degenerate age was underscored by his eschatological despair as his demise approached. He also encouraged his own disciples to engage in austerities: "If there were [but] ten people [among you], who, without regret for life and limb [were willing to] constantly pursue practices of… austerities, I personally would supply whatever you need. It would surely be to our mutual benefit. If there are no such persons, then I will depart far away."[35] Because the practice of austerities was difficult to undertake, his biographer laments that no one spoke up, and so Huisi thereupon dismissed the assembly, gathered his thoughts, and passed away.

Some may wonder just how difficult it is to produce a blood scripture, especially in light of Deqing's blood scripture, which was produced by mixing his blood with gold powder. When the Empress Dowager Li found out about his intention to produce a blood scripture of the *Avataṃsaka Sūtra*, she provided gold powder and paper for his endeavor. One may argue that the practice of using gold powder, as well as the whole phenomenon of blood writing itself, may have been a highly stylized elite activity. Such an assertion of blood writing does bear an element of truth, but from the hundreds of blood scriptures I have examined in China and the actual performance of it that I have witnessed,[36] there is little doubt that the practice involved grave physical pain and danger on the part of the performer, especially in this case, when the text copied was the *Avataṃsaka Sūtra*, or the *Flower Ornament Scripture*, which consists of some six hundred thousand characters.

Deqing identified with Huisi's sentiment for austerities because he lamented the decline of the dharma in the world. Both saw themselves as guardians of the faith: As long as there were those who were willing to engage the body in austerities—or corporeally "embody" the scriptures through blood writing—the demise of Buddhadharma in the world would be avoided. Buddhism would remain in the world only if the wisdom of the scriptures were embodied and realized. This string of logic suggests that self-infliction of violence on the body, as exemplified by blood writing, has the power to maintain the sanctity of religion and prevent moral deterioration. In other words, austerities are instrumental in defending boundaries.

In a postscript written for his friend Xuelang Hong'en's 雪浪洪恩 (1545–1608)[37] disciple, Zhenzhao 真照, who wrote a copy of the *Brahma Net Scripture* in his blood, Deqing laments the demise of dharma and connects blood writing to the attainment of wisdom, or *prajñā*:

> The disciple Zhenzhao has a profound affinity with the practice of *prajñā*. He became a monk at his own will and studied under my dharma brother, Xuelan for some years.... Hearing me lamenting the political state of affairs and the degeneration of the dharma, and that those who engage with the fundamental are few, he was touched by my wish to transmit and recite the [bodhisattva] precepts from the *Brahma Net Scripture*. He begged to receive the [bodhisattva] precepts and generated a profound and weighty vow to prick his tongue for blood to copy this scripture. Moreover, he made a determination to uphold it for the rest of his life. I was moved by his determination. Our original teacher, Vairocana Buddha, whose diligence has never regressed from the inception of his practice until buddhahood, has offered an unspeakable number of life times, using his own skin as paper, bones as pens, and blood as ink to copy scriptures. All of which amounts to as high as Mount Sumeru. Because he emphasized the [preciousness of] the dharma, he was willing to give up his own life

> for it. He [Zhenzhao] knows that it is difficult to transcend birth and death, to sever the root of desire, and anticipate the attainment of buddhahood. Yet, if we rely on the Buddha to practice, in accordance with the vows of the Buddha, why worry about not being able to attain buddhahood? From now on, from one life to the next, use the blood from your body to copy this text so that it amounts to even beyond the height and vastness of Mount Sumeru.[38]

Deqing makes a direct connection between the decline of Buddhadharma and the necessity of self-sacrifice of the bodhisattva and the efficacy of blood writing in the attainment of buddhahood. He cites the *Flower Ornament Scripture's* passage about Vairocana (discussed earlier) to praise Zhenzhao's wish to engage in blood writing at a time when few knew how to genuinely practice it. His point in citing the scripture is to inform Zhenzhao that, as long as the latter emulated Vairocana's former lives as the ultimate bodhisattva exemplar who engaged in blood writing, he, too, would become a buddha. In other words, blood writing and its meritorious power lead to buddhahood. Such a view was shared by many contemporary monastic and lay Buddhists, such as Zibo Zhenke 紫柏真可 (1543–1603) and Ouyi Zhixu, whom I have already discussed, especially when they perceived the possibility of moral degeneration or some eschatological threat.

Ouyi also wrote about the connection between austerities and the continuance of Buddhadharma in his preface to the reprint of the *Sūtra of Twelve Dhūtaguṇa Practice*: "The purpose of *dhūtaguṇas* [austerities] is to slough off the dust-like afflictions. Replete with the twelve practices, the honorable [Mahā]kaśyapa had practiced them for all his life. [For this reason] the World Honored One stated that the perpetuation in the world of the true dharma depended solely on him."[39] Ouyi asserts that Mahakaśyapa was entrusted with the dharma precisely because he engaged in *dhūtaguṇas*, which is a Sanskrit term that the Chinese transliterates as *toutuo* 頭陀 and is interchangeable with painful austerities, or *kuxing*. In the preceding passage Ouyi states that the destruction of afflictions can be accomplished only through austerities. This is a term that most scholars translate as asceticism, which is usually examined through the lens of the Judeo-Christian tradition. I have already detailed the methodological and theoretical problems of doing this in the introduction. What is important to recognize here is that *toutuo* and *kuxing* in the Chinese context are directly connected to physical pain. For this reason I render these terms as painful austerities. For example, Ouyi explicitly describes *kuxing's* painful nature when he advises his lay disciple: "We find it difficult to relinquish [our attachments], especially when it comes to our own bodies in the practice of pricking the tongue for blood to use as ink [in blood writing], which involves extreme pain (*zhongji* 重極)! [Yet] doing so is able to destroy our [attachment to] views of the body."[40] For Ouyi, blood writing was an agentive act predicated on pain. It allowed him to relinquish attachments and attain wisdom.

There are twelve traditional *dhūtaguṇas* instituted in early Buddhist scriptures: (1) dwelling only in the forest; (2) begging for alms; (3) not passing over any house when begging; (4) eating only once a day; (5) limiting one's intake of food; (6) not ingesting liquid food after the midday meal; (7) wearing rag robes; (8) using only three robes; (9) living in a cemetery; (10) sitting at the foot of a tree; (11) dwelling in the open air; (12) sleeping in a sitting position and never lying down. Liz Wilson lists thirteen "*dhūtaguṇas*" in the *Encyclopedia of Buddhism* from modern Theravāda Buddhist context, which provides a different sequence of these practices and has "eating from alms bowl" and "eating in one sitting" replacing the "limiting one's intake of food."[41]

It is important to first note that the original establishment of these practices had more to do with convenience and their cultural acceptance than with soteriology. Second, it is doubtful that many early Indian monastics followed these prescriptions. Those that did, at least from the perspective of the *Mūlasarvāstivāda-vinaya*, tended to be frowned upon as objects of ridicule. They were far from being perceived as saints.[42] I suspect that in China painful austerities were regarded with great reverence because they correlated with the indigenous discourses of sanctity and self-cultivation. This would also explain why no Chinese clerics (at least those that I have come across) practiced all of these twelve or thirteen austerities. While some did follow the practice of eating once a day, not eating after the midday meal, avoiding sexual intercourse, and sleeping in a sitting posture,[43] Chinese clerics drew most of their inspiration from Mahāyāna Buddhist scriptures and their own indigenous practices of self-sacrifice. Blood writing was one example of indigenous practices that the Chinese considered austere. Body slicing and self-immolation were others, and they are discussed in later chapters.[44]

Our view today is that *dhūtaguṇa* or *kuxing* was a standard part of Buddhist self-cultivation. However, evidence shows that such a prescriptive view (mostly derived from the *vinaya*) has clouded our understanding of what actually happened. It would not be far fetched to say that most monastics lived their lives not so differently from the laity. Anyone who actually engaged in any of the austere practices in China would be perceived as unusual. In fact, utilizing various documents that describe in great detail the inventories of monasteries in the area, the processes through which people were ordained, published announcements of monastic affairs that were circulated among the clergy, and so on, we now know that the standard canonical sources on monastic discipline fail—due to their numerous discrepancies with the local sources—to accurately depict how monks and nuns actually went about their lives. The canonical sources are merely prescriptive, not descriptive. Among the most crucial revelations are that many monks and nuns in certain regions of China did not always live in a monastery but stayed at home with their families, frequently drank alcohol, were required to seek permission from secular authorities and pay a fee to be ordained, and paid taxes and performed corvée labor as did any other citizen. All of this flies in the face of *vinaya* regulations and prescriptions. Our perception of how monastics may have lived in medieval and late imperial times needs to be adjusted.[45] During the sixteenth century, most monasteries and monastics were secularized and gentrified. Large monasteries were places to which the educated elite would retreat "to enjoy the [scenic] view, drink wine, compose poetry," far from our view of what monasteries should be.[46] It is no wonder that hagiographical accounts highlight certain traits of eminent monastics, such as taking up vegetarian diets, avoiding sexual intercourse, and engaging in painful austerities. This is probably because these practices were *not* the norm. This would also explain why Ouyi's practices and those who wrote about him described the practices as extraordinary.

Ouyi highlights the relationship between perpetuating the Buddhadharma and the need to attain wisdom through self-inflicted violence. Clear boundaries must be drawn between those who walk the path of wisdom and those who merely talk about it. In his polemical preface for a lay disciple who copied the *Lotus Scripture* in his own blood, Ouyi criticized those whom he believed acted in iconoclastic ways and claimed groundless truths that lacked genuine practice. In his judgment these people were one of the chief causes of what he saw as a decline of Chan Buddhism:

> Those followers of "wild-wisdom" belittle it [blood-writing] as [involving] "corporeality." But among the root causes of beginningless birth and death, none is deeper than the very perception of the body. Among [the practices of] wondrous world-transcending dharma, none precedes destroying the spurious mountain of *satkāya*.[47] When this perverse perception of *satkāya* is destroyed, the wheel of birth and death is forever stilled. This [practice of blood writing] is called

> paying reverence to the Correct Dharma; it is also called using the dharma to make offerings to Buddha. The *Lotus* and *Śuraṃgama* [*sūtras*] have profound praise for incinerating one's limbs and fingers, as well as the merits from burning incense [into one's body]. Some may contend: "How can severing the limb of afflictions and burning the body of ignorance depend on the flesh and blood?" These people do not realize that... this very body is precisely [the husk] of ignorance and afflictions.[48]

In this context Ouyi equates the practice of blood writing with other extreme acts such as incinerating one's fingers and burning one's body. Here, blood writing was used as a countermeasure against those who merely talked of "wisdom" as opposed to actually living and demonstrating it. In other words, engaging the body through blood writing was a remedy for the crisis of spiritual deterioration at the time.

Scholars generally agree that "wild-wisdom" (*kuanghui* 狂慧) refers to the powerful movement of the left wing, the Taizhou 泰州 school of Wang Yangming in the sixteenth and seventeenth centuries, which incorporated into its own teachings the rhetoric of Chan enlightenment and its accompanying Chan "extemporaneous encounter" (*jifeng* 機風 or *chanji* 禪機). An extemporaneous encounter refers to the iconoclastic ways that Chan adepts or masters expressed their enlightened minds. In many cases their unconventional behaviors included shouting and hitting one another. However, people during this time were merely mimicking these behaviors. Contemporary sources refer to their actions as "wild Chan" (*kuangchan* 狂禪).[49] Ouyi also criticized the "crazed" Chan tradition of his time as being confused and corrupted (*hunluan* 混亂).[50] He made this criticism during a period in Chinese history when Chan Buddhism had already been around for close to a thousand years. Its doctrines and methods had been fully integrated into other Chinese traditions.[51] Many prominent and influential figures blurred the boundaries between various philosophical, moral, and religious traditions. They made concerted efforts to unite and reconcile different traditions for their own purposes. To some Buddhist clerics, however, this was perceived as a sign of Buddhism's "degeneration," and some scholars accept this view.[52] However, evidence suggests that this was also a period of great vitality.

During the seventeenth century Linji Chan produced several powerful masters who emphasized the extemporaneous methods and antinomianism of shouting and beating. Jiang Wu argues that this was one result of the extraordinary number of popular Chan literatures that were published during this time. For example, from the late sixteenth century to the end of the seventeenth and the beginning of the eighteenth century, sixty-five new Chan histories of Dharma transmission and biographies of eminent monks were published. Many Chan communities actively read and emulated the practice of shouting and beating, of which Miyun Yuanwu's 密雲圓悟 (1566–1642) Chan lineage was the most aggressive.[53] Chan masters of other lineages, Buddhist masters, and certain influential literati Buddhists were critical of these wild and unconventional behaviors.[54] Seen in this light, then, Ouyi's criticism of wild wisdom or wild Chan can be understood as an attempt to redraw (at least in practice) the boundary that his contemporaries had established and to place it between what he perceived as authentic and benighted forms of self-cultivation.

Modern scholarly consensus generally reproduces the biases of seventeenth-century conservative literati, who caricatured the Taizhou movement of wild Chan as a "perversion" of Wang Yangming thought by later followers, such as Li Zhi (discussed in chapter 1) and other prominent contemporary representatives of the Taizhou School of neo-Confucianism, such as Guan Zhidao 管志道 (1537–1608), Yang Qiyuan 楊起元 (1549–1599), Jiao Hong 焦竑 (1541–1620), and Zhou Rudeng 周汝登 (1547–1629).[55] Yet, the term "wild" during the sixteenth and seventeenth centuries also carried positive implications. In a time when passion and individual expression were celebrated, being wild was perceived by some as being authentic. Jiao Hong, for example, used it to praise Li Zhi, whom he identified as one of the two types of people Confucius preferred to have transmit his teachings when no better candidates were available.[56] Specifically, Jiao Hong spoke of Li as being "wild" to distinguish Li's untrammeled personality and commitment to passion from the "banality" of the conventional Confucians. Opponents of the Taizhou School, however, especially the conservative literati, used the word "wild" negatively to condemn this new trend among the educated elite as indistinguishable from Chan Buddhism, as philosophically anti-intellectual, as the cause of moral disorder, and as heterodox (*yiduan* 異端).[57]

Not surprisingly, many of the Taizhou School proponents had close connections to the very Chan masters who promoted extemporaneous dialogs and the unconventional teaching methods of shouting and beating. For example, when Li Zhi passed away, the center of his community shifted to eastern Zhejiang, where his disciple, Zhou Rudeng, was an active leader who patronized Chan masters such as Miyun Yuanwu.[58] The fusion of Confucian teachings and Chan rhetoric and pedagogy caused a great stir in society. Qian Qianyi 錢謙益 (1582–1664), who was a close friend of Deqing, Zibo, and Ouyi, also vehemently criticized this phenomenon as a sign of the deterioration of the times.[59]

Ouyi unquestionably perceived himself as living in a tumultuous era, beset at every step by events that drove him to reflect deeply and act on his convictions as a Buddhist monk, which impelled him to engage in an urgent moral and practical questioning of what the true and authentic dharma meant. Moreover, his collected writings seem to indicate that his own guilt from repeated failures to personally experience enlightenment[60] and his equally stark conviction that he was living in a degenerate age of the dharma drove him to assiduous observance of the monastic precepts and a life of self-inflicted violence. Thus, his criticism of wild wisdom cannot be simply interpreted as a political decision to side with Confucian conservatives in opposition to Taizhou adherents or as a projection of his own sense of inadequacy onto what he perceived as a sad state of affairs in Buddhist circles. It was a combination of what he witnessed and experienced as a monk. What is clear was his agenda to use the practice of blood writing and other austerities to draw clear boundaries between what he perceived as authentic practice and what was merely empty talk. This perception is succinctly summarized in his earlier statement: The body is the source of ignorance and afflictions. To him the only way to free oneself from *saṃsara* was to carry out specific acts of self-inflicted violence. His blood writing draws on the power of self-sacrifice to engender a renewal of the Buddhist order.

Blood writing may be understood as both boundary making and boundary crossing. It was boundary making because it thwarted the potentially destabilizing disorder of the "wild," located on the margins of what was considered genuine Chan practice. At the same time, it was also boundary crossing because the ability to manipulate the blood flow beyond the body was perceived as an extension of the performer's sanctity. This extension worked like the concept of a "seal," where the potency or authority of one thing is transferred to another object. Blood inside the body manifested life. Like a seal that sanctifies documents and contracts and authenticates deeds, blood from the body authenticated, animated, and sacralized the words of the scriptures outside the body.

As a symbolically potent and multivalent substance, blood empowered performers' writings in ways that no other entity could. In premodern China, blood was thought to have sufficient power to ensure ritual efficacy. Many ancient Chinese rituals involved blood. For example, spilling human blood as a form of sacrifice to heaven (*jitian* 祭天) played a significant role in the Han dynasty.[61] Initiations and faith-sealing covenant rituals often required the shedding of one's blood to substantiate one's commitment.[62] Sometimes a ritual instrument was smeared with human blood in order to sanctify or imbue it with magic powers.[63] During the medieval period, even though vermillion ink, cinnabar, and animal blood were substituted for human blood—for example, in the Daoist and Buddhist production of talismans (*fu* 符) for propitiatory rites[64]—the underlying logic of using blood remained the same.

Blood writing was also believed to have the power to cross boundaries because bloodletting breaches the natural bounds of the body, which normally contains the blood. In blood writing, the blood does not issue randomly or accidentally, as does blood from wounds. It flows purposefully and from a specific source, usually the fingertips, the tongue, or even a place near the heart (as we have seen in the case of Wu Junping), signifying respectfully the weight of the written and spoken words and the sincerity of one's intentions. The breaching of boundaries can be theorized as a form of social and ritual danger. Danger comes from the process of bloodletting both because, if it continues unabated, death will occur and because bloodletting is often associated with warfare, wounding, sacrifice, and depletion. Moreover, blood that is shed during birth and women's menstrual blood were both generally perceived as offensive to the gods and thus had to be properly disposed of to prevent anyone from falling under the influence of supernatural forces.[65] What underlay this social danger appears to have been the presupposition that these losses of blood were improper transgressions of the body's boundaries.

Blood was also was considered dangerous because it can be manipulated in many different ways, from rituals involving blood oaths and sacrifices, to self-flagellation in shamanic practices, to blood writing. When boundaries are transgressed in the case of an individual, it is also considered a transgression of boundaries deemed important to society.[66] Blood in Chinese rituals was considered a vital life fluid that had the power to give life. Red, in the taxonomy of *yin* 陰 and *yang* 陽, symbolizes the *yang* aspect, the light, the male, and the creative principle. In fact, blood was considered to be ultra-*yang*. It represented the element of fire, was the source of life or creative power, and kept away negative things.[67] Since ancient times the color red has had a strong exorcistic, liminal significance. For example, scholars have noted that the royal tombs of the Shang dynasty, such as the one in Wuguancun 武官村, near the ancient Shang 商 city of Anyang 安陽, in Henan province, were filled with as much human blood as possible—as much *yang* energy as possible—in order to guarantee continuing life in the underworld.[68] In addition, regenerative exorcism in these mortuary rituals seems to have depended on physical dismemberment—the spilling of blood and the chopping up of bodies, whether actual or only represented.

Just as Ouyi used blood writing to draw boundaries and criticize what he perceived as heterodox, the literati also engaged in blood writing as a political means to challenge imperial authority. For them, blood writing conveyed a forceful message that defended loyalty and honor, thereby attesting to the public and political life of the literati. The medium and message of their blood memorials asserted an agency beyond ordinary language and mere ink.

Notions of political ideology construct loyalty to the emperor or to the state as a virtue that is parallel to filial piety. The structure of this ideological system was such that the officials served the emperor as sons served a father. The state was itself rhetorically construed as a type of national family (*guojia* 國家). The tension between the demands of one's family and those of the state prompted many debates on the relationship between loyalty to the state and filial piety. There were various historical attempts to ground loyalty to the state on filial piety. For example, the *Classic of Filial Piety* attempts to resolve the conflict between filial piety and political loyalty so as to consolidate monarchial rule. This politicization of the ethics of filial piety was reinforced in the late Ming with the *True Accounts of Filial Devotion* (*Xiaoshun shishi* 孝順事實), supposedly compiled with commentaries by Emperor Chengzu, which praised filial piety.[69] The explicit phrase he used to encourage the conversion of filial piety to political loyalty was "transforming filial piety to loyalty" (*yixiao weizhong* 移孝為忠).[70] The collection of 207 stories of exemplary filial conduct in that text underscores the fundamental assertion that filial piety and political loyalty both stem from the principle of heaven.

In the face of danger, several Donglin Academy members in the seventeenth century demonstrated their loyalty to the emperor through self-inflicted violence. They were portrayed by later compilers as heroes for posterity. In the summer of 1625 a high official, Yang Lian, was falsely arrested, and crowds of tradesmen and commoners supposedly wept and offered sacrifices to him as imperial secret guards escorted him north to Beijing. Five days later Yang was tortured to death.[71] Before he died, he wrote his last words (*juebi* 絕筆) in blood in order to demonstrate his honor and his innocence. Similarly, in 1626, when the imperial police came to arrest the Donglin sympathizer Zhou Shunchang 周順昌 (1584–1626), shopkeepers, laborers, and commoners supposedly rioted in the rain-soaked streets of Suzhou to stop the imperial police from taking him to Beijing.[72] The son of Shunchang, Zhou Maolan 周茂蘭 (seventeenth century), wrote a 144-character memorial to the imperial court with the blood from his own fingers, pleading for the release of his wrongly accused father. Although he was praised and supported by numerous literati and sympathetic friends as extremely pious, his father's life was not spared. Their legend, however, circulated widely during the subsequent Qing dynasty and was included in the *Jade Blood Records* (*Bixie lu* 碧血錄), which included numerous prefaces, comments, and postscripts written by other literati, officials, literary men, and Buddhists.[73]

Ming loyalists writing in the Qing dynasty portrayed Yang Lian and Zhou Shunchang as "martyrs" who were revered by the people in their district for their supposedly righteous character and virtue. Of course, the same Ming loyalists also demonized the eunuch Wei Zhongxian, whose moral credentials and abuse of power Yang Lian and Zhou Shunchang had challenged. Yang Lian, for example, attempted to impeach Wei Zhongxian and wrote a memorial listing twenty-four heinous crimes he had allegedly committed. However, even though some one hundred other officials also denounced Wei, Emperor Xizong stood by his eunuch confidant. Consequently, Wei had his secret police in the Eastern Depot come down hard on Yang Lian and everyone else that stood in his way. Countless civil officials (and even eunuchs) were tortured, and an untold number of people were slaughtered. Ming loyalists portrayed this phenomenon as a fueling of the ongoing crisis of the late Ming, which resulted in the fall of the dynasty.[74] Yang Lian and Zhou Shunchang were just two among some one dozen high-ranking officials whom Wei had tortured or executed.

In his blood memorial to Emperor Xizong, which was, of course, never received, Yang Lian wrote the following:

> Today [Yang] Lian will die under the [punishing] rod! With an obsessed heart I will have repaid [the kindness of] my master [i.e., former emperor Guangzong 光宗]. I have sincerely carried out my relations with others and exerted my body without ever regretting or worrying. I have never tried to escape from danger and death nor resorted to imbibing poison [to take my own life] like Yang Zhen 楊震 [54–124][75]... The thundering rain and [morning] dew—none of them are not the grace of heaven. Living a life of kindness and righteousness, and [then finally] dying in this prison—it is indeed difficult to talk about how underserved this place of death is! Why should I accuse heaven and hold people responsible [for my predicament]? [The sole purpose of] my life is officialdom and I have in the past received the dying words [of Emperor Guangzong]. Confucius once said that a [superior] man [is one] who can be entrusted with the life of an

> orphan [i.e., the crown prince, Xizong] and can take up the responsibility when faced with a major crisis and yet not be deflected [from his purpose].[76] Upholding this single thought, I [can truly say that I] am able to have audience with the former emperors in heaven, stand face-to-face with the two ancestors and ten progenitors,[77] and face the great heaven above and the vast Earth below, as well as the ten thousand ages [to come] under heaven! I laugh aloud again and again at the sword that tries to cut through the eastern wind—why should this have anything to do with me?![78]

Yang Lian's resolve stemmed from his own sense of "righteousness," not unlike a martyr. Perhaps this is why he rhetorically asks why it was fitting for him to suffer an ignominious death after leading such an honorable life. This interpretation is corroborated by the fact that he had promised the dying emperor, Guangzong (Xizong's father), that he would take care of the young prince. On the one hand, it was appropriate for him to die, just like the naturalness of "thundering rain" and "morning dew," because he had failed to make Emperor Xizong step forward and behave as the ideal Confucian ruler his father had wanted him to be. Yang Lian, like other Donglin martyrs, insisted that the crisis of political degeneration could not be solved unless Ming China first undertook a national moral transformation under the personal auspices of its ultimate authority, the emperor. On the other hand, Yang Lian's death could demonstrate the virtue of loyalty, which he sought to embody. That is, failing to change the state of affairs at court, Yang Lian voluntarily submitted to death without any regret in order to publically demonstrate his dignity as a loyal official. In Yang's opinion, like the "grace of heaven," the "thundering rain," and the fleeting "dewdrop," his self-representation of dying as a loyal minister would be redeemed by his martyrdom. By drawing on the power of death, he wrote the blood memorial for posterity in hopes of wresting authority away from the eunuch Wei Zhongxian.

In his sympathetic biographical anthology of leading Donglin personalities (the *Donglin liezhuan* 東林列傳, published in 1711), Chen Ding 陳鼎 (b. 1651) reflected upon the terminal years of the Ming and what the Donglin had done to shape them. He historicized the Donglin martyrs as having resolve and courage (*qijie* 氣節) [79] and asserted that Donglin had changed the whole moral atmosphere (*fengqi* 風氣) of China. He claims that they taught the true "study of the sages" or *sheng*;[80] elucidated "righteous principles"; encouraged "honesty and a sense of shame"; made people look on the dynasty (*guo* 國) as a family (*jia* 家) and on the ruler as a father (*fu* 父); and encouraged people to pursue right like water flowing downhill and to look on death as a return home.[81] From one perspective we can argue that these Donglin personalities were so successful at representing themselves in a particular way that people of later generations could read them only as moral agents. From another perspective, even if their stories were embellished and appropriated by people of later generations for their own purposes, the message conveyed by these acts of the Donglin personalities remains the same: Through self-inflicted violence they acquired sanctity.

Sometimes blood writing was also used to challenge the emperor's authority. An example is Huang Daozhou 黃道周 (1585–1646), who engaged in blood writing as a form of political protest.[82] In 1638 he submitted three memorials condemning (*tanhe* 彈劾) three general officials[83] for engaging in *duoqing* 奪情, claiming that these three people had failed to perform their full filial duties to their deceased parents. *Duoqing* was a practice by which officials whose parents had died would (on imperial order) either shorten or completely forego their mourning periods in order to return to their jobs.[84] He claimed that permitting examples of dereliction of filial duties in the imperial court would lead to the destruction (*bengjie* 崩解) of the imperial and social order. Thus, he indirectly challenged Emperor Chongzhen's authority to request officials to follow *duoqing*. He also implicitly criticized the hypocrisy of the emperor's edicts in earlier years sent to all provinces and counties demanding that local magistrates incorporate the *Classic of Filial Piety* into popular education. Infuriating the emperor, he was, through an oblique political maneuver, charged with the crime of "factionalism" (*pengdang* 朋黨) and sentenced to jail, from which he was released a year later.

In jail, Huang Daozhou engaged in copying more than 120 copies of the *Classic of Filial Piety* as a form of vindication and protest,[85] the final one in his own blood. By this act he sought to legitimize and justify his innocence; it graphically reiterated his conviction that filial piety had to spread widely so that it might rule all under heaven (*tianxia* 天下). Huang Daozhou's blood writing asserted his moral power over his alleged crime. He inflicted violence on his own body even when the text he copied proscribed such an act.

≅

The different cases presented here demonstrate the instrumentality of blood writing and its inseparability from the symbolism that it elicited. Blood writing was a graphic way to demonstrate filial piety, sincerity, and loyalty; it was perceived to have the power to restore and reconstruct religious and political boundaries. It was not merely a symbolic act but a transformative one as well.

To conceive of the ritual of blood writing as merely a "symbolic behavior" that is classified separately from practical, technically effective behavior[86] or actions that require scholarly decoding[87] is to miss its instrumentality in achieving a range of social and religious goals: the preservation and perpetuation of the true dharma in the world; the attainment of *prajñā*; the honoring of deceased parents in hopes of their future rebirth; and the defense of boundaries of sanctity. The multivalent meanings of blood writing in all of the cases discussed here suggest that blood asserted a message stronger than any that could have been created in any other medium. It signaled associations with the creative and exorcistic power and blood sacrifices, blood covenants, and other indigenous rituals. Performers of blood writing drew on these implicit associations to establish their sanctity and negotiate their social lives; their conception of self; their attitudes toward their parents; their political relations with the emperor; and their ability to resist patterns of authority. Their blood writings authored the way others perceived and represented them.

3

Nourishing the Parent with One's Own Flesh

> Li Chong 李翀 was from Xijie 西街.[1] From an early age he practiced the classics on ritual. At one time, Chong's mother, née Tao, had a life-threatening illness (*ji* 疾). The physician said that without [consuming] human flesh [her illness] would not be cured (*fei renrou buliao* 非人肉不療). Chong sliced the flesh from his thigh (*gegu* 割股), cooked it into soup (*geng* 羹), and offered it to his mother. She gradually regained her health.
>
> —Yuan Yingqi 袁應祺 (sixteenth century)

THE PRACTICE OF *gegu* 割股—literally, "slicing a piece of flesh from one's thigh"—was a ritualized filial practice of using one's own flesh to make healing medicine for sick parents or other elders in the family.[2] It was first documented sometime around the Tang dynasty, but by the sixteenth and seventeenth centuries it had become a culturally established expression of filial piety. The increase in the number of cases in numerous provinces and in popular fictional writing during the late Ming indicates that it was part of mainstream society. Similar to the popularity of blood writing, the apparent prevalence of "filial slicing" may have been tied to the renewed interest in filial piety, which began in the fifteenth century and blossomed in the sixteenth and seventeenth centuries.

The general outline of the opening epigraph is apparent: Filial piety requires that people serve their parents to the utmost, including sacrificing their flesh to nourish them. The cases of "filial slicing" discussed in this chapter are representative of a pattern followed by young heroes and heroines who underwent horrific ordeals in their unwavering demonstration of filial piety. Some scholars consider filial acts a "Confucian" practice, but to reduce this practice to a "Confucian imperative" is to rob it of other cultural meanings because it correlated with the larger cultural discourses on medicine, anthropophagy, and self-sacrifice. Filial slicing was bound up in a web of associations in the late imperial era, and people consumed human flesh for many reasons: famine, political intrigues, hatred, medicinal purposes, or even the cult of immortality. Thus filial slicing was not beyond the norm of premodern Chinese culture, so it must be appreciated from this broader perspective. In this chapter we will read about the different strands of influences that have shaped the practice of filial slicing; how performers engaged in it to accomplish different ends; and how writers debated them for their own agendas. Many of the issues discussed in this chapter deal with the social realities of performers and the moral concerns of those who recorded their stories.

Filial slicing flourished in the sixteenth and seventeenth centuries not because this period in Chinese history was a particularly virtuous age but, as discussed in chapter 1, it was a volatile period. The boundaries between inner (*nei* 内) and outer (*wai* 外), between the acceptable and the unacceptable, and between assumed norms and contested preferences were more blurred than they had ever been. The literati touted and praised filial sacrifice in response to social disorder, but their documentation and discussion of it also served other ends. Beneath the discursive veil of filial slicing, the literati romanticized performers to participate in their literary production of "sentiment," or *qing* (discussed in chapter 1). Their published tracts on filial slicing made it an object of debate in a system of moral pedagogy and a vehicle to challenge certain social customs.

On a theoretical level, filial slicing was a way for sons and daughters to use their bodies to give back to parents nourishment in a condensed form as direct recompense for what they had received while in the womb and during childhood. In this sense the central meaning of filial slicing is body substitution. In giving back their own flesh, sons and daughters are giving back life. The currency of this view is evident in many sources. For example, a seventeenth-century son engaged in filial slicing and prayer to the city god so that he could "reduce his own years [i.e. lifespan] so as to increase his mother's."[3] Yet, this practice was more than substitution or reciprocity. People engaged in it to negotiate not only their parents' lives but also their own positions in society. As we will read below, other complex metaphors are also present, including notions of gift, bargaining, exchange, expiation, propitiation, and devotion. Discourses on filial slicing were multifaceted.

The Larger Context of Anthropophagy

The valence of filial slicing is complex and can be understood only in relationship to other Chinese cultural practices of consuming human flesh. Aside from famine and natural disasters, which forced people to engage in cannibalism, three distinct discourses of anthropophagy stand out: political cannibalism, medical cannibalism, and meritorious cannibalism. Indeed, we have ample evidence that cannibalism was practiced throughout different periods of Chinese history as a means of enduring periods of famine, warfare, and political conquest.[4] Scholars have noted that in the seventeenth century, official *Ming History* documents whole regions of China where people engaged in cannibalism due to repeated natural disasters that led to famine.[5] However, there are other cases where the recognizable pattern is that even though cannibalism was tied to hunger in times of famine, it was not always necessarily connected to hunger per se. Below I discuss these three different discourses of cannibalism in order to identify the perceptions embedded in the practice of filial slicing. These discourses, in many cases, overlap, so my categorization is only for heuristic purposes. The important point to realize is that filial slicing, the eating of human flesh from one's children, was not an isolated phenomenon, unique in its logic. It was nested in a complex web of connections to other seemingly unrelated practices of anthropophagy. These associations were established through many centuries of cross-cultural fertilization.

Political cannibalism has its roots in ancient sacrificial rituals, but the practice persisted up to the late imperial times in various disguises. Sometimes eating another human being (part or whole) had to do with revenge, cosmic renewal, and social order or power.[6] Well-known mythic stories of early dynastic crises shed much light on this form of cannibalism. The Yellow Emperor (Huang Di 黃帝), said to be the founder of "civilized" warfare and even Chinese civilization itself, had to defeat the half-monster warrior Chi You 蚩尤, who was cut apart, cooked in a meat stew, and divided among victorious soldiers. The first prehistoric dynasty, Xia 夏 (ca. 2000–1500 B.C.E.), was able to be reestablished only after the defeat of the usurper, the archer Yi 羿, who was fed to his own son by the treacherous minister Han Zhuo 寒浞, who was later overthrown. The Shang 商 was able to replace the Xia only when the founder offered himself up as a sacrifice. The Zhou 周 was able to replace the Shang, according to some texts, only when the dead king was offered up as a sacrifice and, according to others, when its founder had personally killed King Zhou by eating him raw or lapping up his blood.[7]

Consuming the whole human body, whole or parts, was politicized. Sometimes it was done out of revenge. Consider the case of Liu Jin 劉瑾 (1452–1510), one of the powerful eunuchs of the Ming who was consumed by his enemies to seal his defeat. Liu was supposedly cut up into pieces in 1510 for distribution among those officials who detested him.[8] In these cases of political cannibalism, sacrificing the other, whether one's predecessor or one's political opponent, was a means of expiation and regeneration. By eating the former ruler, a new era of rule was able to be established; by eating the eunuch, evil could be eradicated and a renewed balance could flourish in the political state. The objects of sacrifice (former kings or the eunuch) represented sources of power; their very existence denied the sacrificers legitimacy. Power was acquired by incorporating or consuming the life force of the sacrificed. Some of the alternative accounts of these cases of cannibalism in the sixteenth and seventeenth centuries offer conflicting versions of the story. It is certainly plausible that certain of the figures have been euhemerized from early cultural heroes or portrayed in acts they did not commit. But that does not affect the argument here: These stories underline the necessity of regenerative sacrifice and represent cannibalism as not only emotionally fulfilling but also ritually, morally, and politically appropriate.[9]

Medical cannibalism is the second kind of discourse we find in premodern China. Scholars such as Kuwabara Jitsuzō have already historicized the eating of human flesh as part and parcel of the medical practice, which even made it into the larger Chinese culinary arts.[10] In this light we must recognize that Li Chong's filial slicing in the opening epigraph to this chapter shows that offering one's flesh to one's parents may have been a common practice in the field of medicine because physicians prescribed it as a cure for illness.[11]

Here "medicine" does not correspond to our modern conception of the field. Rather, it is intertwined with folk medicine, philosophical cosmology, and religious theories, in particular, the theory of sympathetic resonance or stimulus-response (*ganying* 感應). Physicians prescribed human flesh from the sick person's son or daughter as an effective means of curing the former's sickness. The belief that human flesh, particularly when derived from filial piety, could cure the sick stemmed from a sympathetic view of the universe. Moral action could stimulate the cosmic forces to accomplish many things, including healing the sick. This belief is corroborated by the numerous cases in official and local histories.

In the official histories, the *Jiu Tangshu* 舊唐書 (*Old History of the Tang*) by Liu Xu 劉昫 (887–946), compiled during the later Jin dynasty 後晉 (936–946), provides three of the earliest cases of slicing the body.[12] Only one of them, that of Wang Youzhen 王友貞, was performed for healing parents. He did this at age twenty on the advice of a physician (*yi* 醫). With no other way of curing his ailing mother, he sliced off a piece of flesh from his thigh and mixed it with rice to make a sweet paste (*yi* 飴) and fed it to her. Afterward his mother regained her health. When Empress Wu Zetian 武則天 (634–705; r. 690–705) heard of his act of filial devotion, she sent emissaries to investigate the matter in Wang Youzhen's hometown. After their verification, Wang Youzhe received an imperial honorific tablet (*jingbiao* 旌表) and other rewards for his household.[13]

Wang Youzhen's story suggests that filial slicing probably existed even before the Tang. Medieval Chinese pharmacopeias detailed the medicinal value of different parts of the human body. The view espoused in these texts was steeped in the theoretical assumptions of many other cultural pursuits, such as the shamanistic arts, alchemy, philosophy, astrology, and religion.[14] The efficacy of filial slicing or the belief in its efficacy can be appreciated only in this context.

In Chen Cangqi's 陳藏器 (d.u.) *Bencao shiyu* 本草拾遺 (*Supplement to Materia Medica*), written in 739 C.E.,[15] he explicitly states that human flesh (*renrou* 人肉) was an effective medicine for disease caused by atrophy and emaciation. In the book he promotes medical cannibalism by citing the therapeutic benefits of eating human flesh.

In the late Ming medical compendium, *Bencao gangmu* 本草綱目 (*Hierarchically Classified Materia Medica*), published in 1578, the famous pharmacologist Li Shizhen 李時珍 (1518–1593) declares that, although this practice had a history prior to the publication of Chen Cangqi's pharmacopoeia, it should be condemned because it is immoral:

> In middle of the Kaiyuan era [713–742], in the Tang dynasty (618–907), Chen Cangqi, native of Mingzhou, wrote a book titled *Supplement to Materia Medica*, in which he recorded that human flesh was good for treating atrophy and emaciation (*leizhai* 羸瘵). Henceforth, most of the local villagers would treat those with this sickness with slicing the thigh (*gegu* 割股). But before Chen's time there were already people who practiced slicing the thigh and slicing the liver (*gegan* 割肝) [for medical purposes]... Our bodies, hair, and skin are inherited from our parents and must not be harmed.[16] How could any parent, even if seriously ill, possibly desire their offerings to harm their bodies and limbs, and consume their own flesh and bones? Such [practices] stem from the views of the foolish.[17]

Li Shizhen's criticism would be quickly forgotten as readers went on to read his listing of thirty-seven medicinal benefits of consuming different parts of the human body. For example, eating dried and powdered human gall bladder with tangerine peel treats chronic malaria; drinking powdered penis with wine treats genital wounds; eating baked, then powdered human placenta nourishes the vital energy (*qi* 氣) and cures abdominal disease; imbibing fresh human blood treats dry and scaly skin; and eating stir-fried human hair rolled into a pear-sized mass with ten egg yolks treats convulsions and epilepsy.[18] Given these and other detailed medical prescriptions of human body parts, all "received from one's parents and hence to be protected," it is difficult to take Li Shizhen's criticism as more than lip service, especially when we know that this pharmacopoeia was submitted to the throne for endorsement.

Physicians such as Chen Cangqi and Li Shizhen were recognized by their contemporaries as elite specialists in a field of expertise known as "medicine" *yi* 醫 and were accorded the title of "physician" (the same word for medicine). However, their skills as physicians had their roots in early folk medicine and ancient sacrificial practices of consuming human flesh. Some modern scholars have argued that medical theory and philosophical cosmology began to be integrated even before the Han dynasty and became progressively more secular, consistent, and rationalistic throughout the centuries. Others have also postulated the possible influence of Indian medical lore on Chinese medicine before the sixth century.[19] Regardless of how those claims are evaluated, Li Shizhen's prescriptions for various illnesses still demonstrate that magical, shamanistic, and religious healing never disappeared in the branch of knowledge called medicine.

People were regularly guided by physicians and local healers, who advised pious sons and daughters to perform filial slicing. Aside from Li Chong's case earlier, Peng Yinghong 彭應洪 of Hunan 湖南 province, Changsha 茶陵 prefecture, during the late Ming also engaged in slicing the body at the counsel of a local healer (*fangshi* 方士), who said that only human flesh could cure his mother's sickness. Peng Yinghong sliced his own thigh, cooked it, and offered it to his mother, telling her that it was deer meat. Indeed, she recovered from her illness after consuming it.[20] An easy translation of *fangshi* 方士 (sometimes *fangxiang shi* 方相士) cannot be given as its meaning has changed over time. Some scholars render it "Daoist mystic" or "technician of alchemy"; others translate it as "exorcist." These renderings reflect medieval uses of the term. Here I believe it simply means "local healer" because of their fluid social status, separate from their Daoist origin, and their connection to the "medical" or "healing" arts in late imperial China.[21]

Elite scholar-physicians in the late imperial times, supposedly steeped in the morality of Confucian and neo-Confucian discourse, sought to distance themselves and their expertise from local healers, whom they described as a rabble of quacks and even immoral old women.[22] The expansion of literacy, the reading public, and the production of state-sponsored pharmacopeias led to the polemic against vulgar healing practices. Li Shizhen's criticism should be seen in this light as he tried to distance himself and his expertise from that of his predecessors. However, his rationalized treatment of illnesses inspired by the neo-Confucian discourse on the "investigation of things" does not reinforce the boundary between elite and folk medicines.[23] Common but educated physicians right up to the late imperial times still recommended slicing the body as a legitimate cure for parents' illnesses when ordinary medicine failed.

Medical cannibalism was sometimes about acquiring everlasting power. People ate human flesh for other reasons as well. In medieval Chang'an, the tantric Buddhist master Śubhakarasiṃha (Shanwuwei 善無畏) (637–735)[24] and his Chinese disciple Yixing 一行 (684–727)[25] introduced an esoteric tradition of consuming a person's heart. Śubhakarasiṃha states that "within the human body there is a concretion, which is called human concretion (*renhuang* 人黃). It is like the concretion found in cattle. One who is able to eat it attains the greatest power (*chengjiu* 成就), [such as] circling the world in one day, obtaining anything that one desires, and being able to control people in various ways."[26] The practice is connected to a particular *ḍākinī* mantra given by the Buddha Varirocana in the form of Mahākāla in order to subjugate it. During the Tang dynasty (618–907) Buddhism began to take root in China, especially during the eighth and ninth centuries. Scholars are beginning to note the impact of tantric Buddhism on the educated elite during this time.[27] It is impossible to know for a fact whether and to what extent the practice of consuming human hearts ever influenced, for example, the Chinese pharmacopeia. Nonetheless, we can safely assume that this practice was known among the educated elite, for many of these tantric masters were supported by elite patrons and emperors, and their translated works were read not only by monks but also by the educated lay community.

We have evidence that suggest that Tang emperors, subsequent rulers to those who supported the tantric masters, ate the hearts and livers of children to gain power. The account comes from the Japanese monk pilgrim Ennin 円仁 (794–864), who was trying to leave China when Emperor Wuzong 武宗 (re. 814–846) persecuted Buddhism. In his travelogue he stated that in 845, while in Shandong province, the emperor had sent out an edict demanding the hearts and livers of fifteen-years-old boys and girls. It is uncertain whether this is a historical fact or a fabrication of Buddhists who loathed and demonized the emperor. However, in his diary Ennin wrote that he believed that the emperor was completely fanatical about immortality.[28] From the extent of his outrageous edicts, it is not unthinkable that he sought the hearts and livers of children to feast on as a means of ensuring his immortality.[29] We should note that this supposed incident of Emperor Wuzong eating children's hearts and livers occurred roughly a little more than a hundred years after the influence of tantric Buddhism at the court through masters such as Śubhakarasiṃha and Yixing, who wrote on the practice of eating human concretion to obtain power.

The third kind of anthropophagy is meritorious cannibalism, which correlates with the Buddhist practice of selfless sacrifice. Modern scholars have attributed the spread of filial slicing to the impact of Indian Buddhism on China.[30] I believe it is still difficult to demonstrate the connections between prescriptive Buddhist literature and actual Chinese practice, especially we have few firsthand descriptions of the kinds of events that went on in India.

The closest correlation I have found on the practice of "slicing the thigh" is in the Buddhist *vinayas* (*lü* 律), dating back to roughly three hundred years after the Śākyamuni's passing. The case appears in the *vinayavastu* division on medicine (Skt. *bhaiṣajyavastu*; *yaojiandu* 藥揵度 or *yaoshi* 藥事),[31] which is a collection of narratives detailing how certain precepts came to be established. There, the Buddha supposedly set out various regulations for his monastic followers, which included not eating specific kinds of food. Consuming human flesh was, needless to say, prohibited and in fact was considered a serious transgression, or *sthūlātyaya* (*toulanzhe* 偷蘭遮) because it could potentially lead to *pārājika*, an offense that would lead to a monk's or nun's expulsion from the monastic community.[32] But how this *toulanzhe* precept came to be established is quite interesting.

The story begins with a gravely ill monk in Vārāṇasī (Boluonaiguo 波羅奈國) on the verge of death.[33] He was so sick that he would vomit every time he tried to take any prescribed medicine. A devout Buddhist laywoman (Skt. *upāsikā*; *youposi* 優婆私) named Suppiyā (Subi 蘇卑)[34] inquired about his illness and asked what he needed, to which the monk replied, "Meat."[35] (We must keep in mind that vegetarianism was not practiced by Indian Buddhist clerics.) However, there happened to be a ban on selling or slaughtering animals that day, so she could not procure the meat that was required to cure him.[36] She thought, "If I cannot find meat, then the monk may die, and if he is an *arhat* [liberated person], laypeople like me will miss an opportunity to offer support to the Saṅgha." She then took a sharp knife, sliced a piece of her own flesh from her thigh, and asked her attendant to boil (*zhu* 煮) it in broth (*geng* 羹) and take it to the monk. Not knowing where the meat came from, the monk accepted the offering and subsequently recovered from his illness. Sometime later Suppiyā was lying in bed in intense pain from her wound. When her husband came home, he inquired about her suffering, and she told him what had happened. He was shocked by her action. She asked to make a last offering to the Buddha and the Saṅgha, thinking that she might very well die from the cut. The next day the husband invited the Buddha to their home, and the Buddha quietly accepted and came to the house. As soon as the Buddha arrived, he asked to see Suppiyā. When the husband went to the bedroom to call her, she tried to get up, and suddenly all of her pain stopped. She was miraculously healed. Suppiyā rushed to the Buddha, paid obeisance at his feet, and received his teaching. He praised her for her selfless offering but said that it was inappropriate because a food offering should be made on the principle that it does not inflict suffering on oneself or vex the recipient.

When the Buddha returned to the *saṃgha-ārāma* (dwelling place of the Saṅgha), he went to the monk and asked whether he had received meat broth from Suppiyā, to which the monk said yes. The Buddha asked whether it was delicious. The monk said that it was unusually delicious. Then the Buddha exclaimed, "You fool (*chiren* 癡人)! You ate human flesh," and scolded him for not inquiring about the origin of the meat before accepting the offering. The Buddha then forbade the eating of human meat as a *sthūlātyaya* or *toulanzhe* precept and in addition created a new misdemeanor for accepting an offering of meat without inquiring about its origin (Skt. *duṣkṛta*; *tujiluo* 突吉羅).[37]

This case is repeated in every collection of law codes or *vinayas*: the Sarvāstivādin *vinaya*, the Mūlasarvāstivādin *vinaya*, the Mahāsāṃghika *vinaya*, the Mahīśāsaka *vinaya*, and the Dharmaguptaka *vinaya*.[38] A version of this particular case also appears in a more elaborate form in *sūtras*.[39] While there are minor variations of this case, the plot is basically the same.[40]

The prominent theme in this case of body slicing and self-sacrifice is the idea of merit making (Skt. *puṇya*; *gongde*). The members of the Saṅgha are traditionally considered "fields of merit" (Skt. *dakṣinīya*; *futian* 福田), objects of religious devotion. However, we must remember that, in Buddhism, the objects of offering or fields of merit refer not only to the Three Jewels (Buddha, Dharma, and Saṅgha) but also to parents and those who are poverty stricken.[41] Similar to the mechanism of stimulus-response or *ganying*, where moral action stimulates a blessing from heaven, merit and merit making operate within the larger context of the teaching of karma, in which moral action and ritual performance generate benefits and the buddhas and bodhisattvas grant blessings to those who earn them through their efforts. Once accrued, merits can also be shared with the living and the dead or directed toward a specific goal, such as gaining a good rebirth or realizing enlightenment.

Several interesting correlations exist between the Chinese citations of filial slicing and the supposed Indian case of flesh slicing discussed here. First, the recipient of the offering in both cases is someone worthy of respect. In the case of India, it is a holy monk; in the Chinese case it is a parent. Second, the term used in the *vinaya* is *gebi* 割髀, which is a variation of the Chinese expression for filial slicing, *gegu* 割股. Both *bi* and *gu* refer to the thigh even though, in China, "slicing the thigh" became a stock expression that included many other parts of the body, such as an arm or the chest. Third, if the incident in the *vinayas* can be accepted as historical fact—I see no reason to doubt its veracity—then the Indian practice of slicing one's own flesh out of devotion to save another's life appears to predate the first appearance of this practice in surviving non-Buddhist Chinese sources. All of these *vinayas*, except the *Mūlasarvāstivādin-vinaya*, were translated into Chinese around the same time—the end of the fourth and the first decades of the fifth century—which is roughly a couple of centuries earlier than the textual appearance of filial slicing or *gegu* in China as a filial and medical practice.[42] Also, the earliest of these *vinayas* dates to the precommon era.[43]

Hubert Durt has written on the Buddhist textual precedence for anthropophagy and connects it with the Chinese filial practice of offering flesh to one's parents. He has suggested that "Buddhist circles were eager to support such a development of filial piety" and that the Chinese adopted "this metaphorical and hyperbolic Buddhist motif, the Bodhisattva's offering of his own body, to the quintessentially Chinese and Confucian system of filial piety."[44] His conclusion is mostly based on Japanese secondary scholarship.[45] One is tempted to conclude that Buddhist scriptures and *vinaya* literature were a source of inspiration for filial slicing in China, but we must keep in mind that at least the *vinaya* corpus was theoretically prohibited from circulating among nonmonastics. The *vinaya* is also far from the kind of literature read by the educated elite, for it contains numerous technical terms and transliterations that even the most literate elite would not have been able to understand unless they had spent years studying it. Commentaries on this passage are also silent about flesh slicing and offering.

If we look at the commentaries on the *vinaya* literature by the highly placed and educated Chinese *vinaya* master Daoxuan 道宣 (596–667)[46] of the Tang, we find no direct mention of the Buddhist flesh-slicing incident. However, Daoxuan's commentary on the *vinayavastu* division of medicine includes his advocacy of vegetarianism based on the Mahāyāna scriptures. He argues that if people regularly eat meat, it will eventually lead to eating human flesh.[47] In line with the normative practice of vegetarianism in mainstream Chinese Buddhism, Daoxuan's criticism of meat eating focuses primarily on the perspective of the consumer (one who is eating) and appeals to the authority of the *Mahāyāna Mahāparinirvāṇa-sūtra* and the *Laṅkāvatāra-sūtra* against the eating of any kind of meat. He states that such forbearance will nourish the seeds of compassion for sentient beings and that, since all sentient beings were at one time our own parents, there are numerous reasons not to eat meat.[48] Song dynasty commentaries on the *vinaya* are also silent on this specific case and do not explicitly comment on the significance of slicing one's flesh to feed to others as an offering.[49]

Daoxuan knew about eating human flesh; he also knew of an extreme Indian practice that involves offering one's flesh to parents, mentioned in the *Forest of Pearls in the Garden of the Dharma*.[50] However, his own *vinaya* commentary does not mention the connection between the Buddhist injunction against meat eating (including human flesh) and the practice of filial slicing. Perhaps this silence was due to the fact that anthropophagy was not common enough to single out for commentary, or perhaps his comment on vegetarianism was an implied disapproval of the practice of filial slicing.

It is difficult to say conclusively that the Chinese drew inspiration for filial slicing from the Indian Buddhist practice of slicing one's flesh to feed ailing monks solely on the basis of the limited circulation and the obtuse nature of the *vinaya* literature. We recall from Li Shizhen's words that even pre-Tang physicians recommended filial slicing for medical purposes. Also, as noted earlier, political cannibalism already even in ancient China. The only possible source of inspiration for the Chinese would be texts like the *Forest of Pearls in the Garden of the Dharma*, which contains stories of self-sacrifices by buddhas and bodhisattvas from the *avadāna* literature, or, more likely, Mahāyāna scriptures. The earliest Mahāyāna scripture translated in Chinese that mentions offering flesh would be the third-century scripture *The Buddha Speaks on the Scripture of the Bodhisattva Moon Radiance*, but this short tract may not have had a substantial impact on the Chinese Buddhist community.[51] Other more influential scriptures translated during the fifth century and later, which accrued commentaries, would have made a greater impact on the larger

Chinese society. One of these is the *Mahāparinirvāṇa-sūtra*, which presents a story of offering flesh for medicinal purposes in terms close to what we have seen in the *vinaya* literature.[52]

There is little hard evidence that correlates prescriptive scriptures with descriptive practices, which might show that the Indian Buddhist case of flesh slicing had a direct impact on the Chinese practice of filial slicing. It is nearly impossible to determine the origin of filial slicing. My discussion here merely questions received scholarship and contextualizes several discourses of anthropophagy that may have woven together the multivalent perception and performance of filial slicing in China.

Offering one's own flesh to feed one's sick parents out of devotion, on the one hand, and consuming human flesh for revenge or power, on the other, are categorically different but theoretically similar. All of these acts share the similarity of ritually sacrificing bodies (whole or part) as food in a way that lends intense emotional meaning to human relationships. All of these forms aim at (a hoped-for) renewal, regeneration, and rejuvenation. Nourishing the parents with that which came from them may be conceived of as a form of communion. Cannibalism united the eater and the eaten, which is not completely dissimilar to feeding ailing parents one's own flesh to underscore the ties between children and parents. The contexts differ, but the logic reveals definite similarities, especially if we understand both to be about human relations. Filial slicing in the sixteenth and seventeenth centuries can best understood in the disjunctions and seams where divergent meanings are stitched together by performers and writers. To comprehend these seams, one must unravel the underlying discourses in specific historical cases of filial slicing in the changing social and cultural contexts of this period.

Contentious Representations of Filial Slicing

The lack of institutional control during the sixteenth and seventeenth centuries was exacerbated by new interpretations of morality and changing values. The movement or cult of sentiment celebrated individual expressions of passion and produced stories of filial slicing in the form of regional operas, storytelling traditions, and novels.[53] The ambivalent moral messages and entertaining values embodied in popular novels and these cultural expressions inevitably made filial slicing a topic of debate among writers. This section focuses first on the debates and uses of filial slicing as literary discourse and then on the material and symbolic forces, as well as the social pressures that shaped the lives of the performers, especially women.

The literati passionately wrote of filial slicing by the common people to critique existing social customs, promote the moral reputation of their families, and establish literati networks in their local regions. Their discussions include no social critique of eating human flesh. Instead, they debated the powers that this practice conferred in the affirmation of or challenge to social customs, gender issues, and status. Thus, filial slicing was not about eating human flesh but about the maintenance, regeneration, and production of family ties and the social order. For example, we see in the discourses that surround filial slicing the complex role women could play in the negotiation of their positions in the family. The literati's representations of filial slicing not only provided further impetus for its popularity but also allowed women to use these stories to make a name for themselves "in the world of letters by joining the ranks of other men of letters who were writing accounts like this."[54]

Consider this case of the literatus Wu Jiaji 吳嘉紀 (1618–1684), who wrote about members of his family whose deeds were, as he claimed, exemplars of moral cultivation. One of the members he wrote about was his niece. In his introduction to a poem about her, he says the following:

> My niece, named Changzhong 長仲, is the daughter of my elder brother, Jiashen 嘉紳, and is married to a Mr. Lu 魯. They live right next door to my brother. In the winter of the year of *jiachen* 甲辰 (1664), my brother was ill, and she was four months pregnant. In an anxious hurry, she rushed over to visit [her father], tripped, fell to the ground, and had a miscarriage. Ten days later, my brother's illness worsened. Because custom holds that it is inauspicious for a woman who has given birth [successfully or not] to enter the home of her natal family, my niece was unable to go in. Clutching the doorframe, she wept and said, "Only inches away from my father, and yet I can't even get to see his face!" In grief she wailed and wept, moving all the neighbors. When she returned home, she burned incense and in front of the kitchen god (*zaoshen* 竈神) she sliced flesh from her left thigh (*kui zuogurou* 刲左股肉), placing a dried half-gourd beneath her leg to catch any blood. The knife she used was blunt, but afraid that her family would discover [what was happening], she did not dare to sharpen it. After cutting for a long time, she finally got the flesh loose from her thigh, and yet she did not feel much pain. After sunset, she cooked it into a congee (*mi* 糜) and had it taken to my brother. He ate it, and his illness was cured. The place where my niece had cut herself also subsequently healed. When she looked into the gourd, there was not a single drop of blood. People all said that the gods must have secretly aided her.[55]

Wu Jiaji goes on with his poem:

> A pregnant woman barred from entering the door.
> How hateful is this old custom!
> With tearful eyes she can only glimpse and gaze;
> The doorframe separates one's own bones and flesh.[56]
> "This flesh is of my family;
> I cut it to prepare a soup congee."
> This woman is a common woman.
> She solemnly worships the god,
> Who descends and gives rise to a pure wind.
> The fragrance of her congee pleases the father;
> Her dull blade brings wholeness to the father and children.
> People gather to see the empty gourd.

Wang Jiaji eulogizes his niece for her courageous filial act. In calling her a "common woman" (*yufuren* 愚婦人),[57] he is not degrading her but is putting forth the notion that even a commoner, as a moral agent, can transmit virtue. Such a view, of course, echoes the idea of Wang Yangming's disciple, Wang Gen. As discussed in chapter 1, he was a radical but charismatic teacher of the Taizhou School of Wang Yangming. Son of a salt merchant, he championed the common people and lectured widely to them. One of his slogans was that "even common men and women can access knowledge and put it into action" (*yufu yufu yuzhi nengxing* 愚夫愚婦與知能行); another was that "the Way of the sages is not different from the daily activities of common people. Whoever claims otherwise is heterodox."[58] Not surprisingly, Wang Gen was virtually the only famous man to have come from Wu Jiaji's own home village of Anfeng 安豐 in Taizhou 泰州 prefecture, in southern Jiangsu province.[59]

The notions that everyone had the potential to become a sage and that sanctity must be corporeally demonstrated had great currency during this time. It is worth noting that the term "commoner" (*yu* 愚) in Wu Jiaji's usage may not refer to a person of low intelligence. It should be understood in Wang Gen's sense of someone of nonofficial or nonpolitical social status. Wu Jiaji's writing about the virtues of commoners expresses his identity with them. His implicit claim is that morality is better preserved among uneducated people than among the educated echelons of the governing cultured class. His own family demonstrates this moral authority of the common people.

A cursory glance through the rest of Wu Jiaji's collected poetry suggests that he consciously sought out some of the most ordinary people in his region who acted as bearers of ideal cultural values. These people, his circles of kinship and friends, demonstrated a superior moral aptitude. It appears that he gave agency to common people in order to shame the elite, especially those of a superior social station who lacked the virtues of their presumed inferiors, into conforming to moral ideals.

Wu Jiaji also criticized what he saw as a benighted custom (*fengsu* 風俗) that prevented the natural expression of sentiments, passion, or *qing* between pious children and their parents. This custom of barring pregnant women and those who had just given birth or miscarried from returning home or seeing their parents has a long history in premodern China. Birth—let alone miscarriage—was itself popularly considered both a dangerous and a polluting event to the mother's family.[60] In Changzhong's case, not only did she avoid this month-long seclusion, but she also had a miscarriage, which was most likely perceived as even more pernicious, and yet she still insisted on seeing her father. Wu Jiaji uses the doorframe to symbolize this custom, which barred Changzhong from entering the room to see her biological father. Wu Jiaji's point is clear: Rigid customs, because they are human constructs, are to be relinquished; filial piety, as a natural expression of passion, should be followed.

The notion of filial allegiance seems to be challenged here as well. In medieval Chinese classics, filial piety was represented as a natural human emotion for a son. A woman's filial piety, on the other hand, was a product of cultivation; she was expected to transfer her filial love from her natural parents to her husband's ancestral lineage at marriage. Her attachment to her natal parents was considered "unnatural." However, Wu Jiaji praises Changzhong precisely because she carries out the male ideal of filial piety: She returns to her family and sacrifices herself for her natal father, not her husband's father.

Wu Jiaji's case shows an alternative reality to that portrayed by earlier twentieth-century scholarship, which argues that the late imperial society was dominated effectively by the strict subordination of wives to their affinal relatives.[61] Such a claim can actually be traced back to what scholars would consider "Confucian" texts. For example, in pre-Ming editions of the *Lienü zhuan* 列女傳 (*Biographies of Exemplary Women*) by Liu Xiang 劉向 (76–6 B.C.E.), the "filial women" category is absent. Instead, categories were created for benevolent wisdom (*renzhi* 仁智) and other talents or virtues, such as skill in arguing (*biantong* 辯通).[62] In the Ming editions of the *Guifan tushuo* 閨範圖説 (*Illustrated of Female Exemplars*), which were expanded editions of the original *Lienü zhuan*, however, the situation changes completely.[63] "Filial daughters" as a category was introduced as one of the three important ways to organize records of virtuous women; the other two were "chaste wives" and "self-sacrificing mothers."[64] Because these three categories are all role oriented and favor the affinal family lineage, early scholars claim that representations of virtuous women changed from agents of "intellectual" virtues to bearers of specific "gendered" virtues such as wifely fidelity and ritual propriety. They link this shift to the increasing emphasis on male loyalty in the political realm during the late Ming.[65] In other words, the state supposedly promulgated an effective regime in which wives were subjugated to their affinal lineage. However, did all women fulfill such prescriptive roles so as to transfer their allegiance to the affinal lineage? It seems that Wu Jiaji is arguing otherwise.

Wu Jiaji's account may provide us with a window into the actual dynamics of family relations. Focusing on Changzhong's feeling toward her natal father, he highlights the genuineness of filial devotion toward one's own father. He shows that this passion drives some people to act the way they do and guides their filial piety and loyalty. In other words, passion was the wellspring of moral action. Thus, in her desperation, Chongzhong could find no other way to express her filial devotion but to pray to the gods and engage in filial slicing to heal her father.

The description of Changzhong's performance is devoid of gruesome details, yet symbolically rich. The dramatic focus lies in her uncle's statement that she neither bled nor felt pain. She overcomes the traditional association of women with the biological processes of bodily fluids as a dangerous and polluting threat to order.[66] Also, if she had given birth to a boy rather than miscarried her child, she would have greatly aided her husband's lineage. However, she (presumably) sheds blood inappropriately through miscarriage—a sign of pollution—so she engages in an act of expiation: feeding herself to her natal father.

The symbolism of not bleeding suggests the sanctity of Changzhong and that her boundaries are contained. Instead of depicting the concrete pains and messiness of body slicing, Wu Jiaji incites the reader's imagination with regard to the hidden body. The reader is teased to visualize and fantasize about what is of more importance; that is, the theme of her moral triumph of cultural value is played against her biological imperative as a woman. She is not quite human, and all of her neighbors marvel at the "empty gourd," which attests to the moral power of her filial devotion to win over heaven (or, in her case, the kitchen god).[67] The concealment of blood in these narrative strategies suggests that female blood may have been perceived as polluting. In other words, Changzhong's body is represented as an instrument of concealment.

Modern scholars typically depict filial slicing as a practice performed in "secrecy," invariably hidden from the knowledge of the ailing parent.[68] The performers themselves often state that if the parents find out, they would surely prevent the act or that the act would not be efficacious if the parents were to discover what they were eating.[69] However, because of the widespread circulation of the ideal of filial slicing in popular literature and local histories, there were social pressures on children to perform this filial act. We have one astonishing case of slicing the forearm, where a father actually requested that his son do it for the father's own benefit. The literatus Sun Zhiwei 孫枝蔚 (1620–1687) laments for the foolish father:

> In the world there have been many who have sliced the flesh of their forearms to cure the morbid condition of an illness (*ji* 疾) of their parents. And not all of them did so out of a desire for fame. For in cases where a man's son hopes for his sick parent to remain alive, and there is no other conceivable plan to follow, then and only then may he choose this method—but even then he will conceal what he has done from his parent. And even so, a gentleman will feel disgusted at this. I certainly have never heard of another case [such as this] where a father actually demanded (*zewang* 責望) such an act of his son. In the village of Anfeng in Taizhou (in present-day Jiangsu province), there was a certain Lu Gao 魯高, who married a woman née Wu 吳. When this woman heard that her father-in-law while ill had admired a young man of the village who had sliced his arm (*gegong* 割肱) [to heal his father's illness], she imitated this action in place of her husband. The knife was sharp, and she ended up dying from it.[70]

We have additional details of this case: First, the wife had sliced her forearm because her husband was also sick at the time, and her father-in-law was envious of the neighbor's filial slicing. Second, as a new bride, she was dutiful in maintaining the family sacrifices. Third, she eventually bled to death after twelve days because the knife she used was quite sharp and she had cut her flesh to the bone.[71]

The case of the woman née Wu can be understood on many levels. On the surface it reveals the social pressure to perform filial slicing, which appears to have led to a sort of moral competition among neighbors. It also bespeaks the complex issue of women's kinship loyalty and their ambiguous role in demonstrating a virtue that was traditionally reserved for men, which can be seen as a sort of inversion of the case of Changzhong. We may also be tempted to conclude that the father's envy of a local villager's filial slicing, which prompted him to expect his own son to do the same, was a simple case of envy. However, there may be other social factors at play. We must be mindful that performing virtuous acts (such as filial slicing and female chastity mutilation) had long been enshrined in the Confucian practice of documenting and eulogizing people in official and local histories. The state rewarded filial devotion to one's parents because it paralleled the literati's loyalty to the emperor. The pervasive discourse of self-sacrificing filial virtue was part of the larger cultural ideal for many people. For a family, to have a son embody such an ideal would certainly make the family's "name famous in future ages, and thereby glorify one's parents," as the *Classic of Filial Piety* prescribes. Such a symbolic capital also translated into status and potential imperial reward.

In ancient times the imperial state periodically rewarded performers of filial piety with gifts and state insignia. By the late Ming, it had become a regular imperial practice. These insignias of distinction, consisting of honorary inscriptions over the door to the house or the village gate, were public and part of the state ideology to inculcate virtue in the common people. The practice of rewarding virtuous people has a long history in Chinese culture. The *Rituals of Zhou* 周禮, which supposedly dates from 770 to 476 B.C.E., specified exempting "the worthy and the capable" from corvée labor.[72] During the late Han (25–220 C.E.), a system of honoring people was already established: "In order to promote good behavior, honorific tablets shall be placed at the doors of all pious sons, obedient grandsons, chaste women, righteous wives, and those who cancel debts owed to them or provide relief in times of disaster."[73]

Insignias of virtue were issued to the populace on occasions of accession to the throne, the beginning of a new reign, important sacrifices, the pacification of rebels, and even unpropitious political situations or periods of dwindling dynastic charisma. In this sense, rewarding filial slicing was nothing new but was rather another act added to the list of virtues that the state promoted. The state continued to assert its prerogatives to determine what counted as virtuous behavior over the centuries. What seems to have been special during the sixteenth and seventeenth centuries was that instances of such rewards were extremely numerous, reaching to the thousands annually. We can only imagine the uncountable cases of slicing the body that never made it into the histories.

Despite the imperial reward for filial slicing, the literati officials had always been divided on this practice. In his criticism of a case in which a certain person named Guo Yi 郭儀 from Hu 鄠, or modern-day Xi'an 西安 city in Shaanxi 陝西 province, was imperially rewarded for his practice of slicing the body, Han Yü 韓愈 (768–824) contended that slicing the body was an impious act because filial devotion should go no further than the provision of proper medicines and treatment. Han Yü argued that harming one's body was without precedent among the ancient sages; it was innately repulsive, and those who performed the act ran the risk of death.[74] Nonetheless, there is plenty of evidence of literati of this period and later who wrote eulogies praising the pious performers of filial slicing.[75]

The famous Yuan poet Yang Weizhen 楊維楨 (1296–1370), for example, eulogized a young boy who performed filial slicing but was still unable to save his mother:

> People say that many who slice their limbs succeed in saving their mothers. Does not the boy's failure indicate that he became famous for nothing? To this I reply, this boy knew how to be solicitous of his parent, and this is an indication of the lack of falseness in his heaven[ly nature]. By slicing his limb to save his mother, he showed that he was thinking of his parent and not thinking of his own body. How could one claim he was thinking of becoming famous? Among the evil citizens of this age there are those who cut their limbs or chests so as to evade taxation and compulsory service. How would a young boy do such a thing out of worry about taxation and services? Slicing his limb came from the boy's heaven[ly nature]. Whether or not the mother was in fact saved or not also lies with heaven. I happen to live next door to the boy, so I am an eye-witness to this affair. Since it can be used to promote moral teaching on a broader scale I have written this poem about it.[76]

Filial slicing was a topic of debate. This passage suggests that there were charlatans who performed body slicing just to avoid paying taxes, but others (even young boys) performed it out of genuine feelings of filial piety. Yang argues that a boy could not possibly think of taxes when he was slicing his body, but we cannot rule out the fact that the boy may have been pressured to do it by adults because, during the Song period, the state instituted a law that stated that, if a member of a household was awarded an honorific insignia, the whole household would be exempt from taxation and labor services. A provisional prefect in 1109 stated the following:

> According to the provisions of the decree of February 1, 1106, those who from this time forth cut up their own liver (*gegan* 割肝) [to make

> medicine] for [sick] grandfathers and grandmothers shall be given five lengths of silk, one hectoliter (*dan* 石) of rice and flour,[77] and two deciliters (*dou* 斗) of wine.[78] I would observe that in the subprefectures of this prefecture reports are repeatedly being made that all sorts of persons have cut up their livers [for this purpose]. When the officials investigate, it is frequently found that there is a slight scar on their ribs. If they had really damaged their internal organs, it would not be in the nature of things for the healing to be so complete. The people in their ignorance wish to profit from the imperial gifts and falsely injure themselves. I would request the court to consider the abolition of the above provision.[79]

The practice of imperially honoring the slicing of one's body seems to have been abolished, but it was revived not long after this statement with a stricter investigation of each case by local subofficials. Each case also had to be approved by the whole community in that region.[80]

As the controversy over false cases of filial slicing continued, people's views on this matter became even more divided. Yet the state continued to reward those who supposedly engaged in filial slicing unabated. The whole imperial reward system was steeped in the economy of social and legal coercion.

During the early part of the Ming, slicing the body was banned after a man named Jiang Bo'er 江伯兒 (ca. fourteenth century) from Shandong tried to heal his sick mother by feeding her pieces of his own flesh. When this failed, he killed his three-year-old son as a sacrifice to Mount Tai 岱嶽 (another name for Taishan 泰山), which supposedly cured his mother. When the local authorities commended the man for his filial piety to the state, hoping to use it as an example of filial virtue, Emperor Taizu became furious and stated that Jiang Bo'er was actually destroying the norm of ethics (*miejue lunli* 滅絕倫理). The emperor sentenced Jiang Bo'er to a hundred lashes and sent him into military exile on Hainan Island.[81] After the Taizu and Chengzu eras, however, the central government made little effort to regulate filial slicing; most of the decisions to bestow rewards were left to local magistrates. By the sixteenth and seventeenth centuries, the rules and investigation process were so lax that performers were regularly rewarded by the local authorities.

Another issue that needs to be addressed in Wu Jiaji's story is spousal fidelity, which is an integral characteristic of the devoted wife. Some modern analyses of the family system in late imperial China claim that the traditional role of women in the family was limited to the continuation of the patrilineal line by producing male heirs. Women had no permanent social place of their own; their presence in the family institution was functional and substitutable. Largely anonymous, women bore no distinct mark of their own.[82] They were confined to the domain of the inner—regardless of their literary achievements during this time.[83] Their presence was altogether barred from the realm of the outer—the sphere of politics. This model of analysis rests on the rhetoric of spatial and social segregation, which dates back to classical times. However, such an ideal does not fully account for the wife's own subjective position in the dangerous practice of filial slicing and intense spousal fidelity. The performance of self-sacrifice by the woman née Wu not only reflects the duty of the devoted wife but may also shed light on the central role of women as keepers of virtue and loyal subjects of the patrilineal family. Perhaps women's practice of self-sacrifice allows us to see that passivity and assertion, affine and agnate, were for them two sides of the same coin.

On the surface, it would seem that Wu's performance of slicing her body on behalf of her husband was an expression of fidelity. Yet, given her important and expected role as the progenitor or perpetuator of male descendents, to risk her life by cutting herself—and eventually dying from it—was more than what was required of her. The act threatened her fulfillment of maternal duty. One way to understand her act is to see it as an assertion of her own agency, in which her integrity as a woman took precedence over her limited role as a mere wife. Her sacrifice was productive, regardless of whether it led to her death. If the practice did not kill her, she would have concretely demonstrated her moral superiority to her family. If she died, she would be praised and remembered for her spousal devotion. The potential recognition of imperial honor on the household of pious daughters and extraordinary women institutionalized centuries earlier elevated these women from private to social virtue. Wu's act aligned her with the ranks of other cultural heroines who had preceded her. It was her name that will be remembered in posterity, not that of her natal or affinal families.

Women could receive honor and imperial recognition through self-inflicted violence, which may be comparable to men's success at the latter through civil examinations. Their acts could easily translate into a kind of social mobility. From this perspective, the wife's act of filial slicing was more than the imposition of male expectations projected onto the passive female body or the victimization of women by the patriarchal system.[84] Women's self-inflicted violence may have been for them a means of staking their claim to moral power and improving their social conditions.

Obviously, many factors—personality, the tenor of family relationships, and her personal history—contributed to Wu's individual response to her father-in-law's request for filial slicing. Incoming brides, such as Wu, had no preexisting ties to their new families, and relations between insiders and outsiders were often difficult. We do not know whether Wu was physically ill treated, but it can be assumed that she found herself outside her own home for the first time as a very junior member of the hierarchy, which was likely exacerbated by her seclusion in the inner domain of the family and the realities of women's lives in general at this time. These realities were shaped by skewed sex ratios, poverty, economic changes, and shifting social practices, all of which may have influenced women's self-image and integrity. A new bride's hope lay in the future, in becoming a respected wife and mother and eventually a matriarch, mistress of her own household. It is not unimaginable that our young bride, as with many young brides during the sixteenth and seventeenth centuries, resorted to drastic measures in order to gain this respect.

The woman née Wu in our example also bespeaks a unique view of social role and gender. In contrast to contemporary Western discourse on gender that rationalizes the necessity and coherence of gender difference by arguing the primacy and certainty of biological difference between male and female, the only two sexes recognized in this discourse, the emphasis in Confucian China was on demonstrating the natural and social logic of symmetrical gender roles.[85] The representation of Wu demonstrates that performing a social role of a pious son was more important to social order than ensuring her congruity of biological and social identity. Stepping up to engage in filial body slicing when her husband was unavailable to do so shows that there might have been more societal toleration for individuals who put aside expected gender roles in order to achieve higher ritual or familial ends.[86]

Women's demonstration of certain kinds of virtue was precisely what inspired historians and writers to eulogize them, as in the case of Sun Zhiwei. We know that during late imperial times women were portrayed in literature as cultural icons, untainted by the scholarly frustrations, sacrifices, and moral compromises demanded by participating in the bureaucratic system.[87] In vernacular fiction, for example, women were represented as enacting roles traditionally reserved for their male counterparts; they often redeemed the moral authority of orthodox values and imperial bureaucracy, both of which had become debased through their conflation with men's career ambitions. This is clearly seen in our case, in which Wu usurped the expected role of the pious son. It was she who assumed the moral authority of engaging in the act of self-sacrifice.

Yet, one can also argue that women's loyalty to the patrilineal family was the result of male portrayal and representation of such virtue and that it was the educated men who were obsessed with eccentric expressions of filial piety or spousal devotion and magnified them many times over. For example, the contents of the "exemplary women" genre of literature grew narrower in focus and more intense in their acts of self-inflicted violence; violence was increasingly a staple of the literature, and suicide the common outcome.[88]

Also, different from the case depicted earlier by Wu Jiaji, which conceals the gruesome details of filial slicing and highlights instead his niece's moral aptitude and miraculous feat, Sun Zhiwei calls attention to the corporeality of her practice and her bleeding profusely for twelve days until she finally dies. Sun's shifting of perspectives from the supernatural to the dangers of filial slicing should not be overlooked. His concluding remarks about this case actually chastise Wu Jiaji, his friend and colleague, for not warning readers of the dangers of this practice: "My friend Wu Binxian 吳賓賢 [aka Wu Jiaji] [also] has a poem of lamentation [for her death]. Although in her heart there was loyalty and righteousness, [his poem] lacks a cautionary admonition for later generations [about slicing the body]. Therefore, my intent differs somewhat from his."[89]

Clearly, the same practice of filial slicing was used for different purposes. One literatus praised its embodiment of virtue and sentiments, while another warned of its dangers. Both of these examples come from writings of local educated elite; they bespeak a complex of social and symbolic associations beyond the orchestration of the state. Filial slicing did not promulgate a simple morality. Changzhong's body was a site for contestation over the perception of commoners, the proper roles for women in their families, and their agency. The woman née Wu may have exercised her agency by usurping her husband's filial role, but these stories were written by men who turned filial women into objects of literary debate.

Miracles, Divinities, and Healers

The practice of filial slicing also appears in sixteenth- and seventeenth-century popular literature, local gazetteers, drama, and fiction, showing that the practice was firmly entrenched in the public cultural domain at this time. The discourse on filial slicing was at once a product of social institutions and their preconditions. Many of the tales, fiction or nonfiction, confirm the symbiotic relationship between gods and humans. Popular literature was an active agent in shaping societal values, which further strengthened the normative view that the gods were deeply concerned about humanity. In novels, filial slicing was often ritualized and replete with proper routines of prayers and resulting visions. Descriptions often include divinities communicating with performers in both waking and dream states through apparitions or mysterious voices from the sky. Sometimes performers would engage in this act in front of images of deities or in temples. Wounds would be healed, and lives would be extended, all of which attests to the efficacy of this practice that aimed to stimulate a cosmic response. Even the *Classic of Filial Piety* states, "Filial piety is the principle of heaven, the duty of earth, and the standard conduct of humans. Since it is heaven and earth's principle, people copy it. By doing so, they imitate heaven's brilliance and follow the earth's advantages, thereby harmonizing all under heaven." Also, "When filial piety and brotherliness reach their height, they communicate with the gods (*shenming* 神明)."[90] Proof texts such as these were widely circulated and understood by the people, who grew up memorizing these and similar passages.

In the seventeenth-century novel *Marriage Bonds to Awaken the World* (*Xingshi yinyuan zhuan* 醒世因緣傳) by Xi Zhou Sheng 西周生,[91] when Chao Liang 晁梁, one of the protagonists in the novel, hears that slicing the body can cure illness, he goes to a local earth god temple to cut the flesh from his thigh so that he can prepare a curative soup (*tang* 湯) for his caregiver and mother figure, the woman née Chao (Chao *furen* 晁夫人). The earth god intervenes and sends him a message that there is no need for him to slice his body because that night his mother will be cured.[92] Going to the earth god temple to engage in such an act was natural as the earth god was generally thought of as the lesser god "bureaucrat" in charge of village affairs. The act was a form of testimonial and an announcement to the deity.

Elsewhere in the novel, two daughters-in-law simultaneously perform filial slicing of their bodies for their mother-in-law after hearing that the practice is a panacea that will "bring back [a parent back] to life when the dying process has already begun (*qisi huisheng* 起死回生)." Together they pray fervently to the gods above and below, vow to become vegetarians, ritually change their clothes, cut the flesh from their left arms, and prepare a stew (*gengtang* 羹湯). They give the stew to their mother-in-law, saying that the meat is pork. As a result of their sincere prayer, the mother-in-law eats it, at which point she regains her appetite and begins to eat regularly again. She lives an additional year and eight months and finally dies at the age of seventy-eight.[93]

This novel received considerable attention from the literati. Many extant editions clearly suggest that it was reprinted many times.[94] Given the sixteenth- and seventeenth-century context of the widespread production and reception of morality books and ledgers based on notions of karma, the novel's persistent emphasis on retribution, miracle healings, and divine intervention would suggest that such ideas were familiar to many people at the time.[95]

Scholars also confirm that intervening divinities in stories of filial slicing are also prominent in local gazetteers.[96] According to a late Ming Jinhua

County 金華縣 gazetteer, there was a man named Ni Riheng 倪日亨, whose mother, née Fan 范氏, was gravely ill at age sixty-two. In tears Riheng cried out to the gods, vowing to use his body to substitute his mother's pain (*yuanyi shendai* 願以身代). Then he sliced a piece of his flesh, made a curative broth with it, and offered it to his mother. After that he lay on the ground in great pain from the deep wound (*shangzhong mendi* 傷重悶地) and wanted to die (*yujue* 欲絕). Then he heard a voice from the sky say, "A pious son cures the parent; your lifespan will be increased twenty-four years (*erji* 二紀)."[97]

Divinities also manifested in dreams that involved predictions about people's lives. In 1694 a ten-year-old girl named Fang Futou 方福妵 of Zhejiang province, Yongkang 永康 prefecture, diligently served her ailing mother, née Feng 馮氏, but no medicine could cure her. Futou worried day and night, trying to think of ways to help her mother. One night she dreamed about a certain "white-robed woman" (*baiyi nü* 白衣女) holding a shaving knife, which startled her so much that she woke up. She understood the meaning of the dream, however. The next morning, seeing her mother on the threshold of death, Futou went upstairs to the shrine, lit the lamp, and prayed reverently in front of the altar. She then took a knife and sliced a piece of flesh from her left arm (*ge zuobi rou* 割左臂肉), made a soup with it (*jiantang* 煎湯), and then offered the soup to her mother. The mother's health was immediately restored (*lisu* 立甦). A local government official sent generous amounts of fabric and silver to Futou's family as a result.[98]

Numerous works on dream interpretation existed in late imperial times, many of them written by women, forming a special literary genre on the topic.[99] The popular Ming book on dream interpretation, the *Comprehensive Collection of the Duke of Zhou's Explanation of Dreams* (*Zhougong jiemeng quanshu* 周公解夢全書), states that dreaming of a female holding a knife is an auspicious harbinger of fortune.[100] In the case of Fang Futou, it certainly became a reality. Not only was the mother healed by Futou's flesh, but the family also received official recognition and rewards.[101]

The "white-robed woman" who manifested herself to Futou is a ubiquitous motif that appears in many miracle stories connected to popular religious cults from the tenth century onward.[102] It was also a popular theme in late imperial Chinese paintings. Scholars generally agree that most white-robed female forms that appear in artistic renderings and visions are the white-robed Guanyin or Bodhisattva Avalokiteśvara. However, this is not to say that she was exclusively understood as a "Buddhist" deity. Instead, she was popularly understood as the goddess of mercy. In late imperial times several "precious scrolls" (*baojuan* 寶卷) and hagiographies were devoted to Guanyin, some of which include explicit references to Daoist and thaumaturgical elements.[103]

She was also regularly worshipped at non-Buddhist altars.[104] These works demonstrate her widespread popularity during the sixteenth and seventeenth centuries. In addition, literary and iconographic materials (fiction, drama, and essays) produced during this time were remarkably cavalier and elastic in their reproduction of Guanyin images.[105]

It is no surprise that the white-robed goddess Guanyin came to be connected with self-maiming and themes of filial piety. In popular legends she herself engaged in similar acts that led to her apotheosis. It is conceivable that some people engaged in filial slicing, patterning their self-mutilations after the selfless offerings of this goddess. One such example is the legend of Miaoshan 妙善, the human incarnation of Guanyin. This legend, which was familiar to everyone at this time, tells of a devoted daughter named Miaoshan, who offered her own eyes and hands to aid the recovery of her ailing father—an act that later caused her to become transformed into a goddess[106]—and was symbolically reincorporated into her natal family. This legend takes place in Henan province, but Miaoshan is the incarnation of Guanyin, whose holy site is in Zhejiang province, on whose coast Mount Putuo is located—not far from Futuo's residence and arguably one of the most celebrated and widely known sites associated with the cult of Guanyin.[107] In her discussion of the cult of Guanyin, Yü Chün-fang cites several stories of filial piety and self-maiming that involve this deity. In these stories Guanyin not only appears in the performers' dreams, often the night before the filial act, but also explicitly encourages people to engage in the act and guides them in the "operation."[108] Given the proximity of Futou's residence to Mount Putuo and Guanyin's connection to the filial practice of slicing the body, it is almost certain that Futou was already aware of the connection of Guanyin, her story as Miaoshan, and her acts of filial piety.

In premodern China the visible and invisible worlds were inseparable. Various "signs" were understood as part of the social reality in which people lived. People of all social classes (from emperors on down to commoners) understood themselves as living in a world populated by an entire pantheon of spiritual beings who communicated with them through miracles, dreams, visions, and portents. The boundaries between the world of the living and that of the dead were blurred. People had an acute awareness of the importance of omens, dreams, and visions. These signs were not interpreted as purely psychological phenomena; they were proof that everything was interrelated and part of the "habitus" that guided people's decisions.

The variety of filial-slicing cases discussed here demonstrates that this was a multifaceted practice orchestrated by performers and writers for different purposes. Performers engaged in the practice to assert claims on moral power and sanctity and to negotiate their social circumstances. Rather than promulgating a simple morality of filial piety, filial slicing was an occasion for debates over proper roles in the family, genuineness of natal devotion, social conventions, and even the agency of women. Writers of the sixteenth and seventeenth centuries represented the filial slicing in ways that served their own agendas. I have shown that they indirectly advanced the idea that these exemplars of moral action were better preserved among the uneducated than among the upper echelons of the elite class, using their own kin and friends, like Wu Jiaji did, to demonstrate moral sanctity. Some authors portrayed heroic filial slicing as a practice that transcended the usual strictures of kinship relations, enabling daughters to reclaim an otherwise proscribed relationship with their natal families. Some may argue that these two stories of women who performed filial slicing actually reified the roles of women as subordinate. However, it is precisely because women were subjected by social norms that they established their subjectivity. They were active agents in relation to the mechanism of society by means of their conscious acts,[109] which attracted the literati to write about and debate their practices.

Complex notions of sacrifice, gift, substitution, regeneration, and devotion were simultaneously present in the practice of filial slicing. The cultural dimensions cannot be separated from the religious elements. Writers debated these topics. Their differing positions show that the body itself was a site of contention and that its instrumentality was productive of an enormous metaphoric complex. The theme of miracles, divinities, and portents figures quite prominently in the accounts discussed in this chapter, which suggests that filial slicing cannot be separated from the performers' beliefs that divinities responded to their actions. In the next chapter—on female chastity—we continue to explore the multivalent practice of self-inflicted violence. Young women and widows asserted their agency (even after death) and defended their chastity through self-mortification and suicide. The educated writers wrote about and debated these women's stories for didactic and entertainment purposes. However, from a different angle, popular cultural expectations and beliefs disclose a darker side of these practices. The unnatural deaths of chastity suicide were perceived as forms of disorder and objects of great concern. There is some evidence that the state and the literati eulogized deceased widows out of fear of their revenants.

4

Chaste Widows as Entertainment and Revenants

If I should suddenly die before you, you have
such an impetuous personality that I fear that you will
not understand this principle of death
[and will commit suicide].

—Yang Jisheng 楊繼盛 (1516–1555)

IN THE PREVIOUS chapters I have shown how sixteenth- and seventeenth-century performers of blood writing and filial slicing, and those who wrote about them, asserted different claims to negotiate their social and cosmic conditions. In this chapter I explore how young chaste women and widows engaged in the practices of chastity mutilation and suicide to resist rape and remarriage. In contrast to other scholarly studies of these women's acts of self-violence, I discuss them on both discursive and performative levels from the broader perspective of the larger milieu of the time. I argue that didactic works on these acts were also a form of entertainment but that the practices of self-inflicted violence themselves may have been a way for young chaste women to forge their agency as subjects of sanctity. Chastity mutilations were instruments of change that substantiated cultural and religious values in times of threat. Chastity suicides transformed them as unforgiving revenants who avenged themselves on those who wronged them.

There are several historical studies on the topic of female chastity in late imperial China,[1] which can be grouped into three approaches. The first is the politicization of female chastity: Some scholars argue that wifely fidelity was equated with political loyalty (*zhong* 忠) and emphasize that officials during the sixteenth and seventeenth centuries began to make explicit connections between female chastity and male loyalty to the state. For example, early Ming compilers of the official *Yuan History* placed the motifs of fidelity and resistance to rape together and listed twice as many records of faithful women as any previous dynastic history. These records point to the fact that many of the assailants were Yuan soldiers, which demonizes the non-Han Mongols.[2] The same state strategy occurred during the Qing dynasty, when Ming loyalists appropriated female chastity to symbolize their political allegiance to the fallen empire. During the fall of the Ming dynasty, Ming loyalists spoke of themselves as "faithful wives of the Ming" and identified themselves with women who were loyal to their dead husbands, as they were loyal to the Ming state.[3]

The second approach concerns the literati debates and social effects of chastity mutilation and suicide: Modern scholars have historicized the narratives of the lives of these women and detailed how writers and compilers of gazetteers documented thousands of "virtuous" women in their own local region.[4] These writers debated the women's individual subjectivity and personal circumstances. Some criticized these women, while others identified with their heroines by writing about the passionate conjugal love between men and women as a cause for suicide or self-mutilation.[5] As the epigraph to this chapter illustrates, Yang Jisheng had to strongly warn his loving (but impetuous) wife not to commit suicide after his death. His exhortation was to no avail, however: On the same day that Yang was executed in the marketplace his wife, Zhang Zhen 張貞, committed suicide.[6] Of course, other social issues were also at play in the lives of these women. Some women were coerced into chastity mutilation; others engaged in it to avoid certain responsibilities. Most would not even consider these options of self-inflicted violence.[7]

Third is the didacticism of female chastity: Historians have noted that in many novels, dramas, and poems the educated elite promoted female chastity to transform the moral climate of the time (*lishi* 勵世).[8] Lü Kun, for example, sought ways to popularize the virtue of conjugal loyalty by writing and publishing didactic work for women. However, as we read below, the popularity of his work had other, unintended social effects. Literary works, such as morality tracts, poetry, and especially illustrated books, were entertaining to their readers in the way they dramatized and illustrated accounts of women's lives. In this sense they contributed to the aestheticization of "fierce women" (*lienü* 烈女) as heroines.

These scholarly approaches are integrated into this present chapter, but I propose other, more nuanced ways of reading the practices of female chastity, especially those involving self-inflicted violence. For example, early scholars took a top-down approach to show how the official state discourse encouraged female chastity. Yet, it was through popular literature that the notion of chastity became a widespread cultural phenomenon. Works such as novels, dramas, and poetry seldom focused on its moorings in the principles of patrilineality. Instead, they honed in on the passion and individual expressions involved in the dramatization of self-mutilation and suicide, which made female chastity a runaway favorite among writers. Moreover, the thriving trade in illustrated books and vernacular literature during this time often complicated the didactic rhetoric of the chastity ideal. "Exemplary women" now appeared in compendiums of their own; their stories, preceded by full-page woodblock illustrations, were encapsulated by the compiler's pithy commentary. Compilations of stories of chaste women were widely published and actively read by people of all social classes. These vividly illustrated tales reached more homes and hearts than did Confucian classics; they dramatized the loftiest ideals of morality, which were at the core of literati mores in ways that appealed to a general audience. The purported aim of these didactic works was to inculcate the general populace with the moral lesson of being faithful to one's husband. They presented chastity as a female virtue. Yet, the descriptive language and the strong sexual overtones of the illustrations in these literary pieces often heighten the drama-like performance of female chastity. The supposedly unambiguous narrative of resistance to remarriage often concentrates on the heroine's youth and sexual attractiveness. This dramatization complicates the narratives' seemingly straightforward moral agenda. The conflicting tension between the moral agenda and the entertainment value of chastity stories can be understood only in the context of an age that championed individual passions and alternative interpretations of morality.

Popular works on female chastity suicides dramatize deceased women who, due to their strong passion, continue to exert tremendous spiritual power to engage in romance with their living lovers[9] or to come back as vengeful spirits to haunt those who had harmed them. Plays and dramas proliferated in the sixteenth and seventeenth centuries, and many of these detail the indivisibility of the world of the living and that of the dead. They were both products and producers of the discourse and utter terror of ghosts during this time.[10] Popular religion and healing practices regularly involved rituals meant to counteract spirits as malignant forces that spread disease and death.[11] In fact, many of the religious practices were concerned with appeasing malevolent ghosts, who sought revenge on mortals. These rituals, which included the burning of incense, prayers, fasting, communications through mediums, and the placing of spirit walls to prevent the entry of evil spirits through a doorway, were part of people's everyday existence.[12]

While scholars have noted the significant presence of the discourse of ghosts and revenants in popular culture, no one has yet connected them with the literati and imperial state eulogies for deceased widows as a possible way to appease their highly ambiguous vengeful ghosts. However, as we read later, I have found several sources, including illustrated books, local gazetteers, and miscellaneous jottings by the literati, which support this claim.

This chapter embeds the practice of female chastity mutilation and suicide in the larger milieu of the sixteenth and seventeenth centuries. It explores various issues surrounding these practices by considering the social realities of women, the literary constructions of chastity, and the religious ideals of the time. It raises several questions: How does the moral message of championing female chastity correlate with the richly illustrated books on female exemplars? How does the wide circulation of these illustrated books affect the discourse of chastity mutilation and suicide in the larger cultural milieu of the day? What is the relationship between written texts on and actual performance of chastity mutilation and suicide? Does the literary dramatization of female revenants that come back to haunt the living have an effect on women' choices for suicide? Were texts performative in the lives of chaste widows?

The Practical and Conceptual Implications of Female Chastity

The Chinese term used throughout late imperial times for widows who refused to remarry was *shoujie* 守節, "to be chaste," although the term translates literally as "preserving one's moral fidelity." However, other terms that highlighted different shades of meaning in the practice of female chastity were also used. For example, "pure moral fidelity," or *zhenjie* 貞節, was used to convey the sense of purity and meant not "losing one's body" or virginity (*shishen* 失身). This latter term was a symbolic expression for not losing one's "sexuality" (*jie* 節) by transferring one's procreative power to a man other than one's husband.[13] Ultimately, being chaste suggested that wives should "follow their husbands in death" (*xunsi* 殉死).[14] The opposite of sexual fidelity would be "defilement by illicit sex" (*jianwu* 姦污).

The loss of virginity was of great concern to parents who wished to marry off their daughters. A girl had to be given to her future husband in pristine condition so as to guarantee the purity of the ancestral line.[15] Even if the husband (or husband-to-be) died, a young widow would still be considered "chaste" as long as she maintained the integrity of her body and showed wifely loyalty to her family and proper social conduct after her husband's death.[16] The value of polluted girls (for example, those who had been raped), on the other hand, was much lower; they often became concubines or prostitutes because it was difficult for them to marry into well-to-do families.

In the economy of marriage, maintaining purity of one's body was a difficult but lucrative venture. If a young woman was chaste, not only did she gain social acceptance and prestige, but both her natal and her husband's families also benefited. However, if she did things that were considered licentious, then both families would be affected.[17] The frequent trafficking of females that Susan Mann and Dorothy Ko described in the Ming and Qing markets for young women guaranteed that a young widow's parents-in-law or natal parents could readily find buyers for her.[18] Thus the prestige of chastity might have translated into economic prosperity.

Those who refused to transfer their sexual and reproductive powers to other men or to be a part of the economy of marriage made sure that they could not be placed on the market by disfiguring their faces or bodies or committing suicide. Such acts were concrete "declarations of determination" (*mingzhi* 明志) and "pledges of commitment" (*xinshi* 信誓). More often than not, parents or in-laws who forced these women to remarry were said to be "robbing her determination" (*duoqizhi* 奪其志).[19] This language suggests that, for these young widows, sexuality and chastity were assets, tools, and rights that could be deployed by a variety of actors in a complex system of exchange or negotiation.

The value placed on chastity can be seen in the extent to which women tried to damage or destroy their bodies in order to cut themselves off from the marriage economy. In late imperial China, widows who practiced female chastity would de-eroticize their bodies by cutting off their nose (*gebi* 割鼻, *yibi* 劓鼻, or *jiebi* 截鼻), ears (*ge'er* 割耳), or fingers (*duanzhi* 斷指) and branding their faces with words (*qingmian* 黥面).[20] To a lesser degree than mutilations, sometimes these women would cut off their hair (*jiefa* 截髮 or *duanfa* 斷髮).[21] Sometimes beautiful widows purposefully made themselves look like vagabonds by smearing dirt on their faces (*yintu tumian* 垔土塗面), letting their hair hang loose (*pengtou* 鬅頭), or not wearing shoes (*sanzu* 散足). These were means of protecting themselves from courting rogue males or bandits.[22] Those women who went a step beyond mutilation to committing suicide either to resist forced marriage or rape were considered by most of the literati and state officials as martyrs (*lieshi* 烈士). This term in premodern Chinese usage has a political overtone reserved for men who sacrificed their lives out of loyalty to the state.[23]

It is important to note that, in medieval times, virtuous women were described as *lie* 列, "exemplary." However, in late imperial times, while the term "exemplary" was still used as a topical category in gazetteers and in expanded biographies of chaste women, the meaning of the word shifted to its homophone, *lie* 烈, "fierce." According to *Explicating the Written Characters*, the first comprehensive lexicon of Chinese characters, all of the phrases that contain *lie* 烈 (including the fire radical) connote "staunch," "vehement," and "fierce," such as a "blazing fire" (*liehuo* 烈火), a "scorching sun" (*lieri* 烈日)—a term usually reserved for martyrs.[24] Late imperial sources make this distinction quite clear by using the term "fierce women" (*lienü* 烈女) to describe women who committed suicide. It is not surprising that chaste women who did not commit suicide but instead remained widows for the rest of their lives were considered exemplary women (*lienü* 列女).[25]

Scholars have long discussed the changing historical discourses on female chastity, focusing on genres of literature about female chastity. There is no need to repeat all of their conclusions here except to state that the earliest record of this practice can be traced back to the Han dynasty work of Liu Xiang 劉向, titled *Biographies of Exemplary Women* (*Lienü zhuan* 列女傳),[26] and that the elevation of chaste widowhood was part of the larger Confucian orthodox view of female virtue that originated in the Song. For example, neo-Confucian thinkers in the Song detailed the abstract theoretical underpinnings of a wife's fidelity to her deceased husband as part of the discourse that justified chastity in terms of the economic interests of the husband's patrilineage. Because Song widows inherited substantial property from their fathers in the form of a dowry, which remained separate from the property of their husbands' families, widows often returned to their natal family with this property (and whatever they had accumulated during their marriage) after their husbands had died. Neo-Confucian literati criticized this practice as subverting the prosperity and ritual integrity of the patrilineal line. Instead, they encouraged widows to use their dowries to support their affinal families and to remain with their patriline until death. This ideal was officially established as a state policy for the first time during the Yuan period due to the impact of neo-Confucianism on Yuan rulers and officials.[27] The Yuan state supported chaste widows and prohibited women from taking any property from their first marriage if they returned to their natal families or remarried. During this time, marriage theoretically became a permanent transfer of a woman's body and property to her husband's family.[28] The practice continued into the Ming, which made a definite impact on women's lives in the economy of female chastity.

Performing Chastity as Passion (Qing)

In the sixteenth and seventeenth centuries the discourse on female chastity was fully entrenched in the mainstream value that celebrated individual expression that involved a corporal demonstration of virtue.[29] Yet, virtue during this time was ambiguous. This period witnessed an unprecedented shift in moral values. Writers and thinkers explored human desires and passion. The virtue of chastity became bound up with these issues. Of course, the motif of the beautiful young widow as virtuous was not a sixteenth-century invention; it had already been enshrined in the Confucian discursive practice of reading a woman's desire for her lover as allegorical of a worthy literatus's desire for political recognition. Yet, this motif exploded during the sixteenth and seventeenth centuries to such an extent that even courtesans and prostitutes were held up as emblems of moral integrity if they passionately engaged in self-inflicted violence. Novels that detail these women's chastity mutilations and suicides were championed as demonstrations of genuine *qing* or passion, the basis of all moral virtues.

Popular representations of chastity mutilation and suicide were contested. For the conservative literati, female chastity narratives were intended to serve as moral lessons in female fidelity for the readers to perpetuate. In their writings, female passions should be contained to preserve the conservative norms of ideal behavior.[30] Yet, what lurks behind their endorsement of violent chastity practices as markers of authentic moral performance is their fear of women's sexual promiscuity. Moreover, even though didactic works are supposed to promote conservatism, they are filled with illustrations and descriptions of attractive female bodies. In an age of commercialization, where literary and publishing strategies were used to dramatize, illustrate, and ultimately sell the literati's books, their didacticism was greatly overshadowed by incongruity, utility, and aestheticization of female chastity as enjoyable stories to read. Reading illustrated books on chaste women might have been a form of leisurely "entertainment" for the rest of the population.

Representations of the female body as a site of contestation appear in the seventeenth-century didactic work *Illustrated Female Exemplars* (*Guifan tushuo* 閨範圖說), edited with commentaries by Lü Kun. He brought arcane stories of women in the past to life for his readers by reorganizing and reclassifying the original stories of *Biographies of Exemplary Women* (*Lienü zhuan* 列女傳). He also used the language of the marketplace instead of that of officialdom, which led to its wide circulation and popularity.[31] For example, the young widows in this work ranged from sixteen to thirty years of age. Lü thus focuses on their youthful or sexual attractiveness. Widows' physical appearances are described as "voluptuous and becoming" (*rong yu se* 榮於色), "extremely alluring" (*po you se* 頗有色),[32] "beautiful" (*youzi* 有姿),[33] and with "adorable demeanor" (*mei yu xing* 美於行).[34] These characterizations gave the female body unique possibilities as a theater for entertainment for male readers and their imagination.[35]

In the following case of Gao Xing 高行, whose life was represented in all Ming editions and expansions of female exemplar books, the heroine refused remarriage not only to a nobleman but also to a king:

> Gao Xing ["Lofty Conduct"] was the widow of Liang. Her physical appearance was voluptuous and her demeanor was adorable. Her husband died early, but she refused to remarry. Noblemen of Liang vied to obtain her, but all were unsuccessful. When the king of Liang heard of this, he ordered his minister to propose a betrothal with gifts; many attempts were made. Gao Xing said, "My late husband was unfortunate; he died early [and had an impoverished burial]. I have been taking care of his young child, therefore it would be difficult for me to remarry. Moreover, the propriety of women is to stay in her marriage without changing [her fidelity]. How can I consider myself a human if I prize my own survival and abandon my indebtedness to my late husband, or relinquish righteousness to gain benefit?" She looked into a mirror and grabbed a knife to cut off her nose. She said, "I have just inflicted punishment on myself.[36] The reason I did not kill myself is because I cannot bear to leave my weak young child orphaned. The king desires me for my beauty. Now that I am punished [and have maimed myself],[37] I can finally be released." The minister reported to the king what had happened. The king excused her from conscript labor and bestowed on her an honorific title, "Lofty Conduct."[38]

Even though this dramatic case aims to advance the virtue of female chastity, the narrative focuses on Gao Xing's voluptuous body. Her vulnerable widow's beauty complicates the narrative's seemingly straightforward moral agenda. Because Gao Xing's physical beauty was the object of men's desire, she had to destroy it to fend off their advances. The drama hinges on the unconsummated tension between the male desire for beauty and Gao Xing's destruction of it. Her body was a site where resistance to invasion was acted out. She could have accepted the king's proposition (which included gifts, prestige, and other material benefits—all of which would be desirable to those who lived in poverty), but she refused to barter her body. Even though she was poor, her chastity was worth more to her than any material gift. In her defacement—the most visible and precious feature of her beauty—she proved her commitment to chastity in front of the minister and his attendants beyond any doubt.[39] She declared this to him: "Now you will be able to explain the situation to the king [so he will no longer desire me]."[40] The minister could only gesture his reverence for her act.

Gao Xing's undeniable sanctity is dramatized by the woodblock illustration in figure 4.1 (p. 98), which is evident in the respectful gestures of the minister and of her own child. They gaze with awe upon her body as a sight and a site. Their respectful gestures approve her act with admiration, indirectly eliciting the approval of the reading public. In the illustration Gao Xing sits looking into the mirror on the table in front of her as she cuts off her nose. Her son (to her left) and the minister (in front) press their palms together in reverence as they watch her. They do not attempt to stop her; they just watch her performance. The author endorses this self-inflicted violence and exalts it as an expression of unquestionable sanctity; he transforms her body into an object that is both admired and rejected.

Surely Gao Xing was unable to retaliate; with regard to the mainstream social group her status was marginal—she was not fully a member but not completely separate, either. Her humble origin is depicted in the illustration by the shabby house and ruined walls. In fact, the narrator states that her household could not even afford a proper burial for her husband. In her resistance to the king's proposition, her marginal, apolitical status in comparison to the king meant that she could only resort to, in her words, "self-punishment" (*xing* 刑). Had she not performed this act, she would have been punished anyway. Thus, her self-inflicted violence was a preemptive strategy, one that possibly saved her life.

The sixteenth-century *Illustrated Female Exemplars* aims to solve the perceived degenerate social crisis of sexual promiscuity by holding up the victim Gao Xing as an "exemplar" and granting her a higher status beyond ordinary human capability. Lü Kun's comment praises her sanctity, which subverts the socially superior minister and demands his admiration. Her sacrality is nested in danger, threat, and violence.[41] In making Gao Xing out to be an extraordinary being and an exemplar for all to emulate, Lü Kun revived ancient personae (but departed freely from the original accounts) such as Gao Xing to stand in for people of his period.

We must also consider the significance of this Ming edition of the *Illustrated Female Exemplars*, from which this rich illustration is taken, and

Figure 4.1 A woodblock illustration of Gao Xing cutting her nose, from Lü Kun's 吕坤 (1536–1618) *Guifan tushuo* 闺范图说, *juan* 3, 52a. Reprinted with the permission of the publisher. © Beijing: Xueyuan chubanshe, 1998.

the motives of its compiler, Lü Kun. His many comments about women's uncontrolled passion and sexuality certainly demonstrate that his work is a puritanical attempt to control women. For example, elsewhere in the work Lü Kun compares passions to the uncontrollable torrents of water (*yushui* 鬱水) that are let loose when a dike breaks:[42] "When the passions of the people overflow, restricting them is difficult... and as unbearable as cutting two toes joined together or a tumor."[43] He not only disapproved of gender disorder and illicit sexual relations but also lamented the degenerate state of society, where commoner and elite women behaved "almost like prostitutes" (*changjia* 倡家).[44] For Lü Kun the purity of a woman's body was the measure of her virtue and was to be taken very seriously:

> Guarding the physical body for a woman is like holding up a jade vase or carrying [a container] full of water with both hands. If her heart is not steadfast, then it will be distorted by the ears and eyes; if the effect of her [actions] is not resolute, then family members and outsiders will be suspicious. Only then will a woman complete the preservation of her moral fidelity and establish her purified body. Why? Because a man's enterprise lies in the harmony of the six directions,[45] as long as he does not defile human relations. Even though he may commit some minor flaws, he can still redeem himself. A woman's name and integrity, however, lie in her body; the slightest blemish cannot be concealed by ten thousand good deeds.[46]

Lü Kun's prescription against polluting the chaste body should be understood in the context of conservative Confucian discourse, which sought to control the seductive power of the female body.[47] We should remember from our discussion in chapter 1 that it is precisely because of the widespread anxiety and the deep sense of loss of control that some literati wrote stringently about sex.[48] That is, behind the literati's puritanical criticism of passion as a dangerous disruption of moral fidelity lurks the promiscuous nature of female sexuality. For example, Feng Menglong 馮夢龍 (1574–1646), a famous playwright, novelist, and thinker of the time, acknowledged this when he wrote about a young, beautiful widow named Shao, who took a vow of chastity but later was unable to resist being tempted by her young servant boy and became pregnant by him.[49] This is a case of "failed chastity," where a young girl's sexual desire could not be contained. Scholars have also noted that some widows had affairs with servants for economic interests, especially those widows who lacked the financial resources to pay for work done to maintain their homes.[50]

Lü Kun was responding to what he perceived as the degeneracy of the age, but he chose to use fire against fire: By stirring up people's feelings in his work, he could teach them about morality.[51] Yet, in his endeavor it is difficult to untangle feelings from sincerity, passion, and genuine determination. Gao Xing becomes a visual and discursive field that blurs the boundaries between veneration and desire, commoner and elite, and text and practice.

Many writers during this time produced vernacular fiction, especially in scholar-beauty fiction, which explored the possibilities of individual passion and the chaste female body as the quintessential site of human passion and individualism.[52] By the sixteenth century, the neo-Confucian orthodox view of female chastity had completely fused with this movement of sentiment, resulting in hybrid representations that functioned as potent symbols of virtue and vice. Sometimes the outcome led to improbable twists of plot. For example, the seventeenth-century romance *The Fortunate Union* concludes triumphantly with proof of the heroine's chastity.[53] Tang Xianzu's (1550–1616) *Peony Pavilion* depicts the heroine giving herself to her lover in a dream, which allows her to retain chaste.[54] The narrative's insistence on demonstrating the sexual attractiveness and the potential for licentious desire in female protagonists could be seen as a clash with the writers' didactic intent. Perhaps the merging of the two discourses of virtue and vice stemmed from the perceived importance ascribed to human passions during this time. We know that numerous apologetic literati attempted to reconcile the relationship between Confucian imperatives and passion.

A contemporary moralist, Yuan Huang 袁黄 (1533–1606) had these words to say about passion:

> In ancient times, the sages kept order under heaven by setting a good example of self-cultivation. Such was nothing more than making full use of the passion of an individual. Human beings are born because of passions... [this is why] those good at motivating [others] turn to passion; when connected to passion, people will live in perfect harmony; if one is motivated by passion to go [somewhere], one will travel a thousand miles as if under strict order; if one is compelled by passion to die, one will go through all kinds of dangers as if death meant nothing... this is why those rich in passion are sages; those good at using passion are wise men.[55]

This passage defends passion in terms of its usefulness for self-cultivation and promotion of the social order. In other words, passion undergirds virtue and moves the general reader on a visceral level.

In his *History of Emotions* Feng Menglong claims that it is precisely passion between men and women that structures the Confucian imperative of loyalty and filial piety. He provides moving accounts of numerous men and women, both historical and fictional, whose actions of love and courage demonstrated the highest ideal of Confucian morality. For example, he elaborates on the case of a courtesan who married a literatus, was stolen back by her procurer, remained faithful to her husband even in a brothel, and was finally reunited with him and bore him sons: "She who is without passion cannot be a chaste wife to her husband."[56] Feng states that "in terms of all acts of loyalty, filial piety, chastity, and martyrdom, if they are performed out of moral reasoning then they are strained; but if they stem from utmost passion (*zhiqing* 至情) then they must be considered sincere."[57] Genuine passion legitimated one's actions. It is thus not surprising that Feng recommended that widows commit suicide immediately upon bereavement, when they were in the full glory of their grief.[58]

Indeed, popular literature at the time frequently portrayed an ambiguous image of the female body, attesting to the contentious nature of chastity and questioning its apparent virtue. For example, in Pu Songling's 蒲松齡 (1640–1715) *Strange Stories*, a widow abandons her young son and daughter after the death of her husband; she also sells all of their property, pockets the money, and marries another man—leaving her children in the care of their aunt.[59] Also, the eighteenth-century *Story of One Gentleman and Two Sisters* fictionalizes the complex life of Wang Cuiqiao 王翠翹 (ca. mid-sixteenth century), a young, beautiful, and chaste girl who later became a promiscuous "woman who slept with ten thousand men" (*wanren qi* 萬人妻).[60] Early in the story Wang Cuiqiao launches into a speech to explain why she rejected premarital sex. Her speech echoes that of Lü Kun: "A woman should protect her body like a fragile vase. Once the vase is broken, it can never be repaired. Once a woman's body is stained, how could it regain its chastity? Then what kind of body could I present to you on our wedding night?"[61] Ironically, Wang Cuiqiao became a prostitute and sacrificed the very body (*sheshen* 捨身) she had tried so hard to protect. She did this in order to earn the money necessary to save her father, who had been wrongly implicated in a robbery. Later she became a concubine and finally the wife of a pirate leader. Although the novel shows how she was forced to offer her body to earn money, she never failed to point out that she was selling only her "corporeal body" (*roushen* 肉身) and that her true or "chaste body" would never be for sale. A commentator on the novel states that allowing her chaste body to be defiled was another way of asserting her chastity (*rushen zhi wei jieshen* 辱身之為潔身).[62] This text repeatedly draws attention to Wang Cuiqiao's body, portraying it as a site where the meanings of passion are contested and inscribed.[63]

Reading Female Chastity as Entertainment

Didactic stories of female chastity may be read as unambiguous stories of virtue or a conscious strategy to promote conservatism. However, given the milieu in which these texts circulated, when the literary celebration of passion was at its peak, the explosion of passion and sexuality in vernacular literature as entertaining tropes may have spilled over into the genre of didactic works. In other words, the forms in which female chastity was represented, with their dramatic content and emotional appeal, may also have colored the meaning of these stories far more than any underlying moralizing intent. Representations of chastity were transformed into objects of connoisseurship and entertainment by the very process of their production.

If we read Lü Kun's *Illustrated Female Exemplars* as a didactic production and nothing more, we overlook the complexity of its historical context. Scholars have noted the concessions Lü Kun made to broaden the appeal of his work. Apparently Lü Kun's work was well received; it was widely circulated and went through many editions even during his lifetime. His *Illustrated Female Exemplars* alone went through several editions while he still lived and presumably many more in the eighteenth century.[64] The work contains his pithy comments, which readers find easy to remember, and also contains full-page woodblock illustrations for each case so that they would provide "instant gratification." In the historical contexts of the growing interest in antiquarianism, connoisseurship,[65] and rise in literacy—a context of edification-cum-entertainment—the virtue of female chastity was permanently transformed.

Indeed, illustrated books on female exemplars were well received because of their attractive value. For example, figure 4.2, from the *Illustrated Biographies of Fierce Women* (*Huitu lienü zhuan* 繪圖烈女傳), shows a young woman reading the *Biographies of Exemplary Women*.

This illustration of the young widow is essentially an image of self-promotion. The book she is reading is the *Biographies of Exemplary Women*, or *Lienü zhuan* and her own case is included in the expanded version of the same work.[66] If we examine this illustration, we find that it does not depict any specific virtue. Rather, the effect is to graphically illustrate the hoped-for popularity of the *Biographies of Exemplary Women*.

This illustration also shows that the text was used as a model both of and for exemplary behavior. It is one of the most explicit examples of hagiographers claiming the prescriptive/descriptive function of their own hagiographies. The female-exemplar genre prescribes how exemplary women should live. By depicting one of the text's protagonists reading her own tale in the inner quarter, this

FIGURE 4.2 An illustration of a woman reading the *Biography of Exemplary Women*, from *Huitu lienü zhuan* 繪圖烈女傳, *juan* 11, 1068–1069. Reprinted with the permission of the publisher. © Taipei: Zhengzhong shuju, 1971.

illustration is authorizing the text in a most explicit way. Who better to legitimize the text's contents than a woman who actually lived one of the lives therein?

Moreover, figure 4.2 reveals the wide audience the text reached. There were several domains of reading publics in the late Ming, when China had a population of more than 120 million. These groups, which included imperial examinees, general urban readers, and women, were not entirely mutually exclusive but overlapped in the books they read, especially those pertaining to practical issues and entertainment. Vernacular literature, plays, short stories, ritual manuals, and female-exemplar works made general reading for everyone. Readers did not necessarily create hard delineations among the types of books they read. This "culture of the reading public," as one scholar has pointed out, blurred traditional boundaries between literatus and merchant, male and female, fiction and reality, and morality and perversion.[67]

The physical appeal of many late-Ming expanded and illustrated editions of this genre of literature attracted a wide readership because they included full-page illustrations (sometimes in two-page spreads, as in the *Illustrated Biographies of Fierce Women* in figure 4.2) and ornate renderings of a dramatic moment in each narrative.[68] From the vantage point of both connoisseurship and profit-seeking publishers, editions of this kind allowed illustrations to be selected on the basis of their beauty or expediency regardless of how they fit the narrative to which they were attached.[69] We should remember that these stories became popular during the full bloom of the sixteenth- and seventeenth-century technology of woodcut printing.[70] In a market overrun by illustrated books, a seventeenth-century Hangzhou publisher explicitly stated that, in those days, books without pictures "simply did not sell."[71]

Indeed, the function of illustrations may have been very different from the didactic aims of the narratives. The illustration of Gao Xing, for example, not only depicts her dispositions and emotions as a dramatic icon of "virtue" but also includes considerable use of ornamental details on trees, clothing, furniture, walls, and architecture. Just as Hollywood films embellish true stories for popular consumption, the beautifully illustrated case of Gao Xing was aestheticized, which could be seen as being incongruent with the narrative's sterile and conservative viewpoint on chaste widows. Placed next to the narrative, the illustration encourages readers to envision Gao Xing's beauty and virtue.

The vivid imagery that the illustrations convey must have enhanced the reader's pleasure.[72] Sometimes Lü Kun's own comments provide many images designed to stimulate the reader's imagination. For example, with regard to Gao Xing, he states that her determination was like a "golden rock" (*jinshi* 金石) and that it caused "shivers like ice and frost" (*lin ruo bingshuang* 凜若冰霜).[73] Elsewhere, in his comments on a sixteen-year-old widow who cut off her left ear and placed it in her deceased husband's coffin, Lü Kun states:

> The woman née Fang was only sixteen; yet she raised her only son, served her mother-in-law, and remained chaste for the rest of her life. Isn't this difficult! She cut off an ear and cast it into the coffin [to demonstrate her determination]. On the one hand, this single [gesture] became a pledge for their eternal separation; on the other hand, it was a strategy to end the possibility of forced remarriage. This chaste widow's heart is like a golden rock, or similar to a whetstone [able to sharpen any knife].[74]

In order to appeal to his audience, Lü Kun's comments had to be concise and stimulating. In fact, he had to evoke the very passion he feared. If we consider the scope of his readership, we can appreciate the need to make all of his works as entertaining as possible.

In this larger context, the female-exemplar genre, with its themes of female heroism and pathos, was well suited to display both the moral *and* the entertaining sensibilities of its chroniclers. Writers hoped not only to instruct their readers but also to make their own name in the world of literature by joining the ranks of other writers who were producing similar accounts. It is the need to produce moving works of literature with evocative illustrations, as well as the ever-widening readership, that makes the dramatic stories of chastity a form of entertainment.

Chastity Suicides and Vengeful Revenants

Another way to read female chastity suicide is to imagine what it was like from the perspective of the performers themselves. Their control of circumstances and the significance of their suicides must have given them a degree of power and autonomy to transcend their prescribed roles as mere wives. Modern scholars may attribute the cause of chastity suicides to frustrated literati, arguing that women were oppressed and persuaded to perform these acts by imperial rewards and praise from the literati. They may also claim that those "vulnerable" women committed suicide because they believed that "those who committed suicide for reasons of filial piety and marital fidelity were exempted from the torment in hell."[75] These interpretations present women as passive victims of oppressive external power and false belief. Yet, the reality of their actions must have been more complex than we can even begin to imagine. The supposedly oppressive power that the state and the literati exerted on chaste women pales in comparison to the powerful acts that exerted their agency. Power is never a simple condition external to actors, nor can it be exclusively identified with the actor as subject. If chastity suicides are to be understood as a powerful statement of those women's agency, then the mutual dependence of the performer, her action, and those who wrote about them is precisely the site where power is created.[76] As we read below, evidence suggests that when these women were forced to commit suicide either through their own choice or by their assailant, their suicides were considered to be an occasion for them to return as a ghost to exact their revenge. Such an interpretation can be better appreciated in the religious milieu of the sixteenth and seventeenth centuries.

Modern scholars have already marked out the state mechanism for rewarding and eulogizing deceased widows. The state's criteria for officially rewarding a virtuous widow for committing suicide hinged on the age of the particular widow and the circumstances of her actions. Mark Elvin details the ritual procedures for bestowing such an honor.[77] If a widow committed suicide as a result of forced remarriage or rape, she would be honored. However, if she killed herself for other reasons, then her act was considered "treating life lightly." The supposed aim of honoring dead widows was to make them "martyrs." Their martyrdom may be read as an ideological tool that promoted "respect and encouragement for [the] moral norm."[78]

Instating deceased widows as martyrs also subtly transforms their gender, which involves two interrelated cultural ideals. The first is the notion of *wen* 文, which included cultured behavior and a mastery of literary skills. The second is the idea of *wu* 武, which included martial prowess, strength, and violence.[79] Both of these two opposites, represented respectively by the scholar-official and the military-official or warrior, constituted masculine identity.[80] Deceased widows the cultural ideal of *wu*. For example, when women demonstrated martial prowess, they were described as "manly" (*zhangfu* 丈夫).[81] If a daughter fulfilled a son's filial responsibilities and took revenge on those who had killed her father, she would be described as "manly," fierce, and worthy of praise because she acted from a higher order of virtue.[82] In other words, gender was based more on performance than on biological anatomy. Similarly, it was common for men to engage in homosexual behavior[83] and for eunuchs to have wives and adopt children[84] without having their manliness questioned so long as their public performance did not threaten the patriarchal Confucian family structure. It is the public performance that determines masculinity or femininity, not sex.[85] Sex-linked symbols appear to be secondary to more fundamental principles of moral action.[86]

Yet, a close reading of the language used by the state and the literati in their promotion of deceased women as "martyrs" who acted as "men" reveals another layer of discourse; evidently, more than just promoting social order was at stake; cosmic order was as well. Imperial rewards, martyrdom, and literati eulogies were meant to allay the potential threat posed by these women's unnatural deaths. Violent suicides and homicides of chaste women were feared. In mainstream literature, the wrongly killed, such as the chastely martyred women, were portrayed as vengeful revenants with the ability to roam the world of the living. Their ambiguous identities shifted according to different narratives about them—from saints to martyrs to ghosts and even gods. These narratives were unequivocally integrated into society through centuries of theatrical dramas and legends (such as that of Mulian and Miaoshan, which I discuss below) that may have served as models for chaste widows who resorted to suicide.

Modern scholars in different fields have studied the phenomenon of ghosts in Chinese culture,[87] but the phenomenon of chaste widows who committed suicide and returned as vengeful ghosts has yet been studied. Scholars who are interested in Chinese ritual have generally emphasized imperial or court rituals, or else they have focused on the rituals of local cults while exploring the involvement of local officials only peripherally. Scholars of social or literary history typically do not pay attention to religious beliefs and practices.[88] Yet, supernatural elements are ubiquitous in state-sponsored texts and writings of the educated elite that deal with chastity suicides or homicide.

Consider the following cases The first one (figure 4.3) is a widely circulated Song story included in the seventeenth-century *Illustrated Biographies of Fierce Women*:

> In the fourth year of Jianyan (1130), a rebel soldier Yang Jiu 楊就 invaded the south of Jianzhou.... He passed by the village of Xiaochang and singled out the wife of a villager. He wanted to [rape and] humiliate her. But she resolved to die before she would be humiliated. He raped and killed her, then abandoned her corpse (*shi* 屍) on the side of the road. The bandit [rebel soldier] left. People collected and buried the corpse where it lay. Yet, the imprint (*ji* 跡) of her corpse where

FIGURE 4.3 An illustration of the non-disappearing silhouette of a woman's corpse, from *Huitu lienü zhuan, juan* 11, 1042–43. Reprinted with the permission of the publisher. © Taipei: Zhengzhong shuju, 1971.

> she lay never disappeared. Whenever it would rain her silhouette [on that spot] would be dry; whenever the weather was clear, the silhouette would be wet; if scraped away, the silhouette would reappear; if covered with dirt from elsewhere, the silhouette would appear more prominent. Noblemen praised her fierce chastity (*zhenlie* 貞烈) and lamented her misfortune. The *Analects* says, "[N]ot surrendering the will; not humiliating the body (*buxiang qizhi buru qishen* 不降其志、不辱其身)."[89] This would be an example of this saying.[90]

Like many widows who resisted rape or remarriage, this young woman died a violent death. She was violated and murdered, and her corpse was then abandoned and hence polluted. Left on the roadside to wither away after the rebel soldier had raped and killed her, she was robbed of the chance of receiving offerings. According to Ming law, if raped, a female victim could not be canonized as a chaste martyr even if she had resisted.[91] This illustration openly acknowledges that the wrongful death of a chaste woman can have supernatural effects on the visible world. We cannot ascertain exactly how people understood this work, but considering its wide circulation and its readership, as well as similar stories that circulated among the reading public, the belief must have been quite pervasive. For example, another story tells of a widow née Chen, who hung herself under a trellis in a vegetable garden during a thunderstorm; her corpse did not get wet.[92] Also, another widow née Huang, hung herself on a hot summer day, yet even a day later she still looked alive, and fragrance permeated the room where she had committed suicide.[93] The non-disappearing presence of these women suggests that their inexhaustible life force continued to be a palpable manifestation in the visible world of the living. These tangible signs are precisely the kind of cultural markers that signal the presence of unjustly killed spirits (*yuanhun* 冤魂) or vengeful ghosts (*ligui* 厲鬼) in popular culture. I return to this point below.

The second anecdote, which is also from the late imperial period, illustrates the perceived power attributed to the vengeful ghost of dead widows. The anecdote appears in the writing of an early Ming literatus named Yang Weizhen 楊維禎 (1296–1370).[94] He recounts that at one time he wrote a poem criticizing the widow née Wang 王, who committed suicide after resisting rape following the death of her husband. Yang Weizhen's disparagement caused the ghost of the dead widow to appear in his dream, explaining that the reason he had no son was that his poem had censured her act. When he awoke, he quickly wrote and published another poem extolling her virtue as a chaste widow. Shortly thereafter he was rewarded when his wife bore him a son.[95]

In the third Ming case, a courtesan was wrongly sentenced to death because she was captured along with several bandits. The magistrate never bothered to examine her case in detail even though he knew that she might have been innocent. A month after her execution, the ghost of the blameless courtesan came to the magistrate in a dream. She told him that he had killed her unjustly and that her outrage could not be assuaged. She then suddenly swooped into his mouth. The magistrate awoke and then collapsed as if he had been struck by epilepsy. When he came to, his head was completely twisted around backward. He died four days later. His family also received harsh karmic retribution: The household grew increasingly poor; his son died young; and his grandson became a vagabond.[96] A similar theme of karmic retribution appears in one of Feng Menglong's short stories, in which the beautiful courtesan Du Shiniang 杜十娘 drowns herself in a river after finding out that her lover has sold her to a merchant. After her death, her lover becomes insane, and the merchant dies a month after her death.[97]

The fourth case involves a sixteenth-century essay about a chaste woman née He, who drowned herself to avoid being raped as she was fleeing a battle. The dead woman appeared to the head of the village in a dream and demanded that he build a ghost altar (*litan* 厲壇) and make offerings to her at the site of her death. Note that the character "*li*" in *litan*, or ghost altar, is the same character used to describe a "vengeful ghost" (*ligui* 厲鬼). An altar was subsequently established for her, and sacrificial offerings were regularly made. Yet the essay recast her in a poem as a "martyr of virtue" instead of a vengeful ghost.[98] Later an assistant commissioner in the province had the poem engraved on a stele at her shrine, thus ensuring her changed status. This is direct evidence that the local government and the literati worked together to transform the status of a deceased woman from a vengeful ghost to a martyr exemplar. It is noteworthy that local vengeful-ghost altars held an important place in people's lives. For example, a chastity shrine in Jiangsu province was quite famous for its efficacy in answering all kinds of prayers.[99]

Other cases besides these four also demonstrate the powerful and continuing presence of deceased widows in the lives of the living. They were documented in the writings of local elites as local gazettes or as records of things witnessed and heard—not fictional stories. Their verity is not what I wish to highlight. Instead, these cases demonstrate the larger cultural acceptance of the existence of life after death and the perception that deceased chaste widows as revenants wielded extraordinary power over the living.

The female ghost is a common literary trope in novels. Interestingly, one seldom comes across stories of male ghosts. As Judith Zeitlin notes, this may be a part of "the widespread fascination with the death of beautiful, talented women in the sentimental culture of the period."[100] The man is the normal human protagonist, and the woman is almost always depicted as the beautiful, talented, sensual, and sometimes virtuous representative of another (nonhuman) realm. It is no accident that, in anthologies such as Feng Menglong's *History of Emotions*, not one of the thirty-eight stories listed under the heading "ghosts of love" (*qinggui* 情鬼) concerns a male ghost.[101]

Widows who committed suicide were complicated because this form of death was perceived as a disruption of life as it was intended to be lived. The official rhetoric of the state as witnessed in edicts and local gazetteers asserts that the cosmos was made whole and balanced through values such as filial piety, loyalty, and female chastity. These values were understood as forces that supposedly unified people with heaven. When people aligned themselves with these virtues, they could affect the gods and stimulate a favorable response from heaven. Conversely, when the relationship between people and heaven was disrupted, danger could ensue. In this interdependent world of the living and the dead, deceased widows who committed suicide or were killed during rape were particularly dangerous.

The belief that those who died wrongly, such as in premature deaths, homicides, suicides, and drowning, can continue to haunt the living as vengeful ghosts was widely accepted. Deceased widows could be considered vengeful ghosts or *ligui* because they harassed the living (*zuosui* 作祟); they believe that the living have either forgotten about or have harmed them. Restless in the world of the dead, they come back to haunt the living until they are offered sacrifices. Traces of their malevolent power over the living are evident in the ritual sacrifices described in the literature on widow chastity. The *Illustrated Biographies of Fierce Women* explicitly states that libations (*sijiu* 賜酒) and sacrifices (*ji* 祭) must be offered to deceased widows[102] at the numerous altars (*tan* 壇) and shrines (*lienümiao* 烈女廟)[103] established by the state.

The state's effort may be interpreted as a political strategy to transform potential social disruptions into favorable situations. However, its attempts to shower titles and honors on deceased widows can also be understood as efforts to appease their spirits and avoid potential harm to the living. The flipside of appeasement is, of course, to turn them into objects of reverence. We have evidence of how the state tried to eliminate the worship of vengeful ghosts by converting existing altars dedicated to them into official altars of the state cult (*sidian* 祀典; lit., register of sacrifice), which simply reinforces the notion that the wrongfully dead are dangerous to the living and need to be appeased.[104] These "converted altars" began appearing in the early years of the Ming dynasty, when Emperor Taizu decreed that one such altar be established in every community of one hundred households and that sacrifices be offered twice a year.[105]

The official cult was established to ritually place vengeful ghosts under the jurisdiction of the city gods (Chenghuang 城隍). Interestingly, in 1371 the city gods became formally recognized as officials in charge of the dark world (*mingguan* 冥官). In theory, every city-god temple was intended to house an altar for vengeful ghosts.[106] It appears that the state's effort to convert these altars had little effect on the popular worship of these spirits. The worship practice persisted well into at least the nineteenth century because the state made repeated efforts to issue and reissue edicts on this matter. In 1723 Emperor Yongzheng had to reissue a decree that altars dedicated to martyrs of loyalty, filial piety, and chastity must be established in every province.[107] Again in 1851 Emperor Xianfeng reissued a decree that altars for vengeful ghosts should be limited to the northern suburb of each administrative center.

In an effort to contain and transform the worship of vengeful ghosts, the following imperial decree makes it clear that the ritual imperative of honoring dead widows was an important way to coerce heaven to maintain cosmic order so as to promote the state's agendas:

> Since last year's winter solstice there has been little moisture from the melting snow. The weather has been very dry and parched. Since the beginning of spring, cold and hot have come in unseasonable fashion.... We are aware that the people depend on Us and have constantly examined Our conscience, being deeply fearful that Our institutions may not yet be appropriate, and that We are not able to induce a harmonious response from heaven above.... Hitherto widows who committed suicide when their husbands died have not been permitted to have an award, in the absence of such circumstances as a forced remarriage obligating them to safeguard their fidelity with a swift death.... If we honor them, this will... sharpen respect for moral norms.[108]

It appears that the propitiation of deceased widows had a meteoric affect.[109] Making offerings at altars dedicated to these women uplifted the moral climate of the people, who believed that, in turn, heaven would bestow its blessings. The connection between hoped-for harmony and the perceived crisis of natural calamity hinged on a sympathetic, moral universe. In honoring deceased widows, the emperor's rhetoric and accentuation of the people's dependency on the state had three main objectives. The first was pedagogical. The widows' supreme sacrifice constituted a guide for the populace and implied an imperative to remember them with gratitude. It will "sharpen respect for moral norms," the edict claimed. The second purpose of this decree was directly linked to natural phenomena, in this case unstable weather. Moral actions, people believed, had an effect on the weather. There is a long history of rainmaking practices followed by shamans, emperors, officials, and Buddhist monks. Chapter 5 is devoted to this topic. Finally, the decree had a third purpose. The emperor commemorated deceased widows in shrines through offerings to appease their vindictive nature. The logic is simple: Since these women were moral, they must be venerated. Our laxity in doing so has resulted in our punishment through drought. Appease them and heaven will look with favor upon the populace.

Honoring dead widows could be seen as stemming from fear of the volatile nature of the deceased widows' malevolent spirits. Actually the belief that the vengeful ghost of a person unjustly killed can harm the living is quite old in Chinese culture.[110] Such a view was held by people at all levels of the social hierarchy. In the late imperial times one conservative literatus commented that a deceased widow can transpire as either a ghost or a deity (*tongyu guishen* 通與鬼神).[111] Also, Yuan Mei 袁枚 (1716–1779), a well-known novelist, poet, and social commentator, stated that "The things that are close to immortals and deities are efficacious; so are those who are close to chastity and martyrdom."[112]

In this context, chastity suicides and the ritual of veneration or worship at chastity shrines meant something very different from the mere promotion of moral values. As seen earlier in the different cases cited, a widow's ghost had the power to exact revenge on the men who had wronged her. Shrines dedicated to such women had just as much to do with appeasing their dangerous spirits as with honoring their virtue.[113] As Emily Martin Ahern reminds us, worship and fear are inseparable parts of the Chinese religious experience.[114] It is important to recognize that notions of karma, rebirth, and a world populated with (especially) female ghosts were intricately woven into the very fabric of Chinese culture regardless of differences in people's social status.[115] In chapter 1, I discussed the distinctively new, performance-based interpretations of karma and merit in the morality books and the ledgers of merit and demerit produced during the sixteenth and seventeenth centuries. Here I will only theorize about a possible model of emulation for those chaste women who took their own lives.

The Chinese popular belief in ghosts can be seen as an amalgamation of the ancient soul theory, the concerns of ancestral worship, and popular

Buddhist understandings of reincarnation through the cycle of karmic retribution. Even conservative Confucians during this time incorporated Buddhist notions of karma.[116] In this amalgamation, only certain Buddhist components were drawn into indigenous Chinese beliefs of the afterlife.[117] These beliefs, already widespread by medieval times, were disseminated by popular operas[118] and the performative uses of "transformation texts."[119]

Perhaps no story served as a model for chastely martyred women more than the popular legend of Miaoshan as discussed in the previous chapter. Comparing this legend to the cases of chaste widows, the focus on acts of violence clarifies not only the ambivalent origin of many Chinese gods and goddesses but also the productiveness of suicide. Just as in the literature on Miaoshan, who wished to avoid the travails of wifehood and defied her father's wish for her to marry, some late imperial women also sought to preserve their autonomy through suicide. Moreover, just as Miaoshan cut off parts of her body to cure her father, chaste widows sliced off their noses, ears, or other body parts to demonstrate their resolve. Even though Miaoshan's performance stems from filial piety, chaste women may have emulated her as their role model for marriage refusal.[120]

The literature on Miaoshan involves the deliverance of the dead, those who do not have descendants to care for them in the rites of ancestral worship and details the way to transcendence through self-inflicted violence. Miaoshan refuses to marry, dies prematurely, and becomes a ghost who wanders through the world of the dead. Only when she performs an act of catholic deliverance of the unfortunate beings who wander in hell is she transformed into the Bodhisattva Guanyin. As Guanyin, she protects and saves the anomalous dead, particularly those who do not have descendants to care for them in the rites of ancestral worship. Her redemption and supernatural ability necessitate her death, which became the key to her deification. This motif is inextricably linked to young women martyrs in late imperial China.

"Many gods," argue Shahar and Weller, "share the kind of premature and violent deaths, often by suicide, that typify malevolent ghosts" and "draw upon the power of the margins, of death, and of the outside."[121] In our case, the female ghosts of the rape victims drew on the posthumous superhuman power of the negative and the disenfranchised. Even though these chaste women were unable to defend themselves against their assailers and believed that the only way to retain their honor and dignity was through death, it was by dying that they came back as vengeful ghosts to punish the living.[122] Evidence shows that these wronged women were well aware of their potential power as ghosts.[123]

Paola Zamperini places the phenomenon of female suicide within the long Chinese tradition of venerating the good or honorable dead. She argues that, for fictional heroines who were wronged or alienated by their inability to fulfill their desires in life, suicide was "a revitalizing self-assertion" that signified "a moment of control and power... an act of self-construction."[124] Through natural, violent deaths such as suicide, chaste women could acquire the potent power of either vengeful ghosts or benevolent goddesses[125] to redeem their unjust circumstances.

≅

My focus on the various discursive constructions of female chastity—highlighting the promiscuous representation of chaste widow mutilations and the vengeful nature of their ghosts—allows us to appreciate another richly contingent and contested aspect of self-inflicted violence. Female chastity practices and representations of them detail the significance of these women's lives, which were fully embedded in the larger culture and discourses of the sixteenth and seventeenth centuries. In a culture fascinated by demonstrating genuine passion in extreme forms, their chastity mutilations and suicides served not only as antidotes to an ailing society for the state and conservative literati but also as topics of discussion, illustration, and imagination for the general populace. At the same time, from the perspectives of the women themselves, their chastity suicide may have been a way for them to assert their agency by returning as spirits to take revenge on those who had wronged them. Those who documented the efficacious power of the deceased widows and the vengeful altars dedicated to them blurred the boundaries between the worlds of the living and the dead.

5

Exposing and Burning the Body for Rain

> Recently, people pray for rain but do not know the [method of] utilizing *yin* to beseech *yin*, nor do they engage in the seven affairs. They only ask Buddhist monks and Daoist clerics to write talismans, perform sacrifice, and hold incense to burn candles and talismans. They do not know that the ancients, in order to relieve drought, had to employ female shamans.
>
> —TANG SHUNZHI 唐顺之 (1507–1560)

RAINMAKING RITUALS WERE many and widespread during the sixteenth and seventeenth centuries in China. However, these phenomena are difficult to study because their historical complexity, variations within different ritual traditions, and diversity of performers with a range of social backgrounds have placed them at the margins of most scholarly discussions.[1] What scholars have revealed is that rainmaking rituals lack any coherent ideological content; therefore, it is almost impossible for scholars of Chinese history and religions to place rainmaking within a single conceptual framework.[2] Current explanations of rainmaking practices still tend to privilege what Sinologists understand as the "official ideology" of China—namely, Confucianism—and focus on state rainmaking rituals. Yet, performers from different walks of life engaged in this practice, including emperors, local officials, Buddhist monks, Daoist clerics, and community shamans. Their practices may provide different models of understanding rainmaking rituals, each replete with its own set of ritual technologies and logic. Despite the diversity of performers, what underlies the various rainmaking practices is a performance-centered understanding of a sympathetic universe. There is an incontestable thaumaturgical dimension in all of the performers of rainmaking, especially the practices of ritual exposure and self-immolation.

As suggested by the epigraph at the beginning of this chapter, many methods existed as early as the seventeenth century. They range from reciting spells, to burning talismans, to praying at mountain altars, to burying frogs and lizards, to placating dragon deities. The most extreme (and perhaps efficacious) rituals were exposing one's naked body to the blazing sun and self-immolation. In addition, the available sources provide no fixed term for rainmaking rituals. Some of the expressions used were "praying for rain" (*qiyu* 祈雨), "beseeching rain" (*qiuyu* 求雨), "petitioning for rain" (*qingyu* 請雨), and "bringing rain" (*xingyu* 行雨 or *zhiyu* 致雨). These expressions and others appear in nearly every genre of Chinese literature in later China, such as official histories, local gazetteers, administrative handbooks, novels, and collectanea, as well as in every religious textual tradition such as Daoist ritual manuals and Buddhist scriptures.

These texts embody the various agendas that stem from the theological and ideological persuasions of the redactors who recorded and described rainmaking rituals. Official documents, for example, often cast rainmakers into two dichotomous camps of performers: those belonging to the category of the *yin* principle and those who were characterized as being overbearingly *yang*. In the early part of the Ming dynasty, Emperor Taizu penned a treatise called *On the Three Teachings*, in which he states that the *ru* 儒 is the way of *yang* or material virtue and that Daoism and Buddhism are *yin*, or hidden virtue, and are secret aids of the sage-king way.[3] The aim of the treatise, aside from favoring the *ru* ideology, was to unifying dissimilar religious institutions under his imperial rule. What is interesting is his characterization of Buddhist and Daoist clerics as epitomes of the *yin* principle and of those trained in the Confucian classics as *yang*. Even though Taizu was himself once a Buddhist monk before he became emperor, his caricature is telling of the perceived cosmic roles assigned to different performers.

In his scheme, emperors and officials are representatives of ancient "sage kings," epitomes of the *yang* principle. Official records, that is, the histories produced by the imperial court and the official elite, corroborate this view with accounts of purportedly "successful" rainmaking events, which showed the power of the emperors' and officials' sincerity (*cheng* 誠) to move heaven (*gentian* 感天). Even failed rainmaking attempts are presented as failures to demonstrate the utmost sincerity. The sage-king model is discussed later. Suffice it to say that this model involves emulating ancient (idealized) rulers and their selfless care for the people, which could mean harsh self-introspection, penance, or any degree of self-sacrifice. Modern scholars have followed this sort of rhetoric and historicized various performers' success, which rested on sincerity and virtue (*de* 德). They see this model as different from the logic of efficacy (*ling* 靈) evoked in popular rites.[4] They also show how sometimes these official records are outright repressive of popular rainmaking rites performed by shamans, Buddhists, and Daoists.[5]

My argument is that official and popular rainmaking rituals were not so dissimilar, especially when we look beyond the normative markers and rhetorical tropes, and that scholarly categories often turn out to replicate emic discourses that veil deeper dimensions of the practice. For example, many performers of popular ritual exposure and self-immolation—local village healers, Buddhists, and Daoists—presented themselves as altruistic heroes who were acting out of sincerity and great compassion in their desire to alleviate the people's sufferings, just like emperors and officials who engaged in the rituals. In other words, they elicited the model of the so-called benevolent sage king. Even the writings of the educated elite offer different opinions of the appropriate forms of rainmaking. Sixteenth- and seventeenth-century observers criticized official rainmaking performers as being excessively *yang*; thus, they were unable to draw the *yin* rain. More important, emperors and their surrogates, the officials, in their ritual penance and appropriation of occult methods of rainmaking, may be understood as the ultimate religious specialists. Their thaumaturgical practices drew on the strategies of female shamans and ancient shaman kings. Thus, it is extremely difficult to draw clear boundaries between different emic categories of rainmaking.

Drought is a grave matter that profoundly affects communities, so rainmaking was the jurisdiction of local officials. It may seem paradoxical that thaumaturgical practices would be called upon to support state agendas and local governance, but this was precisely what happened. This thaumaturgical dimension of rainmaking practices—particularly the kind that involves ritual exposure and self-immolation—exposes certain biased assumptions that seem to becloud our perceptions of religiosity in China. It is not so much that officials were "inclusive" in their attempts to bring rain by appropriating occult technologies and soliciting the assistance of different religious professionals. Rather, I argue that the emperors, officials, and other rainmaking performers were themselves thaumaturgists.

No comprehensive taxonomy of rainmaking rituals is provided here. Instead I focus on two specific practices of ritual exposure and self-immolation. I show that whether the particular rainmaking ritual was performed out of sincerity, penance, or a compassionate desire to save others, all of the performers tapped into an undeniable thaumaturgical power that affected the larger economy of moral meteorology. Thaumaturgy is my heuristic category for describing the processes of ritual efficacy, sympathetic resonance, and materially constituted magic. Thaumaturgists include the wonder worker, the occult and the ritual specialist, someone whose power is legitimated materially and cosmologically, someone who is able to mediate both the visible and the invisible worlds. In scholarly literature, the thaumaturgist is usually presented as someone on the margins of the society. However, as I show in this chapter, these individuals are most often in the center of the mainstream culture. Emperors, Buddhist and Daoist clerics, and literati-officials also acted like thaumaturgists. In using this term, I am challenging notions that the thaumaturgist (and similar concepts such as shaman, magician, and sorcerers), as an analytical category, is predominantly made out to be the antithesis of the rational and state ideology of Confucianism.[6]

This thaumaturgical dimension not only runs through multiple rainmaking discourses, in effect blurring their presumed boundaries, but also reveals the centrality of the human body and its potential power to change the natural world. The body may be variously described in different premodern sources as either *yin* or *yang*, malevolent or virtuous, upright or deformed, but its power as a conduit for social and cosmic transformation is never denied. This chapter also argues for the centrality of thaumaturgy to the overall spiritual and cosmological ideas of premodern Chinese people in general. In this chapter I take the liberty of citing relevant early and medieval texts and rituals to contextualize the two late imperial practices of ritual exposure and self-immolation to bring the rain. I show the continuity of various cultural assumptions and practices and provide a historically nuanced and embodied understanding of ritual efficacy.

The Thaumaturgist and Ritual Exposure

Prolonged exposure to the sun as a ritual practice has complex roots in ancient China. Emperors and officials who performed it represented themselves as heirs to the ancient sage kings, who sacrificed their lives for the benefit of the common people. They drew on the powerful discourse of the benevolent ruler, who was supposedly in perfect alignment with heaven. In this conception, prosperity and peace were signs of heaven's approval of the ruler's moral power; natural disasters, on the other hand, were signs of heaven's disapproval. Rulers had to undergo physical deprivation and suffering in times of natural disasters, such as drought, to atone for the wrongs of the people and to engender heaven's sympathy so the universe could again be brought back into alignment. The success of their contrition and penance rested on their supposed sincerity, but beneath the rhetoric of sincerity lurked a darker and contentious discourse of sage kings and shamans.

The sage-king paradigm centers around the myth of two sage kings and their voluntary austerity to benefit the people: the ruler of Xia 夏 dynasty (ca. 2100–1600 B.C.E.), Yü the Great (Dayu 大禹), and the founder of the Shang dynasty (ca. 1600–1046 B.C.E.), King Tang 商湯王. Scholars typically focus on their heroic, self-inflicted violent practices of penance, rebuke, and sacrifice for the benefit of the people. Instead of detailing their supposed compassion, I focus on the thaumaturgical discourses of their narrative because they figure prominently in late imperial rainmaking practices.

It is said that, to help his community, Yü the Great labored for ten years without rest to control flooding. During this time he endured every possible ailment, including one that crippled him so badly that he could no longer lift one leg past the other to walk.[7] The legend of Yü's lameness survives into late imperial times in the form of shamanic expiatory dances called the "steps of Yü" (Yü *bu* 禹步).[8]

Similarly, King Tang was supposedly the ideal model ruler who was guided by his moral propriety and concern for the common people:

> In the era of Tang there was a severe drought for seven years, and divination was made for humans to be sacrificed to heaven. Tang said, "I will make a divination myself, and I will offer myself as a sacrifice on behalf of my people. For is this not what I ought to do?" Then he ordered an official to prepare a pile of kindling and logs. He cut off his hair and fingernails, purified himself with water, and laid himself on the woodpile in order to be burnt (*zifen* 自焚) as a sacrifice to heaven. Just as the fire was taking hold, a great downpour of rain fell.[9]

Note in this passage the discourse of divination, suffering, self-sacrifice, and self-immolation. These were tropes that sixteenth- and seventeenth-century performers adopted for their own rainmaking acts. Many performers, including Ming emperors, officials, and religious clerics, drew on the penitential motif of the sage kings.

Scholars have suggested that these mythic sage kings may have been connected to female shamans. Following the argument of the modern scholar Chen Mengjia, Edward Schafer hypothesizes that the word for "king" (*wang* 王), particularly a king who suffers from lameness, is associated with the term for a "crippled" female shaman, or *wang* 尪. A crippled female shaman also had semantic connections to "madness" (*kuang* 狂) and "deception" (*kuang* 誑).[10] This interpretation is also suggested by Marcel Granet, who observed that both the mythical sage kings Yü the Great and King Tang are depicted as having physical weaknesses. Both sacrificed themselves for the benefit of their people.[11] Yet, these features were also attributes of shamans.

China scholars, past and present, do not agree on the religious roles of the shaman and the spirit mediums and their sometimes overlapping and sometimes distinct relationships to one another.[12] The question of whether shamans in ancient times were male or female adds another layer of complexity to the debate. The term *wu* 巫 generally denoted a woman,[13] as opposed to *xi* 覡, which designated a man.[14] This distinction is important in view of later debates about whether a man or a woman is more efficacious in sacrificial rainmaking. I render the word *wu* as "female shaman" unless it is clear from the context of the sources that it is referring to a man.

King Tang's act of self-immolation is more than a mere act of benevolence. His deed is the same as that of the female shaman. Modern scholars such as Judith Butler have suggested that the body is socially constructed; even the "materiality" of the body is socially constructed through the ritualized, repetitive performance of social norms.[15] If the body is constructed through one's performance and socialization, such as public perceptions and expectations, does this not make King Tang a shaman? The *Commentary to the Spring and Autumn Annals* states that during a drought in 639 B.C.E., the Duke of Lu 魯 wanted to perform the ritual of "burning the female shaman and the crippled" (*fen wuwang* 焚巫尪) in order to produce rain.[16] Such a rainmaking practice was also connected to the ancient rainmaking ritual called *chi* 赤, meaning "stripped naked," which was carved on the Shang oracle bones. It also appears to be connected to the rituals of "exposing the [naked] female shaman" in the sun (*puwu* 曝巫) or "burning the female shaman" (*fenwu* 焚巫) mentioned in the *Rituals of Zhou*[17] and the ritual of "exposing the crippled" (*puwang* 曝尪) described in the *Classic of Rites*.[18] The female shaman was intimately connected to rainmaking.

In these contexts King Tang's act of self-immolation—doing "what he ought to do"—is not so different from that of the female shaman. Perhaps he perceived his own act of ritual self-sacrifice as being related to the ritual exposure of the crippled female shaman. He may have been a sage king to later generations of Confucians, but his acts exemplify the paradigmatic crippled individuals in his own time. This hypothesis is corroborated by the fact that in ancient China the shaman assumed the relatively high social status of a diviner, a healer, and a minister-advisor to rulers and kings. In other words, their status derives from their thaumaturgical powers. The female shamans' exalted position in the ever-shifting cyclical cosmos comes from their special physical endowments—their deformity and *yin* body marked their sanctity. For example, in order to attract the *yin* principle of rain and to invoke heaven's sympathy, rulers would subject the nude (*lou* 裸) body of the female shaman to the pain of prolonged ritual exposure (*tan* 袒 and *lu* 露) in the blazing sun. It is said that, before this was done, her nails and hair were cut. King Tang's own act of cutting off his hair and fingernails before immolating himself is not so different from what rulers imposed on female shamans. There is a high degree of shared identity in their power to mediate between unseen forces of nature and humanity.[19]

In fact, the inheritors of the sage- or shaman-king tradition, the *ru* followers—what scholars usually refer to as the "Confucian" tradition—is intimately bound up with practices that were the provenance of shamans and sorcerers.[20] According to *Explaining Simple and Analyzing Compound Characters*, the earliest comprehensive dictionary in China, *ru* 儒 means to yield (*rou* 柔). It also refers to a technician or person with occult powers (*shushi* 術士). If we look up *xu* 需, part of the compound of *ru*, we get *xu* 䇓, or someone with whiskers who stands and waits for the rain (*li er dai* 立而待).[21] These semantic associations suggest that, in ancient times, *ru* signified an occult technician or a master of mantic arts who engaged in rainmaking.[22]

Turning to the Ming dynasty, we see that many of these associations with occult technologies continue in official rainmaking rituals performed by emperors and officials. Consider the account of Emperor Taizu, founder of the Ming dynasty, who supposedly practiced ritual exposure not only to set an example for subsequent officials of the Ming but also to display the extent to which he himself as the ultimate religious specialist could wield power over nature:

> During the sixth month of 1370 the drought persisted. Taizu said to the secretariat,[23] "One who rules under heaven cannot rule a single day without his people; one who provides sustenance for his people cannot do so without a single day of food. Yet, food depends on agriculture and agriculture depends on the year's [harvest]. Since midsummer there has been no rain and this has really caused the farmers to worry. Affairs dealing with [rain] prayer and sacrifice are part of the propriety [of the ruler] and cannot be ignored. I have already selected a time to go to the altar of mountains and rivers to personally offer ritual supplications. Thus, you should write to the various officials to report the [drought to the deities at] different shrines and inform the empress

> and the concubines to personally execute the rainmaking ritual, so that the farmers will be able to produce food. Make sure that the crown prince and the other kings make ritual offerings at the shrines." When the day arrived, the four drums were sounded and Taizu put on plain garments and straw sandals and traveled on foot to the mountain and river altar. [There,] a straw mat was set up and he sat exposed to the [blazing] sun, without moving for an instant. At night he lay on the ground without loosening the girdle [of his gown]. The prince made ritual offerings of vegetarian food, such as the miscellaneous sesame, barley wheat, beans, and grains. In three days, heavy rain came down. The four directions were sufficiently saturated.[24]

Different measures were taken to prepare for and assist Taizu's rain prayers. However, it was Taizu's ritual exposure that supposedly caused the meteorological change. The narrative presents Taizu as a benevolent and powerful emperor who voluntarily endured suffering for his people, an act that mimics the self-inflicted violence of King Tang and Yü the Great. His act stimulated a response from heaven in the form of rain, which legitimated the emperor's spiritual authority and sanctity.

We do not know whether Taizu actually stripped naked or simply wore plain garments for this rite. It would seem unlikely that an emperor would strip naked publicly, but we cannot rule out the possibility.[25] The words "he sat there exposed" (*luzuo* 露坐) and the statement that during the day he "exposed" (*pu* 曝) himself are the same ones used to record the exposure of female shamans in ancient China, which suggests a conscious decision on the part of the writers to draw a direct link to ancient practices. Taizu's other acts—including donning plain garments and straw sandals and walking to various shrines on foot instead of sitting in a sedan chair to offer prayers, both of which gestures lowered his status before heaven—only further his identity with the ancient shaman kings. These rhetorical markers signal penance and expiation, the pinnacle of which would have been self-sacrifice. Key to this entire ritual endeavor is Taizu's agency as the ultimate ritual specialist, an intermediary, one who communicates with the gods and heaven.

Taizu as the "son of heaven" was the gateway to heaven's sympathy and the pivot of the triad of heaven, earth, and humanity and thus was ultimately responsible for upholding the entire cosmic order. His actions were portrayed by his own imperium and by his subjects as constituting the universe within which all vied for relative status and power. His genealogy traced back to figures such as Yü the Great and King Tang. Like these mythical kings, his actions were able to harmonize the proper sequence of the weather, transform and nourish the multitude, and serve as an intermediary between heaven and the people. Such a mandate to rule was written in edicts (note Taizu's rhetoric of the unity of himself, as the son of heaven, and his people) and embodied with every performance of sacrifice.

As an intermediary, the emperor, through his spiritual and political supremacy, extended beyond the mundane world into the realms of the gods. The earlier passage indicates that Taizu dispatched edicts to his officials to report the drought to local deities of different shrines, as if these deities were also his officials. Modern scholars have argued that, in premodern China, gods and spirits existed in a parallel universe governed by a similar bureaucracy.[26] While this bureaucratic model has been challenged in recent scholarship,[27] there is ample evidence that shows that emperors often treated local deities as subjects and that local officials treated them as equals. For example, many emperors in Chinese history not only bestowed and revoked the deities' official titles but also "coerced" them by ritually exposing their statues (*pushen* 曝神) to the blazing sun during droughts.[28] The logic was that if the deity in question got a "taste" of the blazing heat, it would become sympathetic to the suffering of the people and send rain.[29]

Again, we have a clear example from Taizu, who punished a local god for not sending rain during a drought. He exhibits the marks as the ultimate religious specialist:

> When Taizu stationed his troops at Chu [i.e., modern-day Anhui province], there was a great drought, which caused him to worry. Yuan Gao said, "In the south-east, Mt. Feng, there is a dragon temple by the Bozi Lake that always responded to [rain] prayers. After prayers sometimes fish would jump or turtles would float up [on the surface], all of which are omens of rain." Taizu then fasted, bathed, and went there to pray. [After his prayer] he stood on the western bank of the lake, but after a long time nothing happened. Then he bent his bow and set up his arrow and made an oath, "The deity lives off this soil, but you have no sympathy toward my people. I order that there must be rain in three days. If there is no rain, then the temple dedicated to you shall be destroyed!" He shot three arrows in succession to the lake and returned [to his camp]. By the appointed day, rain indeed came.[30]

Such coercive measures were intended to demonstrate the emperor's superior authority over the local deities, who were made out to be local magistrates in the parallel system of spiritual bureaucracy. In this system, deities were subordinates to heaven and to its chief agent, the son of heaven.

Officials also mimicked the religious authority of emperors and threatened those deities who were responsible for rain. During a drought in Henan province in 1578, the late Ming official Tu Long stated that his prayers at the temples devoted to the city god and the dragon king had repeatedly failed to bring rain. After seeking the help of the village's female shaman, who tried to summon the rain spirit but to no avail, he decided to personally expose his naked body to the sun in the courtyard (*chiri bao zhongting* 赤日暴中庭). From dawn to dusk he exposed his body for two days. However, his effort did not prevail. At last he wrote a memorial to a particular deity, prostrated himself three times, and apologized for what he was about to do. Then he ordered the statues of the deity be removed from the temples and exposed to the afternoon sun. By evening, the clouds had formed, and in the morning rain poured down and continued for another day.[31]

How was it possible for Tu Long, a licentious magistrate, to draw on the discourse of moral virtue when he was well known in literati circles as someone who pursued sensual pleasures? His close friends included some very famous novelists and dramatists, such as Tang Xianzu (1550–1616).[32] Tang, for example, wrote Tu Long a poem that joked about his "sores of love" or syphilis (*lin* 淋). We do have to give him some credit, however, because at least he was deeply aware of his liberalist view of sex and the perils of desire in his didactic writings.[33] A few years after the success in bringing rain (albeit through coercion), Tu Long was promoted to the position of secretary in the Ministry of Rites in Beijing. However, he was impeached after only a year due to his sexual misconduct.[34] Was it because heaven disproved his licentious behavior that it did not respond to his prayers for rain? Or was his downfall perhaps a punishment from heaven for his behavior?

Even though ritual exposure and self-immolation were highly scripted, discursive performances that followed a clear set of rhetorical markers and cultural *topoi*, just going through the ritual protocols did not guarantee rain. Genuine sacrifice was needed. For example, in an earlier Han example, Zhu Liang 祝良, the magistrate of Luoyang, "exposed his body" (*baoshen* 暴身) in the tiered palace courtyard during a severe drought. He "proclaimed his sincerity" (*gaocheng* 告誠) and publicly "rebuked his own faults" (*yinzui* 引罪). Just at that moment, "purple clouds rose in billows and sweet rain (*ganlu* 甘雨) poured down."[35] Also, during the drought in Shandong and Hebei provinces in 724, which began in the spring and lasted for several months, Emperor Xuanzong 玄宗 (re. 712–756) of the Tang dynasty personally took up the ritual responsibility to bring rain. He set up an altar (*she tanxi* 設壇席) in the palace, just like King Tang did, and exposed himself to the blazing sun for three days.[36] These notions of penance, self-rebuke, and self-sacrifice harked back to the thaumaturgical practices of shamans. It is important to understand that the bodily austerities of these discursive performances were socially sanctioned and routinized. They revealed larger fields of bodily action and symbolic communication that were at once socially recognizable and intelligible to everyone, who in turn expected these performers to carry out their acts in such a way. Generations of emperors and officials (and records of their spiritual feats) have transmitted and replicated the sacrificial acts of the paradigmatic shaman kings.

Self-sacrifice and self-inflicted violence were key to bringing rain. Jeffrey Snyder-Reinke has correctly shown that the success of rainmaking was not necessarily based on the discourse of "virtue," or *de*, but on "sincerity," or *cheng* 誠.[37] While sincerity was certainly the term used by the officials, any efficacious penance that actually brought rain would have been interpreted by the common people as the result of sacrifice and self-inflicted violence. Local histories and gazetteers describe the willingness to self-sacrifice as the cause of rain. Donald Sutton, for example, shows that, when various folk rainmaking practices did not work, Feng Zhong, the prefect of Yangzhou, engaged in official penitence. It was only then that the rain fell.[38] Only his expiatory ritual brought rain; others brought no results at all. Sometimes we read cases of how the austerity was so taxing on the officials' bodies that they died during the rain prayer even though their deaths were often followed by rainfall.[39] These texts highlight the darker, violent side of their ritual exposure and their supposed cultic prowess. Their acts unquestionably made them authorities in religious matters.

Compilers of official history, usually educated men, were curators of such sanctity. They ensured the correct interpretations of ritual exposure that would legitimate their own vested interest in "Confucianizing" the moral and cosmic order. Yet it is important to recognize that the realities of these performances were much more complex. On the one hand, officials may have seized the opportunity to demonstrate their moral power by documenting themselves as exemplars in local histories. On the other hand, they were also impelled by their duties to perform rainmaking rituals. Failure or refusal to perform ritual exposure—which the common people actually expected of them—would not only continue the drought but would be proof of their corruption and moral incompetence, the consequences of which were believed to have brought about the drought in the first place. Thus, providing hagiographic records of themselves successfully bringing rain sealed their moral power and innocence. The expectations placed on them also attest to the socially constructed and contested nature of rainmaking ritual discourses.

In nearly all late imperial sources on ritual exposure, performers emulated the paradigm of the shaman kings. Some members of the literati were particularly polemical in reminding their readers of this. They insisted that female shamans rather than surrogates should be employed, just like in ancient times. They advocated a materialist means of bringing rain through the *yin* principle. The late Ming official Tang Shunzhi,[40] for example, provided a list of essentially ineffective means of bringing rain and complained in his *Discourse on Rain Ritual* that:

> Beside the seven affairs,[41] the ancients relieved drought by relocating the market from the city, proscribing animal slaughter,[42] breaking fans,[43] and having officials sit [outdoors] exposed to administer the affairs of the district. All of these can be done. Recently, people pray for rain but do not know the [method of] utilizing *yin* to beseech *yin*, nor do they engage in the seven affairs. They only ask Buddhist monks and Daoist clerics to write talismans, perform sacrifice, and hold incense to burn candles and talismans. They do not know that the ancients, in order to relieve drought, had to employ female shamans. Today Buddhist monks and Daoist clerics are used. Even if the [rainmaking] technique is conducted to its perfection, if the person employed is overbearingly *yang*, he will not be able to procure rain. People of later generations privilege the Buddhist monk and Daoist cleric, but in ancient times the Buddhist monk and Daoist cleric were nonexistent. Today ritual prayers for people should be performed by female shamans. If there are counties and cities that seek to quickly relieve drought, but cannot obtain a female shaman, then a female Daoist cleric or a Buddhist *bhikṣuṇī* [i.e., nun] can be used. This is to use *yin* to beseech *yin*.[44]

Tang Shunzhi's contentious words echo the arguments found in *Luxuriant Gems of the Spring and Autumn Annals* by Dong Zhongshu 董仲舒 (179–104 B.C.E.), the Han dynasty scholar who first articulated the notion of *yin* attracting *yin* in rainmaking rituals. The *yin* and the *yang* principles describe the correspondences of the forces in nature: light and dark, motion and stillness, male and female, life and death. According to him, the five phases of wood, fire, earth, metal, and water, the *yin* and *yang* principles, defined all of the material constituencies in the world. Understanding their workings allowed people to control and manipulate nature. It was because of the material connections between the body and the cosmos that the female shaman or the shaman kings was able to garner enough power to change the course of natural events. In this scheme of things, water and rain were *yin*. So, by sacrificing a female shaman, the epitome of the *yin* principle, drought would end because heaven would send down the rains. She was responsible for ensuring the productivity of the land and particularly for bringing seasonable rainfall.[45] This sympathetic resonance or the mechanism of stimulus-response means that "things of the same genus incite each other."[46] In modern theoretical terms this is the notion of contagion.

The correspondence of similar things in the universe, such as that of the *yin* energy and rain, is explicitly expressed in chapter 57, "Things of the Same Genus Incite Each Other" (*Tonglei xiangdong* 同類相動) of Dong Zhongshu's work:

> If water is poured on level ground it will avoid the parts which are dry, and move towards those that are wet. If [two] identical pieces of firewood are exposed to fire, the latter will avoid the damp and ignite the dry one. The hundred [i.e., myriad] things reject what is different [from themselves] and follow what is the same.... The experiential proof of this is extraordinarily clear. Try tuning musical instruments. The *kung* note or the *shang* note struck upon a lute will be answered by the *kung* or the *shang* note from other stringed instruments. They sound by themselves. This is nothing miraculous (*shen* 神) but the five [musical] notes being in relation... things summon each other.... Heaven embodies *yin* and *yang*; humans also embody the *yin* and *yang*. When the *yin* energy arises in heaven and earth, the *yin* energy in humans also arises. When the *yin* energy dominates in humans, the *yin* energy of heaven and earth responds and arises. Thus it is said they are one. Anyone who understands this principle and hopes to bring about a fall of rain will stir up the *yin* energies so as to stimulate *yin* [since rain is associated with *yin*]; and anyone who wishes to stop rain falling will stir up the *yang* energies to stimulate the *yang* [since the sun is associated with the *yang*]. We find that inducing a fall of rain is not due to the spirits; this principle is indeed subtle and marvelous.[47]

In another chapter, titled "Beseeching Rain," in the same text, Dong Zhongshu advises readers to expose the female shaman and the crippled for nine days in the sun when an autumn drought occurs.[48] Dong saw "nothing miraculous about" using the female shaman to draw rain: She was the embodiment of *yin*, and anyone who needed rainfall had to use *yin* to attract *yin*. This interpretation appears to have little connection to the workings of deities and spirits[49] because the mechanism of this sympathetic resonance was material and corporeal.

The interesting point here is that the female shaman was able to affect change in the weather by material means. Like bodies of water that attract each other on level ground or one musical note resonating with another note on the same scale, there need be nothing moral or ethical about these phenomena. The female shaman's *yin* body and her corporeal form, which can be interpreted as abnormal, marginal, disordered, and hence dangerous, attract rain. If we take her deformity into consideration, getting rid of her abnormal body by sacrificing would restore normality and the balance of things in the natural world (good weather).[50] This notion of contagion, which operates on the logic of likeness—the *yin* body attracting the *yin* rain—and undergirded the practice, was quite prevalent and conveyed in other ways as well.

The discourse of altruism also operated on the notion of contagion. For example, a ruler's altruistic rainmaking ritual directly corresponded to the benevolent workings of a sympathetic heaven (and its celestial bureaucrats). Similar things attract. The moral heaven responds to people who exhibited moral powers. By using corporeal suffering to demonstrate their utmost sincerity and acting as representatives of humanity, emperors and officials restored the order of the cosmos and reestablished the supposedly breached relationship. They had to expiate any fault that may have caused the drought. Hence, they punished themselves. Heaven was perceived as benevolent, so the ruler must also be. A drought was then understood as a sign of certain moral problems of the ruler. This logic would explain why Tu Long in the earlier example was unable to stimulate a response from heaven during his prayer. Even though the mechanisms of sympathetic resonance in female shaman sacrifice and official benevolence may seem different, both operated on the notion of contagion and were enacted through mimetic action.

In the previous pages we noted that Tang Shunzhi accepted his contemporaries' practice of sitting exposed (*luzuo* 露坐) to the sun, but he lamented their ignorance of his more effective means of bringing rain: the ritual exposure of the female shaman. Tang Shunzhi's discourse could be read as an argument for the social and political necessity of female shamans. Yet, in the late imperial times female shamans were regularly criticized and persecuted. Official sources typically marginalize them as suspect religious professionals who wielded dangerous powers; any mention of them in these sources was about persecution. We are tempted to believe that their social status diminished drastically. However, if we look at other types of literature, we see that their influence at the local level did not diminish at all. The invisibility of female shamans in official sources may simply reflect the fact that the imperium categorized shamans along with other suspect religious specialists. Consider, for example, the late Ming case of Madame Chen, who was active in Suzhou. Even though she was a shaman, she claimed to be the incarnation of the Tiantai master Lezi 泐子, who was a disciple of the famous Tiantai master Zhiyi 智顗 (538–597).[51] From the perspective of the officials, who likely saw her as a quasi-Buddhist nun, her status as a shaman was no different from that of a Buddhist nun. Certain female shamans were able, for the most part, to avoid the radar of official persecution because they integrated themselves into mainstream culture.

The social status and occult power of the female shaman was widely recognized, particularly in the domestic religion of the late Ming—a time most associated with women. They were not known as "female shamans," or *wu*, but instead as female healers, midwives, old grannies, or other appellations—women who had special powers in spiritual matters.[52] Female healers at the court, such as midwives and old grannies, were simultaneously feared and respected due to their marginal and ambiguous social status. In certain literature, for example, some of these healers were also physically marked by their deformed asexual bodies, an implicit literary allusion to the female shaman of old.[53] Part of their perceived powers, I believe, stemmed from their ambiguous social status and their *yin* bodies.

In medical lore, the female body was characterized as polluting because of its connections to *yin* and menstrual blood, which was always unstable and crossing boundaries, open to sexual penetration, and leaking and depleting blood, which cannot be contained.[54] Pollution posed a potential threat to the moral and cosmic order. A midwife who mastered the polluting substance became herself the site of potential danger to social and individual systems insofar as the status of the *yin* menstrual blood was taken to be unstable and untamed. This point is discussed later in the section titled "The Power of the Body." For the moment suffice it to say that, even though the power of female healers, grannies, and female shamans was feared, these women were also utilized by emperors and officials, who both feared and endorsed them.[55]

Historians have confirmed this widespread contradictory phenomenon. The late imperial state was particularly impressed by and apprehensive of the occult powers of religious professionals. Even though the Ming legal codes explicitly outlawed sorcery and heresy, such powers were utilized and respected, though not without caution. For example, Susan Naquin writes of a Buddhist nun named Lu, with a large local following, who warned the emperor and his troops about continuing their travel toward the location of an uprising. The emperor noted her "mark of sanctity" and saw her as a source of religious authority. He took her advice and was saved from a potential threat on his life. Afterward the emperor brought her back to the capital and built her a temple, which became known as the "Temple of the Illuminate Maiden." She was lavishly rewarded.[56]

Another case illustrates the popular perception of the similarities between Buddhist nuns and female thaumaturgists. By "popular" I do not mean a perception held only by the unlettered. Far from it, for this perception was also held by the state and its officials. A woman warrior named Tang Sai'er, also known as the "Buddha Mother," was an infamous knight errant of the Ming. She led an insurrection during the reign of Emperor Yongle, and she and her army captured several walled cities and took over the blockades in Shandong province. Her source of military prowess supposedly derived from her magical power to create soldiers out of paper cutouts, talismans, and visions of unseen forces that transmitted sacred texts to her.[57] The state tried for years to capture her but to no avail. That searches were conducted in Buddhist monasteries and nunneries is indicative of how she was regarded by state officials and how individuals like Tang Sai'er were able to escape detection by the state, as many of them had no official religious affiliation.

Immolating the Body for Rain

Both the female shaman and the sage king as ritual specialists constructed their sanctity through penitential sacrifices of prolonged naked exposure to the heat of the sun. If this did not work, self-immolation, an alternative practice, was performed. Self-immolation (*zifen* 自焚), the voluntary practice of setting one's body on fire, has a long and rich history. It was connected to the shamanic rainmaking rituals of King Tang, but later it was also conflated with the Buddhist practice of relinquishing the body (*sheshen* 捨身). James Benn has detailed many cases of Buddhist self-immolators over a span of a thousand years from medieval times to the twentieth century. He shows that, as a concept, self-immolation (or "autocremation," as he calls it) accomplished different ends: rebirth in the Pure Land, attainment of immortality, and political unification.[58] Instead of summarizing all of the Buddhist practices of self-immolation, I focus on cases that occurred in earlier periods but later circulated widely in China. Remarkably, early thaumaturgical themes continued into later China despite different conceptions of thaumaturgy in various religious texts.

In rainmaking rituals there is a natural progression from ritual exposure to self-immolation in the sense that the latter is typically practiced as a last resort. For example, during a great drought in 90 C.E., Han official Dai Feng 戴封, who occupied a central political position, "prayed [for rain] fervently without result, so he piled up firewood and sat in the middle to self-immolate. When the flames arose, heavy rain came down violently and he was uninjured. People far and near were all in awe."[59] He was later appointed to the office of Taichang and was placed in charge of all matters pertaining to magic and divination, with shamans staffing his department.[60] The editors of cases such as this made sure that the "sincerity" of official immolators was powerful enough to guarantee rain, but what stands out was the motif of self-sacrifice, self-inflicted violence, and, in this case, Dai Feng's thaumaturgical powers. Consider also the case of the mid-fifteenth-century official named An Yu 安郁, who was a constable (*dianshi* 典史)[61] in Pujiang County in Sichuan province. During a drought one year and after repeated failure to bring rain, An Yu fasted, bathed, and went to the Daoist Temple of Purple Ultimate (Ziji guan 紫極觀). He gathered firewood, piled it up, and made an oath: "If it does not rain, I will burn myself." Before he set himself aflame on the appointed day, heavy rain came down.[62] The phenomenon of rain arriving before the performer's self-immolation is a common trope in early official records.

What is curious is that An Yu attempted self-immolation at a Daoist temple, presumably under its auspices. Was he a Daoist adept himself? Why was the self-immolation held at a Daoist temple? Unfortunately, our source is silent on these matters. Daoists performed rainmaking rites right up to Ming times, but their methods seldom involved self-immolation. Yet, when we examine the broader pattern of ritual protocol associated with self-immolation, we see that these practices all had connections to the making of a transcendent or *xian*.

An Yu's body was ritually prepared for the practice of self-immolation. He "fasted and bathed" before setting himself aflame. These two actions were part of the ritualization of the body, which not only purifies it but also suggests the inherent biocosmological power within the body that can be unleashed through ritual. Much of the technology of transforming the constituents of the body through diet had already become common knowledge by the fifth century.[63] People from all walks of life in late imperial times certainly knew of these practices because they were part of the larger cultural topoi in popular novels and literature.[64] Even in medieval times, Buddhist monks who immolated themselves prepared their bodies by abstaining from grain. Some went a step further by ingesting fragrant oil and incense—a practice that emulates the Bodhisattva Medicine King of the *Lotus Scripture*, who performed self-immolation as an offering to the Buddha. The special dietary restriction was practiced for a sufficiently long time to ensure that, when the body burned, it would make a more suitable fragrant offering.[65] Abstention from grain and cereal was also a way to cultivate longevity and transcendence through physical and spiritual purification. The method strengthened and refined the body to its essence and starved the supposed "cadavers" who lived in the body and hindered immortality.[66]

According to ancient Chinese lore, fasting is an essential component of bodily purification. People believed that the body is a replica of the cosmos and hence thoroughly divine. Yet, they also believed that it is doomed to decay and die from the time of one's birth because of the mother's diet of grains, the putrefaction of which damages the embryo's nature and defiles the newborn body, causing it to lose its natural divinity. Further, the body is populated with, among other demons, the "three cadavers," which gnaw at the organism and render it vulnerable to disease. For Daoists, it is through fasting that these bodily demons are starved to death and divinity is regained. Dietary regimens like periodic fasting were also used to remake the body, most often to cause it to become lighter and purer.[67]

One's biocosmological power can also be seen in another story that circulated widely in the seventeenth century. It involves an earlier Daoist adept named Gan Ji 干吉, from the Eastern Han (25–220 C.E.). His hagiography must have inspired the popular imagination with regard to the efficacy of self-immolation. Gan Ji was an extremely diligent practitioner. Once he contracted a chronic illness. From morning to dusk he prayed to heaven, and his sincerity moved the Lord Lao 老君, who had an elderly immortal impart a scripture to him. After Gan Ji received the scripture and presumably followed its recommendations, he not only overcame his illness but also learned the secrets of immortality and acquired the ability to deliver other people as well. Whenever someone was ill or a disaster befell the community, he brought cures and peace to the person or the community without fail. Later a general named Ce (Ce jiangshi 策將士) contracted a sickness. Gan Ji cured him by spurting water from his mouth. Later, when a drought occurred, the general bound (*fu* 縛) Gan Ji and exposed him to the sun (*baori* 暴日)—just as the ancients had done to female shamans during rainmaking rituals—and heavy rain came down as a result. Gan Ji was a thaumaturgist in tune with the workings of nature. His body, similar to that of a female shaman, had the ability to summon rain. We are told that the general later became jealous of Gan Ji's shamanic powers, so he had him assassinated, but Gan Ji's corpse was never found. After a hundred years Gan Ji reappeared to the people as a transcendent or *xian*. It was said that his countenance resembled that of a child and that he attained immortality on Mount Zhuyu 紵嶼山.[68]

In the sixteenth century there lived a Buddhist cleric by the name of Zhoufu 周福. Despite his Buddhist affiliation, local people referred to him as "Zhou the Transcendent (Zhouxian 周仙)" or "Master Zhou the Perfected Man" (Zhougong zhenren 周公真人). Both appellations have, for lack of a better word, "Daoist" connotations, but the fact that these terms were used in a Buddhist hagiographical text suggests that the author had no qualms about them.[69] Zhoufu was an esoteric practitioner who specialized in *maṇḍala* offerings, recitation of *vaipulya sūtras*, and the employment of spells, or *dhāraṇī*. At the end of his life, he is said to have told his followers that the time had come for him to "follow the example of the Buddha and join the bath of fire." He then stacked up firewood, sat down on top of the pile, and started chanting spells. Flames suddenly burst from his body. He then said to his followers that "If there is ever a drought in the future, call my name and rain will fall heavily!" It is said that, from the Wanli period on, when villagers prayed for rain they simply called out his name, "Zhou the Transcendent!" and rain would pour down. And when it did, it would be accompanied by the sound of wooden fish being struck (similar to the way they are used during the chanting of scriptures) and a voice that chanted spells.[70]

James Benn describes this case and connects the practice of "autocremation" to the attainment of *samādhi*, or mental concentration, through either recitation of the Buddha's name or meditation.[71] Yet, what is striking in this case is the explicit connection of self-immolation to the motif of burning shamans in early China as discussed earlier. Even though Zhoufu engaged in self-immolation to join the ranks of the Buddhas, he nevertheless knew that the practice had the power to summon rain in times of need. Self-immolation's connection to rain is evident in the case of another Ming Buddhist cleric who explicitly guaranteed the efficacy of his self-sacrifice.

The *Miscellaneous Record of the Ming* details a Buddhist ascetic monk named Yonglong 永隆 (1359–1392), who bartered with Emperor Taizu to exchange his self-immolation for the freedom of thousands of monks from conscription into the army. Because these monks had failed the basic exam for monkhood and had shown their ignorance of scriptures in their own tradition, Taizu wanted to draft them; however, he accepted Yonglong's offer. While the logic behind this exchange is not discussed in the sources, it becomes clear when we read that Yonglong supposedly gave a plaque to certain officials that read "the wind and rain will be favorable" (*fengtiao yushun* 風調雨順) and urged them to present it to the emperor in times of drought. He was certain of the cosmic efficacy of his act.

When Yonglong immolated himself, Taizu freed the monks. That Taizu believed in Yonglong's spiritual power suggests the spiritual efficacy of expiatory rites. Sometime later, when a drought occurred, Taizu remembered Yonglong's predictions and used the plaque to pray for rain. We are told that the region was rewarded with a heavy downfall that very evening. Delighted, Taizu exclaimed, "This is the rain from Yonglong!" Because of Yonglong's meteorological mastery, the emperor publicly eulogized him by writing an imperial poem titled "The Monk Who Shed His Soul" (*luoposeng* 落魄僧).[72] In Yonglong's case, his expiation and self-destruction not only freed the monks but also brought rain.[73]

The explicit connection between self-immolation and rainmaking is fascinating but not surprising. Burning oneself to bring the rain had been a widely accepted form of self-inflicted violence since ancient times, which may be one reason that our sources are silent as to why Zhoufu or Yonglong would explicitly make that connection. I believe he did so because self-immolation was already widely recognized as a practice for summoning rain. These records thus had no need to explain it.

Another way to understand self-immolation is to cast it in a broader Asian cultural context in the discourse of *tapas*, or magical heat. In an Indian Buddhist context, *tapas* is something that flows through the performer of austerities and endows the person with extraordinary power. Traditional Indic concepts of *tapas* include not only the creative force that generates life but also the force of destruction.[74] While the two dimensions of creation and destruction are interrelated, it is the destructive power of *tapas* that interests us here. This power, as seen in the *Ṛg Veda*, is connected to the process of purification.[75] This association was likely inherited by the Buddhists in the form of various scriptural similes, such as "burn away greed, hatred, and ignorance through the fire of one's *samādhi* and *prajñā*," and likening the passions themselves to heat or flame that scorches sentient beings.[76]

What is curious is that only during late imperial time were self-immolators such as Zhoufu portrayed as having the ability to "autocremate" without external aid. That is, they were supposedly able to light themselves on fire solely through the power of their internal heat. Yet, Zhoufu was not your typical "Buddhist." At least in the eyes of the local villagers, he was a thaumaturgist and a *xian*, or transcendent. We must assume that such a power was not the preserve of Buddhists alone if we expand our perspective to shamanic practice in different parts of the world[77] and other religious traditions. For example, one Daoist rainmaking meditation technique could also generate body heat to produce perspiration. The location of the sweat would indicate to the meditator the direction from which the rain would come. This practice is discussed in the next section.

These immolators' implicit link to thaumaturgical practices is undeniable. Despite their religious affiliation, most common people perceived them as wonder workers and occult specialists. Not surprisingly, sometimes they were criticized as such by the elite Buddhist clerics themselves. To these critics, some practices of self-immolation were heterodox, the result of misguided ignorance and demonic possession. For example, master Yunqi Zhuhong 雲棲袾宏 (1535–1615) states the following:

> There are those demons who pour oil [on themselves] and pile firewood to immolate themselves alive. Those who witness this are awed and sigh [in praise], believing that such people have attained the way. How erroneous is this! Those who still have attachments will give birth to demons [from their attachments]. A single thought of admiration toward those who immolate themselves alive will continue the thought of admiration without end, allowing demons to enter their hearts without self-awareness. As for those who sit in flames as if they don't feel any pain, they don't know that [such immunity to pain] comes from the temporary power of demons. Once they expire the demons will leave their bodies. Then their [spirit] will experience miserable, poisonous, and unspeakable suffering.[78]

Zhuhong was an outspoken critic of various kinds of Buddhist and non-Buddhist practices. His criticism of self-immolation in Zhejiang province suggests that the practice may have been quite prevalent during his time. He not only alludes to the sensational effect that this performance had on the audience but also expresses his opinion of it as "demonic." Compared to his own programs of Buddhist charity work, recitation practice, and other milder forms of self-cultivation, he argued for an orthopraxy that avoided extremes. Yet Chinese Buddhist clerics continued to engage in this self-destructive practice because it was deeply ingrained in the Chinese cultic life. In other words, Zhuhong's milder practices might not have been the only "norm" of the day. Inflicting pain on the body—using its instrumentality to substantiate truths—as seen in this and the previous chapters was accepted as a valid part of the larger Chinese culture.

The Power of the Body

The practices of ritual exposure and self-immolation are inextricably tied to an extraordinary conception of the human body. In order for us to appreciate the thaumaturgical dimension of ritual exposure and self-immolation, it is necessary to explore the perceived connections between the body and the cosmos, the workings of nature, social etiquette, and ritual performance.

As the following examples show, the materiality of the body in premodern China was believed to be able to efficaciously control the cosmos. Its positive and negative powers included the ability to influence heaven, bring rain, ward off ghosts, destroy artillery, counteract sorcery, and predict future events. Many of these ideas appear in early medieval and late imperial records. However, more important was the belief that such powers could be cultivated and unleashed through dietary, meditational exorcises, and other rituals in that these powers rested in historically constituted practical knowledge. In other words, people believed that one could change the weather by biological means.[79]

Even in early Chinese texts, the body was ritualized to accomplish different ends. These texts seem to suggest that the body was not perceived simply as a passive recipient of ritual, as if it were only clothed in cultural ideals. Rather, the body was perceived as an instrument, capable in achieving a range of human objectives. For example, the *Analects* states that a paronomastic connection exists between the word "body" (*ti* 體) and the word "ritual" (*li* 禮) and that a syntactic parallel exists between "body" (*shen* 身) and "life" (*shen* 生): "The determined person [of service] and the benevolent person would not seek life by harming their benevolence. There are those who kill their own bodies in order to complete their benevolence."[80] Mark Lewis notes that the description of life here as something that can be killed suggests that the character *shen* referred to the corporeal body and that it was equated with the self.[81] The *Analects* also celebrates the willingness to sacrifice oneself by fasting in the name of integrity.[82] This is an important point because it shows that selfhood and subjectivity were corporeally conceived and that moral integrity was required to be ritually embodied and performed.

Notions that the body wielded vast potential powers held great currency in later China. This power was bound to the cosmos by the materiality of the body. A medical text corroborates the relationship between the microcosmic body and the macrocosmic body. An observer named Wang Kuei 王逵 (ca. fourteenth–fifteenth centuries) asserts the following:

> That the human body accords with heaven and earth is the clearest. Just as heaven and earth have *si*, *wu*, *shen*, and *yu* [duodenary cyclical

> characters] in front and above, so the human heart and lung are located in front and above. In the heavens *hai*, *zi*, *yin*, and *mao* are below and behind, so the human kidney and liver are at the back and underneath. In addition the four limbs and the hundred bones all accord with [the dispositions of] heaven and earth. The human body is the most spiritual of all living things.[83]

The body was conceived of as an organic replica of the cosmos: Internal organs are matched with the disposition of the cosmos. The microcosmic body as an organism is placed into a relation of a structural homology to macrocosmic reality.

People believed in the efficacious technologies of the body. During the Ming, they used a particular Daoist method for predicting rainfall by observing the perspiration of the body. A Daoist manual titled *Supreme Oneness Three Mountains Mulang Rain Praying Incantation* states that an adept can engage in a special kind of south-facing, seated meditation in order to generate bodily heat until various parts of the adept's body begin to sweat. The location of the sweat indicates the direction from which the rain will come. If the adept's body sweats on the chest, then rain will fall in the south; if the left side of his body sweats, then rain will fall in the east, and so forth.[84] This biocosmological equivalence of sweat and rain rests on the logic of likeness between the microcosmic body of the individual and the macrocosmic "body" of the universe.

Sometimes the powers of the body, which represent those of the negative, impurity, danger, and transgression, seem to be innate in certain figures and can be unlocked by rituals. Recall that the female shaman not only was the embodiment of the *yin* principle but also had associations with the female drought demon and that part of her prowess stemmed from her unique, de-eroticized, and deformed body. Ritual exposure of her naked body violated the norm of civility and ordinary conduct. This interpretation is corroborated in the *Classic of Rites* and its commentaries, which stipulated that ritual exposure of part or all of the body at certain intervals in funeral rites in Zhou times was essential to ensure the success of the rituals. Specifically, such ritual exposure of the (male) body would exorcise the ghost of the deceased and other unfriendly spirits.[85]

The exorcistic power of the body is evident in late imperial times as well. A Ming historical chronicle details a provincial graduate named Li Guangdian 李光壂 (1596–1662), who led the late Ming troops at Kaifeng in 1642 to fight off attacks by Li Zicheng 李自成 (1606–1645). One day Li Zicheng's bandit troops (*zei* 賊) sent out women, perhaps female shamans, to expose their naked bodies (*furen chishen* 婦人赤身) on the battlefield in front of the city wall. He had them vehemently "shout imprecations" (*jiaoma* 叫罵) at the

Ming army inside the wall. The result was apparently successful because Li Guangdian's army tried to fire its artillery at the women but failed (*diao dapao xidaoxie* 點大砲, 悉倒洩). His army then countered this magical "attack" by sending out Buddhist monks, who stripped naked and stood (*ling sengren luoli* 令僧人裸立) at the bulwark, where they admonished Li Zicheng's troops. Apparently the counterattack broke down the artillery of Li Zicheng's forces as well.[86] If it is true that both women and Buddhist clerics belong to the principle of *yin*, as Taizu stated in his treatise discussed earlier, then this magical warfare was a competition between two *yin* forces. It is worth noting that the recording of this incident does not appear in some "religious work" but in the writing of the supposedly educated elite.

Accounts of the insurgency of 1774, the Boxer Uprising, in Shandong also demonstrate the body's magical powers. It is stated that when the imperial defenders became fearful of the magical attacks of Wang Lun's 王倫 troops of boxers—with their strange spells, leaping and shouting, and women soldiers waving white fans—an old soldier suggested to the general, "Let a prostitute go up on the wall and take off her underclothing... we will use *yin* to counter their spells." When this proved successful, several other women were sent up on the wall. They stood or sat on the battlements, loosened their hair,[87] and stripped naked. This apotropaic technique forced Wang Lun's army to withdraw.[88] These women's behavior is reminiscent of the madness, frenzy, and shouting of female shamans in ancient ritual performances.

Modern scholars have also noted elsewhere that naked, menstruating, or urinating women could negate ritual and magical efficacy.[89] In the Song folklore, a literary work known as the *Yijian zhi* 夷堅志 tells the story of a shaman (*wuxi* 巫覡) who exorcised a girl possessed by a serpent in a cave by doing the "steps of Yü." The shaman discarded his cap and other garments until he was naked. It is important to note here that ritual nudity was essential for exorcism because it demonstrated the naked body's inherent exorcistic powers.[90]

These public, complex, and widely recognized powers of the exposed body would explain the logic of ritual exposure and self-immolation. As shown in this and other chapters, there were many understandings and uses of the body, much more complex than what we are led to believe by earlier studies on China, which tend to replicate normative prescriptions and ideological truth claims. Self-immolators and those who performed ritual exposure utilized their bodies in a visceral way to negotiate concrete, meteorological changes. No matter who performed them, the same recurring thaumaturgical themes of penitence, self-sacrifice, and magic emerge. Scholars who study state rituals have argued that official rainmaking practices were "performer-centric," rather than liturgy driven in that "no single liturgy governed rainmaking activities from start to finish."[91] I understand rainmaking and other self-inflicted violent practices as "performance-centric." Victor Turner argues that certain rituals not only function as "social dramas" because they embody a dramatic element that highlights their performativity but also show others what they are doing or have done.[92] Judith Butler has also written about the performative nature of social roles, arguing that the subjectivity of individuals is "not fixed" but is continually created through actions, gestures, and other social signs, signs that do not simply represent states of affairs but also bring them about.[93] These theories explain why it doesn't matter who performed ritual exposure and self-immolation. What was important was the perceived efficacy of the performance itself.

≅

In premodern China, rainmaking practices of ritual exposure and self-immolation were predicated on the assumed power of the body to change the course of events in nature. Representations of different types of rainmaking rituals overlap somewhat. We need not consider them as distinct forms of rainmaking, especially when the various records of performances were produced by the same educated men. Even though redactors did distinguish between and debate the mechanisms of moral efficacy and which performers were more effective in bringing rain, their thaumaturgical power was never questioned. Whether the performers were emperors, officials, Buddhist or Daoist clerics, or female shamans, there was essentially little difference in the underlying mechanisms of power. Self-inflicted violence as a socially sanctioned ritual allowed for the manifestation of this biocosmological power.

Conclusion

THE DISCUSSIONS ON self-inflicted violence in this book have focused on the performative impact of personal, social, and religious change. As a category, self-inflicted violence allows us to appreciate its diverse manifestations, which are deeply rooted in sixteenth- and seventeenth-century Chinese culture. Performers engaged in many extreme somatic practices to exercise their power to influence social situations and cosmic conditions. Practices such as blood writing, filial slicing, chastity mutilations and suicides, ritual exposure, and self-immolation were both producers and products of moral values during this time. On the one hand, these practices affected real changes in people's lives. On the other hand, the discourses about them that either validate or challenge certain cultural values are inseparable from the complex milieu that shaped the lives of the performers.

The aim of this book is to give extreme bodily practices a prominent place in the history of sixteenth- and seventeenth-century China. The theme running through the different chapters is that self-inflicted violence, in the form of socially sanctioned and routinized bodily mortifications, was widespread and highly visible. Even though it took many forms and cannot be topologically pigeonholed as a single religious tradition or discourse, the four practices discussed in this book were structured, ritualized, and cut across religious divides. In short, self-inflicted violence was not the specific provenance of any one cultural option, as defined either indigenously or by scholarly taxonomy. Rather, as a distinctive refrain, it cut across and ran through multiple options, in effect blurring their presumed boundaries. My analysis in this book exposes the rich repertoires of exemplary trope and narrative (including exemplary tales that are often repeated in a variety of media) that quite often accompany the different practices. I show that self-inflicted violence had a living history that shaped and was itself shaped by the lives of many different performers and texts.

Explanations that attempt to define the essence of a particular phenomenon in a strict typology sometimes fail to appreciate the complexity of the ways in which that phenomenon both absorbed and affected various social forces as it developed, transforming them as it was in turn transformed. In the practice of blood writing I show that it was not only an accepted, meritorious act of filial piety that negotiated living and deceased parents' lives but also a political act that either supported or challenged patterns of imperial authority. This is evident in the blood writing of Huang Daozhou, who copied the *Classic of Filial Piety* to shame Emperor Chongzhen for his hypocrisy in advocating filial piety while at the same time refusing to allow his own officials to fully perform their filial duties.

Blood writing was also a form of self-sacrifice that substantiated the authenticity of religious orthodoxy during times of perceived spiritual degeneracy. For example, the Buddhist cleric Ouyi Zhixu utilized his blood scriptures to publicly criticize what he perceived as unorthodox Chan practice. Blood writing for him was a way to create boundaries because it demarcated authentic spiritual attainment from the potentially destabilizing impact of "wild Chan" on the Buddhist community. Such boundary making can also be understood as boundary crossing since his blood writing breached the natural bounds of his body, graphically transferring the act of sanctity to the text, animating and sacralizing it. These negotiations were possible because of the complex symbolism of writing in blood, which was understood as the source of creative and exorcistic power. Moreover, the shedding of blood was believed to influence the workings of the cosmos.

The practice of filial piety was also quite complex in the moral economy of the sixteenth and seventeenth centuries. Practitioners not only engaged in blood writing to generate merit to shape the fate of their parents but also used their own flesh as nourishment to heal ailing parents. Such filial anthropophagy elicited metaphors of gift, bargain, exchange, expiation, propitiation, and devotion. But they were not merely metaphors. The practice of filial slicing was bound up in a web of associations in the late imperial time. Consuming human flesh for longevity, nourishment, and power were simultaneously elicited in the practice of filial slicing. Thus, filial slicing was not beyond the norm of premodern Chinese society. Also, rather than reducing it to a "Confucian" or "Buddhist" practice or to any other singular frames of reference, filial slicing may have meant many different things to various people. This is suggested by the ways that members of the literati eulogized and debated the practice. Some used it as a literary trope in their novels to debate *qing*, or passion. Others wrote about it in order to critique existing social customs or to promote their families' moral reputation. As we have seen, Wu Jiaji wrote about his niece Changzhong as a true moral agent. His message is clear: Exemplars of moral action, a fundamental cultural value, are more widespread among commoners than among the cultured governing class. Thus, at least for these literati, filial slicing was not about the consumption of human flesh. Instead, it was about social issues and the power of this practice to reaffirm or challenge the social hierarchy.

In my discussion of female chastity, specifically as self-inflicted violence in which young girls and widows mutilated themselves or committed suicide to resist rape and remarriage, I focus on the tension between women as moral agents and women as objects of desire. This tension is prominent in illustrated didactic works such as the *Illustrated Biographies of Fierce Women*, which utilize the rhetoric of sexual fidelity and innuendos of the chaste widow. Their focus on the female body as a marker of authentic moral performance may be interpreted as the literati's fear of women's sexual promiscuity. Writers and publishers during the publishing boom of the sixteenth and seventeenth centuries also dramatized female chastity in the interest of commercialization and entertainment. Thus, explicit portrayals of widows who resisted forced marriage as beacons of female virtue often lavishly depict young, beautiful, and sensual maidens to increase the marketing and entertainment value of these works. The female body was a site of both virtue and vice. The complicated representations of chastity mutilations and suicides were discussed at length in the case of Gao Xing, whose voluptuous body problematized the otherwise straightforward moral agenda of her didactic narrative. Her physical beauty aroused men's desire, so she resolved to destroy it by slicing off her nose. By permitting this violence or by exalting it as an expression of unquestionable sanctity, the object of desire—Gao Xing's body—was transformed into an object of violence.

Another issue I explore is the religious valence of women's gender roles in their representations as martyrs and vengeful ghosts. Many women committed suicide in order to avoid rape or forced remarriage. Writers viewed these acts as "manly" and "fierce"—representing the women as martyrs. However, through their narratives we also get a glimpse of how women controlled their circumstances and the possible interpretation of their violent suicides, which allowed them a degree of agency. Through this interplay of factors, women demonstrated the ability to transcend their prescribed roles as mere wives. Sometimes they controlled the circumstances of their chastity suicide to come back as ghosts and exact revenge on those who had wronged them. Popular literature conveyed the idea that women who suffered wrongful deaths were dangerous and vengeful and that, as revenants, they wielded an enormous power over the living. Shrines were built, and eulogies were written to honor the deceased chaste widows. However, evidence suggests that these shrines and eulogies were meant to appease their vengeful ghosts. For example, the state made a concerted effort to convert the altars of vengeful ghosts into shrines for virtuous widows. Obviously it saw a correlation between the two; perhaps it feared that the deceased chaste maidens would become vengeful ghosts if they were not placated. In one case, a female revenant haunted the dream of a local magistrate because he had wrongly sentenced her to death for a crime that she did not do. Widely accepted discourses on life after death, karmic retribution, and rebirth also helped to reinforce the possibility of revenge by women who were wrongly killed. These ideas have wide currency and a long history in China and appear not only in religious tracts but also in novels, dramas, and legends. All of these various venues must have informed women of their choices in taking their own lives.

In my discussion of the prolonged ritual exposure to the sun and its extension, self-immolation, I show that regardless of whether the rainmaking practice was performed out of sincerity, penance, or the desire to save others, the manner in which the performers summoned the rain reveals an undeniable thaumaturgical dimension. Emperors modeled themselves on the ancient sage kings; officials exposed their naked bodies to the blazing sun in hopes of soliciting the sympathy of heaven, which would then send rain; and influential Buddhist clerics burned themselves to save the lives of their fellow monks. Their actions mimic the ritual sacrifice of female shamans in ancient times. Some writers criticized these acts because people failed to recognize that by ritually exposing only the *yin*, a female shaman would attract the *yin* rain, but the thaumaturgical dimension underlying these debates remains unchanged. This dimension cuts across religious divides and various rainmaking discourses, in effect blurring the presumed boundaries and the identity of performers. It also reveals the sanctity of the microcosmic body, which is directly and materially related to the larger macrocosm.

Manipulating the body could not only bring rain but also ward off ghosts, destroy artillery, counteract sorcery, and predict future events. The exorcistic body, particularly the naked one, was thought to have these powers because it was part of the fabric of the material world. Magical and contagious, it could be cultivated through dietary, meditational, and other ritual exercises. The biocosmological power explains the logic behind ritual exposure and self-immolation in the moral economy of meteorology.

The history of self-inflicted violence is systematic, rule governed, and replete with meaning for both the performer and the audience. It was quite productive in challenging imperial authority, negotiating social relations, and questioning social customs and patterns of authority. If we free "violence" from our modern presumption that it is limited to external aggression and conflict, we can appreciate the important roles that self-inflicted violent practices have played within the enduring elements of Chinese cultural life, mythologies, rituals, cosmologies, family dynamics, and religious sanctity. The practices examined in this book were highly structured, socially recognizable, and intelligible phenomena. They validated and negotiated accepted values such as filial piety, religious sanctity, loyalty, political authority, and chastity. Premodern writers who discussed and documented these doings did so with the assumption that they were meaningful in their lives—even when others regarded them with disapproval. This book provides a window into the lives of specific performers, their social-cosmic relationships, their conceptions of the potential of the human body, and the ways in which they utilized it to affect the world around them.

Character Glossary

aishen ya 愛身崖
baiyi nü 白衣女
baojuan 寶卷
baori 暴日
baoshen 暴身
Bencao gangmu 本草綱目
Bencao shiyu 本草拾遺
bengjie 崩解
biantong 辯通
biji 筆記
Boluonaiguo 波羅奈國
buxiang qizhi buru qishen 不降其志、不辱其身
changjia 倡家
Changzhong 長仲
chanji 禪機
Chao *furen* 晁夫人
Chao Liang 晁梁
Chen Cangqi's 陳藏器 (d.u.)
Chen Ding 陳鼎 (b. 1651)
Chen Jingze 陳敬則 (sixteenth century)
Chen Que 陳確 (1604–1677)
Chen Que ji 陳確集
Chen Xinjia 陳新甲 (d. 1642)
cheng 誠
Chenghuang 城隍
chengjiu 成就
chengxin kuxing 誠心苦行
chi 赤
Chi You 蚩尤
chiren 癡人
chiri bao zhongting 赤日暴中庭
chuanji 傳記
Chunqiu fanlu zhuzi suoyin 春秋繁露逐字索引
Dai Feng 戴封 (d.u.)
daifu si 代父死
Dajun 大軍
Dajun zhangzhe 大軍長者
dan 石
Daojiao 道教
Daojie 道階 (1866–1934)
Daoxuan 道宣 (596–667)
daoxue 道學
de 德
de 得
dianshi 典史
Dong Zhongshu 董仲舒 (179–104 B.C.E.)
Donglin 東林
dou 斗
Du Shiniang 杜十娘
duanfa 斷髮
duangu 斷穀
duanzhi 斷指
duoqing 奪情
duoqizhi 奪其志
erji 二紀
erzhang 二障

Fang Futou 方福妵 (ca. seventeenth century)
fangshi 方士
fangxiang shi 方相士
fangzhi 方志
fannao zhang 煩惱障
Fayuan zhulin 法苑珠林
fazhi 法執
fei renrou buliao 非人肉不療
feili 非禮
fen wuwang 焚巫尪
Feng En 馮恩 (1491–1571)
Feng Menglong 馮夢龍 (1574–1646)
Feng Xingke 馮行可 (1521–ca. 1609)
Feng Youlan 馮友蘭
fengqi 風氣
fengsu 風俗
fengtiao yushun 風調雨順
fenwu 焚巫
Fojiao 佛教
fu 符
fu 縛
fu 父
furen chishen 婦人赤身
futian 福田
Gan Ji 干吉 (d.u.)
ganlu 甘雨
ganqing 感情
ganying 感應
ganying chuan 感應傳
Gao Panlong 高攀龍 (1562–1626)
gaocheng 告誠
Gaoseng zhuan heji 高僧傳合集
Ge Hong 葛洪 (283–343)
gebi 割鼻
gebi 割臂
gebirou 割髀肉
ge'er 割耳
gegan 割肝
gegong 割肱
gegu 割股
geng 羹
gengtang 羹湯
geqi birou 割其髀肉
geru 割乳
gewu 格物
gexi 割膝
gexie 割脅
gexin 割心
gexiong 割胸
gongguoge 功過格
gongsheng 貢生
Gu Qiyuan 顧起元 (1565–1628)
Guan Zhidao 管志道 (1537–1608)
guanxiang 觀想
Gui Youguang 歸有光 (1507–1571)
Guifan tushuo 閨範圖説
guo 國
Guo Jujing 郭居敬 (fl. 1295–1321)
Guo Yi 郭儀
guojia 國家
Han Yü 韓愈 (768–824)
Han Zhuo 寒浞
hanba 旱魃
Hanshan Deqing 憨山德清 (1546–1623)
He Xinyin 何心隱 (1517–1579)
Hong Mai 洪邁 (1123–1202)
Huang Daozhou 黃道周 (1585–1646)
Huang Di 黃帝
Huang Shiji 黃奭輯 (eighteenth century)
Huang Yu 黃煜 (seventeenth century)
Huang Zongxi 黃宗羲 (1610–1695)
huishang 毀傷
huitu 繪圖
Huitu lienü zhuan 繪圖烈女傳
hunluan 混亂
huo 臛
huofen 活焚
ji 疾
ji 祭
jia 家
Jiang Pingjie 蔣平階 (seventeenth century)
jiangxue 講學
jiantang 煎湯

jianwu 姦污
Jiao Hong 焦竑 (1541–1620)
jiaoma 叫罵
Jiashen 嘉紳
jie 節
jiebi 截鼻
jiedu shi 節度使
jiefa 截髮
jieyi 節義
jifeng 機風
jilei 祭酹
Jin Shengtan 金聖嘆 (1608–1661)
Jingang jing 金剛經
jingbiao 旌表
jinshi 金石
jitian 祭天
juebi 絕筆
kuang 狂
kuang 誑
kuangchan 狂禪
kuanghui 狂慧
kui zuogurou 刲左股肉
kuigu 刲股
kuxing 苦行
leishu 類書
leizhai 羸瘵
Lezi 泐子
li 理
li 禮
li er dai 立而待
Li Guangdian 李光壂 (1596–1662)
Li Shizhen 李時珍 (1518–1593)
Li Zhi 李贄 (1527–1602)
Li Zicheng 李自成 (1606–1645)
Liang Fu 諒輔 (d.u.)
Liao Dongxun 遼東巡 (d.u.)
libai 禮拜
lie 列
lie 烈
liehuo 烈火
lienü 列女
lienü 烈女
lienümiao 烈女廟
lieri 烈日
lieshi 烈士
ligui 厲鬼
lin ruo bingshuang 凜若冰霜
Lin Zhao'en 林兆恩 (1517–1598)
lishen 立身
lishi 勵世
lisu 立甦
litan 厲壇
Liu Baonan 劉寶楠 (1791–1855)
Liu Benzun 柳本尊 (b. 855)
Liu Jin 劉瑾 (1452–1510)
Liu Xiang 劉向 (76–6 B.C.E.)
lou 裸
lu 露
lü 律
Lu Gao 魯高
Luo Guanzhong 羅貫中 (ca. 1330–1400)
Lü Kun 呂坤 (1536–1618)
luoposeng 落魄僧
luzuo 露坐
Lüzi yishu 呂子遺書
manyue 滿月
mei yu xing 美於行
Meng Ke 孟軻
mi 糜
Miaoshan 妙善
miejue lunli 滅絕倫理
mingguan 冥官
Minghe 明河 (1588–1641)
Mingxing zaji 明興雜記
mingzhi 明志
mofa 末法
Mulian 目連
muyi 母儀
Nanyue Huisi 南嶽慧思 (515–577)
Ni Riheng 倪日亨 (d.u.)
Ouyi Zhixu 蕅益智旭 (1599–1655)
Peng Yinghong 彭應洪 (d.u.)
pengdang 朋黨
pengtou 髿頭

po you se 頗有色
pu 曝
Pu Songling 蒲松齡 (1640–1715)
pushen 曝神
*puwang*曝尫
*puwu*曝巫
qi 氣
qijie 氣節
qing 情
qinggui 情鬼
qingkuang 情況
qingmian 黥面
qingshi juwang 情識俱忘
qingyu 情欲
qingyu 請雨
qipin 七品
qisi huisheng 起死回生
qiuyu 求雨
qiyu 祈雨
renhuang 人黃
renyu hengliu 人慾橫流
renzhi 仁智
rong yu se 榮於色
rou 柔
roushen 肉身
ru 儒
rushen zhi wei jieshen 辱身之為潔身
sajiaye 薩迦耶
sanjiao heyi 三教合一
sanzu 散足
shangdi 上帝
*shangxiang*上香
shangzhong mendi 傷重悶地
shanshu 善書
Shanwuwei 善無畏 (637–735)
she tanxi 設壇席
shen 身
shen 生
sheng 聖
shenjian 身見
shenming 神明
Shenxian zhuan 神仙傳
sheshen 捨身
sheshen 捨身品
shi 詩
shi 屍
Shi Nai'an 施耐庵 (1290–1365)
Shimi 十迷
shishen 失身
Shizheng lu 實政錄
shoujie 守節
shushi 術士
sidian 祀典
sijiu 賜酒
Sima Qian 司馬遷 (ca. 145–86 B.C.E.)
Subi 蘇卑
Sun Zhiwei 孫枝蔚 (1620–1687)
suozhi zhang 所知障
Taishan 泰山
Taiyu 岱嶽
Taizhou 泰州
tan 壇
tan 袒
tang 湯
Tang Shunzhi 唐順之 (1507–1560)
Tan Wuchen 曇無讖 (385–433)
Tang Xianzu 湯顯祖 (1550–1616)
tanhe 彈劾
ti 體
tian 天
tianming 天命
tianxia 天下
toulanzhe 偷蘭遮
toutuo 頭陀
Tu Long 屠龍 (1543–1605)
Tudi gong 土地公
Tudi Shen 土地神
tujiluo 突吉羅
wang 王
Wang Cuiqiao 王翠翹 (sixteenth century)
Wang Gen 王艮 (1483–1541)
Wang Kuei 王逵 (ca. fourteenth–fifteenth centuries)
Wang Lun 王伦 (eighteenth century)

Wang Shouren 王守仁; see Wang Yangming
Wang Yangming 王陽明 (1472–1529)
wanren qi 萬人妻
wanrou 剜肉
Wei Zhongxian 魏忠賢 (1568–1627)
wu 巫
wu 舞
wu 武
Wu Jiaji 吳嘉紀 (1618–1684), aka Wu Binxian 吳賓賢
Wu Junping 吳君平 (sixteenth century)
Wu Zetian 武則天 (634–705; r. 690–705)
Wuguancun 武官村
Wuji 無際 (1381–1446)
Wuji Mingxin 無極明信 (1512–1574)
wuxi 巫覡
xi 覡
xian 仙
xiangfa 像法
xianming 賢明
xiao 孝
Xiao jing 孝經
xiaoshuo 小説
xiejing 血經
xieshu 血書
xing 刑
Xingmi lun 醒迷論
xingyu 行雨
xinshi 信誓
xiucai 秀才
xu 需
xu 頊
xunsi 殉死
yajiang 牙將
yang 陽
Yang Cichang 楊嗣昌 (1588–1641)
Yang Jisheng 楊繼盛 (1516–1555)
Yang Lian 楊漣 (1571–1625)
Yang Pu 楊黼 (d.u.)
Yang Qiyuan 楊起元 (1549–1599)
Yang Weizhen 楊維楨 (1296–1370)
yangming 揚名
yanji 驗記
yaojiandu 藥揵度
yaoshi 藥事
yebao 業報
Yi 羿
yi 醫
yibi 劓鼻
yiduan 異端
yin 陰
yinshu 淫書
yintu tumian 垔土塗面
yinzui 引罪
yipo 醫婆
yitiao bian fa 一條鞭法
yixian fumu 以顯父母
yixiao weizhong 移孝為忠
Yixing 一行 (684 – 727)
Yonglong 永隆 (1359–1392)
youposi 優婆私
youxun 由旬
youzi 有姿
yu 愚
Yu *bu* 禹步
Yu Qian 喻謙 (nineteenth century)
Yuan Hongdao 袁宏道 (1568–1610)
Yuan Huang 袁黄 (1533–1606)
Yuan Zhongdao 袁中道 (1570–1624)
yuanhun 冤魂
yuanwen 願文
yuanyi shendai 願以身代
yufu yufu yuzhi nengxing 愚夫愚婦與知能行
yufuren 愚婦人
yujue 欲絕
Yunqi fahui 雲棲法彙
Yunqi Zhuhong 雲棲袾宏 (1535–1615)
yushui 鬱水
zaoshen 竈神
zei 賊
zewang 責望

zhairi 齋日
Zhancha jing 占察經
Zhang Juzheng 張居正 (1525–1582)
Zhang Zhen 張貞 (sixteenth century)
zhangfu 丈夫
Zhao Zhifeng 趙智鳳 (1159–1249)
Zheng'e ji 正訛集
zhengfa 正法
zhengshi 正史
zhenjie 貞節
zhenle 真樂
zhenlie 貞烈
zhenqie 真切
zhenqing 真情
zhenshun 貞順
zhi liangzhi 至良知
Zhi Qian 支謙 (fl. 223–253)
zhiqing 至情
zhixiao 至孝
zhixing heyi 知行合一
Zhiyi 智顗 (538–597)
zhiyu 致雨
Zhizhi 智止
zhong 忠
zhongji 重極
zhongshen jingxiao 終身盡孝
Zhou Maolan 周茂蘭 (seventeenth century)
Zhou Rudeng 周汝登 (1547–1629)
Zhou Shunchang 周順昌 (1584–1626)
Zhoufu 周福 (seventeenth century), aka Zhouxian 周仙
Zhougong jiemeng quanshu 周公解夢全書
Zhouyi Chanjie 周易禪解
zhu 煮
zhu 祝
Zhu Xi 朱熹 (1130–1200)
Zhu Yizun 朱彝尊 (1629–1709)
Zibo Zhenke 紫柏真可 (1543–1603)
zifen 自焚
Ziji guan 紫極觀
zuosui 作祟

Notes

INTRODUCTION

1. See below for my discussion of *de* 德 and *ling* 靈.
2. See, for example, Timothy Brook, "Rethinking Syncretism: The Unity of the Three Teachings and Their joint Worship in Late-Imperial China," *JCR* 21 (Fall 1993): 13–44; Cynthia Brokaw, "Yuan Huang (1533–1606) and the Ledgers of Merit and Demerit," *HJAS*, 47 (1) (June 1987): 137–95. The idea of syncretism in late-imperial China, specifically the late Ming period, also appears in numerous chapter introductions to historical and intellectual studies pertaining to this period.
3. See Kenneth Dean, *Lord of the Three in One: The Spread of a Cult in Southeast China* (Princeton, NJ: Princeton University Press, 1998), 9–11; 21–27. Scholars rely heavily on the writings of the literati elite, those writers who were particularly strong in articulating the dominant ideology of their own tradition over against others. So, for example, when scholars historicize the long and inexorable "decline" in Buddhism and Daoism from the Song dynasty (960–1279) until their "revival" in the sixteenth and seventeenth centuries in the form of syncretism, they are actually repeating the grand repression by the Confucian elite writers. For the "decline" or "renewal" of Buddhism see, for example, Timothy Brook, *Praying for Power: Buddhism and the Formation of Gentry Society in Late-Ming China* (Cambridge, MA: Harvard University Press, 1993), 3; Chün-fang Yü, *The Renewal of Buddhism in China: Chu-hung and the Late Ming Synthesis* (New York: Columbia University Press, 1981), 2–6. Brook's work, *Praying for Power*, for example, argues that the Buddhist revival during the late Ming was the result of the gentry's patronage of monasteries. Their backing provided a public "arena" in which they could convert status into power. As power could not be seized from the imperial state (due to the overabundance of scholars during this time and the few official positions available to them), it could be taken surreptitiously only by withdrawing to the monastic realm, where they promoted themselves as a unified, refined elite whose power derived not from the state but from their own conduct. In essence, Buddhism was moribund, intellectually

bankrupt, socially ineffectual, and politically irrelevant. In Brook's view, the revival of Chinese Buddhism in the late Ming hinged on no intrinsic conditions within Buddhism at all. In his grand thesis he tries to show how monastic patronage worked to the benefit of the gentry but fails to explain why they chose to support monasteries. They could have chosen to fund schools and public works, which they did. Were the Ming gentry so beholden to the state that *only* Buddhist monasteries could provide a basis for their autonomy and power? Brook is not unique in upholding this deeply flawed theory (which is based on the perspectives of certain Confucians or gentry he studies) of the "revival" of Buddhism. His work is also regularly cited, unchallenged, by Sinologists and historians whose own work is "Confucian-centric." Such a thesis—that only the elite Confucian gentry defined the social, cultural, and political direction of Chinese society—is an example of what happens when scholars imbibe wholesale the writings of Confucian literati.

4. Several scholars have problematized our understanding of "religion." The most famous one is perhaps, Jonathan Z. Smith, "Religion, Religions, Religious," in *Critical Terms for Religious Studies*, ed. Mark Taylor (Chicago: University of Chicago Press, 1998), 269–84. I have found Talal Asad's critique of religion particularly poignant; see his *Genealogies of Religion: Discipline and Reasons of Power in Christianity and Islam* (Baltimore: Johns Hopkins University Press, 1993), 27–54.
5. For Ouyi's practice of self-inflicted violence see chapter 2; for the criticism of self-inflicted violence or austerity, specifically self-immolation, see Yunqi Zhuhong 雲棲株宏 (1535–1615), "Burning [Oneself] Alive" (*huofen* 活焚), in *Zheng'e ji* 正訛集 (Collection of Orthodoxy and Heterodoxy), excerpts from *Yunqi fahui* 雲棲法彙 (Collection of Master Yunqi's Teachings), J. no. B277, 33:77b21–29. James Benn has translated a section of this text; see "Where Text Meets Flesh: Burning the Body as an Apocryphal Practice in Chinese Buddhism," *HR* 37 (4) (May 1998): 295–322.
6. See, for example, the introduction to the newest translation of the classic of filial piety by Henry Rosemont Jr. and Roger T. Ames, *The Chinese Classic of Family Reverence: A Philosophical Translation of the* Xiaojing (Honolulu: University of Hawaii Press, 2009).
7. See Robert Ford Campany, *Making Transcendents: Ascetics and Social Memory in Early Medieval China* (Honolulu: University of Hawaii Press, 2009), 33–34.
8. See Jonathan Z. Smith, *Imagining Religion: From Babylon to Jonestown* (Chicago: University of Chicago, 1982), xi. While Smith provides some good insights into the scholar's task, he fails miserably in taking seriously the notion that behind any "religious" phenomenon a kind of complex theology is at work. This is analogous to analyzing legal life while leaving out the moral conceptions that underlie it and concluding that the law is merely a means of resolving disputes.

9. A clear articulation of the instrumentality of ritual can be found in Talal Asad's critique of anthropology of religion, *Genealogies of Religion*, 55–79, esp. 58, 76. I discuss the "body" below.
10. Peter Brown has articulated a similar idea of the holy man as playing certain "roles" in the society; see "The Rise and Function of the Holy Man in Late Antiquity," *Journal of Roman Studies* 61 (1971): 80–101.
11. For a summary of how violence is theorized in contemporary religious studies see Fritz Graf, "Violence," in *Encyclopedia of Religion*, ed. Lindsay Jones et. al. (Detroit: Macmillan Reference USA, 2005): 9595–9600. For an example of an externalist and negative interpretation violence see Mark Juergensmeyer, *Terror in the Mind of God* (Berkeley: University of California Press, 2000). Scholars of East Asian religions also understand violence as various forms of injury, aggression, or the taking of life—in other words, violence as understood from an externalist perspective; see Mark Edward Lewis, *Sanctioned Violence in Early China* (New York: State University of New York Press, 1990). Even cultural theorists subtly consider violence in religions as a form of conflict; see Bryan Rennie and Philip L. Tite, *Religion, Terror, and Violence: Religious Studies Perspectives* (New York: Routledge, 2008); Bruce Lincoln, "Conflict," *Critical Terms for Religious Studies* (Chicago: University of Chicago, 1998), 55–69.
12. Sanctioned violence as a phenomenon is pervasive in premodern societies. Christian and to a lesser extent Muslim history is full of religious wars, most conspicuously the Crusades, which turned against the Orthodox Christian Byzantium, and the European wars of religion that followed the Reformation, such as the Thirty Years War (1618–1648). In China, sanctioned violence has always been part and parcel of law, religion, and social norm, at least until late imperial times. Aside from the various cases I discuss in this book, historians and anthropologists have also noted that violence appears to be at the foundation of political, social, and cosmic order. For the case of Islam see John Kelsay, *Arguing the Just War in Islam* (Cambridge, MA: Harvard University Press, 2007); for China, see Paul A. Cohen, *History in Three Keys: The Boxers as Event, Experience, and Myth* (New York: Columbia University Press, 1997); Joanna Waley-Cohen, *The Culture of War in China: Empire and the Military under the Qing Dynasty* (London: Tauris, 2006); Jon Abbink, "Preface: Violation and Violence as Cultural Phenomena," in *Meanings of Violence: A Cross-Cultural Perspective*, ed. Göran Aijmer and Jon Abbink (Oxford: Berg, 2000), xi–xvii; Göran Aijmer, "Introduction: The Idiom of Violence in Imagery and Discourse," in *Meanings of Violence*, 1–22; Virgil Kit-yiu Ho, "Butchering Fish and Executing Criminals: Public Executions and the Meaning of Violence in Late Imperial and Modern China," in *Meanings of Violence*, 141–60; and the most recent article by Barend ter Haar, "Violence in Chinese Culture," in *The Blackwell Companion to Religion and Violence*, ed. Andrew R. Murphy (Oxford: Wiley, 2011), 249–62. The collection of essays in this book shows that violence is

integral to and constitutive of premodern and modern societies. However, it still conceives of violence as external or interpersonal aggression or force.

13. See Geoffrey Galt Harpham, *The Ascetic Imperative in Culture and Criticism* (Chicago: University of Chicago Press, 1987), xi–xii.
14. This criticism is noted by Oliver Freiberger in examining extra-, inter-, and intra-ascetic criticisms (i.e., from non-ascetics, between different groups of ascetics, and within the same ascetic community, respectively). See Oliver Freiberger, *Asceticism and Its Critics: Historical Accounts and Comparative Perspectives* (Oxford\: Oxford University Press, 2006).
15. Peter Brown examines the variety of attitudes toward the body and sexuality in light of theology, culture, and the relationship between individual and society. See Peter Brown, *The Body and Society: Men, Women, and Sexual Renunciation in Early Christianity* (New York: Columbia University Press, 1988), 222–23, 235–37. It appears that Brown's study of Christianity was in turn influenced by the work of scholars such as Aline Rousselle and Michel Foucault on topics of sexuality, desire, and gender in Greco-Roman antiquity. See Aline Rousselle, *Porneia: On Desire and the Body in Antiquity*, tr. Felicia Pheasant (Oxford: Blackwell, 1988); Michel Foucault, *History of Sexuality: An Introduction*, vol. 1; *The Use of Pleasure*, vol. 2; *The Care of the Self*, vol. 3, trans. Robert Hurley (New York: Vintage, 1988–1990); see also Elizabeth Clark, "Foucault, the Fathers, and Sex," *JAAR* 56 (1988): 619–41.
16. See Caroline Walker Bynum, *Holy Feast and Holy Fast: The Religious Significance of Food to Medieval Women* (Berkeley: University of California Press, 1986), 208–18. See also John G. Gager, "Body-Symbols and Social Reality: Resurrection, Incarnation, and Asceticism in Early Christianity," *Religion* 12 (1982): 345–63; Vincent L. Wimbush and Richard Valantasis, eds., *Asceticism* (New York: Oxford University Press, 1995); William E. Deal, "Ascetics, Aristocrats, and the Lotus Sūtra: The Construction of the Buddhist Universe in Eleventh-Century Japan," PhD diss., Harvard University, 1988. These scholars are reacting to older models of asceticism best represented by E. R. Dodds, *Pagan and Christian in an Age of Anxiety* (Cambridge: Cambridge University Press, 1990).
17. Explicitly rejecting earlier characterizations of asceticism as body hating and dualistic, Peter Brown argues that early Christian asceticism by its nature included matter and the body in spiritual process. See Brown, *Body and Society*, 222–23, 235–37. In theorizing asceticism, scholars have also complicated our understanding of the body and avoided the Cartesian fallacy of polarizing it against an exclusive category of mind even though within the Western academy there are few resources for describing such a concept of the body that does not succumb to a version of the body-mind dichotomy.
18. See Brown, *Body and Society*, 219.
19. Ibid., 222.
20. See Bynum, *Holy Feast and Holy Fast*, 223.

21. See Teresa M. Shaw, *The Burden of the Flesh: Fasting and Sexuality in Early Christianity* (Minneapolis: Fortress, 1998), 2–3, 29–33.
22. See John Kieschnick, *The Eminent Monk: Buddhist Ideals in Medieval Chinese Hagiography* (Honolulu: University of Hawaii Press, 1997), 16–66. James Benn has questioned the applicability of "asceticism" in the study of self-immolation in China (2007, 196). Nonetheless, the categories of "asceticism," "ascetic practice," and "ascetics" are still used throughout his book to describe various Indian and Chinese Buddhist practices such as *dhūta* or *toutuo* 頭陀 and those who engaged in them; see Benn, *Burning for the Buddha: Self-Immolation in Chinese Buddhism* (Honolulu: University of Hawaii Press, 2007), 33, 92–93, 97, 101, 128, 140, 192, 209, 213, 217, 233. William E. Deal critiques the universalist and phenomenological definitions of asceticism and calls for a reading that focuses on the "politics of asceticism." However, his underlying assumption of asceticism is that it involves acts of self-denial and self-discipline; see his "Toward a Politics of Asceticism: Response to the Three Preceding Papers," in *Asceticism*, ed. Vincent L. Wimbush and Richard Valantasis (New York: Oxford University Press, 1995), 424–42. For other examples see Stephen Eskildsen, *Asceticism in Early Taoist Religion* (Albany: State University of New York Press, 1998); Steven Collins, "The Body in Theravāda Buddhist Monasticism," in *Religion and the Body*, ed. Sarah Coakley (Cambridge: Cambridge University Press, 1997), 185–204; and Robert Campany, who defines ascetics as "people who, following the norms of a tradition or master, renounce certain key elements, behaviors, and roles in their environing culture in order to undergo a transformation" (2009, 31). While Campany is using the term to argue against the notion that ascetics were somehow withdrawn from society, his definition still portrays an ascetic as a "renunciant" in terms that are indistinguishable from those used by scholars of Late Antiquity. I discuss *kuxing* 苦行 or painful austerity in chapter 2.
23. Michel Foucault, "Afterword," in Hubert L. Dreyfus and Paul Rabinow, *Michel Foucault: Beyond Structuralism and Hermeneutics*, 2nd ed. (Chicago: University of Chicago Press, 1982), 212.
24. Foucault, *Use of Pleasure*, 27; Richard Valantasis, "Constructions of Power in Asceticism," *JAAR* 63 (1995): 783.
25. See Foucault, *History of Sexuality: An Introduction*, 92–93.
26. For *ganying*, see Feng Youlan 馮友蘭, *A History of Chinese Philosophy*, vol. 2 (Princeton, NJ: Princeton University Press, 1983), 30; Dong Zhongshu 董仲舒 (ca. 179–104 B.C.E.), *Chunqiu fanlu zhuzi suoyin* 春秋繁露逐字索引 ed. D. C. Lau (Taipei: Commercial Press, 1994), 13.2; Robert Sharf, *Coming to Terms with Chinese Buddhism: A Reading of the Treasure Store Treatise* (Honolulu: University of Hawaii Press, 2002), 77–133. The Chinese premodern, "sympathetic" conception of the world may be compared to what Lucien Lévy-Bruhl in 1923 called "participation." This idea also assumes the interpenetration of the unseen

and the seen worlds, the presence of the supernatural in the natural. According to Lévy-Bruhl, who held an evolutionary bias against "primitive religions," the conception confuses the distinctions between persons and between the one and the many and appears not to operate according to the principle of identity or the logic of noncontradiction. According to him, it was at variance with "modern" mentality and ways of conceptualizing. While such a comparison between "participation" and "sympathetic resonance" is possible, I would caution against the evolutionary assumptions in his reading. What is needed is to theorize these ideas, to the best of our abilities, while being attentive to their native usage. See Jill Robbins, "Sacrifice," in *Critical Terms for Religious Studies*, 289–90; Lucien Lévy-Bruhl, *Primitive Mentality*, trans Lilian A. Clare (Boston: Beacon, 1966).

27. Dean, *Lord of the Three in One*, 26. Dean presents an interesting theoretical model of supernatural power by polarizing *sheng* and *ling* as opposites. He draws on the work of Stephen Feuchtwang, "School-Temple and City Gods," in *The City in Late Imperial China*, ed. G. W. Skinner (Palo Alto: Stanford University Press, 1977), 581–608. I disagree with Dean and Feuchtwang in their popularization of these two terms, attributing the former to Confucianism and the latter to popular religions. See my discussion below.
28. A. C. Graham, *Disputers of the Tao: Philosophical Argument in Ancient China* (La Salle, IL: Open Court, 1989), 497.
29. See, for example, Laurence G. Thompson, *Chinese Religion: An Introduction*, fifth ed. (Belmont: Wadsworth, 1996), 2–3.
30. For example, in his provocative article Kenneth Pomeranz sets up a polarity between "official" and "popular" forms of rain-making rituals. He argues that for officials, such rituals operated on the principle of *de*, which he translates as "virtue." For local communities, these rituals rested on the principle of *ling*, which he renders as "magical efficacy." See Kenneth Pomeranz, "Water to Iron, Widows to Warlords: The Handan Rain Shrine in Modern Chinese History," *LIC* 12 (1) (1991): 65, 75–76. The bifurcation is dealt with in more detail in chapter 5; also, in theorizing about the "syncretic field" of Chinese religions, Kenneth Dean polarizes the principles of *de* and *ling*; see Dean, *Lord of the Three in One*, 30–63, 273–95; also Edward L. Davis, *Society and the Supernatural in Song China* (Honolulu: University of Hawaii Press, 2001), 212–13.
31. For issues relating to the interactions of Western hegemony and internal signs of "modernity" in the later part of the Qing dynasty, see David Der-wei Wang and Shang Wei, *Dynastic Crisis and Cultural Innovation from the Late Ming to Late Qing and Beyond* (Cambridge, MA: Harvard University Press, 2005), esp., the introduction and part 3.
32. The idea that heaven or some other kind of cosmic force responds to the moral actions of human beings is ubiquitous in premodern China and has become part of the larger cultural repertoire to describe events and people. In this worldview, humans were not counterposed to a transcendent god. Instead, the cosmos was

tuned in, as it were, on humanity. The vast cosmos appears to be organically threaded onto the lives of exceptional individuals, so that everything in the way of illness, spiritual degeneration, political crisis, or droughts happens in concordance with their actions. The performers' power to affect the world was actualized by manipulating their body through the logic of sympathetic resonance. The macrocosm of the universe was accessed through the microcosm of the human body. Even debates over who or what was efficacious were steeped in the same cultural logic of sympathetic resonance. People may have had different views on who had the most efficacious power, but the beliefs that the cosmos responds to human actions and that bodily behavior affects the cosmic order were not challenged.

33. For an excellent monograph on foot binding see Dorothy Ko, *Cinderella's Sisters: A Revisionist History of Footbinding* (Berkeley: University of California Press, 2005).
34. I borrow this phrase from Foucault's "technology of the body." See Michel Foucault, *Discipline and Punish: The Birth of the Prison*, trans. Alan Sheridan (New York: Vintage, 1995), 24. Foucault borrowed the term from Marcel Mauss.
35. See Mary Douglas, *Purity and Danger: An Analysis of Concepts of Pollution and Taboo* (London: Ark, 1984 [originally published in 1966]), 115.
36. See Pierre Bourdieu, trans. Richard Nice, *The Logic of Practice* (Cambridge: Polity, 1990), 52–65.
37. See Marcel Mauss, "Body Techniques," in *Sociology and Psychology: Essays*, trans. Ben Bruster (London: Routledge and Kegan Paul, 1979), 95–123.
38. See Douglas, *Purity and Danger* (1984). For a critique of Douglas and other anthropological readings of the body see Talal Asad, "Remarks on the Anthropology of the Body," in *Religion and the Body*, ed. Sarah Coakley, 42–52 (Cambridge: Cambridge University Press, 1997).
39. This is called "analogical verification" by Elaine Scarry in *The Body in Pain: The Making and Unmaking of the World* (New York: Oxford University Press, 1985), 14.
40. A more detailed discussion of this appears in chapter 1.
41. See Michel Foucault, *Discipline and Punish*, 11.
42. This is an admittedly dramatic simplification of Butler's theories because she herself has altered her position. However, her earlier work nonetheless remains useful for my research on self-inflicted violence; see Judith Butler, *Bodies That Matter: On the Discursive Limits of "Sex"* (New York: Routledge, 1993), 1–55.
43. I discuss these books later.
44. See R. H. Van Gulik, *Erotic Colour Prints of the Ming Period: With an Essay on Chinese Sex Life from the Han to the Ch'ing Dynasty, b.c. 206–a.d. 1644* (Leiden: Brill, 2004), 105–204.
45. Talal Asad has cogently argued that "the body taught over time to listen, to recite, to move, to be silent, engaged with the acoustics of words, with their sound, feel, and look" is a deep and richly textured "disciplining of the senses"; see his *Formation*

of the Secular: Christianity, Islam, Modernity (Palo Alto, CA: Stanford University Press, 2003), 37–38.

46. In the late 1990s two scholars worked on Chinese Buddhist asceticism. John Kieschnick argues that the ascetic Buddhist monk was one of the archetypes in the medieval era who gained religious sanctity by isolating himself from other social groups in sexual, dietary, and sumptuary practices and, in extreme cases, self-mutilation and ritual suicide; see Kieschnick, *Eminent Monk*, 16–66. He also argues that the Buddhist practice of blood writing derived its power from the "doctrine of merit, veneration for physical suffering, and the powerful symbolism of blood as a mark of sincerity"; see Kieschnick, "Blood Writing in Chinese Buddhism," *JIABS* 23 (2) (2000): 193. James Benn, in his book *Burning for the Buddha* furthers these arguments by closely examining self-immolation, or "auto-cremation," in the *Gaosengzhuan* (*Biographies of Eminent Monks*) genre. He shows that self-immolation played a central role in the creation of "Chinese bodhisattvas," or enlightened saints, as narrated in the Indian scriptures through "apocryphal practices." The strength of their works is that each in his own way opens the field of religious and Buddhist studies of China to new possibilities; they have furthered earlier works by scholars such as Jacques Gernet and Jan Yün-hua; see Jacques Gernet, "Les suicides par le feu chez bouddhistes chinois de Ve au Xe siècle," *Mélanges publiés par l'Institut des Hautes Études Chinoises* 2 (1960), 527–58; Jan Yün-hua, "Buddhist Self-Immolation in Medieval China," *HR* 4 (1965): 243–65. I am indebted to them for their work. However, their approach is either restricted to a particular period or to a particular genre of texts, making the practice of austerities (or what I call self-inflicted violence) hermetically sealed within the medieval world of Buddhist piety. I see these Buddhist austerities as part of the larger pattern of self-inflicted violent practices in China (and East Asia).
47. As scholars have noted, historical periodization is problematic; it is often imposed on the past by historians for specific interpretive or strategic purposes. For this reason I have avoided the terms "late Ming" and "early Qing." Although I follow established academic practice of marking 1550 as the beginning of late Ming, I do not assume that a fundamental change or changes occurring in that year drew an unmistakable line of demarcation between 1550 and the periods that came before and after it. However, as I show in chapter 1, contemporary writers knew that they were living in a period of rapid changes and uncertainty.
48. For more information see, for example, Ray Huang, "The Lung-ch'ing and Wanli Reigns, 1567–1620," in *The Cambridge History of China*, vol. 7, pt. 1, ed. Frederick W. Mote and Denis Twitchett (Cambridge: Cambridge University Press, 1988), 511–84; and William Atwell, "The T'ai-ch'ang, T'ien-ch'i, and Ch'ung-chen Reigns, 1620–1644," in ibid., 585–640.
49. Robert Ford Campany, *To Live as Long as Heaven and Earth: A Translation and Study of Ge Hong's Traditions of Divine Transcendents* (Berkeley: University of California Press, 2002), 101.

50. See, for example, Bynum, *Holy Feast and Holy Fast*, 299–302; Felice Lifshitz, "Beyond Positivism and Genre: 'Hagiographical' Texts as Historical Narrative," *Viator* 25 (1994): 95–113; James Howard-Johnston and Paul Antony Hayward, ed., *The Cult of Saints in Late Antiquity and the Middle Ages: Essays on the Contribution of Peter Brown* (Oxford: Oxford University Press, 1999).
51. For an analysis of the extent to which the seventeenth-century Chinese novel can be taken as a guide to contemporary reality see Daria Berg, *Carnival in China: A Reading of the Xingshi yinyuan zhuan* (Leiden: Brill, 2002), 17; Glen Dudbridge, "A Pilgrimage in Seventeenth-Century Fiction: T'ai-shan and the *Hsing-shih yin-yuan chuan*," *TP* 77 (4–5) (1991): 226–52.
52. See Andrew Plaks, "After the Fall: *Hsing-shih yin-yüan chuan* and the Seventeenth-Century Chinese Novel," *HJAS* 45 (2) (1985): 543–80, 564. For an example of scholarship that denies the realistic integrity of novels see Maram Epstein, *Competing Discourses: Orthodoxy, Authenticity, and Engendered Meaning in Late Imperial Chinese Fiction* (Cambridge, MA: Harvard University Asia Center, 2001), 2. For a discussion on the relationship and construction of fictional and historical evidence outside of the China field see Suzanne Gearhart, *The Open Boundary of History and Fiction: A Critical Approach to the French Enlightenment* (Princeton, NJ: Princeton University Press, 1984), 5–8, 204.
53. Catherine Bell articulates this process as "ritualization," the strategic mode of practices that "produces nuanced relationships characterized by acceptance and resistance, negotiated negotiation, and redemptive reinterpretation of the hegemonic order." See *Ritual Theory, Ritual Practice* (New York: Oxford University Press, 1992), 196.

CHAPTER 1

1. For more information see for example Ray Huang, "The Lung-ch'ing and Wanli Reigns, 1567–1620," in Frederick W. Mote and Denis Twitchett, eds., *The Cambridge History of China*, vol. 7, pt. 1 (Cambridge: Cambridge University Press, 1988), 511–84; and William Atwell, "The T'ai-ch'ang, T'ien-ch'i, and Ch'ung-chen Reigns, 1620–1644," in ibid., 585–640.
2. Chinese historians' moral "decline" paradigm typically characterizes the decadence of the Wanli emperor, the corruption of the bureaucracy, and the profligacy of the society. These historians' strategy is to preserve and emphasize the correlation between political decline and human decadence. For an example of specific cases that undermine this paradigm, see Joanna Handlin Smith, *The Art of Doing Good: Charity in Late Ming China* (Berkeley: University of California Press, 2009), 161–92.
3. See Ray Huang, *1587, a Year of No Significance: The Ming Dynasty in Decline* (New Haven, CT: Yale University Press, 1981); Mi Chü Wiens, "Socioeconomic Change during the Ming Dynasty in Kiangnan Area," PhD diss., Harvard University,

1973. Scholars have also noted the increased interest among the population in the many uprisings and lay-oriented religious groups, which produced new kinds of literature, such as the *baojuan* 寶卷 or precious scrolls; see Sawada Mizuho 澤田瑞穂, *Hōkan no kenkyū* 寶卷の研究 (Tokyo: Kokusho Kankōkai, 1975); Daniel L. Overmyer, *Precious Volumes: An Introduction to Chinese Sectarian Scriptures from the Sixteenth and Seventeenth Centuries* (Cambridge, MA: Published by the Harvard University Asia Center: Distributed by Harvard University Press, 1999); Tanaka Masatoshi, "Popular Uprisings, Rent Resistance, and Bondservant Rebellions in the Late Ming," in *State and Society in China: Japanese Perspectives on Ming-Qing Social and Economic History*, ed. Linda Grove and Christian Daniels (Tokyo: University of Tokyo Press, 1989), 79–100.

4. For a more judicious overview of interpretations of the late Ming social tensions see Martin Heijdra, "The Socio-Economic Development of Rural China during the Ming," in *The Cambridge History of China*, vol. 8, *The Ming Dynasty, 1368–1644*, part 2, ed. by Frederick W. Mote and Denis Twitchett (Cambridge: Cambridge University Press, 1998), 417–578.
5. See Dwight H. Perkins, with the assistance of Yeh-chien Wang, Kuo-ying Wang Hsiao, and Fung-ming Su, *Agricultural Development in China, 1368–1968* (Chicago: Aldine, 1969), 33; Evelyn Sakakida Rawski, *Agricultural Change and the Peasant Economy of South China* (Cambridge, MA: Harvard University Press, 1972), 1–100; Mark Elvin, *The Pattern of the Chinese Past* (Palo Alto, CA: Stanford University Press, 1973), 268–84.
6. See Timothy Brook, *The Confusions of Pleasure: Commerce and Culture in Ming China* (Berkeley: University of California Press, 1998), 81–82, 89; William S. Atwell, "Another Look at Silver Imports into China, ca. 1635–1644," *Journal of World History* 16 (4) (December 2005): 467–89.
7. See Andrew H. Plaks, *The Four Masterworks of the Ming Novel* (Princeton, NJ: Princeton University Press, 1987), 14; Liang Fang-chung, *The Single Whip Method (I-T'iao-Pien Fa) of Taxation in China*, trans. Wang Yü-ch'uan (Cambridge, MA: Harvard University Press, 1956); Ray Huang, *Taxation and Governmental Finance in Sixteenth-Century Ming China* (London: Cambridge University Press, 1974), 120, 299.
8. See summary by Plaks, *Four Masterworks of the Ming Novel*, 3–52.
9. See Willard J. Peterson, *Bitter Gourd: Fang I-Chih and the Impetus for Intellectual Change* (New Haven: Yale University Press, 1979), 69.
10. See Barend ter Haar, *The White Lotus Teachings in Chinese Religious History* (Leiden: Brill, 1992), and Daniel L. Overmyer, *Precious Volumes: An Introduction to Chinese Sectarian Scriptures from the Sixteenth and Seventeenth Centuries* (Cambridge, MA: Published by the Harvard University Asia Center: Distributed by Harvard University Press, 1999).
11. See Mi Chü Wiens, "Cotton Textile Production and Rural Social Transformation in Early Modern China," *Journal of the Institute of Chinese Studies of the Chinese University of Hong Kong* 7 (2) (1974): 515–35.

12. See Hanchao Lu, "Arrested Development: Cotton and Cotton Markets in Shanghai, 1350–1843," *Modern China* 18 (4) (October 1992): 468–99.
13. See Joanna F. Handlin, *Action in Late Ming Thought* (Berkeley: University of California Press, 1983), 22.
14. On the demographic changes in the sixteenth century, see Ho Ping-ti, *Studies on the Population of China, 1368–1953* (Cambridge, MA: Harvard University Press, 1959), 262; Michel Cartier, "Nouvelles données sur la démographie chinoise à l'époque des Ming, 1368–1644," *Annales: Économies, Sociétés, Civilisations* 28 (6) (November–December 1973): 1341–59. For developments in urban areas see Michael Marmé, "Population and Possibility in Ming Suzhou: A Quantified Model," *MS* 12 (Spring 1981): 29–64.
15. See Elvin, *Pattern of the Chinese Past*, 269–71.
16. See Lü Kun, *Shizheng lu*, in *Lüzi yishu* 18–24 *ce*, 3:42b–43a.
17. For the distance between the elite and the commoners, see von Glahn's study of social reform movements and popular protests against the elite in Jiangnan cities; Richard von Glahn, "Municipal Reform and Urban Social Conflict," in *JAS* 50 (2) (May 1991): 280–307.
18. See Wang Lanyin 王蘭蔭, "Mingdai zhi xiangyue yu minzhong jiaoyu 明代之鄉約與民衆教育," *Shida yuekan* 師大月刊 21 (1935): 103–22.
19. See Lü Kun 呂坤 (1536–1618), *Shizheng lu* 實政錄, in *Lüzi yishu* 呂子遺書 18–24 *ce*, 2:18b; 2:16a–b. For the wide expansion of millenarian groups see footnote 3 in this chapter and Haar, *White Lotus Teachings in Chinese Religious History*, 114–246.
20. In the next chapter I discuss the blood writings of Yang Lian and others. For a biography of Yang Lian 楊漣 (1571–1625), see Chen Ding 陳鼎 (b. 1651), *Donglin lie zhuan* 東林列傳 (Taipei: Mingwen shuju, 1991), 157–61.
21. See Benjamin A. Elman, *A Cultural History of Civil Examinations in Late Imperial China* (Berkeley: University of California Press, 2000), 38.
22. See Timothy Brook, *Praying for Power: Buddhism and the Formation of Gentry Society in Late-Ming China* (Cambridge, MA: Council on East Asian Studies, Harvard, and Harvard-Yenching Institute: Distributed by Harvard University Press, 1993), 218. Although I agree with Brook's general observation of the revival of Buddhism during the late Ming, I disagree with his claim that such a revival was merely a public "arena" in which the gentry could convert status into power because, since power could not be seized from the imperial state, it could be taken only surreptitiously by funding Buddhist temples.
23. See Angela Ki Che Leung, "Elementary Education in the Lower Yangtze Region in the Seventeenth and Eighteenth Centuries," in *Education and Society in Late Imperial China, 1600–1900*, ed. Benjamin A. Elman and Alexander Woodside (Berkeley: University of California Press, 1994), 381–416, esp., 393–94; Evelyn Sakakida Rawski, *Education and Popular Literacy in Ch'ing China* (Ann Arbor: University of Michigan Press, 1979), 140. For a summary of the contents of the Four Books

and other classics for youth, see Elman, *Cultural History of Civil Examinations in Late Imperial China*, 272–73.

24. See John Meskill, trans., *Ch'oe Pu's Diary: A Record of Drifting across the Sea* (Tucson: University of Arizona Press for the Association for Asian Studies, 1965), 155.
25. See Rawski, *Education and Popular Literacy in Ch'ing China*, 23; Ellen Widmer, "The Epistolary World of Female Talent in Seventeenth-Century China," *LIC* 10 (2) (December 1989): 1–43; *LIC*, "Symposium on Poetry and Women's Culture in Late Imperial China," special issue, 13 (1) (June 1992).
26. On family-instruction books and the control of women see Charlotte Furth, "Patriarch's Legacy: Household Instructions and the Transmission of Orthodox Values," in *Orthodoxy in Late Imperial China*, ed. Kwang-Jing Liu (Berkeley: University of California Press, 1990), 196–97, 202 [187–211]. Furth also suggests (202) that women's ability to read religious texts may have represented one source of their potential "heterodoxy" in the family.
27. See John Dent-Young and Alex Dent-Young, *The Marshes of Mount Liang: A New Translation of the Shuihu zhuan or Water Margin of Shi Nai'an and Luo Guanzhong* (Hong Kong: Chinese University Press, 1994–2002).
28. Modern scholars concur that this development was spearheaded by figures such as Li Zhi 李贄 (1527–1602), the Yuan 袁 brothers, Tang Xianzu 湯顯祖 (1550–1616), and Feng Menglong 馮夢龍 (1574–1646); see Chun-shu Chang and Shelley Hsueh-lun Chang, *Crisis and Transformation in Seventeenth-Century China: Society, Culture, and Modernity in Li Yü's World* (Ann Arbor: University of Michigan Press, 1992), 162–66; Pi-Ching Hsu, *Beyond Eroticism: A Historian's Reading of Humor in Feng Menglong's* Child's Folly (Lanham, MD: University Press of America, 2006), 58–75; Martin W. Huang, *Desire and Fictional Narrative in Late Imperial China* (Cambridge, MA: Harvard University Press, 2001), 35–56; Richard G. Wang, "The Cult of Qing: Romanticism in the Late Ming Period and the Novel *Jiao Hong Ji*," *MS* 33 (August 1994): 15–17.
29. The term *qing* 情, which has been convincingly studied by Paolo Santangelo, should not be anachronistically contrasted with "reason" (*li* 理). The term *qing* basically means feelings or affective states of mind (*ganqing* 感情), inclination or affection (*qingyu* 情欲), circumstances (*qingkuang* 情況), and authenticity (*cheng* 誠). For example, the idea of *ganqing*, which we usually understand as emotions, passions, or sentiments, also includes a propensity for or an inclination toward something and an original, characteristic, and intrinsic nature, but it lacks any sense of being opposed to "reason." Thus, the term was used to convey a range of affective states, such as filiality and loyalty. Writers of this time even elevated it to the same metaphysical status as that of the principle of heaven; see Paolo Santangelo, *Sentimental Education in Chinese History: An Interdisciplinary Textual Research on Ming and Qing Sources* (Leiden: Brill, 2003), 149.

30. See Plaks, *Four Masterworks of the Ming Novel*, 20; Liu Hui 劉輝 and Yang Yang 揚揚, eds., *"Jin Ping Mei" zhi mi* 金瓶梅之謎 (Shumu wenxian chubanshe, 1989), 220–22.
31. See Martin Huang, *Desire and Fictional Narrative in Late Imperial China*, 5–22; Chen Dongyou 陳東有, *Reyu de jiefang: Ming Qing shehui jingji bianqian yu dazhong shenmei* 人欲的解放：明清社會經濟變遷與大衆審美 (Nanchang: Jiangxi gaoxiao chubanshe, 1996); Wang Yuji 王育濟, *Tianli yu renyu* 天理與人欲 (Ji'nan: Qi Lu shushe, 1992), 194–431; Mizoguchi Yūzō 溝口雄三, *Chūgoku zen kindai shisō no kussetsu to tenkai* 中国前近代思想の屈折と展開 (Tokyo: Tōkyō Daigaku Shuppankai, 1980); Chung-ying Cheng, "Reason, Substance, and Human Desire in Seventeenth-Century Neo-Confucianism," in Wm. Theodore de Bary, ed., *The Unfolding of Neo-Confucianism* (New York: Columbia University Press, 1975), 469–509.
32. See Patricia Sieber, "Turning Lethal Slander into Generative Instruction: Laws, Ledgers, and Changing Taxonomies of Fictional Production in Late Imperial China," in *The Magnitude of Ming: Command, Allotment, and Fate in Chinese Culture*, ed. Christopher Lupke (Honolulu: University of Hawaii Press, 2005), 214–15.
33. The scholar in question was Jin Shengtan 金聖嘆 (1608–1661). As a result of the widespread influence of his interpretation, he was beheaded by the state. See Sieber, "Turning Lethal Slander into Generative Instruction," 219–20.
34. See Chen Que 陳確, "Wuyu zuo sheng bian" 無欲作聖辯, in *Chen Que ji* 陳確集 (Beijing: Zhonghua shuju, 1979), 461.
35. See Elman, *Cultural History of Civil Examinations in Late Imperial China*, 261.
36. See Brook, *Praying for Power*, 119–26; Yü Chün-fang, *The Renewal of Buddhism in China: Chu-Hung and the Late Ming Synthesis* (New York: Columbia University Press, 1981), 11–15. Many Buddhist clerics during the Ming dynasty had close associations with the literati; some identified themselves as such. Their literati disciples often blended teachings and methods of cultivation from different traditions. Many of those who were part of the network of late Ming monks and laymen participated in the *qing* literature movement, according to Jennifer Eichmann in "Spiritual Seekers in a Fluid Landscape: A Chinese Network in the Wanli Period (1573–1620)," PhD diss., Princeton University, 2005.
37. See Martin Huang, *Desire and Fictional Narrative*, 36.
38. See Li Zhongfu 李中馥, "Liancai haoju 憐才豪舉," in his *Yuan Li erzai* 原李耳載, in Wang Wenru 王文濡, comp., *Shuoku* 說庫, vol. 2 (Shanghai, 1915; reprinted in Hangzhou: Zhejiang guji, 1986), 7.
39. For example, the life of Tang Xianzu 湯顯祖 (1550–1616); see Xu Shuofang 徐朔方, "Tang Xianzu nianpu" 湯顯祖年譜 in *Xu Shuofang ji* 徐朔方集 (Hangzhou: Zhejiang guji, 1995), 4: 201–469.

40. See, for example, the observation of a late Qing–early modern thinker, Liang Qichao 梁啓超 (1873–1929), *Intellectual Trends in the Ch'ing Period* (*Qingtai xueshuo gailun* 情代學説概論), translated with introduction and notes by Immanuel C. Y. Hsü. Foreword by Benjamin I. Schwartz (Cambridge, MA: Harvard University Press, 1959), 28.
41. For a general survey of some of the neo-Confucian thinkers, see Willard Peterson, "Confucian Learning in Late Ming Thought" in *The Cambridge History of China*, ed. Denis Twitchett and John K. Fairbank, vol. 8, *The Ming Dynasty*, part 2, 708–88 (Cambridge: Cambridge University Press, 1998).
42. See Okada Takehiko 冈田武彥, *Ō Yōmei to Minmatsu no jugaku* 王陽明と明末の儒學 (Tokyo: Kōmeisha 1970).
43. For an excellent summary of Wang Yangming's students, including He Xinyin, see Peterson, "Confucian Learning in Late Ming Thought."
44. On the popular presentation of the syncretism, see, for example, Judith Berling, "Path of Convergence: Interactions of Inner Alchemy, Taoism, and Neo-Confucianism," *JCP* 6 (2) (June 1979): 123–47.
45. For a good summary of late imperial tendency toward syncretism, see Timothy Brook, "Rethinking Syncretism: The Unity of the Three Teachings and Their Joint Worship in Late Imperial China," *JCR* 21 (Fall 1993): 13–44.
46. Late Ming men like Lin Zhao'en 林兆恩 (1517–1598) and Jiao Hong 焦竑 (1541–1620) developed new kinds of "syncretic logic," asserting that the three teachings "possessed the integrity of a single entity"; see Edward T. Ch'ien, *Chiao Hung and the Restructuring of Neo-Confucianism in the Late Ming* (New York: Columbia University Press, 1986), 14; for the influence and subsequent development of Lin Zhao'en's thought up to modern times see also Kenneth Dean, *Lord of the Three in One: The Spread of a Cult in Southeast China* (Princeton, NJ: Princeton University Press, 1998).
47. See Brook, "Rethinking Syncretism," 27–33.
48. The well-known Buddhist cleric Ouyi Zhixu 蕅益智旭 (1599–1655), for example, was famous not only for his self-inflicted violent practices (discussed in the following chapter) but also for his eclecticism. His writings reveal substantial knowledge not only of Buddhist scriptures but also of Confucian classics and Daoist works. He wrote a work titled *Chan Interpretation of Zhou Changes* (*Zhouyi Chanjie* 周易禪解), which explicated the hexagrams of the *Book of Changes* in terms of various states of *samādhi*, or meditative absorption, and *prajñā*, or wisdom. In this work he ascribes Buddhist attributes to the hexagram lines and shows that the deeper meanings of the *Book of Changes* can be explained only through the Buddhist teachings. In the introduction he unabashedly states, "I am explicating the *Changes* for no other reason than to use Chan to penetrate *ru* 儒—in order that those who subscribe to it [might then] be encouraged to know Chan [Buddhism]." Thus, despite the syncretism, the text was an effort to assert the supremacy of

Buddhism. Even though his commentary contained much intertextuality and mutual appropriation of rituals and religious language, the identities of the three teachings were still distinct. See Douglas Alan White, "Interpretations of the Central Concept of the I-Ching during the Han, Sung, and Ming Dynasties," PhD diss., Harvard University, 1976, 183–86; see also Thomas Cleary, *The Buddhist I Ching* (Boston: Shambhala, 1987).

49. See Cynthia Brokaw, *The Ledgers of Merit and Demerit: Social Change and Moral Order in Late Imperial China* (Princeton, NJ: Princeton University Press, 1991); and a more recent study, Joanna Handlin Smith, *The Art of Doing Good*, 255–62. For confessions see Rodney L. Taylor, "The Centered Self: Religious Autobiography in the Neo-Confucian Tradition," *HR* 17 (3–4) (February–June 1978): 266–84; Wu Pei-yi, "Self-Examination and Confession of Sins in Traditional China," *HJAS* 39 (1979): 5–38. Many of the Ming Buddhist clerics also wrote tracts on merit and demerit; see Yunqi Zhuhong's *Record of Self-Knowledge* in Yü Chün-fang, *Renewal of Buddhism in China*, 238, 249–50. The Buddhist monk Ouyi Zhixu 溝益智旭 (1599–1655) also wrote on divination practices based on an apocryphal scripture (*Zhancha jing* 占察經), in relation to changing one's fate; see, for example, *Lingfeng zonglun* 靈峰宗論 (Taipei: Shihua guoji gufen youxian gongsi, 2004), and Sheng Yen's study of Ouyi, Zhang Shengyan 張聖嚴, *Minmatsu Chūgoku Bukkyō no kenkyū: toku ni Chigyoku o chūshin to shite* 明末中國佛教の研究: 特に智旭を中心として (A Study of Chinese Buddhism at the End of the Ming Dynasty and Master Ouyi Zhixu) (Tōkyō: Sankibo Busshorin, 1975), 204, 245; Beverley Foulks, "Living Karma: The Religious Practices of Ouyi Zhixu (1599–1655)," PhD diss., Harvard University, 2009; and May-Ying Mary Ngai, "From Entertainment to Enlightenment: A Study on a Cross-Cultural Religious Board Game with an Emphasis on the Table of Buddha Selection Designed by Ouyi Zhixu of the Late Ming Dynasty," PhD diss., University of British Columbia, 2011. In the next chapter I discuss Ouyi's engagement with self-inflicted violence.

50. See Sieber, "Turning Lethal Slander into Generative Instruction," 209–15; Brokaw, *Ledgers of Merit and Demerit*, 35. For a discussion of the complexity of morality books as a genre see Catherine Bell, "'A Precious Raft to Save the World': The Interaction of Scriptural Traditions and Printing in a Chinese Morality Book," *LIC* 17 (1) (1996): 160–61.

51. This interest in calculation may be connected with the literati's renewed interest in numerology. For example, one of the three distinct contributions of *Yijing* 易經 scholarship during the Yuan and Ming eras was the technical "arts of calculation." The Ming dynasty alone produced more than six hundred major commentaries on this classic; see Richard Smith, *Fathoming the Cosmos and Ordering the World: The Yijing (I Ching, or Classic of Changes) and Its Evolution in China* (Charlottesville: University of Virginia Press, 2008), 140–79; 157.

52. See chapter 3 for a case of "filial slicing."

53. See Karl S. Y. Kao, "*Bao* and *Baoying*: Narrative Causality and External Motivations in Chinese Fiction," in *Chinese Literary Essays* 11 (December 1989): 115–38.
54. For a study of filial piety, see Keith Nathaniel Knapp, *Selfless Offspring: Filial Children and Social Order in Medieval China* (Honolulu: University of Hawaii Press, 2005), 4. These stories were regularly cited in the sixteenth and seventeenth centuries.
55. On this "dilemma," see Frederick Wakeman Jr., "Price of Autonomy: Intellectuals in Ming and Ch'ing Politics," *Daedalus* 101 (Spring 1972): 35–70.
56. See Goodrich and Fang, *Dictionary of Ming Biographies*, 1325; and Xu Shuofang, "Tu Long nianpu," 341–48; citation from Martin Huang, *Desire and Fictional Narrative in Late Imperial China*, 18.
57. See Martin Huang, *Desire and Fictional Narrative in Late Imperial China*, 8.
58. See Brook, *Confusions of Pleasure*. While providing some original scholarship, Brook covers much of the same ground as "Communications and Commerce," in Denis Twitchett and Frederick W. Mote, eds. *The Cambridge History of China*, vol. 8, *The Ming Dynasty, 1368–1644* (Cambridge: Cambridge University Press, 1998), part 2, 579–707, and Shigeta Atsushi, "The Origins and Structure of Gentry Rule," in *State and Society in China: Japanese Perspectives on Ming-Qing Social and Economic History*, ed. Linda Grove and Christian Daniels (Tokyo: University of Tokyo Press, 1984), 335–85.

CHAPTER 2

1. See below for the full citation.
2. The most extensive study of blood writing in the Buddhist context is Zhang Shengyan, *Minmatsu Chūgoku Bukkyō no kenkyū*, 224–30. Shengyan documents twenty-one people, both lay and monastic, during the late Ming who engaged in the practice. See also John Kieschnick, "Blood Writing in Chinese Buddhism," *JIABS* 23 (2) (2000): 177–94. Most of the theoretical and doctrinal points in Kieschnick's article have already been covered by Shengyan. Other scholars, such as Sung-peng Hsu, *A Buddhist Leader in Ming China* (University Park: Pennsylvania State University Press, 1979, 72–75) discuss the practice only in passing. I have found only one author who discusses blood writing from other than a Buddhist perspective: Daphne P. Lei, "The Blood-Stained Text in Translation: Tattooing, Bodily Writing, and Performance of Chinese Virtue," *Anthropological Quarterly* 82 (1) (2009): 99–128. Lei speculates briefly on the practice of blood writing for women, arguing that for them this practice "heightened the feminine sexual allure for male viewers" and provided them with an auteurship that had bestowed control as author, director, and performer (119–20) of blood writing. The problem with this interpretation is the failure to see that records of blood writing come to us already theorized and theologized by mostly male authors and redactors. Women are subordinated to

men in premodern Chinese literature in that they are consistently made subservient to men by the very structure of the narratives in which they appear.

3. For examples of scholarship that propose this normative viewpoint, see the introduction to the newest translation of the classic of filial piety by Henry Rosemont Jr. and Roger T. Ames, *The Chinese Classic of Family Reverence: A Philosophical Translation of the* Xiaojing; for a textbook account of "Confucianism" and the role of filial piety in the Chinese kinship system, see Laurence G. Thompson, *Chinese Religion: An Introduction* (Belmont: Wadsworth, 1996), 31–52.
4. Premodern China was a graphocentric culture, an "empire of the text," in that text and textualization dominated the mainstream culture. See Christopher Leigh Connery, *The Empire of the Text: Writing and Authority in Early Imperial China* (Lanham, MD: Rowman and Littlefield, 1998); Mark Edward Lewis, *Writing and Authority in Early China* (Albany: State University of New York Press, 1999).
5. See the first chapter of the *Xiaojing* 孝經 (*Classic of Filial Piety*). For this translation I have revised that of James Legge, *The Sacred Books of China: The Texts of Confucianism*, part 1, *The Hsiâo King* (New York: Scribner, 1899), 465. For an alternative translation see Patricia Ebrey, ed., *Chinese Civilization: A Sourcebook* (New York: Free Press, 1993), 64–68. For the dating of *The Classic of Filial Piety* see William G. Boltz, "Hsiao Ching," in *Early Chinese Texts*, ed. Michael Loewe, 141–53 (Berkeley: Society for the Study of Early China, 1993), 142–44; Itano Chōhachi 板野長八, *Jukyō seiritsushi no kenkyū* 儒教成立史の研究 (Tōkyō: Iwanami Shoten, 1995), 1–50; Keith N. Knapp, *Selfless Offspring: Filial Children and Social Order in Medieval China* (Honolulu: University of Hawaii Press, 2005), 90; Watanabe Shinichirō 渡部信一朗, "Kōkyō no seiritsu to sono haikei 孝經の成立とその背景," *Shirin* 69 (1) (1986): 53–86; Chen Tiefan 陳鐵凡, *Xiaojingxue yuanliu* 孝經學源流 (Taipei: Guoli bianyiguan, 1986), 41–60; and Ikezawa Masaru 池澤優, "The Philosophy of Filial Piety in Ancient China," PhD diss., University of British Columbia, 1994, 117–46; 198–244.
6. See, for example, assertions of Wang Gen (1483–1540) in William de Bary, *Learning for Oneself: Essays on the Individual in Neo-Confucian Thought* (New York: Columbia University Press, 1991), 164.
7. In translating this, I have consulted Legge's translation in *Sacred Books of China*, 485. For an alternative translation see Keith N. Knapp, *Selfless Offspring: Filial Children and Social Order in Medieval China* (Honolulu: University of Hawaii Press, 2005), 91. For stimulus-response see Feng Youlan 馮友蘭, *A History of Chinese Philosophy*, vol. 2 (Princeton, NJ: Princeton University Press, 1983), 2: 30; Dong Zhongshu 董仲舒 (ca. 179–104 B.C.E.), *Chunqiu fanlu zhuzi suoyin* 春秋繁露逐字索引, ed. D. C. Lau (Taipei: Commercial Press, 1994), 13.2; Robert Sharf, *Coming to Terms with Chinese Buddhism: A Reading of the Treasure Store Treatise* (Honolulu: University of Hawaii Press, 2002), 77–133.
8. For a fuller discussion see the next chapter, which discusses filial body slicing.

9. Scholars have also pointed out that during the late Ming numerous people sacrificed their own lives for their ailing parents in the hope of bringing cosmic reward to them. The "cliff for abandoning life" (*sheshen ya* 舍身崖), near the top of Mount Tai (*taishan* 泰山), for example, was the site of many filial suicides. People believed that if they sacrificed themselves by jumping off this cliff, the mountain deities would look kindly upon the merits accrued by this act of "filial duty" and restore the ailing parent to health. They believed that a sick parent's life could be extended only through a reciprocal shortening of the life of the youngest child. The practice became so prevalent that in 1523 the governor of Shandong, He Qiming 何起鳴, ordered that a wall three hundred feet long and fifteen feet high be erected at the top of the cliff in order to prevent people from jumping off the precipice. An inscription on the wall stated, "False sacrifice is false love." He also changed the name to "cliff for loving life" (*aishen ya* 愛身崖). However, despite the wall, the warnings, and the renaming, people continued leaping to their death from this cliff as late as 1924. See Brian R. Dott, *Identity Reflections: Pilgrimages to Mount Tai in Late Imperial China* (Cambridge: Harvard University Asia Center, 2004), 69; Nie Qin 聶欽, *Taishan daoli ji* 泰山道里記 (*An Itinerary of Mount Tai*) (Taipei: Yiwen yinshu guan, 1968), 23; Édouard Chavannes, *Le T'ai chan: Essai de monographie d'un culte chinois. Appendice: Le dieu du sol dans la Chine antique* (Paris: Leroux, 1910), 63; Dwight Condo Baker, *T'ai Shan: An Account of the Sacred Eastern Peak of China* (Shanghai: Commercial Press, 1925), 144–45.
10. The three scriptures in question are *Fumu en nanbao jing* 父母恩難報經, *Fumu en zhong jing* 父母恩重經, *Fumu enzhong nanbao jing* 父母恩重難報經; see Yü Chün-fang, *Kuan-yin: The Chinese Transformation of Avalokiteśvara* (New York: Columbia University Press, 2001), 346–47.
11. Hanshan Deqing and Ouyi Zhixu mention and wrote prefaces for numerous clerics and laymen in their day who copied Buddhist scriptures in blood; see *Bashibazu daoying zhuanzan* 八十八祖道影傳贊, X. no. 1608, 86: 644b11, for the case of Songying Ran chanshi 松隱然禪師 (ca. fourteenth century). For Daguan Zhenke 達觀真可 (1543–1603), who wrote "若不究心。坐禪徒增業苦。如能護念。罵佛猶益真修" in 647c15 (also recorded in a stele dedicated to him), see *Hanshan laoren mengyou ji*, X. no. 1456, 73: 653b03, and *Zibo zunzhe quanji* 紫柏尊者全集, by Hanshan Deqing in X. no. 1452, 73: 263a3–b21, 272b2–c14, 273a3–a16). See also the case of the head monk Foling Gan 佛嶺乾首座, who copied the *Avataṃsaka Sūtra*, *Hanshan laoren mengyou ji* 憨山老人夢遊集 (*Collection of the Dream Roaming of the Old Man, Hanshan*), X. no. 1456, 73: 480b24. Other cases in this collection include the case of Haikuo Chan man 海濶禪人, who copied the *Avataṃsaka Sūtra*, in 520b09; the case of Xingchu Xingyuan Chan man 惺初性元禪人 in 521a1; the case of Danju Fakai 澹居法鎧, a disciple of Zhenke (X. no. 1456, 73: 608c6), who copied the *Classic of Filial Piety* (*Xiaojing* 孝經) when he was still a layman and later copied the *Brahma Net Scripture* (*Fanwang jing* 梵網經), 665c24; his biography is

summarized in an epigraphy: X. no. 1456, 73: 665c13–666c16; the case of layman Zhengguang 正光居士, who copied the *Diamond Sūtra*, *Samatabhadra's Vows*, and chapters from the *Lotus Scripture*, 669c22–3; the case of Miaofeng Fudeng 妙峰福登, who copied the *Avataṃsaka Sūtra* with blood from his tongue, 675b23; the case of the Chan man Lin 麟禪人, who copied the *Avataṃsaka Sūtra*, 681c07; the case of Jia Xueren 賀學仁居士, who copied the *Diamond Sūtra*, 682a15; the case of the śramaṇa Fanjue 方覺沙彌, who copied the *Diamond Sūtra*, 682b13; the case of Changshou Sanfeng bhikshu 常熟三峰比丘, who copied the *Lotus Scripture*, 682c02; the case of the Chan man Gongquan 公全禪人, who copied the *Lotus Scripture*, 682c12; the case of Xuelang Hong'en 雪浪洪恩 (1545–1608), who copied the *Brahma Net Scripture* (*Fanwang jing* 梵網經) with blood from his tongue, 683a05; the case of layman Zhang An 張安, who copied the *Diamond Sūtra*, 698a21; the case of a novice, Zuanzhu 選諸, who copied the *Avataṃsaka Sūtra*, 827c10; another novice monk at Caoxi 曹溪, who copied a chapter from the *Avataṃsaka Sūtra*, the "Samatabhadra's Practice and Vows" (Puxian xingyuan ping 普賢行願品), 828a10; and Deqing's own votive text, excerpted from the *Avataṃsaka Sūtra* and inspired by reading Nanyue's 南嶽 votive text, written in his blood, 758c11, and the whole *Avataṃsaka Sūtra* itself, see *Bashibazu daoying zhuanzan*, X. no. 1608, 86: 649a3 and 651b10.

See Ouyi Zhixu, *Lingfeng zonglun* 靈峰宗論 (Taipei: Shihua guoji gufen youxian gongsi, 2004), 540, 785, 786, 1094.

12. See chapter 1 for a discussion of the movement of *qing*, or passion. Scholars of Chinese literature claim that this movement to express individual subjectivity and genuineness became a cult of sentiment. In Raymond Williams's term, this cultural shift is best described as a change in the "structures of feeling" of a society, where the "particular quality of social experience and relationship, historically distinct from other particular qualities…gives the sense of a generation or of a period"; see Raymond Williams, *Marxism and Literature* (Oxford: Oxford University Press, 1977), 131.
13. See *Jingang chiyan ji* 金剛經持驗紀 by Zhou Kefu 周克復 (date unknown; hereafter as d.u.), X. no. 1635, 87: 548b; *Jushi zhuan* 居士傳 by Peng Shaosheng 彭绍升 (1740–1796), X. no. 1646, 88: 204c.
14. For related scriptural miracle tales, or the *yanji* 驗記 genre of Buddhist literature, see, for example, *Dafangguang fo huayanjing ganying zhuan* 大方廣佛華嚴經感應傳 by the layman Wusheng 無生居士 (d.u.), T. no. 2074, 51: 173b3–178b10, esp. 177a14. Many popular Buddhist scriptures in East Asia had miracle tales associated with them. Most of these tales are not necessarily commensurate with the particular scripture's doctrinal position. Below, I argue for the connection between the message and the medium of Buddhist scripture.
15. See *Jushi zhuan* 居士傳, X. no. 1646, 88: 204c22.
16. Buddhist apologists, both clerical and lay, have facilitated this blending of indigenous Chinese value with Buddhist self-sacrifice. In one widely circulated seventh-century Buddhist collectanea (*leishu* 類書), the *Forest of Pearls in the Garden of*

the Dharma, a special section is devoted to filial piety, in which the practice of "devoting all of one's life to being entirely filial (*zhongshen jingxiao* 終身盡孝)" is considered "the splendor of state building" and "the means to repay the kindness of parents for giving birth to one's flesh and body (*roushen* 肉身)." See *Fayuan zhulin* 法苑珠林 (*Forest of Pearls in the Garden of the Dharma*) by Daoshi 道世 (d. 682) in 668, T. no. 2122, 53: 654c13–17. For a study of this text and its author see Chen Yuzhen 陳昱珍, "Daoshi yu *Fayuan zhulin* 道世與法苑珠林," *ZHFXXB* 中華佛學學報 5 (July 1992): 233–62. The *Fayuan zhulin* makes explicit connections between demonstrating parental fealty and perfecting Buddha's wisdom. Citing more than thirty disparate scriptures and treatises, this work details the crucial relevance of filial piety for Buddhists. These scriptures include the *Scripture of King Malla* (*Foshuo moluowang jing* 佛說末羅王經), T. no. 517, 14; *Increased by One Āgama Sutras* (*Zengyi ahan jing* 增一阿含經), T. no. 125, 2: 549a–830b; *Scripture of Forty-Two Sections* (*Sishierzhang jing* 四十二章經), T. no. 784, 17: 722c1–5; *Sūtra of the Repository of Miscellaneous Treasures* (*Zabaozang jing* 雜寶藏經), T. no. 203, 4; *Scripture of Great Expedient Means in the Buddha's Compassionate Recompense* (*Dafangbian fo baoen jing* 大方便佛報恩經), T no. 156, 3: 124–67; *Selected Collection of One Hundred Avadāna Tales* (*Xuanji baiyuan jing* 撰集百緣經), T. no. 200, 4: 203–257; *Scripture on Upāsaka Precepts* (*Youpose jie jing* 優婆塞戒經), T. no. 1488, 24: 1034a–1075b; *Scripture on the Correct Dharma of the Foundations of Mindfulness* (*Zhengfa nianchu jing* 正法念處經), T. no. 721, 17: 1a–417c; in *Sarvāstivāda Treatise* (*Suopoduo lun* 薩婆多論), it is unclear which Sarvāstivāda treatise (*Suopoduo lun* 薩婆多論) the *Fayua nzhulin* 法苑珠林 is referring to; *Great Wisdom of Transcendence Treatise* (*Dazhi du lun* 大智度論), T. no. 1509, 25: 57c–756b; and *New Bhāṣā Treatise* (*Xin bosha lun* 新婆沙論): It is unclear which *Vibhāṣā-śāstra* it is, but I believe it refers to the *Apidamo da piposha lun* 阿毘達磨大毘婆沙論; Skt. *Abhidharma-mahāvibhāṣā-śāstra* in 200 *juan* by Kātyāyanīputra 迦多衍尼子 (d.u.), probably composed in Kashmir around 100 C.E., trans. Xuanzang 玄奘 (600–664) between 656 and 659, T. no. 1545, 27: 1a–1004a. Michihata Ryōshū has done an excellent study on some of the scriptures cited in this note; see Michihata Ryōshū 道端良秀, *Chūgoku Bukkyō to Jukyō rinri kō to no kōshō* 中国仏教と儒教倫理孝との交渉, in *Chūgoku Bukkyō shi zenshū* 中国仏教史全集, vol. 9 (Tōkyō: Shoen, 1985), 83–101.

17. See, for example, Edward Conze, *The Perfection of Wisdom in Eight Thousand Lines and Its Verses* (Bolinas, CA: Four Seasons Foundation, 1973), 104–106; Burton Watson, *The Lotus Sutra* (New York: Columbia University Press, 1993), 324; and the *Da fangguang fo huayan jing* 大方廣佛華嚴經 (*The Great Vaipulya Buddha Flower Ornament Scripture*; Skt., *Buddhāvataṃsaka-mahāvaipulya-sūtra*), trans. Prajñā 般若 ca. 800, T. no. 293, 10: 845c.
18. Gregory Schopen has argued, for example, for the connection between Mahāyāna texts, using the *Diamond Sūtra* as an example, and the cult of books; see Gregory

Schopen, "The Phrase 'sa pṛthivīpradeśaś caityabhūto bhavet' in the Vajracchedikā: Notes on the Cult of the Book in Mahāyāna," in *Figments and Fragments of Mahayana Buddhism in India: More Collected Papers* (Honolulu: University of Hawaii, 2005), 25–62.

19. My translation is based on Edward Conze; see Edward Conze, *Buddhist Wisdom Books: Containing the Diamond Sutra and the Heart Sutra* (New York: Harper and Row, 1972; originally published 1958), 56. Original passage in *Jinggan bore boluomi jing* 金剛般若波羅蜜經, T. no. 235, 8: 750c21–23. Schopen also discusses this passage in "The Phrase 'sa pṛthivīpradeśaś caityabhūto bhavet' in the Vajracchedikā," 26–30.
20. See Conze, *Perfection of Wisdom in Eight Thousand Lines*, 116–17. This translation is of the *Aṣṭasāhasrikā-prajñāpāramitā Sūtra* or *Daoping bore jing* 道行般若波羅蜜經 (T. no. 224, 8), which is the oldest *Prajñāpāramitā* literature surviving in China.
21. See, for example, Ruben L. F. Habito, "Bodily Reading of the *Lotus Sūtra*," in Stephen Teiser and Jacqueline Stone, eds., *Readings of the Lotus Sūtra* (New York: Columbia University Press, 2009), 186–208.
22. See *Da fangguang fo huayan jing* 大方廣佛華嚴經 (Skt., *Buddhāvataṃsaka-mahāvaipulya-sūtra*), T. no. 293, 10: 845c.
23. "Sumeru" is a Sanskrit word; it translates into Chinese as "wondrously tall mountain" (*miaogao shan* 妙高山). In Buddhist cosmology, it is a towering mountain in the center of a great ocean, on a golden wheel, in the center of the universe. The mountain rises eighty thousand *yojanas* (an ancient Indian measurement of distance, approximately either four or nine miles; the issue is disputed) above sea level. It is surrounded by nine mountains and eight seas. The sun and moon circle it, and the six destinies and various heavens are around and above it. On its peak is *Trāyastrimśa*, heaven, where Indra lives. For Sumeru, see Mochizuki Shinkō 望月信亨 (1869–1948), ed., *Mochizuki Bukkyō daijiten* 望月佛教大辞典 (Tokyo: Sekai Seiten Kankō Kyōkai, 1954–1963), 2513a, 4437b; for *yojanas* or *youxun* 由旬, 737b, 4926a.
24. Passages of this sort also made it into the Chinese collection of monastic rules as an injunction, where all who seek to receive the bodhisattva precepts should aspire to do the same; see *Fanwang jing* 梵網經 (*Sūtra of Brahma's Net*), attributed to Kumārajīva (350–409) in 406, T. no. 1484, 24: 1009a. For translations of this work in Western languages, see Hui Seng, *Buddha Speaks the Brahma Net Sutra: The Ten Major and Forty-Eight Minor Bodhisattva Precepts* (Ukiah: Sino-American Buddhist Association, 1982); J. J. M. de Groot, *La Code du Mahâyâna en Chine: Son influence sur la vie monacale et sur le monde Laique*, bilingual ed. (Amsterdam, 1893). For a discussion of this work see Paul Groner, "The Fan-wang ching and Monastic Discipline in Japanese Tendai: A Study of Annen's Futsū jubosatsukai kōshaku," in *Chinese Buddhist Apocrypha*, ed. Robert E. Buswell Jr. (Honolulu: University of Hawaii, 1990), 251–89.
25. Among the two dozen or so contemporary performers who engaged in blood writing mentioned by the late Ming Buddhist monks Deqing and Ouyi, the *Lotus*

Scripture and the *Flower Ornament Scripture* were the most popular texts to copy. In the section titled "The Technology of Blood Writing" I hypothesize that performers usually chose a scripture to copy based not on doctrine but on the length of the text.

26. See L. Carrington Goodrich and Chao-ying Fang, eds., *Dictionary of Ming Biography* (New York: Columbia University Press, 1976), 445–48.
27. See my discussion of Wang Yangming in chapter 1; for an excellent study of and source citation on the impact of Wang Yangming in the intellectual, social, and political spheres of late Ming, leading to the downfall of the dynasty, see Jianhuang Chen 陳劍鍠, "Yangming houxue suo chansheng zhi zhu wenti 陽明後學所產生之諸問題 (The Various Problems That Arose from the Subsequent Followers of [Wang] Yangming)," *BMQS* 5 (2001): 161–200.
28. See *Gujin tushu jicheng* 古今圖書集成 by Chen Menglei 陳夢雷 (b. 1651) et al. (Taipei: Dingwen shuju, 1977), category: "human relationships" (*Minglun huibian* 明倫彙編), section: "government service" (*Guanchang dian* 官常典), under "Biographies of Eminent Officials" (Mingchen liezhuan 名臣列傳), *juan* 357, *ce* 284, 37.2. Hereafter, citations from *Gujin tushu jicheng* will be abbreviated as *GJTSJC*, followed by category, section, *juan*, *ce*, and page number.
29. See L. Carrington Goodrich and Chao-ying Fang, eds., *Dictionary of Ming Biography* (New York: Columbia University Press, 1976), 447.
30. See *Cixie shujing yuanwen* 刺血書經願文 ("A Votive Text on Drawing Blood to Write Scriptures") in *Lingfeng zonglun*, 26.
31. Ouyi Zhixu, *Lingfeng zong lun*, 791. More details on this doctrine can be found in *Yogācārabhūmi-śāstra* 瑜伽師地論 by Asaṅga (fourth century), T. no. 1579, 30: 327a19; *Cheng weishi lun* 成唯識論 (*Treatise on the Demonstration of Consciousness-Only*; Skt. **Vijñaptimātratāsiddhi-śāstra*) by Xuanzang 玄奘 (600–664) in 659, T. no. 1585, 31: 1a12; and scholarly studies by Stefan Anacker, *Seven Works of Vasubandhu* (Delhi: Motilal Banarsidass, 1984), 221–30; Charles Muller, "The Yogācāra Two Hindrances and Their Reinterpretations in East Asia," *JIABS* 27 (2004): 207–35; and Paul L. Swanson, "Chih-I's Interpretation of *Jñeyāvaraṇa*: An Application of the Three-Fold Truth Concept," *Annual Memoirs of the Otani University Shin Buddhist Comprehensive Research Institute*, vol. 1 (Kyōto: Ōtani Daigaku Shinshū Sōgō Kenkyūjo, 1983), 51–72.
32. For the vows by Huisi of Nanyue 南岳 or 南嶽慧思 (515–77) see *Nanyue Si dachanshi lishi yuanwen* 南嶽思大禪師立誓願文 by南嶽慧思 (515–577), T. no. 1933, 46: 786b. One of Huisi's vows was to engage in austere practices for the next fifty-six million years in all future rebirths so that the degeneration of dharma (*mofa* 末法) would never arrive.
33. This is recorded in his *Zixu nianpu* 自序年譜 autobiography written in 1622. See *Hanshan laoren mengyou ji*, X. no. 1456, 73: 836b1–836b4. For a brief discussion of the occasion in which Deqing engaged in blood writing and of his sponsor, Empress Dowager Li, see Sung-peng Hsu, *A Buddhist Leader in Ming China*, 72–75.

34. For a study of Nanyue Huisi's life and thought see Paul Magnin, *La vie et l'œuvre de Huisi (515–577): Les origines de la secte bouddhique chinoise du Tiantai* (Paris: École Française d'Extrême-Orient, 1979); Jan Nattier, *Once upon a Future Time: Studies in a Buddhist Prophecy of Decline* (Berkeley, CA: Asian Humanities Press, 1991), 110–11; and Daniel B. Stevenson, "Nanyue Huisi (515–577)—Recollections, Works, and Motifs," in *The Meaning of the Lotus Sūtra's Course of Ease and Bliss*, ed. Daniel B. Stevenson and Hiroshi Kanno (Tokyo: Meiwa, 2006), 3–182.
35. Translation by Stevenson, "Nanyue Huisi (515–577)—Recollections, Works, and Motifs," 41.
36. In the summer of 2007 my two months of research in China and Japan allowed me not only to view several hundred copies of Buddhist scriptures in private monastic libraries, public research libraries, and national museums but also to interview performers who engaged in blood writing. I conducted this research at the Yongquan Monastery 湧泉寺 on Mount Gu 鼓山 in Fujian province; the Beijing National Library; and the Sōtō temple, Fuzai-in 豊財院, in Ishikawa province, Japan, which houses the complete *Prajñāparamita Sūtra* in 600 *juans* in 700 accordion books. My monk informants are Huikong 慧空, who is one of the senior priors (*jianyuan* 監院) at Yongquan Monastery, and Weihui 惟慧, who was in charge of the temple collection of blood writings at Yongquan Monastery. I also interviewed Cao Zhengqun 曹正群, an elderly laywoman who lived and worked at the monastery and who offered blood for a resident monk named Renyi 仁一 to copy the *Diamond Sūtra* in 2004. Yongquan Monastery houses more than seven hundred copies of blood scriptures. According to the Weihui, the monastery began its collection of blood scriptures at least as early as the eleventh century but lost its entire collection to fire in the early Ming. Thus, the earliest blood scripture it now has dates only to 1638, the late Ming. The *sūtra* is the *Scripture on the Names of the Buddha as Expounded by the Buddha* (*Foshuofoming jing* 佛說佛名經) in twelve *juans* (T. no. 440, 14). I was also able to witness a blood-writing performance by a monk named Chuanfa 傳法, who resided near Yongquan Monastery. He used a simple razor blade and pricked and sliced the sublingual vessels of the underside of his tongue for blood. Blood flowed out freely, along with strands of tissue or fiber, down to three cups that held the blood. The practice is unquestionably painful.
37. Xuelang Hong'en was one of the most celebrated of the monks who promoted the *Flower Ornament Scripture* in the Jiangnan area. Xuelang and Hanshan both studied the *Flower Ornament Scripture* under Wuji Mingxin 無極明信 (1512–1574) at Bao'en Monastery in Nanjing. Later in his life he was drawn to Chan teachings. See Shengyan, *Mingmo fojiao yanjiu*, (Taipei: Dongchu chu ban she, 1987), 217; Liao Zhaoheng 廖肇亨, "Xuelang Hong'an chutan: Jianti Dongjing Neige wenku suocang 'Guxianglu' 雪浪洪恩初探: 兼題東京內閣文庫所藏'谷響錄,'" *Hanxue yanjiu* 漢學研究 14 (2) (December 1996): 35–57.
38. See "Postscript to the Brahma Net Scripture" (Xieshu Fanwang jing ba 血書梵網經跋), in *Hanshan laoren mengyou ji*, no. 1456, X 73: 683a19–683b.

39. See *Foshuo shi'er toutuo jing* 佛說十二頭陀經 (*The Buddha Explains the Twelve Dhūtaguṇas*), trans. Guṇabhadra (394–468), T. no. 783, 17: 720c. For Ouyi's preface see *Ke shi'er toutuo jing ba* 刻十二頭陀經跋 ("Postscript to the Carving of the Scripture of the Twelve Dhūtaguṇas") in *Lingfeng zonglun*, 786.
40. See Ouyi Zhixu, *Lingfeng zong lun*, 799.
41. See Liz Wilson, "Ascetic Practices," in *The Encyclopedia of Buddhism*, ed. Robert E. Buswell Jr. (New York: Macmillan, 2004), 32–34.
42. See Gregory Schopen, "Art, Beauty, and the Business of Running a Buddhist Monastery in Early Northwest India," in *Buddhist Monks and Business Matters: Still More Papers on Monastic Buddhism in India* (Honolulu: University of Hawaii, 2004), 26.
43. See, for example, those cases detailed by John Kieschnick, *The Eminent Monk: Buddhist Ideals in Medieval Chinese Hagiography* (Honolulu: University of Hawaii Press, 1997), 33–36.
44. Body slicing is discussed in chapter 3, and self-immolation in chapter 5. For an excellent study of Buddhist self-immolation see James Benn, *Burning for the Buddha: Self-Immolation in Chinese Buddhism* (Honolulu: University of Hawaii Press, 2007). Kieschnick argues that, by the tenth century, such "self-inflicted assaults on the body were an established form of ascetic practice"; see Kieschnick, *Eminent Monk*, 37.
45. See, for example, Hao Chunwen 郝春文, *Tang houqi wudai Songchu Dunhuang sengni de shehui shenghuo* 唐后期五代宋初敦煌僧尼的社會生活 (*The Social Life of Buddhist Monks and Nuns in Dunhuang during the Late Tang, Five Dynasties, and the Early Song*) (Beijing: Zhongguo shehui kexue chubanshe, 1998).
46. For how Buddhism has become completely "gentrified," which is a view that I do not altogether agree with, see Timothy Brook, *Praying for Power: Buddhism and the Formation of Gentry Society in Late-Ming China* (Cambridge, MA: Council on East Asian Studies, Harvard University, and Harvard-Yenching Institute: Distributed by Harvard University Press, 1993), 107–26; also, Timothy Brook, "Xu Guangqi in His Context: The World of the Shanghai Gentry," in Catherine Jami, Peter Engelfriet, and Gregory Blue, eds., *Statecraft and Intellectual Renewal in Late Ming China: The Cross-Cultural Synthesis of Xu guangqi* (Leiden: Brill, 2001), 72–98, esp. 93.
47. The word *sajiaye* (薩迦耶) is a transliteration of the Sanskrit word *satkāya*, which means the "body" and has the connotation of body as self. In the Chinese Buddhist context, it is usually coupled with the word *dṛṣṭi*, which can be translated as "perception" or "view." Since the text is speaking of *shenjian* (身見), I understand *sajiaye* as a reiteration of the perception or view that identifies the body as an object of one's self-attachment.
48. Ouyi Zhixu, *Lingfeng zong lun*, 791.
49. For a discussion of the relationship of wild-Chan, wild wisdom, and Li Zhi, see Mao Wenfang 毛文芳, "Wanming 'Kuangchan' tanlun 晚明「狂禪」探論,"

HXYJ 漢學研究 19 (2) (2001): 171–200. For contemporary criticism of wild-Chan, see Huang Zongxi 黃宗羲 (1610–95), *Mingru xue'an* 明儒學案 (Beijing: Zhonghua shuju, 1985), 703; for an English version of the criticism, see Julia Ching with the collaboration of Chaoying Fang, *The Record of Ming Scholars* (Honolulu: University of Hawaii Press, 1987), 165.

50. See Ouyi Zhixu, *Lingfeng zong lun*, 659.
51. Many literati during this time thought of the teachings of Buddhism and Confucianism as complementary. One literati commented in 1601 that scholars in his day were so familiar with Buddhist teachings that they used their literary style freely in their writings and treated them as the equal of Neo-Confucianism; see Yu Jideng 余繼登, *Diangu jiwen* 典故紀聞 (*Hearsay Notes on Statuary Precedents*) (Beijing: Zhonghua shuju, 1984; reprint), 134–35; see also Timothy Brook, *Praying for Power: Buddhism and the Formation of Gentry Society in Late-Ming China* (Cambridge, MA: Harvard University Press, 1993), 57–63.
52. Some modern scholars have accepted this normative view and characterized this period as a "decline" of Chinese Buddhism. Even though scholars sometimes do not explicitly use the word "decline," the structure through which they historicize Chinese Buddhism uses the trope of decline; see Arthur F. Wright, "Buddhism and Chinese Culture: Phases of Interaction," *JAS* 17 (1) (November 1957): 17–42; Sung-peng Hsu, *A Buddhist Leader in Ming China*. Jiang Wu, however, calls the seventeenth century the "third golden age of Chan Buddhism"; see Jiang Wu, *Enlightenment in Dispute: The Reinvention of Chan Buddhism in Seventeenth-Century China* (Oxford: Oxford University Press, 2008), 6.
53. Jiang Wu states that Miyun alone produced twelve successors and that, through these heirs and within twenty years, his second-generation successors numbered 495, while the third generation reached 1,168, numbers that are unsurpassed in Dharma transmission in Chan history; see Jiang Wu, *Enlightenment in Dispute*, 5–7.
54. See, for example, Jiang Wu, *Enlightenment in Dispute*, 131; Qian Qianyi 錢謙益 (1582–1664), *Liechao shiji xiaozhuan* 列朝詩集小傳, vol. 4, fascicle 12 (Shanghai: Zhonghua shuju, 1961), entry on Tan Yuanchun 譚元春 (1585–1637); Darryl Cameron Sterk, "Chan Grove Remarks on Poetry by Wang Shizhen: A Discussion and Translation," master's thesis, University of Toronto, 2002, 117–19; Lian Ruizhi 連瑞枝, "Qian Qianyi de Fojiao shengya yu linian" 錢謙益的佛教生涯與理念, *Zonghua Foxue xuebao* 中華佛學學報 7 (1994): 331–34.
55. See Araki Kengo 荒木見悟, *Mindai shisō kenkyū: Mindai ni okeru Jukyō to Bukkyō no kōryuū* 明代思想研究: 明代における儒教と佛教の交流 (Tokyo: Sōbunsha, Shōwa, 1972), 130–39, 237–43. For Jiao Hong see Edward T. Ch'ien, *Chiao Hung and the Restructuring of Neo-Confucianism in the Late Ming* (New York: Columbia University Press, 1986), 45.
56. See *Analects* 13: 21; for an English translation of this passage see D. C. Lau, *The Analects (Lun yu) / Confucius* (New York: Penguin, 1979), 122; also Julia Ching,

To Acquire Wisdom: The Way of Wang Yang-Ming (New York: Columbia University Press, 1976), 25–27.

57. See Zhu Yizun 朱彝尊 (1629–1709), *Jingzhiju shihua* 静志居詩話, vol. 2 (Beijing: Renmin wenxue chubanshe: Xinhua shudian Beijing faxing suo faxing, 1990), 431; Chen, Jianhuang 陳劍鍠, "Yangming houxue suo chansheng zhi zhu wenti 陽明後學所產生之諸問題."
58. See Jiang Wu, *Enlightenment in Dispute*, 252.
59. See ibid., 131, and Qian Qianyi, *Liechao shiji xiaozhuan*.
60. See Ouyi Zhixu, *Lingfeng zong lun*, 657.
61. See Michael Loewe, *Chinese Ideas of Life and Death: Faith, Myth, and Reason in the Han Period (202bc–ad 220)* (London: Allen and Unwin, 1982), 21, 128, 130, 133.
62. For blood covenants see *Chunqiu Zuo zhuan zhengyi* 春秋左傳正義, Duke Ding year five, in *Shisan jing zhushu* 十三經註疏 (Beijing: Zhonghua shuju, 1979) 54, 435; Burton Watson, *The Tso Chuan: Selections from China's Oldest Narrative History* (New York: Columbia University Press, 1989), 185. For blood rituals see Gil Raz, "Blood Rites and Pure Covenants: Lineage Construction in Early Daoist Ritual and Narrative," paper presented at the American Academy of Religion, San Antonio, November 20–23, 2004; also James Benn, "Where Text Meets Flesh: Burning the Body as an Apocryphal Practice in Chinese Buddhism," *HR* 37 (4) (May 1998): 297. While many of these practices persisted into late imperial times, they can be dated to as early as the third century B.C.E.
63. For talismans written in blood and ways of smearing objects with blood, see *Lingshu* 48, 8.1a–b, partly cited in Donald Harper, *Early Chinese Medical Literature: The Mawangdui Medical Manuscripts* (London: Kegan Paul International, 1998), 63. A fuller citation appears in Li Jianmin 李建民, "Zhongguo gudai 'jinfang' kaolun" 中國古代"禁方"考論, *BIHP* 歷史語言研究所集刊 68 (1) (1997 [117–66]), 133. For how it is used today see Tong Chee-Kiong, *Chinese Death Rituals in Singapore* (London: Routledge Curzon, 2004), 123; 174, fn. 43, 44, 45.
64. See Michel Strickmann, *Chinese Magical Medicine* (Stanford, CA: Stanford University Press, 2002), 151–52; Tong, *Chinese Death Rituals in Singapore*, 123. The blood of roosters is still used to consecrate talismans and to make ritual offerings, as shown in a 2003 documentary film of a Daoist ritual in Hunan province, China; see "Han Xin's Revenge: A Daoist Mystery," L'École Française d'Extrême-Orient, DVD, directed by Patrice Fava (France: Le CNRS Images, 2005).
65. See Charlotte Furth, *A Flourishing Yin: Gender in China's Medical History, 960–1665* (Berkeley: University of California Press, 1999), 94, 215. Furth also notes that, according to some Ming pharmacists, menstrual blood, particularly at the midpoint of menstruation, could offer maximal *yang* energy for males.
66. See Mary Douglas, *Purity and Danger: An Analysis of Concepts of Pollution and Taboo* (London: Routledge and Kegan Paul, 1966), 94–128.
67. See Jo Riley, *Chinese Theatre and the Actor in Performance* (Cambridge: Cambridge University Press, 1997), 181–86.

68. See Te-k'un Cheng, *Archaeology in China*, vol. 2 (Cambridge: Heffer, 1960), 73–74. Bagley has said that, in fact, the entire Shang royal cemetery at Anyang has yielded about fifteen hundred human skeletons of people who were slaughtered on the occasion of royal funerals. See Robert W. Bagley, "A Shang City in Sichuan Province," *Orientations* (November 1990: 61.
69. See Chengzu 成祖, *Xiaoshun shishi* 孝順事實, 10 vols. Princeton Rare Books Collection, originally published 1420.
70. Ibid., *juan* 6, 9b.
71. For a biography of Yang Lian 楊漣 (1571–1625), see Chen Ding 陳鼎 (b. 1651), *Donglin lie zhuan* 東林列傳 (Taipei: Mingwen shuju, 1991), 157–61.
72. For a biography of Zhou Shunchang 周順昌 (1584–1626), see ibid., 179–89.
73. See Huang Yu 黄煜 (seventeenth century), *Zhou Duanxiao xiansheng xieshu tiehuang* 周端孝先生血疏貼黃 in *Bixie lu* 碧血錄 (*Jade Blood Records*) (Taipei: Yiwen yinshuguan, 1966, repr.). I refer to several editions of the *Bixie lu*; only this edition has the story of Zhou Shunchang's narrative in the form of an appendix. It is possible that *Zhou Duanxiao xiansheng xieshu tiehuang* circulated independently prior to the compilation of the *Bixie lu*. In Jiang Pingjie 蔣平階 (seventeenth century), ed., *Donglin shimo* 東林始末 (Taipei: Wenyuan shuju, 1964), there are many personal letters that Donglin participants wrote describing their thoughts and feelings to friends and family; personal diaries and autobiographical accounts; and eyewitness records, like that of the anonymous "Beijing guest" who worked undercover as a guard in the prison in Beijing and left a detailed description of the suffering inflicted on six of the Donglin martyrs in 1625. There are also original memorials to the throne, unedited by official court historians and bearing the original dates of submission and rescript. Right after the suicide of eunuch Wei Zhongxian in 1628, published compilations began to appear of personal accounts and official documents, such as the *Bixue lu*, as well as topical histories written to satisfy an evident public appetite for reading material devoted to recent events. For a history of the Donglin phenomenon, see John W. Dardess, *Blood and History in China: The Donglin Faction and Its Repression, 1620–1627* (Honolulu: University of Hawaii Press, 2002); Busch Heinrich, "The Tung-lin Shu-yüan and Its Political and Philosophical Significance," *Monumenta Serica* 14 (1949–1955): 1–163.
74. See Shih-shan Henry Tsai, *The Eunuchs in the Ming Dynasty* (New York: State University of New York Press, 1996), 1–6; 112–13.
75. For Yang Zhen 楊震 (54–124), see "Yang Zhen liezhuan 楊震列傳," in Fan Ye 范曄 (398–445), *Hou Hanshu* 後漢書 (Beijing: Zhonghua shuju, 1965), 1759–1769.
76. This is not an exact quote but a paraphrase of book eight, section six, of the *Analects*. I have consulted several translations of the *Analects*, 8: 6. See, for example, D. C. Lau, *Confucius: The Analects (Lun yü)* (New York: Penguin, 1979), 93.
77. This expression refers to all of the emperors of the Ming dynasty.
78. See Huang Yu 黄煜, *Bixie lu* in *Zhongguo neiluan waihuo lishi congshu* 中國內亂外禍歷史叢書, vol. 15 (Shanghai: Shenzhou guoguang she, 1936), 85.

79. For a discussion of *qijie* 氣節 as the distinct character of the Donglin Academy members and a general description of their political agenda, see Li Zhuoran 李焯然, "Lun Donglin dangzheng yu Wanming zhengzhi 論東林黨爭與晚明政治," in *BMQS* 1 (1) (1985): 63–76. This term is used by Gao Panlong 高攀龍 (1562–1626), as recorded by Huang Zongxi 黃宗羲 (1610–1695), *Mingru xue'an* 明儒學案 (Taipei: Mingwen shuju, 1991), 1433.
80. See my discussion of sage and sanctity in the introduction.
81. Chen Ding 陳鼎 (b. 1651), preface, 1a–2b. Chen states that his manuscript containing all of these stories was stolen while he was staying at an inn in Beijing. In Wuxi he later compiled the *Donglin liezhuan* 東林列傳, which covers some 175 Donglin or Donglin-associated people, not all of them martyrs. Chen also stated that, until he undertook this project, most people of his acquaintance considered the Donglin a "pit of disaster" and were fearful even of discussing it. See *Donglin liezhuan* 東林列傳 (Taipei: Mingwen shuju, 1991).
82. I am indebted to Lü Miaw-fen 呂妙芬 for sharing her 2006 AAR paper with me, which points out the prominent position of the *Classic of Filial Piety* (*Xiaojing* 孝經) in the late Ming era. She demonstrates the variety of ways this work was understood and used. One of the ways was blood writing. See Lü Miaw-fen 呂妙芬, "Zuowei yishixing wenben di Xiaojing: Ming-Qing renshi Xiaojing shijian di gean yanjiu 做為儀式性文本的《孝經》：明清士人《孝經》實踐的個案研究" (paper presented at the 2006 meeting of the American Academy of Religion, Washington, DC, Nov. 18–21), 1–26.
83. The three officials were Yang Cichang 楊嗣昌 (1588–1641), Chen Xinjia 陳新甲 (d. 1642), and Liao Dongxun 遼東巡 (d.u.).
84. Literally the term means "cutting short the emotions" and in its typical traditional usage meant the recall of an official to meet a pressing military need. For a brief discussion of the changing norm of this ritual and its political implications for the state see Norman A. Kutcher, *Mourning in Late Imperial China: Filial Piety and the State* (New York: Cambridge University Press, 1999), 47–110.
85. See Huang Daozhou 黃道周, *Huang Shizai xiansheng wenji* 黃石齋先生文集 (Shanghai: Shanghai guji chubanshe, 1995), *juan* 12, 25b.
86. For rituals as "texts" see Catherine Bell, *Ritual Theory, Ritual Practice* (New York: Oxford University Press, 1992), 45; Talal Asad, *Genealogies of Religion: Discipline and Reasons of Power in Christianity and Islam* (Baltimore: Johns Hopkins University Press, 1993), 29, 58.
87. See Clifford Geertz, *The Interpretation of Cultures: Selected Essays* (New York: Basic Books, 1973), 125.

CHAPTER 3

1. Xijie is in the Guilin district 桂林府 in current-day Yangshou county 陽朔, Guangxi province 廣西省.

2. The term *gegu* during the Ming was connected to a whole cluster of practices including cutting the thigh (*kuigu* 刲股), slicing the arm (*gebi* 割臂), slicing the liver (*gegan* 割肝), slicing the chest (*gexiong* 割胸), slicing the rib (*gexie* 割脅), slicing the forearm (*gegong* 割肱), slicing the breast (*geru* 割乳), slicing the heart (*gexin* 割心), slicing the knee (*gexi* 割膝), and carving a piece of flesh (*wanrou* 剜肉). For the purpose of discussing these practices I use "filial slicing." However, for specific passages I translate *gegu* accordingly.
3. See Mao Qiling 毛奇齡, "Yang Xiaozi zhuan 楊孝子傳," in Zheng Shuruo 鄭樹若, ed., Yu chu xuzhi 虞初續志 (Shanghai: Wenruilou, n.d.), *juan* 9: 11.
4. See, for example, David A. Graff, "Meritorious Cannibal: Chang Hsün's Defense of Sui-Yang," *AS* (3rd ser.) 8, part 1 (1995), 1–16.
5. See Zhang Shengyan 張聖嚴, *Minmatsu Chūgoku Bukkyō no kenkyū*, 6–7.
6. See Kuwabara Jitsuzo *Tōyō bunmei shiron* 東洋文明史論, 132; the book also discusses human flesh as a delicacy, 143–46.
7. Mark Edward Lewis, *Sanctioned Violence in Early China* (Albany: State University of New York Press, 1990), 165–66; 206–10.
8. See Donald Sutton, "Consuming Counterrevolution: The Ritual and Culture of Cannibalism in Wuxuan, Guangxi, China, May to July 1968," *Comparative Studies in Society and History* 37 (1) (January 1995): 150; Shih-shan Henry Tsai, *The Eunuchs in the Ming Dynasty* (New York: State University of New York Press, 1996), 225.
9. Ample evidence in historical records from the Han to the late imperial times reveals not only that was cannibalism practiced (in times of famine and disaster) but also that methods of cooking human flesh were quite similar. The most detailed research so far has been done by Kuwabara Jitsuzō 桑原隲藏 (1870–1931), "Shinajin kan ni okeru shokujin niku no fūshū 支那人間に於ける食人肉の風習," in *Kuwabara Jitsuzō zenshū* 桑原隲藏全集 (*Complete Collected Works of Kuwabara Jitsuzō*), vol. 2, ed. Miyazaki Ichisada 宮崎市定 et al. 6 vols. (Tokyo: Iwanami Shoten, 1969), 153–205. The article is also reprinted in *Tōyō bunmei shiron* 東洋文明史論 (Tokyo: Heibonsha, 1988), 97–168; see also Lewis, *Sanctioned Violence in Early China*, 28, 148; K. C. Chang, ed., *Food in Chinese Culture: Anthropological and Historical Perspectives* (New Haven, CT.: Yale University Press, 1977), 34; Key Ray Chong, *Cannibalism in China* (Wakefield, NH: Longwood Academic, 1990), 153–56.
10. See Kuwabara Jitsuzō 桑原隲蔵, "Shina jinkan ni okeru shokujin niku no fūshū 支那人間に於ける食人肉の風習."
11. Li Chong's story can be found in Yuan Yingqi 袁應祺 (1574 *jinshi*), *Tianyige cang Mingdai fangzhi xuankan* 天一閣藏明代方志選刊, vol. 18 (Shanghai: Shanghai guji shudian yingyin, 1981 printing): *juan* 8, 88–89. Preface dated to 1579.
12. Unlike other scholars who claim that there was only one case of *gegu*, I have found a total of three in the *Jiu Tangshu* 舊唐書; see Qiu Zhonglin 邱仲麟, "Buxiao zhi xiao—Tang yilai gegu liaoqin xianxiang de shehuishi chutan" 不孝之孝—唐以來割股療親現象的社會史初探 (A Sociohistorical Study of the Phenomenon

of "Slicing the Flesh to Heal Parents" from the Tang Dynasty to the Modern Era), *Xin shixue* 新學史 6 (1) (1995): 50. Other scholars repeat his findings. Besides the case of Wang Youzhen 王友貞, the other two cases seem to be unrelated to healing parents. However, the term "gegu" was used, and both cases involved a demonstration of devotion or commitment. The other two cases appear in Liu Xu 劉昫 (887–946) et al. *Jiu Tangshu* 舊唐書 (Taipei: Dingwen shuju, 1979). The first one is found in *juan* 16, 503, listed under the biography of Emperor Muzong, Li Heng 穆宗李恆. In 823 C.E. a company commander (*yajiang* 牙將) named Wang Zhi 王贄 performed slicing of the body to heal a military commissioner (*jiedu shi* 節度使). The second case is listed under the biography of general Li Ji 李勣 in *juan* 67, the section on *liezhuan* 列傳, case no. 17, 2488, where he sliced his own body in order to win the heart of an able prisoner of war. The third case is Wu Zhongyin 烏重胤 in *juan* 161, in the section on *liezhuan*, case no. 111, 4228. It is said that his virtue as a general was so respected that on the day he died more than twenty of his soldiers "sliced their bodies" and offered their flesh along with wine during his funeral (*jilei* 祭酹). For more details of the official titles "company commander" and "military commissioner" see Charles O. Hucker, *A Dictionary of Official Titles in Imperial China* (Palo Alto: Stanford University Press, 1985), 574b and 144b respectively.

13. See Liu Xu 劉昫 (887–946) et al., *Jiu Tangshu* 舊唐書, *juan* 192, 5118.
14. The following works have been particularly helpful in my understanding of premodern Chinese medical lore: Joseph Needham, with the research assistance of Wang Ling, *Science and Civilisation in China* (Cambridge: Cambridge University Press, 1954–2008), esp. vol. 2 (1956), vol. 5, pts. 2–5 (1979, 1980, 1983), and vol. 6, pt. 1 (1986); Manfred Porkert, *The Theoretical Foundations of Chinese Medicine: Systems of Correspondence* (Cambridge, MA: MIT Press, 1974); Nathan Sivin, *Traditional Medicine in Contemporary China: A Partial Translation of Revised Outline of Chinese Medicine (1972): With an Introductory Study on Change in Present Day and Early Medicine* (Ann Arbor: Center for Chinese Studies, University of Michigan, 1987); and his *Chinese Alchemy: Preliminary Studies* (Cambridge, MA: Harvard University Press, 1968); Shigeru Nakayama and Nathan Sivin, *Chinese Science: Explorations of an Ancient Tradition* (Cambridge, MA: MIT Press, 1973); Kenneth J. DeWoskin, trans., *Doctors, Diviners, and Magicians of Ancient China: Biographies of Fang-Shih* (New York: Columbia University Press, 1983).
15. Yü Chün-fang, *Kuan-yin*, 339; T'ien Ju-k'ang, *Male Anxiety and Female Chastity: A Comparative Study of Chinese Ethical Values in Ming-Ch'ing Times* (Leiden: Brill, 1988), 152.
16. This is a passage from the *Classic of Filial Piety*; for a discussion of the full passage see chap. 2.
17. See Li Shizhen 李時珍 (1518–1593), *Bencao gangmu tongshi* 本草纲目通释 (*General Explanation of Compendium of Materia Medica*), ed. Chen Guiting 陈贵廷 (Beijing: Xueyuan chubanshe, 1992), *juan* 52, 2224a–b; cf. the translation

by Luo Xiwen; see Li Shizhen, *Compendium of Materia Medica* (*Bencao gangmu*), six vols. (Beijing: Foreign Languages Press, 2003), vol. 6, 4188–89. There is also an earlier translation of this passage by J. J. M. de Groot, *The Religious System of China: Its Ancient Forms, Evolution, History and Present Aspect, Manners, Custom and Social Institutions Connected Therewith* (Taipei: Ch'eng Wen, 1976), 385–86. The translation in the main text is a modification of Luo Xiwen.

18. See Li Shizhen, *Compendium of Materia Medica* (*Bencao gangmu*), 4187, 4182, 4173, and 4138–39, respectively.
19. See Roy Porter, *Greatest Benefit to Mankind: A Medical History of Humanity* (New York: Norton, 1998), 137, 148.
20. See *GJTSJC*, category: "Confucianism and Literature" (*Lixue huibian* 理學彙編), section: "The Conduct of Life" (*Xuexing dian* 學行典), *juan* 219, *ce* 614, 57.1.
21. See Christopher Cullen, "Patients and Healers in Late Imperial China: Evidence from the *Jinpingmei*," *HS* 31, pt. 2 (June 1993): 99–150, and Yüan-ling Chao, "Medicine and Society in Late Imperial China: A Study of Physicians in Suzhou" (PhD diss., University of California, Los Angeles, 1995), 251–65. Donald Harper argues strongly that in ancient China the group of people called *fangshi*, which he translates as "recipe gentlemen," played a crucial role in the canonization of medicine based on the numerological system of the "five phases" theory. This understanding of the *fangxiang shi* as "gentlemen," however, is fraught with problems because, in the *Rituals of Zhou* 周禮, they were specifically referred to as "manics" (*kuangfu* 狂夫); see Edward Schafer, "Ritual Exposure in Ancient China," *HJAS* 14 (1/)2 (June 1951): 161. For other explanations of *fangshi* or *fangxiang shi* see Stephen R. Bokenkamp, *Early Daoist Scriptures* (Berkeley: University of California Press, 1997), 6–7, 240–42; and DeWoskin, *Doctors, Diviners, and Magicians of Ancient China*; Donald Harper, "Iatromancy, Diagnosis, and Prognosis in Early Chinese Medicine," in *Innovation in Chinese Medicine*, ed. Elisabeth Hsu (Cambridge: Cambridge University Press, 2001), 99–120, esp. 102.
22. In *Doctors, Diviners, and Magicians of Ancient China* DeWoskin gives some idea of how versatile the concept of a healer could be at that time. His book includes biographies of these healers from late imperial China up to the early Han, written by Han historian Sima Qian 司馬遷 (ca. 145–86 B.C.E.). See also Ngo Van Xuyet, *Divination, magie et politique dans la Chine ancienne: Essai* (Paris: Presses universitaires de France, 1976). For *fangshi*, see my discussion below for details. On the range of healers that a well-off client might consult in the late Ming, see Cullen, "Patients and Healers in Late Imperial China." On the tension between the shaman-mediums and the educated elite (including Buddhists, Daoists, Confucians, and physicians), see Yüan-ling Chao, "Medicine and Society in Late Imperial China," 251–65; Donald Sutton, "From Credulity to Scorn: Confucians Confront the Spirit Mediums in Late Imperial China," *LIC* 21 (2) (December 2000): 1–39; and Angela Ki Che Leung, "Women Practicing Medicine in Premodern China," in *Chinese Women in the Imperial Past: New Perspectives*, ed. Harriet T. Zurndorfer

(Leiden: Brill, 1999), 101–34, esp., 110–13. There is clear evidence that during the Ming, the imperial government institutionally supported a variety of women "healers." The generic term for these women was "dames of medicine," or *yipo* 醫婆, but under this rubric were also many other categories. See Victoria Cass, "Female Healers in the Ming and the Lodge of Ritual and Ceremony," *JAOS* 106 (1) (January–March 1986): 233–45.

23. Scholars have analyzed the chemical properties and therapeutic measures of the bodily elements that Li Shizhen used and found them to be based largely on a symbolic relation with folk medicine and thaumaturgical *tours de force*; see W. C. Cooper and Nathan Sivin, "Man as a Medicine: Pharmacological and Ritual Aspects of Traditional Therapy Using Drugs Derived from the Human Body," in *Chinese Science: Explorations of an Ancient Tradition*, ed. Shigeru Nakayama and Nathan Sivin (Cambridge, MA: MIT Press, 1973): 203–72.

24. Śubhakarasiṃha (Shanwuwei 善無畏) (637–735) was a charismatic Indian *paṇḍit* who propagated Buddhist esotericism in China. Born into a royal family in Orissa, he inherited the throne at age thirteen but renounced it when his brothers began a violent struggle over the succession. He became a Buddhist monk, settling in the Veṇuvanavihāra 竹林精舍 at Nālanda monastery 那爛陀寺. At the behest of his master, Dharmagupta 達摩笈多, he embarked on a journey to China via Turfan 吐蕃, arriving in 716. He was met by Emperor Xuanzong 玄宗 in 717 and began translating texts at Ximing Monastery 西明寺. When the emperor relocated in 724, he moved to Loyang, working there with Yixing 一行 on the translation of various scriptures. The *Mahāvairocana-abhisambodhi Sūtra Commentary* was most likely translated there.

25. A student of Śubhakarasiṃha 善無畏 and Vajrabodhi (Jingangzhi 金剛智), Yixing 一行 (684–727) was another influential Tantric master who lived and disseminated teachings in China. His famous disciple, Amoghavajra (Bukong jingang 不空金剛) (705–774), grew up in China and became one of the most influential Tantric masters in China. Amoghavajra had great influence in the imperial court; in 759 he initiated emperor Suzong 肅宗 (711–762) as a *cakravartin* (chuanlun wang 轉輪王). Yixing was also influential at court. His patron was none other than Suzong's father, emperor Xuanzong 玄宗 (685–762). Yixing was a prolific author in the area of esoteric Buddhism. He was also a master of mathematics, astrology, Daoism, and calendrical studies. His secular name was Zhang Sui 張遂, posthumous title 大慧禪師; he was a reformer of the Chinese calendar and author of several works. For a brief account of Yixing and his connection with Daoist astrology see Christine Mollier, *Buddhism and Taoism Face to Face: Scripture, Ritual, and Iconographic Exchange in Medieval China* (Honolulu: University of Hawaii Press, 2008), 141–46; for biographies of Śubhakarasiṃha, Vajrabodhi, and Amoghavajra see Chou Yi-liang, "Tantrism in China," in *Tantric Buddhism in East Asia*, ed. Richard Payne (Boston: Wisdom, 2005), 33–60.

26. This passage appears in Śubhakarasiṃha's commentary to *Mahāvairocana-abhisambodhi Sūtra Commentary* (*Da biluzhena chengfo jingshu* 大毘盧遮那成佛經疏), T. no. 1796, 39: 687b20–22. Translation here by David B. Gray, "Eating the Heart of the Brahmin: Representations of Alterity and the Formation of Identity in Tantric Buddhist Discourse," *HR* 45 (1) (Aug., 2005): 47–8. Gray's main thesis is to show that Indian Buddhists appropriated many heterodox Hindu rituals, in this case the Śaiva Kāpālikas. He is unaware of any lasting impact of Śubhakarasiṃha's commentary in China and does not speculate on the theoretical significance of anthropophagy. For other studies of this commentary see Nobumi Iyanaga, "Daikokuten," in *Hōbōgirin*, ed. Adrien Maisonneuve and Jean Maisenneuve (Tokyo: Maison Franco-Japonaise, 1994), 7:839–920, esp. 857–60; and his "Dākinī et l'Empereur—Mystique bouddhique de la royaut'e dans le Japon medieval," in "Reconfiguring Cultural Semantics: The Construction of Japanese Identity," ed. Fabio Rambelli and Patrizia Violi, special issue, *Versus* (*Quaderni di studi semiotici*) 83/84 (May–December 1999): 41–111, esp. 51–53.
27. Since the mid-1960s Western scholarship has recognized the importance of Vajrayāna, or tantric Buddhism. However, little has been done on this form of Buddhism in East Asia. In the past decade or so there has been a surge of studies on the importance of tantric Buddhism in the spread and formation of East Asian Buddhism. See, for example, Christine Mollier, *Buddhism and Taoism Face to Face*; Richard Payne, ed., *Tantric Buddhism in East Asia*; and particularly Chou Yi-liang, "Tantrism in China," 33, 36.
28. See Edwin O. Reischauer, ed., *Ennin's Diary: The Record of a Pilgrimage to China in Search of the Law* (New York: Ronald, 1955), 386; also Michihata Ryōshū 道端良秀, "Chūgoku Bukkyō to shokuninniku no mondai 中國佛教と食人肉の問題" (Chinese Buddhism and the Problem of Eating Human Flesh), in Fukui Kōjun 福井康順, ed. *Jikaku Daishi kenkyū* 慈覺大師 研究 (original publication Tokyo: Association of the Tendai Sect for Buddhist Studies, 1964; rept., Tokyo: Waseda Daigaku Shuppanbu, 1980), 391–404, esp. 392. For examples of the extent of Emperor Wuzong's belief in Daoism and the damage inflicted during the Huichang persecution, see Reischauer, ed., *Ennin's Diary*, 351–53, 354–55, 388–90; for the consumption of children's hearts and livers by Tang emperors see T. H. Barrett, "The Madness of Emperor Wuzong," *Cahiers d'Extrême-Asie* 14: 173–86.
29. See, for example, Reischauer, ed., *Ennin's Diary*, 354–55.
30. See Chün-fang Yü, *Kuan-yin*, 338–47; T'ien Ju-k'ang, *Male Anxiety and Female Chastity*, 152–53; Ryōshū, "Chūgoku Bukkyō to shokuninniku no mondai 中國佛教と食人肉の問題," 396–404; Hubert Durt, "Two Interpretations of Human-Flesh Offering: Misdeed or Supreme Sacrifice," *Journal of the International College for Advanced Buddhist Studies* (Kokusai Bukkyogagu daigakuin daigaku kenkyu kiyo), 1 (1998): 117–36.

31. For an explanation of the structure of the *vinaya* see Gregory Schopen, "Vinaya," in *Encyclopedia of Buddhism*, ed. Robert E. Buswell Jr. (New York: Macmillan, 2004), 885–89, esp. 888.
32. See Mochizuki Shinkō 望月信 (1869–1948), *Mochizuki Bukkyō daijiten* 望月佛教大辭典 (Tokyo: Sekai Seiten Kankō Kyōkai, 1954–1963), vol. 4, 3668c.
33. Vārāṇasī, present-day Benares, is an ancient Indian state, located west of Magadha 摩揭陀 and north of Kośala.
34. The *Daśa-bhāṇavāra*-vinaya has an *upāsikā* (laywoman) named Mahāsenā 摩訶斯那 (or Dajun 大軍) instead of Suppiyā or Subi. Other versions simply have variant Chinese characters for Subi, except the *Mūlasarvāstivādin-vinaya*, in which Mahāsenā is a male.
35. In the *Mūlasarvāstivādin-vinaya* it is a physician who told the elder Mahāsenā (Dajun zhangzhe 大軍長者), a wealthy *upāsaka* (layman) patron of the Buddha, that the sick monk needed meat. He had his servants buy some meat but was unable to eat it because of the abstention that day, so his wife sliced a piece of flesh from her thigh (*gebirou* 割髀肉). See *Mūlasarvāstivādin-vinaya*, T. no. 1448, 24: 3c16.
36. According to the *Mūlasarvāstivādin-vinaya*, a prince had been born in the kingdom that day, so the king banned all slaughtering for one day. See *Mūlasarvāstivādin-vinaya*, T. no. 1448, 24: 3c20–21. The *Mahāsāṃghika-vinaya* has it that the day was a ritual day (*zhairi* 齋日) or festival day marked by abstention from meat. See *Mahāsāṃghika-vinaya*, T. no. 1425, 22: 486b8.
37. *Duṣkṛta* or *tujiluo* 突吉羅 is rendered in Chinese as 惡作. The lightest class of offenses of the Buddhist precepts requires confession by the offender to only a single good monk or nun.
38. For the Sarvāstivādin *vinaya* see *Daśa-bhāṇavāra-vinaya* or *Shisong lü* 十誦律, trans. Puṇyatara 弗若多羅 (fourth–fifth century) and Kumārajīva 鳩摩羅什 (344–413) between 404 and 405, T. no. 1435, 23: 185c5–186b1; for the Mūlasarvāstivādin *vinaya* see *Mūlasarvāstivādin-vinaya* or *Genben shuo yiqie youbu* 根本說一切有部毘奈耶, trans. by Yijing 義淨 (635–713) in 703–710, T. no. 1448, 24: 3b26–4b1; for the Mahāsāṃghika *vinaya* see *Mahāsāṃghika-vinaya* or *Mohe sengqi lü* 摩訶僧祇律, trans. Buddhabhadra 佛陀跋陀羅 (arrived in China in 406–408) and Faxian 法顯 (320?–420?) during the Eastern Jin (317–420), T. 486a24–c1; for the Mahīśāsaka *vinaya* see *Mahīśāsaka-vinaya* or *Wufen lü* 五分律 (full title: Mishasaibuheshi 彌沙塞部和醯五分律), trans. Buddhajīva 佛陀什 (arrived in China in 423) and Daosheng 道生 (355–434) between 423 and 434, T. no. 1421, 22: 148b10–c11; for the Dharmaguptaka *vinaya* see *Dharmagupta-vinaya* or *Sifen lü* 四分律, trans. Buddhayaśas 佛陀耶舍 (fifth century) and 竺佛念 Zhu Fonian (fourth century) in 408, T. no. 1428, 42: 868c5–869a18. The case also appears in I. B. Horner's English translation of the Vinaya Pitaka, *The Book of the Discipline* (London: Published for the Pali Text Society by Luzac, 1949–1966), vol. 4, 295–98. Because the *vinaya* of the Dharmaguptaka is the most complete in

comparison to others and is the one followed by later Chinese, I use this version as the basis for the following discussion. Other *vinayas* are used as supplements.

39. See, for example, the *Mahāyāna Mahāparinirvāṇa-sūtra* (*Dabanniepan jing* 大般涅槃經) in forty fascicles, trans. in the northern Liang by Dharmakṣema or Tan Wuchen 曇無讖 (385–433) between 416 and 423: "At the castle of Varanasi, there was an *upāsikā* called Mahasenatta, who had already performed various good deeds at the places of innumerable buddhas before. This *upaāsikā*, for ninety days in one summer, invited the saṅgha and offered medicine. At that time there was a monk who was gravely ill. A good physician saw him and prescribed meat. If meat was given, the illness would be dispelled at once. If not, his life would be in danger. Hearing the words of the doctor, the *upāsikā* took gold and went about the town, saying, 'Who can sell me meat? I will give gold for the purchase. For so much meat I will give an equal amount of gold.' She walked all over the city but none gave it. Then, the *upaāsikā* cut off a piece of her own thigh (*geqi birou* 割其髀肉). She cut it up, cooked it into a broth (*huo* 臛), and scented it; then she gave it to the monk. Having partaken of it, he was cured." In the Buddha's meditation, he hears her painful cries of "Namo Buddhāya," which caused the Buddha to feel sympathy for her and to magically send her medicine that instantly healed her wound. The Buddha then telepathically expounded the bodhisattva path to her. See T. no. 374, 12: 458a24–458b4. My translation differs from that of Kosho Yamamoto, *The Mahayana Mahaparinirvana-Sutra: A Complete Translation from the Classical Chinese Language*, vol. 2 (Ube, Japan: Karinbunko, 1973–1975), 385.
40. For example, in other versions of this *vinaya*, the monk is not made to appear foolish but is an accomplished practitioner who, after regaining his health, attained arhathood and miraculously healed Suppiyā.
41. See *Mochizuki Bukkyō daijiten*, 4396b, 4318a, 4420b.
42. Of course, even in the third century, the *Lotus Scripture* or the *Saddharmapuṇḍarīka-sūtra*, which celebrates the bodhisattva's bodily sacrifice, the sanctity of bodily offering was known in China.
43. See E. Frauwallner, *The Earliest Vinaya and the Beginnings of Buddhist Literature*, trans. L. Petech (Rome: Italian Institute for the Middle and Far East [Is.M.E.O.], 1956).
44. See Durt, "Two Interpretations of Human-Flesh Offering."
45. See, for example, Michihata Ryōshū 道端良秀, *Bukkyō to jukkyō rinri: Chūgoku bukkyō ni okeru kō no mondai* 仏教と儒教倫理: 中国仏教における孝の問題 (Kyoto: Heirakuji shoten, 1968), 82; and his "Chūgoku Bukkyō to shokuninniku no mondai 中国仏教と食人肉の問題."
46. Daoxuan is popularly associated with the Nanshan 南山 tradition of *vinaya* (*lü* 律) in China. Daoxuan assisted Xuanzang 玄奘 (600–664) in translating precept texts and biographies of monks. He also completed, in 664, the compilation of the *Da tang neidian lu* 大唐内典錄 (*Great Tang Record of Scriptures*). He worked together with Daoshi 道世 of Ximing Monastery 西明寺, the author of the *Fayuan zhulin*

法苑珠林, in the publication of various *vinaya* texts. For more information see *Mochizuki Bukkyō daijiten*, 3882a, 854b, 2319c, 3999b. For more information on Daoxuan see Huaiyu Chen, *The Revival of Buddhist Monasticism in Medieval China*. New York: Peter Lang, 2007.

47. See Daoxuan 道宣 (596–667), *Sifen lü shanfan buque xingshi chao* 四分律刪繁補闕行事鈔 (*The Abbreviated and Supplemented Commentary on the Conducts from the Vinaya of the Four Sections*), composed between 626 and 630, T. no. 1804, 40: 118a13–17.

48. See *Sifenlü shanfan buque xingshichao*, T. no. 1804, 40: 118a2–a14. There are four translations of the *Laṅkāvatāra-sūtra* or *Lengjia jing* 楞伽經, of which three are extant: (1) *Lengqiejing sijuan* 楞伽經四卷 by Dharmakṣema between 412 and 433, listed in the *Kaiyuan shijiao lu* 開元釋教 錄 at T. no. 2154, 55: 629b11 (not extant); (2) *Lengqie abatuoluo baojing* 楞伽阿跋多羅寶經, 4 fasc. trans. (partial) by Gunabhadra 求那跋陀羅 (T. no. 670, 16); (3) *Rulengqiejing* 入楞伽經, 10 fasc. trans. Bodhiruci 菩提流支 (T. no. 671, 16); and (4) *Dasheng rulengqie jing* 大乘入楞伽經, 7 fasc. trans. Śikṣānanda 實叉難陀 (T. no. 672, 16). Citation from *Digital Dictionary of Buddhism*, "*Laṅkāvatāra-sūtra*" (entry by Charles Muller and M. Radich), http://www.buddhism-dict.net/ddb/. Edition of July 23, 2009. Michihata also discusses this in his "Chūgoku Bukkyō to shokunin-niku no mondai," 402–403.

49. See Zhanran Yuanzhao 湛然元照 (d. 1116), *Sifenlü xingshi chao zichiji* 四分律行事鈔資持記 (*Record on the Particular Practices of the Commentary of the Vinaya of the Four Sections*), T. no. 1805, 40: 377c4–378b2.

50. Daoxuan worked together with Daoshi 道世 of Ximing Monastery 西明寺, the author of the *Fayuan zhulin* 法苑珠林 (*Forest of Pearls in the Garden of the Dharma*), which comments on the Indian *avadāna* of the boy Xusheti 須闍提, who offered his flesh to feed his father and mother when they ran out of food on a journey; see T. no. 2122, 53: 655c11–656c5. *Fayuan zhulin* recognized this *avadāna* as an example of filial piety. See also Michihata, "Chūgoku Bukkyō to shokuninniku no mondai," 398.

51. See *Foshuo Yueming pusa jing* 佛說月明菩薩經 by Zhi Qian 支謙 (fl. 223–253). The basic theme of this scripture is similar to a Jātaka, where the Buddha expounds on one of his past lives, when he offered to sacrifice himself to save a sentient being. In the case of his *sūtra*, the Buddha in one of his past lives was a prince by the name of Zhizhi 智止, who offered a piece of his flesh to save the life of an ailing bhikṣu; see T. no. 169, 3:411c.

52. See note 47; Durt also discusses this in his "Two Interpretations of Human-Flesh Offering," 245–46.

53. See Shi Nai'an 施耐庵 (1290–1365) and Luo Guanzhong 羅貫中 (ca. 1330–1400), *Shuihu zhuan* 水滸傳 (*Water Margins*), *juan* 11, 27, 32, 44 (Beijing: Renmin wenxue chubanshe, 1975), 146, 369–70, 424, 613. For an English translation see Pearl S. Buck, *All Men Are Brothers* (New York: John Day, 1937);

Xi Zhou Sheng 西周生, *Xingshi yinyuan zhuan* 醒世姻緣傳 (*Marriage as Retribution, Awakening the World*), *juan* 52 (Shanghai: Shanghai guji chubanshe, 1981), 759–60. See below for a discussion of the authorship of Xi Zhou Sheng as Pu Songling 蒲松齡 (1640–1715).

54. See Katherine Carlitz, "Shrine, Governing-Class, and the Cult of Widow Fidelity in Mid-Ming Jiangnan," *JAS* 56 (3) (August 1997): 616.
55. See Wu Jiaji 吳嘉紀 (1618–1684), *Louxuan shi* 陋軒詩 (Taipei: Wenhai chubanshe, 1966), *juan* 3, 150–51. My translation slightly differs from that of Jonathan Chaves, "Moral Action in the Poetry of Wu Chia-chi (1618–1684)," *HJAS* 46 (2) (December 1986): 453–54.
56. *Gurou* 骨肉 means one's family members, usually sons and daughters from the perspective of the parents and siblings from the perspective of the children. See *Chongbian guoyu cidian* 重編國語辭典. Taipei: Taiwan shangwu yinshuguan, 1981.
57. For *yu* 愚 as "commoner" instead of "foolish," see *yufu yufu* 愚夫愚婦 in ibid., 5579b.
58. See Wang Gen 王艮 (1483–1541), *Wang Xinzhai quanji* 王心齋全集 (Taipei: Guangwen shuju, 1975), *juan* 1, 2a, 3a; *Chongjuan Xinzhai Wang xiansheng quanji* 重鐫心齋王先生全集. Citation from Lu Guanzhou, "Taizhou xuepai huasu yanjiu 泰州學派化俗研究" (PhD diss., Zhongshan Daxue 中山大學, 2004), 89.
59. See Chaves, "Moral Action in the Poetry of Wu Chia-chi (1618–1684)," 415–16.
60. Early texts indicate that parturient women were moved outside the main house to give birth and remained outside for a month (*manyue* 滿月) after giving birth—until the pollution had dispersed. Further, she was not allowed to leave her room after delivery. See Wang Chong 王充 (27–97?), *Lunheng jiaoshi* 論衡校釋, selected by Huang Hui 黃暉 (Taipei: Taiwan shangwu yinshu guan, 1964), *juan* 23, 971, 973. An English translation is available by Alfred Forke (1867–1944), *Lun-hêng*, 2 vols. (New York: Paragon Book Gallery, 1962; repr. of the 1907 edition). By late imperial times women no longer gave birth outside the house, but the "pollution" still had to be contained within the mother's room. The period of seclusion, however, usually a month, was still in effect. For classic ethnographic analyses of menstrual and birth pollution in China, see Emily Ahern, "The Power and Pollution of Chinese Women," in *Studies in Chinese Society*, ed. Arthur P. Wolf, 269–90 (Stanford University Press, 1978). For an exploration of the historical depth of such beliefs see Gary Seaman, "The Sexual Politics of Karmic Retribution," in *The Anthropology of Taiwanese Society*, ed. Emily Ahern and Hill Gates (Stanford, CA: Stanford University Press, 1981) , 381–96. Charlotte Furth suggests that the emergence in late imperial China of medical theories about "fetal poison" may represent a medicalization of popular beliefs about how a mother's polluting powers after childbirth affected her infant. See Charlotte Furth, "Blood, Body, and Gender: Medical Images of the Female Condition in China 1600–1850," in *Chinese Femininities, Chinese Masculinities: A Reader*, ed. Susan Brownell and Jeffrey N. Wasserstrom (Berkeley: University of California Press, 2002), 291–314.

61. Dorothy Ko also critiques the earlier scholarly portrayal of women as an analytical confusion that mistakes normative prescriptions for experienced realities; see Dorothy Ko, *Teachers of the Inner Chambers: Women and Culture in Seventeenth-Century China* (Stanford, CA: Stanford University Press, 1994), 1–5.
62. The other categories are maternal rectitude (*muyi* 母儀), sage intelligence (*xianming* 賢明), purity and obedience (*zhenshun* 貞順), and chastity and righteousness (*jieyi* 節義). See Liu Xiang 劉向 (76–6 B.C.E.), *Lienü zhuan* 列女傳. Sibu beiyao 四部備要 ed. (Taipei: Taiwan Zhonghua shu ju, 1965). For a discussion of this work see Zhang Jing 張敬, *Lienü zhuan jinzhu jinyi* 列女傳今註今譯 (Taipei: Taiwan shangwu yinshuguan, 1994); Lisa Raphals, *Sharing the Light: Representations of Women and Virtue in Early China* (New York: State University of New York, 1998), 20–112.
63. There were many editions and expansions of the *Lienü zhuan*, which was also one of the first books to be illustrated with woodcut prints. Among the major editions were the *Record of Female Exemplars* (*Guifan tushuo* 閨範圖說) by Lü Kun 呂坤 (1536–1618) (Beijing: Xueyuan chubanshe, 1998) and the *Illustrated Biographies of the Fierce Women* (*Huitu lienü zhuan* 繪圖烈女傳), ed. Wang Geng 汪庚 (1573–1620) and illustrated by Qiu Ying 仇英 (1494–ca. 1552) (Taipei: Zhengzhong shuju, 1971). For more information on other editions, see Raphals, *Sharing the Light*, 114.
64. Related to this was the new category of "filial wives," which was formally established later by the Qing dynasty in 1727. See Mark Elvin, "Female Virtue and State in China," *Past and Present* 104 (August 1984): 127.
65. One of the arguments is that during the turbulent times of the late Ming, when the Han people increasingly lost ground to the strong invading Manchus, loyalty to the Ming court became especially pressing. Scholars of early China have noted the analogy between a chaste wife's fidelity to her husband's familial lineage and an official's political loyalty to his righteous ruler during the classical Warring States period. Scholars of late imperial China argue that this model was revived in the late Ming. See Li-Hsiang Lisa Rosenlee, *Confucianism and Women: A Philosophical Interpretation* (Albany: State University of New York Press, 2006), 101; Lee Cheuk Yin, "Emperor Chengzu and Imperial Filial Piety of the Ming Dynasty," in *Filial Piety in Chinese Thought and History*, ed. Alan K. L. Chan and Sor-hoon Tan (London: RoutledgeCurzon, 2004), 151; Lisa Raphals, "Reflections on Filiality, Nature, and Nurture," in *Filial Piety in Chinese Thought and History*, ed. Alan K. L. Chan and Sor-hoon Tan (London: RoutledgeCurzon, 2004), 222; and Carlitz, "Shrine, Governing-Class, and the Cult of Widow Fidelity in Mid-Ming Jiangnan," 613.
66. See especially Mary Douglas, *Purity and Danger: An Analysis of Concepts of Pollution and Taboo* (London: Ark, 1984); and Emily Martin Ahern, *The Woman in the Body: A Cultural Analysis of Reproduction* (Boston: Beacon, 1992; originally published 1989).

67. Yü Chün-fang also notes the supernatural elements of the filial body-slicing practice during this time in the context of Guanyin miracle tales. While the deities who intervene in the filial practice differ, the essential plot is the same, and these stories attest to the belief in the workings of "sympathetic resonance" or *ganying* 感應. See Yü Chün-fang, *Kuan-yin*, 342–47.
68. See, for example, ibid., 341.
69. See, for example, *Xingshi yinyuan zhuan*, *juan* 36, 474.
70. See Sun Zhiwei 孫枝蔚 (1620–1687), *Gaitang ji* 溉堂集, *houji* 後集 (Shanghai: Shanghai guji chubanshe, 1979) (earlier edition in Library of Congress), *juan* 3, 11. My translation slightly differs from that of Chaves, "Moral Action in the Poetry of Wu Chia-chi (1618–1684)," 466.
71. See Sun Zhiwei, *Gaitang ji*, *juan* 3, 12; Wu Jiaji 吳嘉紀 (1618–1684), *Louxuan shi* 陋軒詩, *juan* 10, 570.
72. See Lin Yin 林尹, *Zhouli jinzhu jinyi* 周禮今註今譯 (Taipei: Taiwan shangwu yinshuguan, 1972), 97–118.
73. See *Hou Hanshu*, 3624.
74. See Han Yü 韓愈 (768–824), "Huren dui 鄠人對" (Response to the People of Hu), in Liu Yuyi 劉於義 (1675–1748) et al., *Shaanxi tongzhi* 陝西通志 in *Yinyin Wenyuan ge Sikuquanshu* 景印文淵閣四庫全書, 556 *ce* (Taipei: Taiwan shangwu yinshuguan, 1983), *juan* 94, 528. Or Han Yü 韓愈 (768–824), *Han Changli quanji* 韓昌黎全集, 2 vols. (Hong Kong: Kwong Chi Book Co.; reprint, n.d.), 2: 493.
75. See, for example, Liu Zongyuan 柳宗元 (773–819), "An Inscription on the Filial Gate" *Xiaomen ming* 孝門銘 in Ouyang Xiu 歐陽修 (1007–1072), *Xin Tangshu* 新唐書, in *Ershiwu shi* 二十五史 (Beijing: Zhonghua shuju, 1975–1981), *juan* 195, 5589. See also Yenna Wu, "Moral Ambivalence in the Portrayal of *Gegu* in Late Imperial Chinese Literature," in *Ming Qing wenhua xinlun* 明清文化新論, ed. Wang Chengmian 王成勉 (Taipei: Wenjin chubanshe, 2000), 250. In later periods numerous cases can be found in the *xiaoyi*, or "filial righteousness" section, of *liezhuan* in the official histories—the *Songshi*, for example. See *Songshi* 宋史 456. 13, 386ff. Citation from Yenna Wu.
76. See Yang Weizhen 楊維楨 (1296–1370), *Tieya xiansheng gu yuefu* 鐵崖先生古樂府, in *Sibu beiyao* 四部備要 (Taipei: Zhonghua shuju, 1965–1966), 6. 43.
77. A *dan* 石 is ten bushels; see *Chongbian guoyu cidian* 重編國語辭典 (Taipei: Taiwan shangwu yinshuguan, 1981), 862b.
78. One *dou* 斗 or *gongdou* 公斗 is a deciliter, which is equal to 10 liters or 2.64 gallons; a *dou* also refers to a "container" of wine; see *Lin Yutang's Chinese-English Dictionary of Modern Usage* (Hong Kong: Chinese University of Hong Kong, 1972), 1078b.
79. See Xu Song 徐松 (1781–1848), *Song huiyao jiben* 宋會要輯本 (*Draft Collection of Song Statues*), vol. 4 (Taipei: Shijie shuju, 1964), *li juan* 61: 1690. An alternate translation appears in Elvin, "Female Virtue and State in China," 117.
80. Elvin, "Female Virtue and State in China," 104.

81. See Zhang Tingyu 張廷玉 (1672–1755) et al., *Mingshi* 明史, *liezhuan* 列傳, *juan* 137, case 25 (Beijing: Zhonghua shuju, 1975–1981), 3946.
82. See Susan Mann, "Widows in the Kinship, Class, and Community Structures of Qing Dynasty China," *JAS* 46 (1) (February 1987): 44. She explains the extent to which women's kinship loyalties had been forced into the patrilineal mold: "Weak ritual ties with her natal family and the unacceptability of a return to her natal home forced the bride into near-complete dependency on her husband's family." This view basically repeats earlier scholarship in anthropology; see Maurice Freedman, *The Study of Chinese Society*, ed. William Skinner (Stanford, CA: Stanford University Press, 1979), 236–37, 245–46; and Margery Wolf, *Women and the Family in Rural Taiwan* (Stanford, CA: Stanford University Press, 1972), 128–57. This model is questioned by Ko, *Teachers of the Inner Chambers*. For earlier periods see Patricia Buckley Ebrey, *The Inner Quarters: Marriage and the Lives of Chinese Women in the Sung Period* (Berkeley: University of California Press, 1993).
83. A few women were accomplished literary writers, and the poems and letters they exchanged have been preserved; these women were able to maintain friendships with other female writers and acquaintances, as well as their own relatives. However, the scope of ordinary women was much more limited. On women's literary accomplishments during this time see Ellen Widmer and Kang-i Sun Chang, eds., *Writing Women in Late Imperial China* (Stanford, CA: Stanford University Press, 1997).
84. T'ien Ju-K'ang argues that ruthless despotism and the hostile sociopolitical environment drove the literati scholars to "direct their own anger and frustration toward perpetrating in women the distortion of an originally deep moral sense to successive levels of fanaticism." He claims that the scholarly literary activity of documenting extreme filial acts served the purpose of "soothing [their] academic frustration." In other words, the literati projected their anxiety onto socially marginalized people, idealizing and transforming them into icons of purity by encouraging them to engage in extreme virtuous acts, such as female chastity and body slicing. T'ien even passed judgment on the extreme acts of filial piety in the late imperial times as a degeneration of and a "parasite" on an "original and pure" Confucian imperative prescribed in the classics. Reducing all literati motivations to status anxiety ignores not only the agency of nonelite actors but also other cultural forces at work. See T'ien Ju-K'ang, *Male Anxiety and Female Chastity*, 149–61, esp. 91, 159–60.
85. For a historical discussion of the intolerance of biological fluidity in the European West, see Thomas Laqueur, *Making Sex: Body and Gender from the Greeks to Freud* (Cambridge, MA: Harvard University Press, 1990).
86. Charlotte Furth has shown that naturally occurring sex changes in late imperial China means biological sex was conceptualized as happening along a continuum. These transformations did not threaten the natural order, itself a cultural

construct based on the knowledge of constantly shifting yin-yang permutations, so long as the person in question was properly stationed in the social order. See Charlotte Furth, "Androgynous Males and Deficient Females: Biology and Gender Boundaries in Sixteenth- and Seventeenth-Century China," *LIC* 9 (2) (December 1988): 1–31. I have also come across a few illustrated stories of a literati widower who was able to feed his infant son milk from his own breast due to his virtue. There are two illustrations in Liang Yannian 梁延年 (1673–1681), *Shengyü xiangjie* 聖諭像解 in *Ming Qing zhenben banhua ziliao congkan* 明清珍本版画资料丛刊, vol. 8, ed. Ma Wenda 马文大 and Chen Jian 陈坚 (Beijing shi: Xueyuan chubanshe, 2003), 35, 36.

87. For a discussion of how the late Ming official Lü Kun identified with women during times of moral uncertainty, see Joanna F. Handlin, "Lü Kun's New Audience: The Influence of Women's Literacy on Sixteenth-Century Thought," in *Women in Chinese Society*, ed. Margery Wolf and Roxanne Witke (Stanford, CA: Stanford University Press, 1975), 13–38, esp. 30–31; Maram Epstein, *Competing Discourses: Orthodoxy, Authenticity, and Engendered Meaning in Late Imperial Chinese Fiction* (Cambridge, MA: Harvard University Asia Center, 2001), 88. For eighteenth-century portrayals of women see Susan Mann, " 'Fuxue' (Women's Learning) by Zhang Xuecheng (1738–1801): China's First History of Women's Culture," *LIC* 13 (1) (1992): 40–62, esp. 42.

88. Female chastity is the topic of chapter 4. Here is it sufficient to cite Katherine Carlitz, who noted with reference to pre-Ming dynastic history, written in early Ming times, that half of the widows listed among exemplary women had committed suicide; that is, to merit inclusion in the dynastic history, extreme forms of chaste devotion were now demanded; see Carlitz, "The Social Uses of Female Virtue in Late Ming Editions of *Lienü Zhuan*," *LIC* 12 (1991): 117–48, esp. 121–22.

89. See Sun Zhiwei, *Gaitang ji*, *juan* 3, 11.

90. This translation is adapted from Keith Knapp's revision of James Legge's translation of *Hsiao King*; see Keith Knapp, *Selfless Offspring: Filial Children and Social Order in Medieval China* (Honolulu: University of Hawaii Press, 2005), 91; for medieval miracles connected to filiality, see 82–112.

91. Xi Zhou Sheng 西周生, "The Scholar of Western Zhou," is the posthumous title of the work. Hu Shi has argued that the author is actually Pu Songling (1640–1715), but this claim is now being challenged. See Epstein, *Competing Discourses*, 122n5; Yenna Wu, *Ameliorative Satire and the Seventeenth-Century Chinese Novel, Xingshi yinyuan zhuan: Marriage as Retribution, Awakening the World* (Lewiston, NY: Mellen, 1999): 73–79.

92. See Xi Zhou Sheng 西周生, *Xingshi yinyuan zhuan* 醒世因緣傳, chapter 36 (Taipei: Liangjin chubanshe, 1986), 474.

93. Ibid., chapter 52, 661.

94. Wu, *Ameliorative Satire and the Seventeenth-Century Chinese Novel*, 79–87.

95. This novel goes into great detail about demonstrating the retributive justice of karma. Many key incidents are presented in such a way that they appear to be readable only in terms of karma, and the reader is periodically reminded of this point not only in the opening verses of many chapters but also at various points in the unfolding of a specific plot segment. See Martin W. Huang, *Desire and Fictional Narrative in Late Imperial China* (Cambridge, MA: Harvard University Press, 2001), 153–57.
96. See for example, Qiu, Zhonglin 邱仲麟. "Buxiao zhi xiao—Tang yilai gegu laioqin xianxiang di shehiushi chutan" 不孝之孝—唐以來割股療親現象的社會史初探 (A Sociohistorical Study of the Phenomenon of "Slicing the Flesh to Heal Parents" from the Tang Dynasty to the Modern Era). *Xin shixue* 新學史 6 (1) (1995): 59.
97. See *GJTSJC*, category: "Confucianism and Literature" (*Lixue huibian* 理學彙編), section: "The Conduct of Life" (*Xuexing dian* 學行典), *juan* 210, *ce* 614, 10.2–11.1. One *ji* is twelve years; for *shouji* 壽紀, see *Chong bian guoyu cidian* 重編國語辭典, 4108a.
98. See *GJTSJC*, category: "Human Relationships" (*Minglun huibian* 明倫彙編), section: "Womankind" (*Guiyuan dian* 閨媛典), *juan* 38, *ce* 398, 5.1.
99. On the religious and medical background of such works up to the Qing dynasty see Michel Strickmann, "Dreamwork of Psycho-Sinologists: Doctors, Taoists, Monks," in *Psycho-Sinology: The Universe of Dreams in Chinese Culture*, ed. Carolyn T. Brown (Washington, DC: Asia Program, Woodrow Wilson International Center for Scholars; Lanham, MD: Distributed by arrangement with UPA, 1988), 25–46; Lin Fu-Shih, "Religious Taoism and Dreams: An Analysis of the Dream-Data Collected in the Yün-Chi Ch'i-Ch'ien," *Cahier d'Extrême-Asie* 8 (1995): 95–112.
100. There were several editions of this work; the one in question is the most comprehensive, boasting 127 *juan* and 1,000 seven-character dream interpretations. For information on *Zhougong jiemeng quanshu* 周公解夢全書 (*Comprehensive Collection of the Duke of Zhou's Explanation of Dreams*) see Wolfram Eberhard, *Moral and Social Values of the Chinese* (Taipei: Zhengwen; distributed by Chinese Materials and Research Aids Service Center, 1971), 80; Fang Jing Pei and Zhang Juwen, *The Interpretation of Dreams in Chinese Culture* (Trumbull, CT: Weatherhill, 2000), 95, 141. The quote in question is from *juan* 5, under the category "Items such as Knives, Swords, Banners, and Bells and Drums." The passage is "女人帶刀大吉慶." I have not been able to locate a hard copy of this edition; my citation comes from the internet; see *Zhougong jiemeng daquan quanshu* 周公解夢大全全書, http://toptech.ira.org.tw/dream/05.htm (accessed Dec. 2, 2011).
101. By the Qing times, hundreds of dream collections were in circulation, dating supposedly from the Shang period to the Ming. They came to epitomize the tradition of Chinese dream interpretation. Compendiums in the eighteenth century were written to collect these cases and works; see Richard J. Smith, *Fortune-Tellers*

and Philosophers: Divination in Traditional Chinese Society (Boulder: Westview, 1991), 245–57, esp., 247–49. For an excellent study of the prevalence and prominent position of dreams in people's lives as seen in novels and dramas of the late imperial times, see Liao Tengye 廖藤葉, *Zhongguo mengxi yanjiu* 中國夢戲研究 (Taipei: Xuesi chubanshe, 2000). For earlier periods see Robert K. Ong, *The Interpretation of Dreams in Ancient China* (Bochum: Brockmeyer, 1985).

102. See Yü Chün-fang, *Kuan-yin*, 247–62; Rolf A. Stein, "Avalokiteśvara/Kouan-yin, un exemple de transformation d'un dieu en déesse," *Cahiers d'Extrême-Asie* 2 (1986): 17–77, esp. 27–37.

103. For Ming *baojuan* 寶卷 literature see Yü Chün-fang, *Kuan-yin*, 260–62; 344–45; also Daniel L. Overmyer, *Precious Volumes: An Introduction to Chinese Sectarian Scriptures from the Sixteenth and Seventeenth Centuries* (Cambridge, MA: Harvard University Press, 1999), 38–39. For Daoist references see the popular version of the legend of Miaoshan contained in the Wanli collection of hagiographies, called *Sanjiao yuanliu soushen daquan* 三教源流搜神大全, and a Daoist version called *Namo Guanshiyin pusa* 南無觀世音菩薩, which was included in the Supplement to the Daoist Canon in 1607; see Glen Dudbridge, *The Legend of Miao-Shan* (London: Ithaca Press for the Board of the Faculty of Oriental Studies, Oxford University, 1978), 57–68; Wilt Idema, *Personal Salvation and Filial Piety: Two Precious Scroll Narratives of Guanyin and Her Acolyte* (Honolulu: University of Hawaii Press, 2008).

104. See Kenneth Dean, *Lord of the Three in One: The Spread of a Cult in Southeast China* (Princeton, NJ: Princeton University Press, 1998), 23.

105. See Judith T. Zeitlin, "The Life and Death of the Image: Ghosts and Female Portraits in Sixteenth- and Seventeenth-Century Literature," in *Body and Face in Chinese Visual Culture*, ed. Wu Hung and Katherine R. Tsiang (Cambridge, MA: Harvard University Asia Center: Distributed by Harvard University Press, 2005), 229–56, esp. 231–32.

106. See Dudbridge, *Legend of Miao-shan*.

107. On Mount Putuo see Yü Chün-fang, *Kuan-yin*, 369–88.

108. Ibid., 342–47.

109. See Michel Foucault, *The Use of Pleasure*, vol. 2 of *The History of Sexuality*, trans. Robert Hurley (New York: Vintage Books, 1990), 27.

CHAPTER 4

1. The most recent publication to date on female chastity in the late imperial times is Lu Weijing, *True to Her Words: The Faithful Maiden Cult in Late Imperial China* (Stanford, CA: Stanford University Press, 2008). This is the first full-length monograph on what the author calls "the cult of the faithful maiden," which spanned roughly the fourteenth through the nineteenth centuries. Her book was published after I had done the majority of my research in 2007, so I was unable

to consult it. However, I have subsequently added some citations from her book that seem to support my own claims, especially on those areas that deal with social history and early Qing cases of female chastity. Her book is primarily a social-historical study of female chastity, with a focus on the cult as a symbol of political loyalty to a state in crisis. It shows how the Qing state appropriated the chastity cult to demonstrate the moral superiority of the Manchus over the Han. See footnotes below for other, earlier works on female chastity.

2. See Mark Elvin, "Female Virtue and the State in China," *Past and Present* 104 (August 1984): 111–52. I have found that the Ming expanded editions of the *Biographies of Exemplary Women* particularly highlight rapes by the Yuan army. In the *Illustrated Female Exemplars* half of the suicide cases were instigated by the Yuan army; in the *Illustrated Biographies of the Fierce Women* more than half of the pre-Ming cases of suicides were also instigated by the Yuan army. Their commonality lies in the fact that the instigators of most suicide cases were non-Han people during times of warfare.
3. See Janet M. Theiss, *Disgraceful Matters: The Politics of Chastity in Eighteenth-Century China* (Berkeley: University of California Press, 2004); Katherine Carlitz, "Shrines, Governing-Class Identity, and the Cult of Widow Fidelity in Mid-Ming Jiangnan," *JAS* 56 (3) (August 1997): 612–40; Susan Mann, "Widows in the Kinship, Class, and Community Structures of Qing Dynasty China," *JAS* 46 (1) (February 1987): 37–56; Ann Waltner, "Widows and Remarriage in Ming and Early Qing China," in *Women in China: Current Directions in Historical Scholarship*, ed. Richard W. Guisso and Stanley Johannesen (Youngstown, NY: Philo, 1981), 143–44; Lu Weijing, *True to Her Words*, 68–100.
4. By the late sixteenth century nearly every local gazetteer had a section on morally "exemplary women" or *lienü* 列女; see Elvin, "Female Virtue and State in China." I have also checked hundreds of local gazetteers that include cases of female chastity mutilations and suicides. I have no reason to doubt the veracity of these cases.
5. Dorothy Ko, for example, shows that these practices were themselves a performative discourse produced by elite women. She demonstrates that those who "follow their husbands in death" were "martyrs of love" by drawing on Ming elite women's death poems. She shows that, at least for some women, love was central to chastity suicides. Without a "cult of conjugal love," it would be hard to explain the apparent enthusiasm with which some widows embraced an ideology that was predicated on the denial of their emotional and sexual needs. See Dorothy Ko, *Teachers of the Inner Chambers*, 185–87.
6. Yang Jisheng was in prison, awaiting sentencing for having written a memorial excoriating the evils of Grand Secretary Yan Song (1480–1565. See Beverly Bossler, "*Final Instructions* by Yang Jisheng, (1516–1555)," in *Under Confucian Eyes: Writings on Gender in Chinese History*, ed. Susan Mann and Yu-Yin Cheng (Berkeley: University of California Press, 2001), 119–32; the epigraphy at the beginning of this chapter appears on p. 122. For other scholars who discuss the literati debates

and social effects of chastity, see Katherine Carlitz, "The Daughter, Singing Girl, and the Seduction of Suicide," in *Passionate Women: Female Suicide in Late Imperial China*, ed. Paul S. Ropp, Paola Zamperini, and Harriet T. Zurndorfer (Leiden: Brill, 2001), 22–46; Paola Zamperini, "Eros and Suicide in Late Imperial Chinese Fiction," in *Passionate Women: Female Suicide in Late Imperial China*, 77–104.

7. In reading their stories, it is important to remind ourselves that not every woman was preoccupied with chastity. Many women carried on adulterous affairs for years without worrying about their reputations. Janet Theiss discusses the various factors of personality, family relationships, and women's personal histories, all of which contributed to their individual responses to rape and forced remarriage. She shows that when assaults were avenged in some manner, the victims seldom committed suicide. The few that did commit suicide were either unusually vulnerable to accusations of impropriety or caught in crimes. For example, one woman was caught in a compromising situation: She was raped because she had been caught stealing fruit; see Theiss, *Disgraceful Matters*, 196–97. In this case suicide was seen as the only means of demonstrating their innocence. Other motives at work may have caused women to resist marriage, and these may have had more to do with the women's experiences than with any prescribed Confucian imperatives.
8. Many of the studies listed in footnotes 3 through 7 also deal with the moralization of female chastity.
9. See Judith T. Zeitlin, *The Phantom Heroine: Ghosts and Gender in Seventeenth-Century Chinese Literature* (Honolulu: University of Hawaii Press, 2007), 16–17; 23–24; 138–40.
10. For the festivities and terror of Mulian drama see David Johnson, ed., *Ritual Opera, Operatic Ritual: "Mu-lien Rescues His Mother" in Chinese Popular Culture* (Berkeley: University of California: Distributed by IEAS Publications, 1989).
11. For shamanic practices and healers practicing during this time see Charlotte Furth, *A Flourishing Yin: Gender in China's Medical History, 960–1665* (Berkeley: University of California Press, 1999), 268–78.
12. See Laurence Thompson, *Chinese Religion: An Introduction*, 5th ed. (Belmont, CA: Wadsworth, 1996), 5.
13. This term, *shishen* 失身, has a long history, dating to Mencius; see D. C. Lau, trans., *Mencius* (Harmondsworth: Penguin, 1970), 125. In late imperial times the term was still in circulation. For example, in the *Illustrated Female Exemplars* of the seventeenth century, Mencius's injunction against contact between the sexes finds expression in the Five Dynasties story of Wang Ning's wife, who cut off her hand when an innkeeper touched it as he pushed her out the door. See Lü Kun 吕坤 (1536–1618), *Guifan tushuo* 闺范图说 (*Illustrated Female Exemplars*) (Beijing: Xueyuan chubanshe, 1998), *juan* 3, 58a–59a.
14. See, for example, "Lienü zhuan" 列女傳 in *Mingshi* 明史 by Zhang Tingyu 張廷玉 (1672–1755), et al. (Beijing: Zhonghua shu ju), 7746.

15. See Matthew H. Sommer, *Sex, Law, and Society: Society in Late Imperial China* (Stanford, CA: Stanford University Press, 2000), 80.
16. See Theiss, *Disgraceful Matters*, 130–31, 152–53.
17. See a discussion of ambiguous attitudes toward female chastity in Jonathan Spence, *The Death of Woman Wang* (New York: Viking, 1978), 60–76.
18. See Mann, "Widows in the Kinship," 44–45; Ko, *Teachers of the Inner Chambers*, 261–62.
19. See, for example, Wang Geng 汪庚 (1573-1620), ed. and Qiu Ying 仇英 (1494–ca. 1552), illustrator, *Huitu Lienü zhuan* 繪圖烈女傳 (*Illustrated Biographies of the Fierce Women*), reprint of *Zhibuzuzhai kanben* 知不足齋刋本 (Taipei: Zhengzhong shuju, 1971), *juan* 13, 1200.
20. In the late Ming a woman, née Ouyang 歐陽, resisted forced remarriage by using a sewing needle to prick the word "chastity" (*jie* 節) into her forehead and then added black ink to the wound—much like the process of tattooing. The townspeople called her "black-head chaste widow." See the 190th case in "Exemplary Biographies" (*liezhuan* 列傳) in *Mingshi*, *juan* 302, 7714. The practice of branding the face with words, or tattooing, was one of the five major imperial punishments (*xing* 刑) of premodern China. See Deborah Sommer, "*Xing* 刑," in *RoutledgeCurzon Encyclopedia of Confucianism*, ed. Yao Xinzhong (London: RoutledgeCurzon, 2003), 694–95. For *qingmian* 黥面 see *Chongbian guoyu cidian* 重編國語辭典, 2958b. A connection definitely exists between the self-inflicted punishment of branding one's face or cutting off one's nose (another of the five punishments), as in the case of Gao Xing, which I discuss below, and female chastity. However, this connection is beyond the scope of this chapter and awaits future research.
21. In premodern China hair was an important cultural marker, and in late imperial times it was a sign of political protest. See Michael R. Godley, "The End of the Queue: Hair as Symbol in Chinese History," *East Asian History* 8 (December 1994): 53–72.
22. See the story of the woman née Wang in Lü Kun, *Guifan tushuo*, *juan* 3, 60a–b.
23. For *lieshi* 烈士 see Morohashi Tetsuji 諸橋轍次 (1883–1982), *Dai Kan-Wa jiten* 大漢和辭典, vol. 7 (Tokyo: Taishūkan Shoten, 1955–1960): 393–94.
24. See Xu Shen 許慎 (30–124), *Shuowen jiezi* 說文解字 (*Explicating the Written Characters*) (Shanghai: Shanghai guji chubanshe, 1981), 180 for *lie* 列 and 480 for *lie* 烈.
25. For a brief history of how *lie* 列 (as in "exemplar") became *lie* 烈 (as in "fierce"), see Sherry J. Mou, "Writing Virtues with Their Bodies: Rereading the Two Tang Histories' Biographies of Women," in *Presence and Presentation: Women in the Chinese Literati Tradition*, ed. Sherry J. Mou (New York: St. Martin's, 1999), 110. The observation of this distinctive usage in late imperial times comes from my reading of several hundred cases of female chastity detailed in local gazetteers.
26. See Lisa Raphals, *Sharing the Light: Representations of Women and Virtue in Early China* (New York: State University of New York, 1998); Katherine Carlitz,

"The Social Uses of Female Virtue in Late Ming Edition of *Lienü zhuan*," *LIC* 12 (1991): 117–48.

27. For remarriage as the norm of society see Waltner, "Widows and Remarriage in Ming and Early Qing China," 143–44.
28. See Bettine Birge, *Women, Property, and Confucian Reaction in Sung and Yuan China (960–1368)* (New York: Cambridge University Press, 2002), 220–82; Beverly J. Bossler, *Powerful Relations: Kinship, Status, and the State in Sung China (960–1279)* (Cambridge, MA: Harvard University Press, 1998).
29. For more detailed discussion on the larger milieu of the sixteenth and seventeenth centuries see chapter 1.
30. See, for example, the writings of Chen Jiru 陳繼儒 (1558–1639), as noted in Jamie Greenbaum, *Chen Jiru (1558–1639): The Background to Development and Subsequent Uses of Literary Personae* (Leiden: Brill, 2007), 119–24.
31. For a brief discussion of the characteristics of *Biographies of Exemplary Women* as a genre and its shift in ideology in later Ming edition and expansions of this work, see Joanna F. Handlin, *Action in Late Ming Thought: The Reorientation of Lü K'un and Other Scholar-Officials* (Berkeley: University of California Press, 1983), 144.
32. See, for example, Lü Kun, *Guifan tushuo, juan* 3, 48a.
33. Ibid., 60.
34. Ibid., 52b.
35. *Se* 色 has two distinct meanings: either facial countenance or sensual beauty. See Keith Knapp, "*Se* 色," in *RoutledgeCurzon Encyclopedia of Confucianism*, ed. Yao Xinzhong (London: Routledge Curzon, 2003), 533–34.
36. The word "punishment," or *xing* 刑 has an association with the five prescribed imperial punishments of branding, cutting off one's nose, amputation of one's feet, castration, and death. See Deborah Sommer, "*Xing* 刑," 694–95.
37. The expression *xingyu zhiren* 刑餘之人 connotes (1) a eunuch, a person who is physically incomplete; (2) a criminal who is punished; (3) and a person whose body is no longer complete after having being punished. See *xingyu* 刑餘 in *Chongbian guoyu cidian*, 3290b.
38. Lü Kun, *Guifani tushuo, juan* 3, 52b–53a.
39. Scholars have noted the real social and legal pressures of gossip and alleged flirtation that widows and women in the absence of their husbands faced. See, for example, Theiss, *Disgraceful Matters*, 193–215.
40. Lü Kun, *Guifani tushuo, juan* 3, 53a.
41. René Gerard defines "sacred" as basic to "archaic society as something really dreadful and destructive and dangerous." For him, the sacred is violence directed at a sacrificial victim; see Markus Müller, "Interview with René Girard," *Anthropoetics: The Electronic Journal of Generative Anthropology* 2 (1) (June 1996): http://www.anthropoetics.ucla.edu/AP0201/interv.htm (accessed Mar. 28, 2007); see also René Girard, *Violence and the Sacred*, trans. Patrick Gregory (Baltimore: Johns Hopkins University Press, 1977), 1–38. I realize that Girard's theory is couched in the very different

religious and cultural contexts of Christianity. I mention his theory here merely to bring to the forefront the perceived sanctity in self-inflicted violence and the ambiguous symbolism of Gao Xing's status as used by the educated elite in this work.

42. See Lü Kun, *Shingingo* 呻吟語 (*Shenyin yu*), ed. Kōda Rentarō 公田連太郎 (Tokyo: Meitoku Shuppansha, 1956), *juan* 5, 734.
43. Ibid., *juan* 4, 647.
44. See Lü Kun's preface in *Guifan tushuo*, 1a–b.
45. The six directions—east, west, north, south, heaven above, and earth below—refer to the universe.
46. Lü Kun 呂坤 (1536–1618), *Guifan tushuo, juan* 2, 2b.
47. Conservative literati did not necessarily disapprove of remarriage, but their views were ambiguous. Chastity versus remarriage was a hotly debated topic, and many sided with remarriage; see, for example, Gui Youguang's 歸有光 essay titled "A Treatise on Chaste Women" (Zhennü lun 貞女論); Gui Youguang 歸有光 (1507–1571), *Zhenchuan xianshengji* 震川先生集 (Shanghai: Shanghai guji chubanshe, 1981), 58–59. He favors marriage on the basis of the *yin* 陰 and *yang* 陽 modalities, the Confucian classics, and the principle of patrilineality. In this essay Gui Youguang argues that the practice of widow suicide was counter to Confucian ritual norms (*feili* 非禮). However, he did write positive eulogies for widows who died from either defending their chastity against bandits or committed suicide out of grief. See also 570–70, 621–26. It seems he was ambiguous about the issue of widow suicide.
48. By the late sixteenth century, the pursuit of individual happiness had reached fever pitch. It became fashionable among high-minded literati to complain that their contemporaries were being overwhelmed by "the overflow of human desire" (*renyu hengliu* 人慾橫流) and that the pursuit of material pleasure had corrupted social mores. See, for example, the often-quoted complaint that "people's behaviors have turned increasingly dissolute while waste and extravagance are becoming the norm in society" in Zhang Han 張瀚 (1511–1593), "Fengsu ji" 風俗記, *Songchuang mengyu* 松窗夢語 (Shanghai: Shanghai guji chubanshe, 1986), 123; Fan Lian 范濂 (b. 1540), *Yunjian jumu chao* 雲間據目抄, *juan* 2 in *Biji xiaoshuo daguan* 筆記小說大觀, vol. 13 (Taipei: Taibei xinxing shuju, 1973), 114; Gu Qiyuan 顧起元 (1565–1628), "Jianye fengsu ji" 建業風俗記, *Kezuo zhuiyu* 客座贅語, *juan* 5, 30b–32a, in *Jinling congke* 金陵叢刻, case 1, in *Baibu congshu jicheng* 百部叢書集成 (Taipei: Yiwen yinshuguan, 1968). For a discussion of "over consumption" see Craig Clunas, *Superfluous Things: Material Culture and Social Status in Early Modern China* (paperback ed.) (Honolulu: University of Hawai'i Press, 2004), 141–65.
49. See Feng Menglong, *Stories to Caution the World: A Ming Dynasty Collection*, vol. 2, trans. Shuhui Yang and Yunqin Yang (Seattle: University of Washington Press, 2005), 607–21; for Chinese, Feng Menglong 馮夢龍 (1574–1646), *Xinping Jingshi tongyan* 新評警世通言 (Shanghai: Shanghai guji chubanshe, 1992), 566–80.

50. See Paola Paderni, "Between Constraints and Opportunities: Widows, Witches, and Shrews in Eighteenth-Century China," in *Chinese Women in the Imperial Past: New Perspectives*, ed. Harriet T. Zurndorfer (Leiden: Brill, 1999), 262–70.
51. See Handlin, *Action in Late Ming Thought*, 149.
52. The most comprehensive study of Yuan and Ming literary romances to date is Chen Yiyuan 陳益源, *Yuan Ming zhongpian chuanqi xiaoshuo yanjiu* 元明中篇傳奇小說研究 (Hong Kong: Xuefeng wenhua shiye gongsi, 1997), esp. 1-18 for a generic description of these texts.
53. See Mingjiaozhongren 名教中人, *Haoqiu zhuan* 好逑傳 (Taipei: Guojia chubanshe, 1990); for English see F. W. Baller, *The Fortunate Union* (Shanghai: American Presbyterian Mission Press, 1911).
54. See Tang Xianzu 湯顯祖 (1550–1616), *Mudan ting* 牡丹亭 (Taipei: Taiwan shangwu yinshuguan, 1972); for an English translation see Zhang Guangqian, trans, *The Peony Pavilion* (Beijing: Foreign Language Press, 2001). For an analysis of the relationship between this drama and the cult of sentiment see Epstein, *Competing Discourses*, 92–103.
55. Yuan Huang 袁黄, "Qingli lun" 情理論 in *Yuan Liaofan xiansheng Liangxing zhai ji* 袁了凡先生兩行齋集. This edition was privately printed by the Yuan family of Jiaxing (*Jiaxing yuanshi jia kanben* 嘉興袁氏家刊本); citation and translation from Martin W. Huang, *Desire and Fictional Narrative in Late Imperial China*, with minor modification, 46.
56. The Chinese is "無情之婦, 必不能為節婦." See the commentary to the story about Zhu Cai 朱蔡, the last story under the first scroll; Feng Menglong 馮夢龍 (1574–1646), *Qing shi* 情史 (*History of Emotions*) (Changsha: Yuelu shushe, 2003), 21.
57. See Feng Menglong, *Qing shi*, 21. Trans. from Paolo Santangelo, *Sentimental Education in Chinese History: An Interdisciplinary Textual Research on Ming and Qing Sources* (Leiden: Brill, 2003), 195.
58. See Hua-yuan Li Mowry, "Ch'ing-shih and Feng Meng-lung" (PhD diss., University of California–Berkeley, 1976), 73.
59. See Pu Songling, *Strange Stories from a Chinese Studio*, trans. Herbert A. Giles (London: Laurie, 1909), 86; 288–90.
60. See Qingxin Cairen 青心才人 (eighteenth century), *Jin Yun Qiao zhuan* 金雲翹傳 (Shenyang: Chunfeng wenyi chubanshe, 1983), *juan* 1, 3. My subsequent citations of this text come from this edition. Wang Shizhen included a biography of Wang Cuiqiao in the "Jinü 妓女" (courtesan) section of his *Yanyi bian* 豔異編 (*Collected Stories of the Romantic and the Strange*), in *Guben xiaoshuo jicheng* 古本小說集成 (Shanghai: Shanghai guji chubanshe, 1990), 1583–87; see Wang Shizhen 王世貞 (1526–1590), *Xu Yanyi bian* 續豔異編, *juan* 6, in *Yanyi bian*; Huang Zongxi, however, anthologizes her under the category of "*lienü* 列女" (female exemplar); see Huang Zongxi 黄宗羲 (1610–1695), *Ming wenhai* 明文海 (Beijing: Zhonghua shuju, 1987), *juan* 414, 4311–12. The biography is titled

"Li Cuiqiao zhuan 李翠翹傳." For a study of *Jin Yun Qiao zhuan* see Chen Yiyuan 陳益源, *Wang Cuiqiao gushi yanjiu* 王翠翹故事研究 (Taipei: Liren shuju, 2001).

61. See Qingxin Cairen, *Jin Yun Qiao zhuan*, *juan* 3, 25.

62. The only existing edition of *Jin Yun Qiao zhuan* with pre-chapter commentaries is the Kangxi edition, which is housed in the Asakusa Bunko 淺草文庫 in Japan. This citation comes from Martin W. Huang, *Desire and Fictional Narrative in Late Imperial China*, 222.

63. See Martin W. Huang, *Desire and Fictional Narrative in Late Imperial China*, 216, 219.

64. In a postscript to a memorial in which Lü Kun pleaded innocent to charges that his *Guifan tushuo* had nefarious intent in certain state controversies, Lü Kun listed four editions of the work and remarked that the literati were circulating *Guifan tushuo* among themselves and that merchants were selling it everywhere. See Handlin, *Action in Late Ming Thought*, 144.

65. See Clunas, *Superfluous Things*.

66. The story is about how she read the *Biographies of Exemplary Women* daily (*Risong Lienü zhuan* 日誦列女傳) as a form of resistance to her uncle and aunt, who tried to force her to remarry. See Wang Geng 汪庚, ed. *Huitu lienü zhuan* 繪圖烈女傳, *juan* 11, 1070.

67. See Ko, *Teachers of the Inner Chambers*, 34–48, esp. 43. Ko also undermines the scholarly equation of illustrated books with women readers; men were equally enthusiastic readers of illustrated texts; see ibid., 51.

68. Full-page illustrations began appearing in the Yuan but did not become a popular format for books, especially novels and dramas, until the sixteenth century. See Victor Mair, *Painting and Performance: Chinese Recitation and Its Indian Genesis* (Honolulu: University of Hawaii Press, 1988), 4.

69. Lisa Raphals has noted that the Ming editions of "female exemplars" deemphasized the importance of intellectual virtue stories. She suggests that this de-emphasis may have something to do with the demands of the Ming publishing market; illustrations of women engaging in admonition or skilled in intellectual discussion were simply less dramatic than pictures of women committing suicide and resisting rape. See Raphals, *Sharing the Light*, 137.

70. By the Wanli period, the competition to increase sales had encouraged booksellers to engage highly skilled professional artists to illuminate their texts. Although we cannot safely identify the illustrator of *Guifan tushuo*, scholars have pointed out that it is clear that, by the late Ming, book illustration had become an independent art form with its own highly regarded specialists. See Robert Hegel, *Reading Illustrated Fiction in Late Imperial China* (Stanford, CA: Stanford University Press, 1998), 193; Chang Bide 昌彼得, ed., *Mingdai banhua xuan* 明代版畫選 (Taipei: Guoli zhongyang tushuguan, 1969), 1–2; Wang Bomin 王伯敏, *Zhongguo banhua shi* 中國版畫史 (Shanghai: Shanghai renmin meishu chubanshe, 1961), 72–83.

71. See Zhang Xiumin 張秀民, *Zhongguo yinshua shi* 中國印刷史 (Shanghai: Shanghai renming chubanshe, 1989), 498.
72. Victor Nell suggests that seeing the movie before reading the book on which it was based often decreased the pleasure of reading since the viewer's memories of the movie would supply many visual details. Similarly, illustrated books on female chastity may have helped the reader to generate mental images of the stories; see Victor Nell, *Lost in a Book: The Psychology of Reading for Pleasure* (New Haven, CT: Yale University Press, 1988), 220–25; citation from Hegel, *Reading Illustrated Fiction in Late Imperial China*, 323.
73. See Lü Kun, *Guifan tushuo*, 53a.
74. Ibid., 57b.
75. See T'ien Ju-K'ang, *Male Anxiety and Female Chastity*, 51–52, 58, 66, 81, 124–125.
76. See Michel Foucault, *The History of Sexuality: An introduction*, vol. 1 of *The History of Sexuality*, 92–3; Judith Butler, *The Psychic Life of Power: Theories in Subjection* (Stanford, CA: Stanford University Press, 1997), 1–16.
77. For those who maintained chastity but continued to live, they had to meet certain criteria to be rewarded. In 1304, the Ministry of Rituals proposed that honorific insignia should be given to widows who had been bereaved before thirty and had attained at least fifty years of age. From 1723 onward, it was necessary only to have maintained fidelity for fifteen years and to be at least forty years old. Later the minimum number of chaste years was further reduced. See Elvin, "Female Virtue and the State in China," 123–24.
78. Ibid., 128, 135.
79. For a specific study of *wu* 武 as an organizing principle in the Chinese conception of the cosmos, see Stephan Feuchtwang, *The Imperial Metaphor: Popular Religion in China* (London: Routledge, 1992).
80. See Kan Louie and Louise Edwards, "Chinese Masculinity: Theorizing *Wen* and *Wu*," *EAH* 8 (1994): 135–48.
81. In premodern China, all human bodies were constituted by the *yin* and the *yang*. Scholars have pointed out that notions of male and female bodies are homologous along a shifting continuum of mixed and interpenetrating energies and forces. This means that multiple possible configurations of *yin* and *yang* are possible within the body and might vary in individuals according to time and circumstances. See Furth, *Flourishing Yin*, 49–50; Raphals, *Sharing the Light*, 169–93, esp. 190–91.
82. See the story of Zhao E 趙娥 in Lü Kun, *Guifan tushuo, juan* 2, 16a. See also a similar story in Wang Geng, ed., *Huitu Lienü zhuan, juan* 14, 1312, where Wang Geng condones and traces the virtue of this act to the *Analects of Confucius*: "[There are those who] would kill themselves for benevolence" 有殺身以成仁. For an alternative rendering of this passage see D. C. Lau, *The Analects (Lun yu)/ Confucius* (Harmondsworth: Penguin, 1979), 133. Sometimes the higher purpose of virtue stems from the martial prowess, or *wu*; see Victoria Cass, *Dangerous*

Women: Warriors, Grannies, and Geishas of the Ming (Lanham, MD: Rowman and Littlefield, 1999), 65–85.

83. See the detailed analysis of this in Matthew H. Sommer, "Dangerous Males, Vulnerable Males, and Polluted Males: The Regulation of Masculinity in Qing Dynasty Law," in *Chinese Femininities, Chinese Masculinities: A Reader*, ed. Susan Brownell and Jeffrey N. Wasserstrom, 67–88 (Berkeley: University of California Press, 2002); also Martin W. Huang's history of famous literati such as Tu Long 屠龍 (1543–1605), Yuan Hongdao 袁宏道 (1568–1610), Yuan Zhongdao 袁中道 (1570–1624), and others in *Desire and Fictional Narrative in Late Imperial China*, 5–22, esp. 11.

84. See Jennifer W. Jay, "Another Side of Chinese Eunuch History: Castration, Marriage, Adoption, and Burial," *Canadian Journal of History* 28 (3) (December 1993): 460–78.

85. See Charlotte Furth, "Blood, Body, and Gender: Medical Images of the Female Condition in China, 1600–1850," in *Chinese Femininities, Chinese Masculinities*, 291–314; see also her *Flourishing Yin* and her "Androgynous Males and Deficient Females: Biology and Gender Boundaries in Sixteenth and Seventeenth Century China," *LIC* 9 (2) (December 1988): 1–31. See also Susan Brownell, *Training the Body for China: Sports in the Moral Order of the People's Republic of China* (Chicago: University of Chicago Press, 1995), 219–22; Ann Anagnost, "Transformations of Gender in Modern China," in *Gender and Anthropology: Critical Reviews for Research and Teaching*, ed. Sandra Morgen (Washington, DC: American Anthropological Association, 1989), 313–42, esp. 321.

86. Modern scholars contend that the categories of sex and gender are different. It is still commonplace in the social sciences today to find scholars using the word "sex" to refer to reproductive anatomy, which is typically either male or female and is perceived as fixed at birth. They use "gender" to refer to the roles, behaviors, and symbols attached to anatomical sex in a particular culture, which is said to be learned and culturally variable. Recognizing that the generic category of "woman" (*funü* 婦女) was a relatively recent concept during the Qing and later Republican-era reformists (1912–1949), these scholars argue persuasively that in late imperial China, gender as a socially constructed concept overshadowed anatomical sex in the definition of the categories "male" and "female." For a summary discussion of gender versus sex, see the introduction to Susan Brownell and Jeffrey N. Wasserstrom, eds., *Chinese Femininities, Chinese Masculinities: A Reader* (Berkeley: University of California Press, 2002), 1–34; for a discussion of the generic category of "woman" (*funü* 婦女), see Tani Barlow, "Theorizing Woman: *Funü, Guojia, Jiating*," in Angela Zito and Tani Barlow, eds., *Body, Subject, and Power in China* (Chicago: University of Chicago Press, 1994), 254. See also her new book, *The Question of Women in Chinese Feminism* (Durham, NC: Duke University Press, 2004), 15, 39–40. Barlow argues that the two kinship terms of *nü* 女 (unmarried woman) and *fu* 婦 (married woman), previously separated nouns, were combined into a single word *funü* 婦女

and glossed as the collectivity of all women in the patrilineal family, beginning in the Qing dynasty, to serve the Confucian imperative of ritual order.

87. The following list is a sample of representative scholarship on the topic of "vengeful ghosts." I list them in chronological order, beginning with the most recent. See Zeitlin, *Phantom Heroine*; Michael Szonyi, "The Virgin and the Chinese State: The Cult of Wang Yulan and the Politics of Local Identity on Jinmen (Quemoy)," *JRS* 19 (1) (2005): 87–98; Sing-Chen Lydia Chiang, *Collecting the Self: Body and Identity in Strange Tale Collections of Late Imperial China* (Leiden: Brill, 2005), 229; Anne Gerritsen, "From Demon to Deity: Kang Wang in Thirteenth-Century Jizhou and Beyond," *TP* 90 (1–3) (2004): 1–31; Stephan Feuchtwang, "The Avenging Ghost: Paradigm of a Shameful Past," in *Xinyang, yishi yu shehui: Disanjie guoji Hanxue huiyi lunwenji. Renleixue zu* 信仰儀式與社會: 第三屆國際漢學會議論文集. 人類學組 (*Belief, Ritual, and Society: Papers from the Third International Conference on Sinology, Anthropology Section*), ed. Lin Mei-rong 林美容 (Taipei: Institute of Ethnology, Academia Sinica, 2003), 7–36; Brigitte Baptandier, "The Lady Linshui: How a Woman Became a Goddess," in *Unruly Gods: Divinity and Society in China*, ed. Meir Shahar and Robert P. Weller (Honolulu: University of Hawaii Press, 1996), 105–49; Liu Yuanru 劉苑如, *Shenti, xingbie, jieji: Liuchao zhiguai de changyi lunshu yu xiaoshuo meixue* 身體·性別·階級: 六朝志怪的常異論述與小說美學 (Taipei: Zhongyang yanjiuyuan Zhongguo wenzhe yanjiusuo faxing, 2002), 105, 109–29; Lin Fushi 林富士, *Guhun yu guixiong de shijie: Bei Taiwan de ligui xinyang* 孤魂與鬼雄的世界: 北臺灣的厲鬼信仰 (Taipei: Daoxiang chubanshe, 1995) 11–21; Yu Kuang-hong, "Making a Malefactor a Benefactor: Ghost Worship in Taiwan," *Bulletin of the Institute of Ethnology* 70 (Autumn 1990): 39–77; C. Stevan Harrell, "When A Ghost Becomes a God," in *Religion and Ritual in Chinese Society*, ed. Arthur Wolf (Stanford, CA: Stanford University Press, 1974), 193–206; Miyakawa Hisayuki 宮川尚志, *Rokuchō shūkyōshi* 六朝宗教史 (Tokyo: Kokusho Kankōkai, 1974), 196–231.

88. The one exception is the recent book by Judith Zeitlin, who explores the elite production of literature on and representation of "ghost" in the seventeenth century; see Zeitlin, *Phantom Heroine*.

89. The original passage in *Lunyu* 論語 refers to Bo Yi and Shu Qi: "*Buxiang qizhi buru qishen, Boyi Shuqi yu* 不降其志,不辱其身,伯夷叔齊與." For an alternative rendering of this passage see Lau, *Analects*, 151.

90. Wang, Geng 汪庚, *Huitu Lienü zhuan* 繪圖烈女傳, *juan* 11, 1042–44. For a discussion of the characteristics of *Illustrated Biographies of the Fierce Women* see Raphals, *Sharing the Light*, 116, 119.

91. By the early sixteenth century the Ming state had begun canonizing "chastely martyred wives and girls (*zhenlie funü* 貞烈婦女) who died by homicide or suicide while resisting rape." See Sommer, *Sex, Law, and Society in Late Imperial China*, 69, 84.

92. See Qian Yiji 錢儀吉 (1783–1850), *Bei zhuanji* 碑傳集 (A Collection of Epitaphs and Biographies) (Taipei: Wenhai chubanshe, 1973), 7101.
93. See Li Zhaoluo李兆洛 (1769–1841), *Yangyizhai wenji* 養一齋文集 (*Collected Works from the Studio for Cultivating Wholeness*), 10 vols. (China: Guangxu wu yin, 1878), 15:9b; see Liu Weijing, *True to Her Words*, 157.
94. His biography may be found in the L. Carrington Goodrich, *Dictionary of Ming Biography, 1368–1644* (New York: Columbia University Press, 1976), vol. 2, 1547–53.
95. See *GJTSJC*, *juan* 493, 527; story citation from Anthony C. Yu, "'Rest, Rest, Perturbed Spirit!' Ghosts in Traditional Chinese Prose Fiction," *HJAS* 47 (2) (December 1987): 430. I have located the first poem by Yang Weizhen 楊維禎 in *Tieya yuefuzhu* 鐵崖樂府註 in *Sibu beiyao* 四部備要 (Taipei: Taiwan Zhonghua shuju, 1965–1966), *juan* 9, 2b.
96. *Gujin tushu jicheng*, *juan* 493, 480.
97. See Feng Menglong, *Stories to Caution the World*, 547–65. For the Chinese, see Feng Menglong, *Xinping Jingshi tongyan*, 508–26.
98. See Carlitz, "Shrines, Governing-Class Identity, and the Cult of Widow Fidelity in Mid-Ming Jiangnan," 634.
99. See Zhang Xiang 張相 (1877–1945), ed., *Gujin wenzong* 古今文綜 (*A Comprehensive Collection of Essays from Ancient and Modern Times*) (Taipei: Zhonghua shuju youxian gongsi, 1962), 17:382a–b.
100. See Judith Zeitlin, "Embodying the Disembodied: Representations of Ghost and the Feminine," in *Writing Women in Late Imperial China*, ed. Ellen Widmer and Kang-I Sun Chang, 242 (Stanford, CA: Stanford University Press, 1997).
101. See Feng Menglong 馮夢龍 (1574–1645), *Qing shi* 情史 (Changsha: Yuelu shushe, 2003), 433–75; Pu Songling was also known for his stories about romances between men and supernatural females; see Judith T. Zeitlin, *Historian of the Strange: Pu Songling and the Chinese Classical Tale* (Stanford, CA: Stanford University Press, 1993); Yu, "'Rest, Rest, Perturbed Spirit!'," 429; Sing-Chen Lydia Chiang, *Collecting the Self*, 25.
102. See, for example, the story of the widow née Zhang in Wang Geng, ed. *Huitu Lienü zhuan* 繪圖烈女傳, *juan* 11, 1058.
103. These are common expressions in the literature on widow chastity; see, for example, in the *Huitu lienü zhuan*, *juan*, 12, 1158. In gazetteers the shrines would sometimes have a general name like *jilieci* 節烈祠, which can be a sacrificial altar dedicated to ancestors, loyal martyrs, chastely martyred women, or filial sons.
104. See Gongquan Xiao (1897–1981), *Rural China: Imperial Control in the Nineteenth Century* (Seattle: University of Washington Press, 1960), 220–24; T'ung-tsu Ch'ü, *Local Government in China under the Ch'ing* (Cambridge, Ma: Harvard University Press, 1962), 164–66; Romeyn Taylor, "Official and Popular Religion and the Political Organization of Chinese Society in the Ming," in *Orthodoxy in Late Imperial China*, ed. Kwang-Ching Liu (Berkeley: University of California

Press, 1990), 126–57; Paul R. Katz, *Demon Hordes and Burning Boats: The Cult of Marshal Wen in Late Imperial Chekiang* (Albany: State University of New York Press, 1995), 60; Guo Qitao, *Exorcism and Money: The Symbolic World of the Five-Fury Spirits in Late Imperial China* (Berkeley: Institute of East Asian Studies, University of California, Berkeley, Center for Chinese Studies, 2003), 42–47; Paola Zamperini, "Eros and Suicide in Late Imperial Chinese Fiction," in *Passionate Women: Female Suicide in Late Imperial China*, 91.

105. These altars were first established by Taizu to commemorate the spirits of men who died in battle; death away from home, in battle, was considered unnatural death. Hence, the spirits of the deceased soldiers needed to be appeased. However, in the later part of the Ming period, deceased widows, whose deaths were also considered unnatural, were also worshipped at these altars. See, for example, the female chastity shrine in Jiangsu province cited above.

106. Guo Qitao, *Exorcism and Money*, 43.

107. See Jin Youli 金友理 (eighteenth century), *Taihu beikao* 太湖備考 (Nanjing: Jiangsu guji chubanshe, 1998), 268.

108. Citation and translation from Elvin, "Female Virtue and the State in China," 129. Original text from Tuojin 托津 et al., *Qinding Da Qing huidian shili* 欽定大清會典事例, completed in 1899 (Taipei: Wenhai chuban she, 1991-1992), *juan* 404, 16b–17b.

109. Sometimes officials and local people were identified as being the "cause" of drought. See Mark Elvin, "Who Was Responsible for the Weather? Moral Meteorology in Late Imperial China," in *Beyond Joseph Needham: Science, Technology, and Medicine in East and Southeast Asia*, ed. Morris F. Low, *Osiris*, 2nd ser., vol. 13 (Chicago: University of Chicago Press, 1999), 213–37.

110. See Alvin P. Cohen, "The Avenging Ghost: Moral Judgment in Chinese Historical Texts" (PhD diss., University of California–Berkeley, 1971), chap. 2; see also his translation of *Yuanhun zhi* in *Tales of Vengeful Souls: A Sixth Century Collection of Chinese Avenging Ghost Stories* (Taipei: Ricci Institute, 1982).

111. See Gui Youguang, *Zhenchuan xiansheng ji* 震川先生集, 622.

112. See Yuan Mei 袁枚 (1716–1779), *Yuan Mei quanji* 袁枚全集 (*Complete Works by Yuan Mei*) (Nanjing: Guji chubanshe, 1993), 8:141. Yuan is not alone in acknowledging the efficacy of deceased widows. Even though some members of the literati would criticize the practice of female suicides, they did not deny the deceased widows' power; see, for example, Yin Huiyi 尹會一 (1691–1748), *Jianyu xiansheng wenji* 健餘先生文集 (*Collected Works of Yin Huiji*) (Taipei: Yiwen yinshuguan, 1966), 239.

113. See, for example, *Huitu lienü zhuan*, *juan* 12, 1158.

114. Emily Martin Ahern, *The Cult of the Dead in a Chinese Village* (Stanford, CA: Stanford University Press, 1973).

115. For an introductory article on the pervasive impact of Buddhist teaching on karma in medieval and late imperial times see Jan Yün-hua, "The Chinese Understanding

and Assimilation of Karma Doctrine," in *Karma and Rebirth: Post Classical Developments*, ed. Ronald W. Neufeldt (Albany: State University of New York Press, 1986), 145–68.

116. See Brokaw, *The Ledgers of Merit and Demerit*, 138–56.
117. For an introduction to and critique of "popular forms" of Chinese religious beliefs and practices see Stephen F. Teiser, "The Spirits of Chinese Religion," in *Religions of China in Practice*, ed. Donald S. Lopez Jr. (Princeton, NJ: Princeton University Press, 1996), 3–37, esp. 21–35.
118. See Stephen F. Teiser, "The Ritual behind the Opera: A Fragmentary Ethnography of the Ghost Festival, A.D. 400–1900," in *Ritual Opera, Operatic Ritual*, ed. David Johnson (Berkeley: University of California: Distributed by IEAS Publications, 1989), 191–223, esp. 211; also by Stephen F. Teiser, *The Ghost Festival in Medieval China* (Princeton, NJ: Princeton University Press, 1988), 107–12.
119. See Teiser, *Ghost Festival in Medieval China*, 170–79.
120. See Glen Dudbridge, *Legend of Miao-shan*, 85–98.
121. Shahar and Weller, "Introduction," *Unruly Gods*, 11.
122. An alternative reading is that it was the force of female pollution that gave the deceased widows their power. Steven Sangren examines the symbolic significance of Guanyin worship in Taiwan and argues that women's marriage refusal is connected to the perception of their "female-pollution." While this may have relevance in contemporary times, there is little evidence that women were perceived as inherently "polluted" in the sixteenth and seventeenth centuries; see Paul Steven Sangren, "Female Gender in Chinese Religious Symbols: Kuan Yin, Ma Tsu, and the 'Eternal Mother,' " *Signs* 9 (1), *Women and Religion* (Autumn 1983): 11–13. My argument does not deal with the issue of pollution but centers around the significance of violent deaths of women.
123. See Theiss, *Disgraceful Matters*, 205.
124. See Zamperini, "Eros and Suicide in Late Imperial Chinese Fiction," 94–95.
125. Fei Siyan 費絲言 cites a case in which a literatus eulogizes a deceased widow as a benevolent deity (*shenming* 神明) who was able to dispel other vengeful ghosts; see Fei Siyan 費絲言, *You dianfan dao guifan: cong Mingdai zhenjie lienü de bianshi yu liuchuan kan zhenjie guannian de yangehua* 由典範到規範: 從明代貞節烈女的辨識與流傳看貞節觀念的嚴格化 (Taipei: Guoli Taiwan daxue chuban weiyuanhui, 1998), 317. In his collected works, Gui Youguang writes about the efficacy of a chaste widow shrine (*zhenlie miao* 貞烈廟) where a county magistrate and other literati prayed for rain after a three-month drought. Great rain came down like torrents as a result of their prayers. See Gui Youguang, *Zhenchuan xiansheng ji* 震川先生集, 422. From these cases we can deduce that chastely martyred widows were also benevolent deities.

CHAPTER 5

1. By far the most thorough study of rainmaking practices, at least official ones, that is, those performed by officials, is by Jeffrey Snyder-Reinke, *Dry Spells: State Rainmaking and Local Governance in Late Imperial China* (Cambridge, MA: Published by the Harvard University Asia Center: Distributed by Harvard University Press, 2009). In addition to this recently published monograph is a monograph on a Yuan-dynasty mural at a Buddhist monastery; see Jing Anning, *The Water God's Temple of the Guangsheng Monastery: Cosmic Function of Art* (Leiden: Brill, 2002). Secondary scholarship on rainmaking in English tends to focus on official rainmaking rituals; see Edward Schafer, "Ritual Exposure in Ancient China," *HJAS* 14 (1–2) (June 1951): 130–84; Mark Elvin, "Who Was Responsible for the Weather? Moral Meteorology in Late Imperial China," in *Beyond Joseph Needham: Science, Technology, and Medicine in East and Southeast Asia, Osiris*, 2nd ser., vol. 13, ed. Morris F. Low (Chicago: University of Chicago Press, 1999), 213–37; Michael Loewe, "The Cult of the Dragon and the Invocation for Rain," in *Chinese Ideas about Nature and Society: Studies in Honour of Derk Bodde*, ed. Charles Le Blanc and Susan Blader (Hong Kong: Hong Kong University Press, 1987), 195–213; Kenneth Pomeranz, "Water to Iron, Widows to Warlords: The Handan Rain Shrine in Modern Chinese History," *LIC* 12 (1) (1991): 62–99; Donald Sutton, "Prefect Feng and the Yangzhou Drought of 1490: A Ming Social Crisis and the Rewards of Sincerity," *Minsu quyi* 民俗曲藝 143 (3) (June 2004): 19–47. Japanese and Chinese scholars tend to focus on rainmaking practices in ancient times; see Akita Shigeaki 秋田成明, "Usai ni tsuite" 雩祭について, *Shinagaku* 支那學 10, special issue (1942–1943): 21–34; Narumiya Kazō 成宮嘉造, "Chūgoku kodai no u nit suite" 中国古代の雩について, *Birin ronshū* 美林論集 5 (1978): 1–14; Fukino Yasushi 吹野安, "Chūgoku kodai shiukō" 中国古代止雨考, *Kokugakuin zasshi* 国学院雑誌 82 (10) (1981): 1–14; Fujita Tadashi 藤田忠, "Kodai usai ni tsuite no kōsatsu" 漢代雩祭についての考察, *Kokushikan daigaku bungaku jinbun gakkai kiyō* 国士舘大学文学部人文学会紀要 21 (1988): 83–99; He Shengdi 贺圣迪, "Daojiao fengyu shu" 道教风雨术, *Shijie zongjiao yanjiu* 世界宗教研究 2 (1991): 49–57; Cui Hua 崔華 and Niu Geng 牛耕, "Cong Han huazhong de shuihan shen huaxiang kan woguo Han dai de qiyu fengsu" 從漢畫中的水旱神畫像看我國漢代的祈雨風俗, *Zhongyuan wenwu* 中原文物 3 (1996): 75–83; Hu Bingzhang 胡炳章, "Cong bianshi dao jilong" 从鞭石到祭龙, *Zhongnan minzu xueyuan xuebao* 2 (1997): 43–45. The few that wrote about late imperial times include Izushi Yoshihiko 出石誠彦, *Shina shinwa densetsu no kenkyū* 支那神話傳說の研究 (Tokyo: Chūō Kōronsha, 1973), 445–89; Ikeda Suetoshi 池田末利, "Jōdai Shina no seiu girei nit suite" 上代支那の請雨儀礼, *Shūkyō kenkyū* 宗教研究 133 (1952): 63–66; Yuan Li 苑利, "Huabei diqu qiyu huodong zhong hanba yu zhan hanba yishi" 華北地區祈雨活動中旱魃與斬旱魃儀式, *Sixiang zhanxian* 思想戰線 27 (3) (2001): 116–17; Zhou Zhiyuan 周致元, "Mingdai junchen daoyu de zongjiao chanshi" 明代君臣祷雨的宗教阐释, *Anhui daxue xuebao* 安徽大学学报, 26 (1) (January 2002): 22–27.

2. Snyder-Reinke, however, does provide a single conceptual framework based on the emic category of "sincerity," or *cheng* 誠; he states that "both officials and commoners considered the pursuit of 'sincerity' the single most important objective in rainmaking activities" (169). While he complicates scholarly constructions of Confucian "virtue" (117) and "orthodoxy" (180–83), his reading of rainmaking rituals as centering around the notion of "sincerity" (117; 169–74) is troubling not only because this notion is deeply entrenched in "Confucian" values but also because the conclusions he draws are skewed by his sources, which are mostly official documents produced by either the officials themselves or the educated elite. These sources would naturally champion "sincerity" as the single most important in producing rain. It is then not surprising that he positions officials as the sole "focal point of community rainmaking efforts" (154). My arguments differ from his. If one examines non-official sources, one realizes that no single framework undergirds rainmaking rituals. See Jeffrey Snyder-Reinke, *Dry Spells: State Rainmaking and Local Governance in Late Imperial China* (Cambridge, MA: Published by the Harvard University Asia Center: Distributed by Harvard University Press, 2009).
3. See Judith Berling, *The Syncretic Religion of Lin Chao-en* (New York: Columbia University Press, 1980):47.
4. For example, Kenneth Pomeranz argues that Confucian rainmaking rituals were qualitatively different from popular ones. He sets up a polarity between "official" and "popular" forms of rainmaking rituals and claims that, for officials, rainmaking rituals operated on the principle of *de*, which he translates as "virtue." For local communities, rainmaking rituals rested on the principle of *ling*, which he renders as "magical efficacy." See Kenneth Pomeranz, "Water to Iron, Widows to Warlords," 65, 75–76. Synder-Reinke concurs with this characterization but complicates it by showing that officials also readily appropriated occult technologies for rainmaking and that "no sacrifices were withheld" as long as they worked; see Snyder-Reinke, *Dry Spells*, 84–118.
5. See, for example, Yu Zhengxie's 俞正燮 (1775–1840criticism of ritual exposure and self-immolation, "Qiuyu shuo 求雨說," in *Huangchao jingshi wenxubian* 皇朝經世文續編, Ge Shijun 葛士濬 (fl. 1888), *juan* 46, "Huangzheng 荒政" (Taipei: Wenhai chubanshe, 1972), 26a–27b. Below I discuss specific examples.
6. I am inspired by the work of Birgit Meyer and Peter Pels, who challenge anthropological writings on "magic" as a way to distinguish "savage" and "primitive" logic from modern Western logic. See Birgit Meyer and Peter Pels, *Magic and Modernity: Interfaces of Revelation and Concealment* (Palo Alto, CA: Stanford University Press, 2003), 38. Bernard Faure has also written on the theme of thaumaturgy in Buddhism, specifically Chan Buddhism. However, he never really defines what he means by the thaumaturgist. Sometimes he uses the term to refer to magicians or anyone with supernatural powers; at other times the term seems to refer to tricksters; see Bernard Faure, *The Rhetoric of Immediacy: A Cultural Critique of*

Chan/Zen Buddhism (Princeton, NJ: Princeton University Press, 1991), 97–131. Likewise, John Kieschnick uses the term to refer to Buddhists who had developed supernatural powers; see his *The Eminent Monk: Buddhist Ideals in Medieval Chinese Hagiography*, 67–111.

7. See Anne Birrell, *Chinese Mythology: An Introduction* (Baltimore: Johns Hopkins University Press, 1993), 146–48.
8. For a modern study of the "steps of Yü" in shamanism, see Donald S. Sutton, *Steps of Perfection: Exorcistic Performers and Chinese Religion in Twentieth-Century Taiwan* (Cambridge, MA: Harvard University Asia Center: Distributed by Harvard University Press, 2003).
9. See Birrell, *Chinese Mythology*, 86.
10. See Schafer, "Ritual Exposure," 160–61n88. Schafer also points to the semantic and religious link between "madness" and an earlier understanding of the *fangxiang shi* 方相士 as someone who was called a maniac (*kuangfu* 狂夫); see ibid., 181.
11. Ibid., 161; Chen Mengjia 陳夢家, "Shangdai de shenhua yu wushu 商代的神話與巫術," Yanjing xuebao 燕京學報 20 (1936): 535; Marcel Granet, *Chinese Civilization* (London: Kegan Paul, Trench, Trübner, 1930), 191.
12. The term "shaman" comes to us through Russian from the Tungusic *šaman*, meaning "one who is excited, moved, raised." See Larry G. Peters and D. Price-Williams, "Towards an Experimental Analysis of Shamanism," in *American Ethnologist* 7 (3) (1980): 408n1. Eliade has provided a very broad (but problematic) definition of shamanism as a "technique of ecstasy." See Mircea Eliade, *Shamanism: Archaic Techniques of Ecstasy*, rev. ed., trans. Willard R. Trask, with a new foreword by Wendy Doniger (Princeton, NJ: Princeton University Press, 1992; originally published 1964), 4. Scholars of China have subsequently either modified or criticized these earlier definitions; see David N. Keightley, "Shamanism, Death, and the Ancestors: Religious Mediation in Neolithic and Shang China (ca. 5000–1000 B.C.)," in *Asiatische Studien/Études Asiatiques* 52 (3) (1998): 766; Stephen F. Teiser, *The Ghost Festival in Medieval China* (Princeton, NJ: Princeton University Press, 1988), 144–45. Some see shamanism (often a rendering of *wu* 巫) as a "substrate" that united Chinese religions. The notion of a "shamanic substrate" was first mentioned by Piet van der Loon, "Les origines rituelles du théâtre chinois," *Journal Asiatique* 265 (1977): 168. Others have vehemently opposed such a view in the context of Chinese religions and argued that the shaman should be distinguished from spirit mediums; see Edward Davis, *Society and the Supernatural in Song China* (Honolulu: University of Hawaii Press, 2001), 2–3. This is not the place to discuss scholarly disputes over the term *wu*. Because this distinction is not prioritized in my sources, I am rendering *wu* as "shaman" as an analytic category to discuss rainmaking.
13. See Schafer, "Ritual Exposure," 152–55; also Wolfram Eberhard, *Chinese Fairy Tales and Folk Tales* (London: Kegan Paul, Trench, Trübner, 1937), 56–58, 311–15.
14. See Schafer, "Ritual Exposure," 158. In later texts the terms *wuxi* 巫覡 occur together with the general meaning of "shamans."

15. See Judith Butler, *Bodies That Matter*, 1–55.
16. See *Chunqiu zuozhuan* 春秋左傳, attributed to Zuoqiu Ming 左丘明 (fifth century B.C.E.), in *Duanju shisan jingwen* 斷句十三經經文 (Taipei: Kaiming shudian, 1984), 43; see also Schafer, "Ritual Exposure," 131.
17. See Chen Mengjia, "Shangdai de shenhua yu wushu," 564–65.
18. For the *Liji* 禮記 passage, see book 2, "The Than Kung," sec. 2, part 3, no. 29, of James Legge, *The Sacred Books of China: The Texts of Confucianism*, part 4, *The Li Kī: The Sacred Books of the East*, vol. 27 (Oxford: Clarendon, 1879–1885), 201.
19. Shirakawa Shizuka 白川靜 contends that, in ancient times, *xu* 需 and *wu* 巫 played identical roles, especially in the practice of ritual exposure; see Shirakawa Shizuka 白川靜 (1910–2006), trans. Kaji Nobuyuki 加地伸行 and Fan Yuejiao 范月嬌, *Zhongguo gudai wenhua* 中國古代文化 (*Ancient Chinese Culture*) (Taipei: Wenjin chubanshe, 1983), 121.
20. See Wu Wenzhang 吳文璋, *Wushi chuantong he rujia de shenceng jiegou* 巫師傳统和儒家的深層結構 (*The Tradition of the Wizard and the Structure of Confucianism*) (Gaoxiong: Fuwen tushu chubanshe, 2001).
21. See Xu Shen 許慎 (30–124) with annotation by Duan Yucai 段玉裁 (1735–1815), *Shuowen jiezi zhu* 說文解字注 (*Annotation to Explaining Simple and Analyzing Compound Characters*) (Taipei: Yiwen yinshuguan, 1966), 370, 580, 505.
22. Some scholars believe that the identity of *ru* as an occultist began only after the Qin and Han dynasties; see Wu Wenzhang, *Wushi chuantong he rujia de shenceng jiegou*, 24–25.
23. For the secretariat see "中書省" in Charles O. Hucker, *A Dictionary of Official Titles in Imperial China* (Palo Alto, CA: Stanford University Press, 1985), 193, entry no. 1606.
24. See Chen Zhiben 陳治本 (d.u.) et. al., *Huangming baoxun* 皇明寶訓 (Taipei: Taiwan xuesheng shuju, 1986), in *GJTSJC*, category: "Celestial Matters" (*Lixiang huibian* 曆象彙編), section: "Strange Phenomena" (*Shuzheng dian* 庶徵典), *juan* 91, *ce* 43, 68–69. The fact that Taizu personally engaged in rain prayer without delegating this task to others suggests that the drought might have occurred around the capital.
25. Official histories are brief and conservative in their description of emperors' performance of ritual exposure, which may suggest that the editors and compilers were trying to conceal the fact that the emperors were naked. Schafer discusses this issue in "Ritual Exposure," 136–37.
26. See Arthur P. Wolf, "Gods, Ghosts, and Ancestors," in *Religion and Ritual in Chinese Society*, ed. Arthur P. Wolf (Palo Alto, CA: Stanford University Press, 1974), 131–82.
27. See, for example, Michael Szonyi, "The Illusion of Standardizing the Gods: The Cult of the Five Emperors in Late Imperial China," in *JAS* 56 (1) (February 1997): 113–35; Meir Shahar and Robert P. Weller, *Unruly Gods: Divinity and Society in China* (Honolulu: University of Hawaii Press, 1996). The theme of celestial

"bureaucracy" is also fully challenged in Robert Hymes, *Way and Byway: Taoism, Local Religion, and Models of Divinity in Sung and Modern China* (Berkeley: University of California Press, 2002).

28. For Qing periods see Alvin P. Cohen, "Coercing the Rain Deities in Ancient China," *HR* 17 (3–4) (February– May 1978): 250; for his accounts of medieval periods see pp. 250–55.
29. Snyder-Reinke argues that "if a deity did not send rain, it was often interpreted to mean that the deity was unaware of people's hardships. Dragging the deity from its shaded shrine into the hot sun allowed the deity to experience the suffering of the people firsthand" (*Dry Spells*, 98). But the opposite could also be argued. There is evidence to suggest that exposing the deities to the blazing sun might have signified punishing the deity.
30. See *Mingwai shi* 明外史 in *GJTSJC*, category: "Celestial Matters" (Lixiang huibian 曆象彙編), section: "Strange Phenomena" (Shuzheng dian 庶徵典), *juan* 96, *ce* 44, 21; see also Cohen, "Coercing the Rain Deities in Ancient China," 247–48.
31. See *GJTSJC*, category: "Celestial Matters" (*Lixiang huibian* 曆象彙編), section: "Strange Phenomena" (*Shuzheng dian* 庶徵典), *juan* 95, *ce* 44, 14. For other late imperial cases of rainmaking by officials see Sutton, "Prefect Feng and the Yangzhou Drought of 1490."
32. See Zheng Run 鄭閏, *Jin Ping Mei he Tu Long* 金瓶梅和屠龍 (Shanghai: Xielin chubanshe, 1994), 160–65.
33. See Martin W. Huang, *Desire and Fictional Narrative in late Imperial China*, 5–8.
34. See L. Carrington Goodrich, ed., and Chaoying Fang, associate ed., *Dictionary of Ming Biographies* (New York: Columbia University Press, 1976), 1325.
35. See Li Fang 李昉 (925–996) et. al., *Taiping yulan* 太平御覽 (Taipei: Taiwan shangwu yinshuguan, 1975), *juan* 11, 185.
36. See Ouyang Xiu 歐陽修 (1007–1072) et. al., *Xin Tangshu* 新唐書 (Beijing: Zhonghua shuju, 1975), *juan* 35, 916.
37. See Snyder-Reinke, *Dry Spells*, 117.
38. See Sutton, "Prefect Feng and the Yangzhou Drought of 1490," 24–28.
39. See Pomeranz, "Water to Iron, Widows to Warlords," 87.
40. Tang Shunzhi 唐順之 (1507–1560) was a well-respected and influential Ming essayist, literary theorist, and an official for most of his lifetime. For a detailed description of his career and contributions to literature see Goodrich and Fang, eds., *Dictionary of Ming Biography*, 1252b–1256b.
41. The "seven matters" (*qishi* 七事) is a further development of the "six matters" (*liushi* 六事) attributed to King Tang, who blamed himself for a drought; the seven are as follows: "Is governance not proper? Have the people been harmed? Is the royal house honored? Are women flourishing? Have there been bribes? Have the meritorious been slandered? Or why has it not rained until now?" In late imperial times,

the six evolved into the seven core responsibilities of an official. See Snyder-Reinke, "Dry Spells," 50, 109–10.

42. Kenneth Pomeranz claims that the state's banning of animal slaughter (*jintu* 禁屠) was meant to be an expression of "benevolence" and that such bans were never reinforced. On the other hand, the banning of animal slaughter in the villages was meant to be "universal because it was a show of popular effort and devotion that was supposed to move the heavens." Such a dichotomy, as attested by this passage, apparently is false. This passage assumes that the banning of animal slaughter was a practice instituted before the late imperial time; see Pomeranz, "Water to Iron, Widows to Warlords," 74–75.

43. I have as yet been unable to find any information on the practice of "breaking the fan."

44. See Tang Shunzhi, "Ping yuyong" 評雩禜 in *GJTSJC*, category: "Political Economy" (*Jingji huibian* 經濟彙編), section: "Ceremonies" (*Liyi dian* 禮儀典), *juan* 659, *ce* 723, 9.

45. See Schafer, "Ritual Exposure," 131; Chen Mengjia, "Shangdai de shenhua yu wushu," 63–566.

46. See chapter 2 on "sympathetic resonance." For a specific discussion of this concept in relation to the natural environment, see Robert P. Weller and Peter K. Bol, "From Heaven-and-Earth to Nature: Concept of the Environment and Their Influence on Policy Implementation," in *Confucianism and Ecology: The Interrelation of Heaven, Earth, and Humans*, ed. Mary Evelyn Tucker and John Berthrong (Cambridge, MA: Distributed by Harvard University Press for the Harvard University Center for the Study of World Religions, 1998), 314.

47. See the chapter on "Tonglei xiangdong" 同類相動 in Dong Zhongshu's 董仲舒 (179–104 B.C.E.) *Chunqiu fanlu* 春秋繁露, ed. Zhong Zhaopeng 鍾肇鵬, *Chunqiu fanlu jiaoshi* 春秋繁露校釋 (Shijiazhuang: Hebei renmin chubanshe, 2005), 809–14. The *Chunqiu fanlu* is a commentary on the *Spring and Autumn Annals* (*Chunqiu* 春秋) and is one of the most important interpretive early works that establish the "Confucian" views on the importance of portents, the exemplary actions of sages, the concept between basic (*ben* 本) and secondary (*mo* 末), the nature of heaven and its relationship with earth and humans, and the ethical ideas of *yin* and *yang* and the five agents. For a brief discussion of the attribution of this work see Loewe, "Cult of the Dragon," 196; Joachim Gentz, "Dong Zhongshu" in *The Encyclopedia of Religion*, 2nd ed., vol. 4, ed. Lindsay Jones, 2418–19 (Detroit: Macmillan Reference USA, 2005); and Sarah A. Queen, *From Chronicle to Canon: The Hermeneutics of the Spring and Autumn, according to Tung Chung-shu* (Cambridge: Cambridge University Press, 1996). On page 5 Queen contends that the work was probably the product of an anonymous compiler who lived sometime between the third and sixth centuries. The quote cited in the main text is also repeated in *GJTSJC*, category: "Celestial Matters" (*Lixiang huibian* 曆象彙編), section: "Strange Phenomena" (*Shuzheng dian* 庶徵典), *juan* 9, *ce* 37, 42–43.

48. The line, which is "秋暴巫尪至九日," appears in the section on "Beseeching Rain" (*qiuyu* 求雨); see *Chunqiu fanlu jiaoshi* 春秋繁露校釋, 998.
49. Such implicit criticism of his contemporaries, who beseeched the deities and spirits for rain, is also evident in late imperial times. Further on in the text we will see how this rather rationalist view was appropriated by later literati in standard manuals on rainmaking.
50. Some modern scholars have hypothesized that the purpose of burning the female shaman in rainmaking rituals was to send them to heaven personally in order to "report" the need for rain. This explanation rests not on the logic of sympathetic resonance but on the bureaucratic model of the cosmos. See Liu Zhixiong 劉志雄 and Yang Jingrong 陽靜榮, *Long yu Zhongguo wenhua* 龍與中國文化 (Beijing: Renmin chubanshe, 1996), 245.
51. See Dorothy Ko, *Teachers of the Inner Chambers*, 200; Zhiyi 智顗 is usually considered the founder of the Tiantai 天台 school of Buddhism in China. He is also regarded as the first major figure to make a significant break from the Indian tradition to form an indigenous Chinese Buddhist system of doctrine and meditation. The most important influence on him was his first teacher, Nanyue Huisi, the Buddhist meditation master who engaged in the painful austerities discussed in chapter 2.
52. For sample stories see Ko, *Teachers of the Inner Chambers*, 200–202.
53. See the character Mama Meng in the Ming opera *The Swallow's Letter*; Charlotte Furth, *A Flourishing Yin: Gender in China's Medical History, 960–1665* (Berkeley: University of California Press, 1999), 272. Mama Meng is a humpbacked grandmother who practiced the medical arts.
54. See Furth, *Flourishing Yin*, 72.
55. Mary Douglas, *Purity and Danger: An Analysis of Concepts of Pollution and Taboo* (London: Ark Paperbacks, 1984; originally published 1966), 94. Douglas clarifies the complex relation of reciprocal involvement and necessary repulsion that existed between the ordering system and that which it had to repel in order to retain its systematicity. She explains that, although the system of order and organization must repel, it must at the same time rely upon and harness this dangerous raw material for its contents, for its recourse.
56. See Susan Naquin, "The Baoming Temple: Religion and the Throne in Ming and Qing China," in *HJAS* 48 (1) (1988): 131–88; Liu Tong 劉侗 (1593–1636), *Dijing jingwu lue* 帝京景物略 (Shanghai: Gudian wenxue chubanshe, 1957), 89–90; also Victoria Cass, *Dangerous Women*, 68–70.
57. See Zhang, Tingyu 張廷玉 (1672–1755) et al., *Mingshi*, *juan* 154, 17b; *juan* 175, 1a.
58. See the excellent article by James A. Benn, "Where Text Meets Flesh: Burning the Body as an Apocryphal Practice in Chinese Buddhism," *HR* 37 (4) (May 1998): 295–322, and his book *Burning for the Buddha: Self-Immolation in Chinese Buddhism*, 19–53, 164–94. Unless otherwise noted, I rely on Benn's translations for my

analysis of Buddhist cases of self-immolation. My analysis, however, differs from his. For non-Buddhist cases of self-immolation see Schafer, "Ritual Exposure"; Qiu Xigui, "On the Burning of Human Victims and the Fashioning of Clay Dragons in order to Seek Rain as Seen in the Shang Dynasty Oracle-Bone Inscriptions," trans. K. Fowler, *Early China* 9/10 (1983–1985290–306.

59. The passage in Chinese is as follows: "其年大旱，封禱請無獲，乃積薪坐其上以自焚．火起而大雨暴至，於是遠近歎服"; see Fan Ye 范曄, *Hou Hanshu* 後漢書 (Beijing: Zhonghua shuju, 1965), 2684.
60. See Schafer, "Ritual Exposure," 139.
61. Hucker, *Dictionary of Official Titles in Imperial China*, 506. It is not clear whether *dianshi* 典史 had implications other than "clerk," an unranked sub-official, in earlier times. This translation is based on the late imperial hierarchical ranking system.
62. See *GJTSJC*, category: "Human Relationships" (*Minglun huibian* 明倫彙編), section: "The Government Service" (*Guangchang dian* 官常典), *juan* 659, 307 *ce*, 50; the story is also repeated in *Mingchen liezhuan* 名臣列傳 (*Biographies of Famous Officials*); see also Schafer, "Ritual Exposure," 140. Schafer states that An Yu performed this act without "depending on the help of [a] local religious specialist." However, in the original sources this information is absent.
63. An example of this widespread practice appears in Ge Hong 葛洪 (283–343), *Shenxian zhuan* 神仙傳 (*Biographies of Divine Transcendents*) (Taipei: Taiwan shangwu yinshuguan, 1983). A study and translation of this work can be found in Robert Campany, *To Live as Long as Heaven: A Translation and Study of Ge Hong's Traditions of Divine Transcendents* (Berkeley: University of California Press, 2002).
64. See the story of Chao Liang 晁梁 in the novel *Marriage Bonds to Awaken the World* (*Xingshi yinyuan zhuan* 醒世因緣傳) by Pu Songling (1640–1715) under the name Xi Zhou Sheng 西周生; Yenna Wu, *Ameliorative Satire and the Seventeenth-Century Chinese Novel, Xingshi yinyuan zhuan-marriage as Retribution, Awakening the World* (Lewiston, NY: Mellen, 1999), 73–79. This story is discussed in chapter 3.
65. See, for example, Benn, *Burning for the Buddha*, 38–39.
66. See Jean Lévi, "The Body: The Daoists' Coat of Arms," in *Fragments for a History of the Human Body*, ed. Michel Feher, with Ramona Naddaff and Nadia Tazi, 105–126 (New York: Urzone, 1989), 110–113.
67. For a more detailed discussion of dietary practices in connection to immortality or gaining transcendence, see Campany, *Making Transcendents*, 62–87.
68. See *Shangyou lu* 尚友錄 as recorded in *GJTSJC*, category: "Human Relations" (*Minglun huibian* 明倫彙編) section: "Clan and Family Names" (*Shizu dian* 氏族典), *juan* 167, *ce* 353, 33. Mount Zhuyu 紵嶼山 is a mythic island mountain in Daoist lore. A discussion is given in Ge Hong's *Baopuzi* 抱朴子; see Luo Zhufeng 羅竹風 et al., *Hanyu da cidian* 漢語大詞典 (Shanghai: Shanghai cishu chubanshe, 1987–1995), vol. 9, 798.

69. My use of this term is not to reify Daoism as a discrete religious tradition with a distinct set of practices. Rather, I show that many of these practices were shared by numerous traditions. For a good discussion of the limitations of Daoism, see Robert Ford Campany, "On the Very Idea of Religions (in the Modern West and in Early Medieval China)," *HR* 42 (4) (May 2003): 287–319.
70. See Daojie 道階 (1866–1934) and Yu Qian 喻謙 (d.u.), *Xinxu gaoseng zhuan* 新續高僧傳, in *Gaoseng zhuan heji* 高僧傳合集 (Shanghai: Shanghai guji chubanshe, 1991), 39: 1197; Benn, *Burning for the Buddha*, 177–78.
71. See Benn, *Burning for the Buddha*, 177–79.
72. See Chen Jingze 陳敬則 (sixteenth century), *Mingxing zaji* 明興雜記, 2 vols. This rare book edition is housed at the Beijing University library. My citation comes from *GJTSJC*, category: "Celestial Matters" (*Lixiang huibian* 曆象彙編), section: "Strange Phenomena" (*Shuzheng dian* 庶徵典), *juan* 96, *ce* 44, 21. This story is also recorded in *Bu xu gaoseng zhuan* 補續高僧傳, by Minghe 明河 (1588–1641), *juan* 20, in *Gaoseng zhuan heji* 高僧傳合集 (*Combined Collection of Eminent Monks*) (Shanghai: Shanghai guji chubanshe, 1991), 738c–739a.
73. James Benn also discusses this case as a recurring theme of influential monks who atoned for the misdeeds of the saṅgha; see Benn, *Burning for the Buddha*, 174–76.
74. For a complete discussion of the creative aspect of *tapas* in early India see Walter O. Kaelber, "*Tapas*, Birth, and Spiritual Rebirth in the Veda," *HR* 15 (1976): 343–86; for the destructive dimension see his "*Tapas* and Purification in Early Hinduism," *Numen* 26, fasc. 2 (December 1979): 192–214.
75. Kaelber, "*Tapas* and Purification in Early Hinduism," 195.
76. See, for example, Leon Hurvitz, trans., *Scripture of the Lotus Blossom of the Fine Dharma* (New York: Columbia University Press, 1976), 61.
77. See Mircea Eliade, *Yoga: Immortality and Freedom* (New York: Pantheon, 1958), 331–32, 337.
78. See Yunqi Zhuhong 雲棲袾宏 (1535–1615), *Lianchi dashi ji* 蓮池大師集 (Taipei: Taiwan yinjing chu, 1955), 136.
79. Here I am drawing on the inspiration of Marcel Mauss, who contended that "there are necessarily biological means of entering into 'communion with God.' "; see his *Sociology and Psychology: Essays* (London: Routledge and Kegan Paul, 1979), 122.
80. See Liu Baonan 劉寶楠 (1791–1855), "Wei Ling Gong," chapter 18, *Lunyu zhengyi* 論語正義 (Taipei: Zhonghua congshu weiyuanhui, 1958), 881.
81. See Mark Lewis, *The Construction of Space in Early China* (Albany: State University of New York Press, 2006), 15.
82. See Liu Baonan, *Lunyu zhengyi*, chap. 1, "Xue er," 18; chap. 2, "Wei zheng," 26–27; chap. 7, "Yong ye," 121; chap. 8, "Shu er," 139, 141, 143, 145; chap. 9, "Tai bo," 169; chap. 17, "Xian wen," 305; chap. 18, "Wei ling gong," 346; chap. 20, "Yang huo," 282.
83. See Wang Kuei 王逵, *Lihai ji* 蠡海集 in *GJTSJC*, category: "Human Relationships" (*Minglun huibian* 明倫彙編), section: "People and Their Attributes" (*Renshi dian* 人事典), *juan* 6, *ce* 385, 33. For an alternative translation see Joseph

Needham, *Science and Civilisation in China*, vol. 2 (Cambridge: Cambridge University Press, 1954), 300.

84. The text in question is *Taiyi sanshan mulang qiyu zhou* 太乙三山木朗祈雨咒. It is currently held in the National Library, Beijing, rare books collection, document number 0508; see Snyder-Reinke, *Dry Spells*, 60–64.
85. The ritual prescriptions also included leaping or dancing. It seems that acts of both exposure and dancing have possible earlier connections to shamanic performances of Shang times; see Schafer, "Ritual Exposure in Ancient China," 145–52. Nakedness was also expressed in Daoist bare-footed ritual dances in medieval times (i.e., the "steps of Yü" or Yü *bu* 禹步); see Kristofer Schipper, "Vernacular and Classical Ritual in Taoism," *JAS* 45 (1) (November 1985): 32. Also see the later information in this chapter for a Ming-dynasty discussion of this practice.
86. See Li Guangdian 李光壂 (1596–1662), *Shou Bian rizhi* 守汴日志 (Zhongzhou: Zhongzhou guji chubanshe, 1987), 7. For a brief discussion of this work and its author see the introduction and postscript by the editor of this edition, Wang Xingya 王兴亚, 1–5, 73–75. For a history of this particular siege see Roger V. Des Forges, *Cultural Centrality and Political Change in Chinese History: Northeast Henan in the Fall of the Ming* (Palo Alto, CA: Stanford University Press, 2003), 222–25.
87. Leaving the hair unbound was characteristic of madmen and ghosts. It was also thought to have the ability to unleash some of an individual's spiritual powers; see Lewis, *Construction of Space in Early China*, 71.
88. See Susan Naquin, *Shantung Rebellion: The Wang Lun Uprising of 1774* (New Haven, CT: Yale University Press, 1981), 100–101.
89. See Paul A. Cohen, *History in Three Keys: The Boxers as Event, Experience, and Myth* (New York: Columbia University Press, 1997), 119–45; for the use of women to suppress gunfire see Joseph W. Esherick, *The Origins of the Boxer Uprising* (Berkeley: University of California Press, 1987), 54.
90. See Hong Mai 洪邁 (1123–1202), *Yijian dingzhi* 夷堅丁志 in the *Biji xiaoshuo daguan* 筆記小說大觀 (Taipei: Xinxing shuju, 1975), *juan* 20, 2379–81; see also Schafer, "Ritual Exposure," 150.
91. See, for example, Snyder-Reineke, *Dry Spells*, 152.
92. See Victor Turner, *The Drums of Affliction: A Study of Religious Processes among the Ndembu of Zambia* (Oxford: Clarendon, 1968), 273–75, and his *From Ritual to Theatre: The Human Seriousness of Play* (New York: Performing Arts Journal Publications, 1982), 61–123.
93. See Judith Butler, *The Psychic Life of Power*, 119–22.

Abbreviations and Conventions

AM	*Asia Major*
BMQS	*Bulletin of Ming-Qing Studies* (*Ming Qing shi jikan* 明清史集刊)
BSOAS	*Bulletin of the School of Oriental and African Studies*
BSOS	*Bulletin of the School of Oriental Studies*
EAH	*East Asian History*
HJAS	*Harvard Journal of Asiatic Studies*
HR	*History of Religions*
HS	*History of Science*
HXYJ	*Hanxue yanjiu* 漢學研究
JAAR	*Journal of the American Academy of Religion*
JAOS	*Journal of the American Oriental Society*
JAS	*Journal of Asian Studies*
JCP	*Journal of Chinese Philosophy*
JIABS	*Journal of the International Association of Buddhist Studies*
JICSCUHK	*Journal of the Institute of Chinese Studies of the Chinese University of Hong Kong*
JRS	*Journal of Ritual Studies*
JWH	*Journal of World History*
LIC	*Late Imperial China*
MC	*Modern China*
MS	*Ming Studies*
PEW	*Philosophy East and West*
TP	*T'oung Pao*
ZHFXXB	*Zhonghua foxue xuebao* 中華佛學學報

References to the *Taishō shinshū daizōkyō* 大正新修大藏經 (85 vols., ed. and comp. Takakusu Junjiro 高楠順次郎, Watanabe Kaigyoku 渡邊海旭, et al., Tokyo: Taisho Issaikyo Kanko Kai, 1924–1934) are abbreviated as T., followed by the work number, volume number, page number, and the registry column (a, b, or c). A * next to a title of a work indicates that the Sanskrit title is a reconstruction from the Chinese.

References to the *Wanzi xuzang jing* 卍 字續藏經 (150 vols., Taiwan: Xinwenfeng chubangongsi, 1968–1970), a reprint of the *Dainihon zokuzōkyō* 大日本續藏經 (150 vols., ed. Nankano Tatsue, Kyoto: Zōkyō shoin, 1905–1912), are abbreviated as X., followed by the work number, volume number, page number, the registry column (a or b), and line.

References to *Ming ban Jiaxing dazang jing* 明版嘉興大藏經 (Xinwenfeng chuban gongsi, 1987) are abbreviated as J., followed by the work number, volume number, page number, the registry column (a or b), and line.

References to the Daoist Canon are abbreviated as *Daozang*, followed by index number based on Kristofer Schipper and Franciscus Verellen, *The Taoist Canon: A Historical Companion to the Daozang* (道藏通考), Chicago: University of Chicago Press, 2004. The Daoist works used are from Zhang Jiyu 張繼禹 et al., *Zhonghua daozang* 中華道藏, Beijing: Huaxia chubanshe, 2004.

References to the *Gujin tushu jicheng* 古今圖書集成 by Chen, Menglei 陳夢雷 (b. 1651), et al. are abbreviated as *GJTSJC*, followed by category, section, *juan*, *ce*, and page number. The *GJTSJC* used for this book is the United Data Banks Digital Publication, Inc., online version as provided by Eastview.com. This database gives page images of the Zhonghua shuju edition of 1934.

Select Bibliography

PRIMARY SOURCES

Works in Buddhist Canons by Title

Apidamo dapiposha lun 阿毘達磨大毘婆沙論 (Skt. *Abhidharma-mahāvibhāṣā-śāstra*) by Kātyāyanīputra 迦多衍尼子 (d.u.). Composed in Kashmir ca. 100. Trans. Xuanzang 玄奘 between 656 and 659. T. no. 1545, 27.

Apidamo jushe lun 阿毘達磨俱舍論 (Skt. *Abhidharmakośabhāṣya*) by Vasubandhu 世親 (fourth century). Trans. Xuanzang 玄奘 (600–664) between 651 and 654. 30 *juan*. T. no. 1558, 29.

Apidamo jushe shilun 阿毘達磨俱舍釋論 (Skt. *Abhidharmakośabhāsya*) by Vasubandhu 世親 (fourth century). Trans. Paramārtha 眞諦 (499–569). 22 *juan*. T. no. 1559, 29.

Bashibazu daoying zhuanzan 八十八祖道影傳贊 (*Eulogies to the Biographies and Images of the Eighty-Eight Ancestors*) by Hanshan Deqing 憨山德清 (1546–1623) in 1620. 4 *juan*. X. 1608, 86.

Buxu gaoseng zhuan 補續高僧傳 (*Supplement to Extended Biographies of Eminent Monks*) by Tairu 汰如 (d.u.). 26 *juan*. X. no. 1524, 77.

Cheng weishi lun 成唯識論 (*Treatise on the Demonstration of Consciousness-Only*; Skt. **Vijñaptimātratāsiddhi-śāstra*) by Xuanzang 玄奘 (600–664) in 659. 10 *juan*. T. no. 1585, 31.

Dabanniepan jing 大般涅槃經 (*Great Nirvana Scripture*; Skt. *Mahāparinirvāṇa sūtra*). Trans. Dharmakṣema 曇無讖 (fifth century) between 416 and 423. 40 *juan*. T. no. 374, 12.

Dafangbian fo baoen jing 大方便佛報恩經 (*Sūtra of Great Expedient Means in the Buddha's Recompense*). Translator unknown. Trans. between 25 and 220. 7 *juan*. T. no. 156, 3.

Dafangguang fo huayan jing 大方廣佛華嚴經 (*The Great Vaipulya Buddha Flower Ornament Scripture*; *Buddhāvataṃsaka-mahāvaipulya-sūtra*). Trans. Buddhabhadra 佛馱跋陀 in 420. 60 *juan*. T. no. 278, 9.

Dafangguang fo huayan jing 大方廣佛華嚴經 (*The Great Vaipulya Buddha Flower Ornament Scripture*; *Buddhāvataṃsaka-mahāvaipulya-sūtra*). Trans. Śikṣānanda 實叉難陀 in 699. 80 *juan*. T. no. 279, 10.

Dafangguang fo huayan jing 大方廣佛華嚴經 (*The Great Vaipulya Buddha Flower Ornament Scripture*; Skt., *Gaṇḍavyūha-sūtra*). Trans. Prajñā 般若 in 798. 40 *juan*. T. no. 293, 10.

Dafangguang fo huayan jing ganying zhuan 大方廣佛華嚴經感應傳 (*Record of Sympathetic Resonance of the Great Vaipulya Buddha Flower Ornament Scripture*) by Layman Wusheng 無生居士 (d.u.), T. no. 2074, 51.

Dayun jing qiyu tanfa 大雲經祈雨壇法. T. no. 990, 19.

Dayunlun qingyu jing 大雲輪請雨經 (*Scripture of [Summoning] Great Clouds and Petitioning for Rain*). Trans. Yixing 一行 (683–727). T. no. 989, 19.

Dazhangfu lun 大丈夫論 (*Treatise of the Great Being*; no Sanskrit equivalent exists). Attributed to Āryadeva 提婆羅. Trans. Daotai 道泰 (d.u.) in the fifth century. 2 *juan*. T. no. 1577, 30.

Dazhidu lun 大智度論 (*Great Perfection of Wisdom Treatise*; Skt. **Mahāprajñāparamita śāstra*). Attributed to Nāgārjuna 龍樹 (150–250). Trans. Kumārajīva 鳩摩羅什 (343/4–413). 100 *juan*. T. no. 1509, 25.

Fayuan zhulin 法苑珠林 (*Forest of Pearls in the Garden of the Dharma*) by Daoshi 道世 (d. 683) in 668. 100 *juan*. T. no. 2122, 53.

Fanwang jing 梵網經 (*Sūtra of Brahma's Net*). Attributed to Kumārajīva (350–409) in 406. 2 *juan*. T. no. 1484, 24.

Foshuo hailongwang jing 佛說海龍王經. Trans. Zhu fahu 竺法護 (Dharmarakṣa; 230?–316). T. no. 598, 15.

Foshuo moluowang jing 佛說末羅王經 (*Sūtra of King Malla*). Trans. Juqu Jingsheng 沮渠京聲 (d. ca. 464) in Liu-Song era (420–450). 1 *juan*. T. no. 517, 14.

Foshuo shi'ertoutuo jing 佛說十二頭陀經 (*The Buddha Explains the Twelve Dhūtaguṇas*). Trans. Guṇabhadra 求那跋陀羅 (394–468). 1 *juan*. T. no. 783, 17.

Gaoseng zhuan 高僧傳 (*Biographies of Eminent Monks*) by Huijiao 慧皎 (497–554) in 519. 14 *juan*. T. no. 2059, 50.

Gaoseng zhuan heji 高僧傳合集 (*Combined Collection of Eminent Monks*) by Huijiao 慧皎 (497–554) et al. Shanghai: Shanghai guji chubanshe, 1991.

Hanshan laoren mengyou ji 憨山老人夢遊集 (*Collection of the Dream Roaming of the Old Man, Hanshan*) Hanshan Deqing 憨山德清 (1546–1623). 55 *juan*. X. no. 1456, 73.

Hongzan fahua zhuan 弘贊法華傳 (*Eulogy to the Biographies Associated with the Lotus Scripture*) by Huixiang 惠詳 (mid-seventh century). 10 *juan*. T. no. 2067, 51.

Jingang jing chiyan ji 金剛經持驗紀 (*Record of the Practice and Experiences Associated with the Diamond Sūtra*) by Zhou Kefu 周克復 (seventeenth century). 2 *juan*. X. no. 1635, 87.

Jinguangming jing 金光明經 (*Scripture of Golden Light*; Skt. *Suvarnaprabhāsauttama sūtra*). Trans. Dharmakṣema 曇無讖 (fifth century). 4 *juan*. T. no. 663, 16.

Jushi zhuan 居士傳 (*Biography of Lay Buddhists*) by Peng Shaosheng 彭绍升 (1740–1796) in 1775 (according to the date of the postscript). 56 *juan*. X. no. 1646, 88.

Lianchi dashi ji 蓮池大師集 by Yunqi Zhuhong 雲棲株宏 (1535–1615). Ed. Sengchan Daxing 僧懺大醒 (twentieth century). Taipei: Taiwan yinjingchu, 1955.

Lingfeng zonglun 靈峰宗論 (*Principle Treatise of Master Lingfeng*) by Ouyi Zhixu 澫益智旭 (1599–1655). Taipei: Shihua guoji gufen youxian gongsi, 2004.

Nanyue Si dachanshi lishi yuanwen 南嶽思大禪師立誓願文 (*The Votive Text of Aspirations of Great Chan Master Nanyue [Hui]si*) by Nanyue Huisi 南嶽慧思 (515–577). 1 *juan*. T. no. 1933, 46.

Sifenlü shanfan buque xingshi chao 四分律刪繁補闕行事鈔 (*The Abbreviated and Supplemented Commentary on the Conducts from the Vinaya of the Four Sections*), composed between 626 and 630 by Daoxuan 道宣 (596–667), T. no. 1804, 40.

Sifenlü xingshi chaozi chiji 四分律行事鈔資持記 (*Record on the Particular Practices of the Commentary of the Vinaya of the Four Sections*) by Zhanran Yuanzhao 湛然元照 (d. 1116), T. no. 1805, 40.

Sishi'erzhang jing 四十二章經 (*The Scripture of Forty-Two Sections*). Trans. attributed to Kāśyapamātaṇga 攝摩騰 (first century) and Dharmarakṣa 竺法蘭 (first century). 1 *juan*. T. no. 784, 17.

Song gaoseng zhuan 宋高僧傳 (*Song Version of the Biographies of Eminent Monks*) by Zanning 贊寧 (919–1001). 30 *juan*. T. no. 2061, 50.

Xinxu gaoseng zhuan 新續高僧傳 (*Newly Extended Biographies of Eminent Monks*) by Daojie 道階 (1866–1934) and Yu Qian 喻謙 (d.u.). In *Gaoseng zhuan heji* 高僧傳合集 (*Combined Collection of Eminent Monks*). Shanghai: Shanghai guji chubanshe, 1991.

Xu gaoseng zhuan 續高僧傳 (*Continuation of the Biographies of Eminent Monks*) by Daoxuan 道宣 (596–667) in 665. 30 *juan*. T. no. 2060, 50.

Xuanji baiyuan jing 撰集百緣經 (*Selected Collection of One Hundred Avadāna Tales*). Trans. Zhi Qian 支謙 (d.u.) between 223 and 228. 10 *juan*. T no. 200, 4.

Youpose jie jing 優婆塞戒經 (*Scripture on Upāsaka Precepts*; Skt. *Upāsaka-śīla-sūtra*). Trans. Dharmakṣema 曇無讖 (385–433/36?) between 414 and 421. 7 *juan*. T. no. 1488, 24.

Yunqi fahui 雲棲法彙 (Collection of Master Yunqi's Teachings) by Yunqi Zhuhong 雲棲株宏 (1535–1615). 10 *juan*. J. no. B277, 33.

Yuqieshi dilun 瑜伽師地論 (*Discourse on the Stages of Concentration Practice*; Skt. *Yogācārabhūmi-śāstra*) by Asaṅga 無著 (fourth century). 100 *juan*. T. no. 1579, 30.

Za baozang jing 雜寶藏經 (*Sūtra of the Repository of Miscellaneous Treasures*; Skt. *Saṃyukta-ratna-piṭaka-sūtra*). Trans. Kekaya 吉迦夜 (d.u.) and Tanyao 曇曜 (d.u.) ca. 472. 10 *juan*. T. no. 203, 4.

Zengyi ahan jing 增壹阿含經 (*Increased by One Āgama Sutras*; Skt. *Ekottara-āgama-sūtra*; Pāli. *Aṅguttara-nikāya*). Trans. Gautama Saṃghadeva 瞿曇僧伽提 (d.u.) in 397. 51 *juan*. T. no. 125, 2.

Zhengfa nianchu jing 正法念處經 (*Scripture on the Correct Dharma of the Foundations of Mindfulness*; Skt. *Saddharma-smṛty-upasthāna-sūtra*). Trans. Gautama Prajñāruci 瞿曇般若流支 (538–543). 70 *juan*. T. no. 721, 17.

Zibo zunzhe quanji 紫柏尊者全集 (*Complete Collection of Venerable Zibo*). Ed. and comp. Hanshan Deqing 憨山德清 (1546–1623) in 1621 (according to preface). 29 *juan*. X. no. 1452, 73.

Daoist Scriptures by Title

Taishang dongyuan shuo qingyu longwang jing 太上洞淵說請雨龍王經 (*Scripture of the Dragon-Kings for Praying Rain, Preached by the Most High, [Lord of] the Abyss*), *Daozang* 362.

Taishang huguo qiyu xiaomo jing 太上護國祈雨消魔經 (*Demon-Slaying Scripture for Protecting the Country and Praying for Rain*). *Daozang* 52.

Taishang Yuanshi tianzun shuo dayu longwang jing 太上元始天尊說大雨龍王經 (*Scripture on the Great Rain-Producing Dragon-Kings, Spoken by the Most High Heavenly Worthy of Primordial Beginning*), *Daozang* 51.

Other Primary Sources by Author

Ban, Gu 班固 (32–92). *Hanshu* 漢書. Repr. Beijing: Zhonghua shuju, 1962.

Chen, Bangyan 陳邦彥 (1603–1647). *Chen Yanye xiansheng ji* 陳岩野先生集. 2 vols. Hong Kong, 1977.

Chen, Ding 陳鼎 (b. 1651). *Donglin lie zhuan* 東林列傳. Taipei: Mingwen shuju, 1991.

Chen, Hanzhen 陳翰珍. *Baixiao tu* 百孝圖. Repr. Taipei: Hanzhen shuju, 1985.

Chen, Menglei 陳夢雷 (b. 1651) et al. *Qinding gujin tushu jicheng* 欽定古今圖書集成. Taipei: Dingwen shuju, 1977.

Chen, Pengnian 陳彭年 (961–1017), et al. *Guang yun* 廣韻. Taipei: Guangwen shuju, 1961.

Chen, Zhiben 陳治本 (d.u.) et al. *Huangming baoxun* 皇明寶訓. Taipei: Taiwan xuesheng shuju, 1986.

Chengzu 成祖 (1360–1424). *Xiaoshun shishi* 孝順事實. Princeton Rare Books Collection; originally published 1420.

Dong, Zhongshu 董仲舒 (ca. 179–104 B.C.E.). *Chunqiu fanlu*, *Chunqiu fanlu jiaoshi* 春秋繁露校釋. Ed. Zhong Zhaopeng 鍾肇鵬. Shijiazhuang: Hebei renmin chubanshe, 2005.

———. *Chunqiu fanlu zhuzi suoyin* 春秋繁露逐字索引. Ed. D. C. Lau. Taipei: Commercial Press, 1994.

Fan, Lian 范濂 (d.u.) *Yunjian jumu chao* 雲間據目鈔. In *Biji xiaoshuo daguan* 筆記小說大觀. Taipei: Taibei xinxing shuju, 1973.

Fan, Ye 范曄 (398–445). *Hou Hanshu* 後漢書. Beijing: Zhonghua shuju, 1965.

Fava, Patrice. "Han Xin's Revenge: A Daoist Mystery." L'École Française d'Extrême-Orient, DVD. France: Le CNRS Images, 2005.

Feng, Menglong 馮夢龍 (1574–1646). *Qing shi* 情史. Changsha Shi: Yuelu shushe, 2003.

———. *Qingshi leilue* 情史類略, comp. Zhanzhan waishi 詹詹外史 (Feng Menglong's pseudonym). Original ed. by Liben Tang 立本堂 (1621–1722). In *Guben xiaoshuo jicheng* 古本小說集成, ed. An Pingqiu 安平秋 et al. Shanghai: Shanghai guji chubanshe, 1990.

———. *Stories to Caution the World: A Ming Dynasty Collection*. 2 vols. Trans. Shuhui Yang and Yunqin Yang. Seattle: University of Washington Press, 2005.

———. *Xinping jingshi tongyan* 新評警世通言. Shanghai: Shanghai guji chubanshe, 1992.

Ge, Hong 葛洪 (284–364). *Shenxian zhuan* 神仙傳. Taipei: Taiwan shangwu yinshuguan, 1983.

Ge, Shijun 葛士濬 (fl. 1888). *Huangchao jingshi wenxubian* 皇朝經世文續編. Taipei: Scripta Sinica Digital Database.

Gu, Qiyuan 顧起元 (1565–1628). *Kezuo zhuiyu* 客座贅語. In *Jinling congke* 金陵叢刻, case 1 (第1函), *Baibu congshu jicheng* 百部叢書集成. Taipei: Yiwen yinshuguan, 1968.

Gu, Yanwu 顧炎武 (1613–1682). *Rizhi lu jishi* 日知錄集釋, ed. Huang Rucheng 黃汝成 (1799–1837). Vol. 18 of *Sibu beiyao* 四部備要, corrected ed. in 100 vols. Taipei: Taiwan zhonghua shuju, 1966–1975.

Gui, Youguang 歸有光 (1507–1571). *Zhenchuan xiansheng ji* 震川先生集. Shanghai: Shanghai guji chubanshe, 1981.

He, Liangjun 何良俊 (1506–1573). *Siyou zhai congshuo* 四友齋叢說. Beijing: Zhonghua shuju, 1959.

Hong, Mai 洪邁 (1123–1202). *Yijiandingzhi* 夷堅丁志. In *Biji xiaoshuo daguan* 筆記小說大觀. Taipei: Xinxing shuju, 1975.

Huang, Hui 黃暉 (27–96?). *Lunheng jiaoshi* 論衡校釋. Taipei: Taiwan shangwu yinshuguan, 1964.

Huang, Yu 黃煜 (seventeenth century). *Bixie lu* 碧血錄 in *Zhongguo neiluan waihuo lishi congshu* 中國內亂外禍歷史叢書, vol. 15. Shanghai: Shenzhou guoguang she, 1936.

———. *Zhou Duanxiao xiansheng xieshu tiehuang* 周端孝先生血疏貼黃 in *Bixie lu* 碧血錄. Repr., Taipei: Yiwen yinshuguan, 1966.

Huang, Zongxi 黃宗羲 (1610–1695). *Mingru xue'an* 明儒學案. Beijing: Zhonghua shuju, 1985.

———. *Ming wenhai* 明文海. Beijing: Zhonghua shuju, 1987.

———. *Mingru xue'an* 明儒學案 . Taipei: Mingwen shuju, 1991.

Ji, Dakui 紀大奎 (1746–1825). *Qiuyu pian* 求雨篇. In *Baibu congshu jicheng* 百部叢書集成. Taipei: Yiwen shuju, 1967.

Jiang, Pingjie 蔣平階 (seventeenth century), ed. *Donglin shimo* 東林始末. Taipei: Wenyuan shuju, 1964.

Jin, Youli 金友理 (eighteenth century). *Taihu beikao* 太湖備考. Nanjing: Jiangsu guji chubanshe, 1998.

Kong, Yingda 孔穎達 (574–648). *Chunqiu Zuo zhuan zhengyi* 春秋左傳正義. In *Shisan jing zhushu* 十三經註疏. Beijing: Zhonghua shuju, 1979.

Li, Fang 李昉 (925–996) et al. *Taiping yulan* 太平御覽. Taipei: Taiwan shangwu yinshuguan, 1975.

Li, Guangdian 李光壂 (1596–1662). *Shou Bian rizhi* 守汴日志. Zhongzhou: Zhongzhou guji chubanshe, 1987.

Li, Shizhen 李時珍 (1518–1593). *Bencao gangmu tongshi* 本草纲目通释, ed. Chen Guiting 陈贵廷. Beijing: Xueyuan chubanshe, 1992.

———. *Compendium of Materia Medica* (*Bencao gangmu*). Trans. Luo Xiwen. Six vols. Beijing: Foreign Languages Press, 2003.

Li, Zhaoluo 李兆洛 (1769–1841). *Yangyizhai wenji* 養一齋文集 (*Collected Works from the Studio for Cultivating Wholeness*). 10 vols. China: Guangxu wu yin, 1878.

Li, Zhi 李贄 (1527–1602). *Fenshu* 焚書. Beijing: Zhonghua shuju chuban: Xinhua shudian Beijing faxing suo faxing, 1961.

Liang, Yannian 梁延年 (1673–1681). *Shengyü xiangjie* 聖諭像解, in *Ming Qing zhenben banhua ziliao congkan* 明清珍本版画资料丛刊, vol. 8. Ed. Ma Wenda 马文大 and Chen Jian 陈坚. Beijing: Xueyuan chubanshe, 2003.

Liu, Baonan 劉寶楠 (1791–1855). *Lunyu zhengyi* 論語正義. Taipei: Zhonghua congshu weiyuanhui, 1958.

Liu, Tong 劉侗 (1593–1636). *Dijing jingwu lue* 帝京景物略. Shanghai: Gudian wenxue chubanshe, 1957.

Liu, Xiang 劉向 (76–6 B.C.E.). *Lienü zhuan* 列女傳. Sibu beiyao 四部備要, ed. Taipei: Taiwan Zhonghua shuju, 1965.

Liu, Xu 劉昫 (887–946) et al. *Jiu Tangshu* 舊唐書. Taipei: Dingwen shuju, 1979.

Liu, Yuyi 劉於義 (1675–1748) et al. *Shanxi tong zhi* 陝西通志. In *Yinying Wenyuan ge Siku quanshu* 景印文淵閣四庫全書, 556 *ce*. Taipei: Taiwan shangwu yinshuguan, 1983.

Lü, Kun 呂坤 (1536–1618), ed. *Shingingo* 呻吟語 (*Shenyin yu*), ed. Kōda Rentarō 公田連太郎. Tokyo: Meitoku Shuppansha, 1956.

———. *Guifan tushuo* 闺范图说. Beijing: Xueyuan chubanshe, 1998.

———. *Shizheng* lu 實政錄. In *Lüzi yishu* 呂子遺書 18–24 *ce*. Preserved in the Far Eastern Library, University of Chicago.

Luo, Guangzhong 羅貫中 (1330–ca. 1400). *Sanguo yanyi* 三國演義. Shanghai: Shanghai guji chubanshe, 1989. Trans. Moss Roberts as *Three Kingdoms: China's Epic Drama*. New York: Pantheon, 1976.

Mingjiaozhongren 名教中人. *Haoqiu zhuan* 好逑傳. Taipei: Guojia chubanshe, 1990.

Ouyang, Xiu 歐陽修 (1007–1072) et al. *Xin Tangshu* 新唐書. In *Ershiwu shi* 二十五史. Beijing: Zhonghua shuju, 1975–1981.

Pu, Songling 蒲松齡 (1640–1715). *Strange Stories from a Chinese Studio*. Trans. Herbert A. Giles. London: Laurie, 1909.

Qian, Qianyi 錢謙益 (1582–1664). *Liechao shiji xiaozhuan* 列朝詩集小傳. Repr. Shanghai: Zhonghua shuju, 1961.

Qian, Yiji 錢儀吉 (1783–1850). *Bei zhuanji* 碑傳集. Taipei: Wenhai chubanshe, 1973.

Qingxin Cairen 青心才人 (eighteenth century). *Jin Yun Qiao zhuan* 金雲翹傳. Shenyang: Chunfeng wenyi chubanshe, 1983.

Shi, Nai'an 施耐庵 (1290–1365), and Luo Guanzhong 罗贯中 (ca. 1330–1400). *Shuihu zhuan* 水滸傳. 100 *juan*. Beijing: Renmin wenxue chubanshe, 1975.

Sun, Zhiwei 孫枝蔚 (1620–1687). *Gaitang ji* 溉堂集, *houji* 後集. Shanghai: Shanghai guji chubanshe, 1979 (earlier edition in Library of Congress).

Tang, Xianzu 湯顯祖 (1550–1616). *Mudanting* 牡丹亭 (*The Peony Pavilion*). Taipei: Taiwan shangwu yinshuguan, 1972.

Tuo, Tuo 脫脫 (1314–1355) et al. *Songshi* 宋史. Beijing: Zhonghua shuju, 1975.

Tuojin 托津 et al. *Qinding Da Qing huidian shili* 欽定大淸會典事例. Compiled in 1899. Taipei: Wenhai chuban she, 1991–1992.

Wang, Chong 王充 (27–97?). Lunheng jiaoshi 論衡校釋. Selected by Huang Hui 黄暉. Taipei: Taiwan shangwu yinshu guan, 1964.

Wang, Gen 王艮 (1483–1541). *Wang Xinzhai quanji* 王心齋全集. Taipei: Guangwen shuju, 1975.

Wang, Geng 汪庚 (1573–1620), ed. Qiu Ying 仇英 (1494–ca. 1552), illustrator. *Huitu Lienü zhuan* 繪圖烈女傳. Repr. of *Zhibuzuzhai kanben* 知不足齋刊本. Taipei: Zhengzhong shuju, 1971.

Wang, Kuei 王逵 (ca. fourteenth–fifteenth centuries). *Lihai ji* 蠡海集. In *Yingyin Wenyuange Siku quanshu* 景印文淵閣四庫全書, 866 *ce*. Taipei: Taiwan shangwu yinshuguan, 1983.

Wang, Shizhen 王世貞 (1526–1590). *Xu Yanyi bian* 續豔異編, *juan* 6, in *Yanyi bian* 豔異編. In *Guben xiaoshuo jicheng* 古本小說集成, ed. An Pingqiu 安平秋 et al. Shanghai: Shanghai guji chubanshe, 1990.

Wang, Yangming 王陽明 (1472–1529). *Chuanxi lu* 傳習錄. Taipei: Taiwan shangwu yinshuguan, 1971.

Wei, Zheng 魏徵 (580–643) et al. *Suishu* 隋書. Beijing: Zhonghua shuju, 1973.

Wu, Jiaji 吳嘉紀 (1618–1684). *Louxuan shi* 陋軒詩. Taipei: Wenhai chubanshe, 1966.

Wu, Yingji 吳應箕 (1594–1645). *Donglin benmo* 東林本末. Beijing: Beijing chubanshe, 2005.

Xi Zhou Sheng 西周生, or Pu Songling 蒲松齡 (1640–1715). *Xingshi yinyuan zhuan* 醒世姻緣傳. Shanghai: Shanghai guji chubanshe, 1981.

———. *Xingshi yinyuan zhuan* 醒世因緣傳. Taipei: Liangjin chubanshe, 1986.

Xie, Zhaozhe 謝肇淛 (1567–1624). *Wuza zu* 五雜俎. 2 vols. In *Biji xiaoshuo daguan* 筆記小說大觀, vols. 6–7. Taipei: Taipei Xinxing shuju, 1975.

Xu, Shen 許慎 (30–124), annot. Duan Yucai 段玉裁 (1735–1815). *Shuowen jiezi zhu* 說文解字注. Taipei: Yiwen yinshuguan, 1966.

Xu, Shupi 徐樹丕 (d.u.). *Shixiao lu* 識小錄. Vol. 4 in *Hanfen lou miji* 涵芬樓秘笈. Taipei: Taiwan shangwu yinshuguan, 1967.

Xu, Song 徐松 (1781–1848). *Song huiyao jiben* 宋會要輯本 (*Draft Collection of Song Statues*), 16 vols. Taipei: Shijie shuju, 1964.

———. *Song huiyao jigao* 宋會要輯稿. Taipei: Xinwenfeng chuban gongsi, 1976.

Yang, Weizhen 楊維楨 (1296–1370). *Tieya yuefuzhu* 鐵崖樂府註, in *Sibu beiyao* 四部備要. Taipei: Zhonghua shuju, 1965–1966.

Yin, Huiyi 尹會一 (1691–1748). *Jianyu xiansheng wenji* 健餘先生文集 (*Collected Works of Yin Huiji*). Taipei: Yiwen yinshuguan, 1966.

Yu, Jideng 余繼登. *Diangu jiwen* 典故紀聞. 1601. Repr. Beijing: Zhonghua shuju, 1984.

Yu, Zhengxie 俞正燮 (1775–1840). "Qiuyu shuo 求雨說." In *Huangchao jingshi wenxubian* 皇朝經世文續編, Ge Shijun 葛士濬 (fl. 1888), *juan* 46, "Huangzheng 荒政." Taipei: Wenhai chubanshe, 1972.

Yuan, Mei 袁枚 (1716–1779). *Yuan Mei quanji* 袁枚全集. Nanjing: Guji chubanshe, 1993.

Yuan, Yingqi 袁應祺 (1574 *jinshi*). *Tianyige cang Mingdai fangzhi xuankan* 天一閣藏明代方志選刊, vol. 18. Shanghai: Shanghai guji shudian yingyin, 1981.

Yuan, Zhonglang 袁中郎 (1568–1610). *Yuan Zhonglang quanji* 袁中郎全集. Taipei: Wenxing shudian,1965.

Zhang, Chao 張潮 (b. 1650). Yu Chu xinzhi 虞初新志. Shanghai: Wenruilou, n.d.

Zhang, Han 張瀚 (1511–1593). "Fengsu ji" 風俗記. In *Songchuang mengyu* 松窗夢語. Shanghai: Shanghai guji chubanshe, 1986.

Zhang, Tingyu 張廷玉 (1672–1755) et al. *Mingshi* 明史. Beijing: Zhonghua shuju, 1974.

Zhang, Xiang 張相 (1877–1945), ed. *Gujin wenzong* 古今文綜. Taipei: Zhonghua shuju youxian gongsi, 1962.

Zheng, Shuruo 鄭樹若. *Yu chu xuzhi* 虞初續志. Shanghai: Wenruilou, n.d.

Zheng, Xuan 鄭玄 (127–200) et al. *Zhouli zhushu* 周禮注疏. Taipei: Taiwan shangwu yinshuguan, 1983.

Zhu, Yizun 朱彝尊 (1629–1709). *Jingzhiju shihua* 静志居詩話. Vol. 2. Beijing: Renmin wenxue chubanshe: Xinhua shudian Beijing faxing suo faxing, 1990.

Zuoqiu, Ming 左丘明 (fifth century B.C.E.). *Chunqiu zuozhuan* 春秋左傳. In *Duanju shisan jingwen* 斷句十三經經文. Taipei: Kaiming shudian, 1984.

Lexicons Listed by Title

Bukkyōgo daijiten 佛教語大辞典, ed. Nakamura Hajime 中村元. Tokyo: Tōkyō Shoseki, 1975.

Chongbian guoyu cidian 重編國語辭典. Taipei: Taiwan shangwu yinshuguan, 1981.

Dai Kan-Wa jiten 大漢和辭典. Ed. Morohashi Tetsuji 諸橋轍次 (1883–1982). 13 vols. Tokyo: Taishūkan Shoten, 1955–1960.

Dictionary of Ming Biography. By L. Carrington Goodrich and Chao-ying Fang. New York: Columbia University Press, 1976.

Dictionary of Official Titles in Imperial China. By Charles O. Hucker. Stanford, CA: Stanford University Press, 1985.

Digital Dictionary of Buddhism, ed. Charles Muller. http://www.buddhism-dict.net/ddb/. Edition of December 26, 2007.

Encyclopedia of Religion, ed. Lindsay Jones et al. Detroit: Macmillan Reference, 2005.

Hanyu da cidian 漢語大詞典, ed. Luo Zhufeng 羅竹風 et al. 13 vols. Shanghai: Shanghai cishu chubanshe, 1987–1995.

Lin Yutang's Chinese-English Dictionary of Modern Usage. Hong Kong: Chinese University of Hong Kong, 1972.

Mochizuki Bukkyō daijiten 望月佛教大辞典, ed. Mochizuki Shinkō 望月信亨 (1869–1948). 10 vols. Tokyo: Sekai Seiten Kankō Kyōkai, 1954–1963.

RoutledgeCurzon Encyclopedia of Confucianism, ed. Yao Xinzhong. London: Routledge Curzon, 2003.

Shuowen jiezi 說文解字. Ed. Xu Shen 許慎 (30–124). Shanghai: Shanghai guji chubanshe, 1981.

SECONDARY SOURCES

Abbink, Jon. "Preface: Violation and Violence as Cultural Phenomena." In *Meanings of Violence: A Cross-Cultural Perspective*, ed. Göran Aijmer and Jon Abbink, xi–xvii. Oxford: Berg, 2000.

Ahern, Emily. *The Cult of the Dead in a Chinese Village*. Stanford, CA: Stanford University Press, 1973.

———. "The Power and Pollution of Chinese Women." In *Studies in Chinese Society*, ed. Arthur P. Wolf, 269–90. Stanford, CA: Stanford University Press, 1978.

———. *The Woman in the Body: A Cultural Analysis of Reproduction*. Boston: Beacon, 1992 (originally published 1989).

———, and Hill Gates, eds. *The Anthropology of Taiwanese Society*. Stanford, CA: Stanford University Press, 1981.

Aijmer, Göran. "Introduction: The Idiom of Violence in Imagery and Discourse." In *Meanings of Violence: A Cross-Cultural Perspective*, ed. Göran Aijmer and Jon Abbink, 1–22. Oxford: Berg, 2000.

Akita, Shigeaki 秋田成明. "Usai nit suite" 雩祭について. *Shinagaku* 支那學 10 (1942–1943, special issue): 21–34.

Anacker, Stefan. *Seven Works of Vasubandhu*. Delhi: Motilal Banarsidass, 1984.

Anagnost, Ann. "Transformations of Gender in Modern China." In *Gender and Anthropology: Critical Reviews for Research and Teaching*, ed. Sandra Morgen, 313–42. Washington, DC: American Anthropological Association, 1989.

Araki, Kengo 荒木見悟. *Mindai shisō kenkyū: Mindai ni okeru Jukyō to Bukkyō no kōryū* 明代思想研究: 明代における儒教と佛教の交流. Tokyo: Sōbunsha, 1972.

Asad, Talal. *Genealogies of Religion: Discipline and Reasons of Power in Christianity and Islam*. Baltimore: Johns Hopkins University Press, 1993.

———. "Remarks on the Anthropology of the Body." In *Religion and the Body*, ed. Sarah Coakley, 42–52. Cambridge: Cambridge University Press, 1997.

———. *Formation of the Secular: Christianity, Islam, Modernity*. Stanford, CA: Stanford University Press, 2003.

Atwell, William. "The T'ai-ch'ang, T'ien-ch'i, and Ch'ung-chen Reigns, 1620–1644." In *The Cambridge History of China*, vol. 7, ed. Denis Twitchett and Frederick W. Mote, 585–640. Cambridge: Cambridge University Press, 1988.

———. "Another Look at Silver Imports into China, ca. 1635–1644." *JWH* 16 (4) (December 2005): 467–89.

Bagley, Robert W. "A Shang City in Sichuan Province." *Orientations* (November 1990): 52–67.

Baker, Dwight Condo. *T'ai Shan: An Account of the Sacred Eastern Peak of China*. Shanghai: Commercial Press, 1925.

Baller, F. W. *The Fortunate Union*. Shanghai: American Presbyterian Mission Press, 1911.

Baptandier, Brigitte. "The Lady Linshui: How a Woman Became a Goddess." In *Unruly Gods: Divinity and Society in China*, ed. Meir Shahar and Robert P. Weller, 105–49. Honolulu: University of Hawaii Press, 1996.

Barlow, Tani. "Theorizing Woman: *Funü, Guojia, Jiating*." In *Body, Subject, and Power in China*, ed. Angela Zito and Tani Barlow, 253–90. Chicago: University of Chicago Press, 1994.

———. *Question of Women in Chinese Feminism*. Durham, NC: Duke University Press, 2004.

Barrett, T. H. "The Madness of Emperor Wuzong." *Cahiers d'Extrême-Asie* 14: 173–86.

Beal, Samuel. Trans. *Si-yu-ki. Buddhist Records of the Western World: Chinese Accounts of India*. 2 vols. London: Trübner, 1884.

Bell, Catherine. "Religion and Chinese Culture: Toward an Assessment of 'Popular Religion.' " *HR* 29 (1) (August 1989): 35–57.

———. *Ritual Theory, Ritual Practice*. New York: Oxford University Press, 1992.

———. " 'A Precious Raft to Save the World': The Interaction of Scriptural Traditions and Printing in a Chinese Morality Book." *LIC* 17 (1) (1996): 158–200.

———. *Ritual: Perspectives and Dimensions*. New York: Oxford University Press, 1997.

Benn, James A. "Where Text Meets Flesh: Burning the Body as an Apocryphal Practice in Chinese Buddhism." *HR* 37 (4) (May 1998): 295–322.

———. "Written in Flames: Self-immolation in Sixth-century Sichuan." *T'oung Pao* 92 (4–5) (2006):117–172.

———. "Fire and the Sword: Some Connections between Self-Immolation and Religious Persecution in the History of Chinese Buddhism." In *The Buddhist Dead: Practices, Discourses, and Representations*, ed. J. Stone and B. Cuevas, 234–65. Honolulu: University of Hawaii Press, 2007.

———. *Burning for the Buddha: Self-Immolation in Chinese Buddhism*. Honolulu: University of Hawaii Press, 2007.

———. "Spontaneous Human Combustion: Some Remarks on a Phenomenon in Chinese Buddhism." In *Heroes and Saints: The Moment of Death in Cross-Cultural Perspectives*, ed. P. Granoff and K. Shinohara, 101–33. Newcastle: Cambridge Scholars Press, 2007.

———. "The Lotus Sūtra and Self-Immolation." In *Readings of the Lotus Sutra*, ed. Jacqueline I. Stone and Stephen F. Teiser, 107–30. New York: Columbia University Press, 2009.

Berling, Judith. "Path of Convergence: Interactions of Inner Alchemy, Taoism, and Neo-Confucianism." *JCP* 6 (2) (June 1979): 123–47.

———. *The Syncretic Religion of Lin Chao-en*. New York: Columbia University Press, 1980.

Birge, Bettine. *Women, Property, and Confucian Reaction in Sung and Yuan China (960–1368)*. New York: Cambridge University Press, 2002.

Birrell, Anne. *Chinese Mythology: An Introduction*. Baltimore: Johns Hopkins University Press, 1993.

Bo, Yuan 伯圓. *Wutai shan shang yi xingzhe* 五臺山上一行者 (*A Practitioner on Mount Wutai*). New York: American Society of Buddhist Studies, 1992.

Bokenkamp, Stephen R. *Early Daoist Scriptures*. Berkeley: University of California Press, 1997.

Boltz, William G. "Hsiao Ching." In *Early Chinese Texts*, ed., Michael Loewe, 141–53. Berkeley: Society for the Study of Early China, 1993.

Boodberg, Peter. "The Semasiology of Some Primary Confucian Concepts." *PEW* 2 (1953): 317–32; repr. in *Selected Works of Peter A. Boodberg*, ed. Alvin P. Cohen, 26–44. Berkeley: University of California Press, 1979.

Bossler, Beverly J. "*Final Instructions* by Yang Jishen (1516–1555)." In *Under Confucian Eyes: Writings on Gender in Chinese History*, ed. Susan Mann and Yu-yin Cheng, 119–32. Berkeley: University of California Press, 2001.

———. *Powerful Relations: Kinship, Status, and the State in Sung China (960–1279)*. Cambridge, MA: Harvard University Press, 1998.

Bourdieu, Pierre. *The Logic of Practice*. Trans. Richard Nice. Cambridge: Polity, 1990.

Brokaw, Cynthia J. "Yuan Huang (1533–1606) and the Ledgers of Merit and Demerit." In *HJAS* 47 (1) (June 1987): 137–95.

———. *The Ledgers of Merit and Demerit: Social Change and Moral Order in Late Imperial China*. Princeton, NJ: Princeton University Press, 1991.

———. "On the History of the Book in China." In *Printing and Book Culture in Late Imperial China*, ed. Cynthia J. Brokaw and Kai-wing Chow, 3–54. Berkeley: University of California Press, 2005.

Brook, Timothy. *Praying for Power: Buddhism and the Formation of Gentry Society in Late-Ming China*. Cambridge, MA: Harvard University Press, 1993.

———. "Rethinking Syncretism: The Unity of the Three Teachings and Their Joint Worship in Late Imperial China." *JCR* 21 (Fall 1993): 13–44.

———. *The Confusions of Pleasure: Commerce and Culture in Ming China*. Berkeley: University of California Press, 1998.

———. "Xu Guangqi in His Context: The World of the Shanghai Gentry." In *Statecraft and Intellectual Renewal in Late Ming China: The Cross-Cultural Synthesis of* Xu guangqi, ed. Catherine Jami, Peter Engelfriet, and Gregory Blue, 72–98. Leiden: Brill, 2001.

Brown, Peter. "The Rise and Function of the Holy Man in Late Antiquity," *Journal of Roman Studies* 61 (1971): 80–101.

———. *The Body and Society: Men, Women, and Sexual Renunciation in Early Christianity*. New York: Columbia University Press, 1988.

Brownell, Susan. *Training the Body for China: Sports in the Moral Order of the People's Republic of China*. Chicago: University of Chicago Press, 1995.

Buck, Pearl S. *All Men Are Brothers*. New York: Day, 1937.

Butler, Judith. *Bodies That Matter: On the Discursive Limits of "Sex."* New York: Routledge, 1993.

———. *The Psychic Life of Power: Theories in Subjection*. Stanford, CA: Stanford University Press, 1997.

Bynum, Caroline Walker. *Holy Feast and Holy Fast: The Religious Significance of Food to Medieval Women*. Berkeley: University of California Press, 1986.

Campany, Robert Ford. *To Live as Long as Heaven and Earth: A Translation and Study of Ge Hong's Traditions of Divine Transcendents*. Berkeley: University of California Press, 2002.

———. "On the Very Idea of Religions (in the Modern West and in Early Medieval China)." *HR* 42 (4) (May 2003): 287–319.

———. *Making Transcendents: Ascetics and Social Memory in Early Medieval China*. Honolulu: University of Hawaii Press, 2009.

Carlitz, Katherine. "The Social Uses of Female Virtue in Late Ming Editions of *Lienü Zhuan*." *LIC* 12 (1991): 117–48.

———. "Desire, Danger, and the Body: Stories of Women's Virtue in Late Ming China." In *Engendering China: Women, Culture, and the State*, ed. Christina K. Gilmartin, Gail Hershatter, Lisa Rofel, and Tyrene White, 101–24. Cambridge, MA: Harvard University Press, 1994.

———. "Shrine, Governing-Class, and the Cult of Widow Fidelity in Mid-Ming Jiangnan." *JAS* 56 (3) (August 1997): 612–40.

———. "The Daughter, Singing Girl, and the Seduction of Suicide." In *Passionate Women: Female Suicide in Late Imperial China*, ed. Paul S. Ropp, Paola Zamperini, and Harriet T. Zurndorfer, 22–46. Leiden: Brill, 2001.

Cartier, Michel. "Nouvelles données sur la démographie chinoise à l'époque des Ming, 1368–1644." *Annales: Économies, Sociétés, Civilisations* 28 (6) (November–December 1973): 1341–59.

Cass, Victoria. "Female Healers in the Ming and the Lodge of Ritual and Ceremony." *JOAS* 106 (1) (January–March 1986): 233–45.

———. *Dangerous Women: Warriors, Grannies, and Geishas of the Ming*. Lanham, MD: Rowman and Littlefield, 1999.

Chan, Wing-tsit, trans. *Instructions for Practical Living and Other Neo-Confucian Writing by Wang Yang-ming*. New York: Columbia University Press, 1963.

Chang, Bide 昌彼得, ed. *Mingdai banhua xuan* 明代版畫選. Taipei: Guoli zhongyang tushuguan, 1969.

Chang, Chun-shu, and Shelley Hsueh-lun Chang. *Crisis and Transformation in Seventeenth-Century China: Society, Culture, and Modernity in Li Yü's World*. Ann Arbor: University of Michigan Press, 1992.

Chang, K. C., ed. *Food in Chinese Culture: Anthropological and Historical Perspectives*. New Haven, CT: Yale University Press, 1977.

Chao, Yüan-ling. "Medicine and Society in Late Imperial China: A Study of Physicians in Suzhou." PhD diss., University of California, Los Angeles, 1995.

Chavannes, Édouard. *Le T'ai chan: Essai de monographie d'un culte chinois. Appendice: Le dieu du sol dans la Chine antique*. Paris: Leroux, 1910.

Chaves, Jonathan. "Moral Action in the Poetry of Wu Chia-chi (1618–1684)." *HJAS* 46 (2) (December 1986): 387–469.

Che, Xilun 車錫倫. *Zhongguo baojuan yanjiu lunji* 中國寶卷研究論集. Taipei: Xuehai chubanshe, 1997.

Chen, Dongyou 陳東有. *Reyu de jiefang: Ming Qing shehui jingji bianqian yu dazhong shenmei* 人欲的解放：明清社會經濟變遷與大衆審美. Nanchang: Jiangxi gaoxiao chubanshe, 1996.

Chen, Huaiyu. *The Revival of Buddhist Monasticism in Medieval China*. New York: Peter Lang, 2007.

Chen, Jianhuang 陳劍鍠. "Yangming houxue suo chansheng zhi zhu wenti 陽明後學所產生之諸問題." *BMQS* 明清史集刊 5 (2001): 161–200.

Chen, John, and Tina Chen. *Chinese Medical Herbology and Pharmacology*. City of Industry, CA: Art of Medicine Press, 2004.

Chen, Mengjia 陳夢家. "Shangdai de shenhua yu wushu 商代的神話與巫術." *Yanjing xuebao* 燕京學報 20 (1936): 485–576.

Chen, Que 陳確 (1604–1677). "Wuyu zuo sheng bian" 無欲作聖辯. In *Chen Que ji* 陳確集. Beijing: Zhonghua shuju, 1979.

Chen, Tiefan 陳鐵凡. *Xiaojingxue yuanliu* 孝經學源流. Taipei: Guoli bianyiguan, 1986.

Chen, Yiyuan 陳益源. *Wang Cuiqiao gushi yanjiu* 王翠翹故事研究. Taipei: Liren shuju, 2001.

———. *Yuan Ming zhongpian chuanqi xiaoshuo yanjiu* 元明中篇傳奇小說研究. Hong Kong: Xuefeng wenhua shiye gongsi, 1997.

Chen, Yuzhen 陳昱珍. "Daoshi yu *Fayuan zhulin* 道世與法苑珠林." *ZHFXXB* 中華佛學學報 5 (July 1992): 233–62.

Cheng, Chung-ying. "Reason, Substance, and Human Desire in Seventeenth-Century Neo-Confucianism." In *The Unfolding of Neo-Confucianism*, ed. Wm. Theodore de Bary, 469–509. New York: Columbia University Press, 1975.

Cheng, Te-k'un 鄭德坤. *Archaeology in China*. Vols. 2–3. Cambridge: Heffer, 1960, 1963.

Cherniack, Susan. "Book Culture and Textual Transmission in Sung China." *HJAS* 54 (1) (June 1994): 5–125.

Chia, Lucille. "Of Three Mountains Street: The Commercial Publishers of Ming Nanjing." In *Printing and Book Culture in Late Imperial China*, ed. Cynthia J. Brokaw and Kai-wing Chow, 107–51. Berkeley: University of California Press, 2005.

Chiang, Sing-Chen Lydia. *Collecting the Self: Body and Identity in Strange Tale Collections of Late Imperial China*. Leiden: Brill, 2005.

Ch'ien, Edward T. *Chiao Hung and the Restructuring of Neo-Confucianism in the Late Ming*. New York: Columbia University Press, 1986.

Ching, Julia. *To Acquire Wisdom: The Way of Wang Yang-ming*. New York: Columbia University Press, 1976.

———, with the collaboration of Chaoying Fang. *The Records of Ming Scholars*. Honolulu: University of Hawaii Press, 1987.

Chong, Key Ray. *Cannibalism in China*. Wakefield, NH: Longwood Academic, 1990.

Chou, Yi-liang. "Tantrism in China." In *Tantric Buddhism in East Asia*, ed. Richard Payne, 33–60. Boston: Wisdom, 2005.

Chow, Kai-wing. "Writing for Success: Printing, Examinations, and Intellectual Change in Late Ming China." *LIC* 17 (1) (June 1996): 120–57.

Ch'ü, T'ung-tsu. *Local Government in China under the Ch'ing*. Cambridge, Ma: Harvard University Press, 1962.

Clark, Elizabeth. "Foucault, the Fathers, and Sex," *JAAR* 56 (1988): 619–41.

Cleary, Thomas. *The Buddhist* I Ching. Boston: Shambhala, 1987.

———. *The Flower Ornament Scripture: A Translation of the Avatamsaka Sutra*. Boston: Shambhala Publications, 1993.

Clunas, Craig. *Superfluous Things: Material Culture and Social Status in Early Modern China* (paperback ed.). Honolulu: University of Hawaii Press, 2004.

Cohen, Alvin P. "The Avenging Ghost: Moral Judgment in Chinese Historical Texts." PhD diss., University of California–Berkeley, 1971.

———. "Coercing the Rain Deities in Ancient China." *HR* 17 (3–4) (February–May 1978): 244–65.

———. Trans. and annotator. *Tales of Vengeful Souls: A Sixth-Century Collection of Chinese Avenging Ghost Stories*. Taipei: Ricci Institute, 1982.

Cohen, Paul A. *History in Three Keys: The Boxers as Event, Experience, and Myth*. New York: Columbia University Press, 1997.

Collins, Steven. "The Body in Theravāda Buddhist Monasticism." In *Religion and the Body*, ed. Sarah Coakley, 185–204. Cambridge: Cambridge University Press, 1997.

Connery, Christopher Leigh. *The Empire of the Text: Writing and Authority in Early Imperial China*. Lanham, MD: Rowman and Littlefield, 1998.

Conze, Edward. *Buddhist Wisdom Books: Containing the Diamond Sutra and the Heart Sutra*. New York: Harper and Row, 1972; originally published 1958.

———. *The Perfection of Wisdom in Eight Thousand Lines and Its Verses*. Bolinas, CA: Four Seasons Foundation, 1973.

Cooper, W. C., and Nathan Sivin. "Man as a Medicine: Pharmacological and Ritual Aspects of Traditional Therapy Using Drugs Derived from the Human Body." In *Chinese Science: Explorations of an Ancient Tradition*, ed. Shigeru Nakayama and Nathan Sivin, 203–72. Cambridge, MA: MIT Press, 1973.

Crooke, William. "Nudity in Indian Custom and Ritual." *Journal of the Royal Anthropological Institute of Great Britain and Ireland* 49 (January–June 1919): 237–51.

Cui, Hua 崔華, and Niu Geng 牛耕. "Cong Han huazhong de shuihan shen huaxiang kan woguo Han dai de qiyu fengsu" 從漢畫中的水旱神畫像看我國漢代的祈雨風俗. *Zhongyuan wenwu* 中原文物 3 (1996): 75–83.

Cullen, Christopher. "Patients and Healers in Late Imperial China: Evidence from the *Jinpingmei*." *HS* 31, part 2 (June 1993): 99–150.

Dardess, John W. *Blood and History in China: The Donglin Faction and Its Repression, 1620–1627*. Honolulu: University of Hawaii Press, 2002.

Davis, Edward. *Society and the Supernatural in Song China*. Honolulu: University of Hawaii Press, 2001.

Deal, William E. "Ascetics, Aristocrats, and the Lotus Sūtra: The Construction of the Buddhist Universe in Eleventh-Century Japan." PhD diss., Harvard University, 1988.

———. "Toward a Politics of Asceticism: Response to the Three Preceding Papers." In *Asceticism*, ed. Vincent L. Wimbush and Richard Valantasis, 424–42. New York: Oxford University Press, 1995.

De Bary, William. *Learning for Oneself: Essays on the Individual in Neo-Confucian Thought*. New York: Columbia University Press, 1991.

Dean, Kenneth. *Lord of the Three in One: The Spread of a Cult in Southeast China*. Princeton, NJ: Princeton University Press, 1998.

Deng, Aimin 鄧艾民. *Chuanxi lu zhushu* 傳習錄注疏. Jilong: Fayan chubanshe, 2000.

Dent-Young, John, and Alex Dent-Young. *The Marshes of Mount Liang: A New Translation of the Shuihu zhuan or Water Margin of Shi Nai'an and Luo Guanzhong*. Hong Kong: Chinese University Press, 1994–2002.

Des Forges, Roger V. *Cultural Centrality and Political Change in Chinese History: Northeast Henan in the Fall of the Ming*. Stanford, CA: Stanford University Press, 2003.

DeWoskin, Kenneth J., trans. *Doctors, Diviners, and Magicians of Ancient China: Biographies of Fang-shih*. New York: Columbia Press, 1983.

Dodds, E. R. *Pagan and Christian in an Age of Anxiety*. Cambridge: Cambridge University Press, 1990.

Dott, Brian R. *Identity Reflections: Pilgrimages to Mount Tai in Late Imperial China*. Cambridge: Harvard University Asia Center, 2004.

Douglas, Mary. *Purity and Danger: An Analysis of Concepts of Pollution and Taboo*. London: Ark Paperbacks, 1984; originally published 1966.

Dudbridge, Glen. *The Legend of Miao-Shan*. London: Ithaca Press for the Board of the Faculty of Oriental Studies, Oxford University, 1978.

———. "A Pilgrimage in Seventeenth-Century Fiction: T'ai-shan and the *Hsing-shih yin-yuan chuan*," *TP* 77 (4–5) (1991): 226–52.

Durt, Hubert. "Two Interpretations of Human-Flesh Offering: Misdeed or Supreme Sacrifice." *Journal of the International College for Advanced Buddhist Studies* (Kokusai Bukkyogagu daigakuin daigaku kenkyu kiyo) 1 (1998): 236–52.

Eberhard, Wolfram. *Chinese Fairy Tales and Folk Tales*. London: Kegan Paul, Trench, Trübner, 1937.

———. *Moral and Social Values of the Chinese*. Taipei: Taiwan, Zhengwen; distributed by Chinese Materials and Research Aids Service Center, 1971.

Ebrey, Patricia Buckley, ed. *Chinese Civilization: A Sourcebook*. New York: Free Press, 1993.

———. *The Inner Quarters: Marriage and the Lives of Chinese Women in the Sung Period*. Berkeley: University of California Press, 1993.

Eichmann, Jennifer. "Spiritual Seekers in a Fluid Landscape: A Chinese Network in the Wanli Period (1573–1620)." PhD diss., Princeton University, 2005.

Eliade, Mircea. *Shamanism: Archaic Techniques of Ecstasy*. Rev. ed., trans. Willard R. Trask, with a new foreword by Wendy Doniger. Princeton, NJ: Princeton University Press, 1992. Originally published 1964.

———. *Yoga: Immortality and Freedom*. New York: Pantheon, 1958.

Elman, Benjamin A. *A Cultural History of Civil Examinations in Late Imperial China*. Berkeley: University of California Press, 2000.

Elvin, Mark. "Female Virtue and State in China." *Past and Present* 104 (August 1984): 111–52.

———. *The Pattern of the Chinese Past*. Stanford, CA: Stanford University Press, 1973.

———. "Who Was Responsible for the Weather? Moral Meteorology in Late Imperial China." In *Beyond Joseph Needham: Science, Technology, and Medicine in East and Southeast Asia, Osiris*, 2nd ser., vol. 13, ed. Morris F. Low, 213–37. Chicago: University of Chicago Press, 1999.

Epstein, Maram. *Competing Discourses: Orthodoxy, Authenticity, and Engendered Meaning in Late Imperial Chinese Fiction*. Cambridge, MA: Harvard University Asia Center, 2001.

Esherick, Joseph W. *The Origins of the Boxer Uprising*. Berkeley: University of California Press, 1987.

Eskildsen, Stephen. *Asceticism in Early Taoist Religion*. Albany: State University of New York Press, 1998.

Fane, Hannah. "The Female Element in Indian Culture." *Asian Folklore Studies* 34 (1) (1975): 51–112.

Fang, Jing Pei and Zhang Juwen. *The Interpretation of Dreams in Chinese Culture*. Trumbull, CT: Weatherhill, 2000.

Faure, Bernard. *The Rhetoric of Immediacy: A Cultural Critique of Chan/Zen Buddhism*. Princeton, NJ: Princeton University Press, 1991.

Fei, Siyan 費絲言. *You dianfan dao guifan: Cong Mingdai zhenjie lienü de bianshi yu liuchuan kan zhenjie guannian de yangehua* 由典範到規範: 從明代貞節烈女的辨識與流傳看貞節觀念的嚴格化. Taipei: Guoli Taiwan daxue chuban weiyuanhui, 1998.

Feng, Youlan 馮友蘭 (1895–1990). "The Rise of Neo-Confucianism and Its Borrowings from Buddhism and Taoism." Trans. Derk Bodde. *HJAS* 7 (2) (July 1942): 89–125.

———. *A Short History of Chinese Philosophy*, ed. Derk Bodde. New York: Free Press, 1966.

———. *A History of Chinese Philosophy*. Trans. Derk Bodde. 2 vols. Princeton, NJ: Princeton University Press, 1983.

Feuchtwang, Stephan. "School-Temple and City Gods." In *The City in Late Imperial China*, ed. G. W. Skinner, 581–608. Stanford: Stanford University Press, 1977.

———. *The Imperial Metaphor: Popular Religion in China*. London: Routledge, 1992.

———. "The Avenging Ghost: Paradigm of a Shameful Past." In *Xinyang, yishi yu shehui: Disanjie guoji Hanxue huiyi lunwenji. Renleixue zu* 信仰儀式與社會: 第三屆國際漢學會議論文集.人類學組 (*Belief, Ritual, and Society: Papers from the Third International Conference on Sinology, Anthropology Section*), ed. Lin Mei-rong 林美容, 7–36. Taipei: Institute of Ethnology, Academia Sinica, 2003.

Fong, Grace. "Signifying Bodies: The Cultural Significance of Suicide Writings by Women in Ming-Qing China." In *Passionate Women: Female Suicide in Late Imperial China*, ed. Paul S. Ropp, Paola Zamperini, and Harriet T. Zurndorfer, 105–42. Leiden: Brill, 2001.

Forke, Alfred (1867–1944). *Lun-hêng*. 2 vols. New York: Paragon Book Gallery, 1962; repr. of the 1907 edition.

Foucault, Michel. "Afterword." In *Michel Foucault: Beyond Structuralism and Hermeneutics*, 2nd ed., by Hubert L. Dreyfus and Paul Rabinow, 208–28. Chicago: University of Chicago Press, 1982.

———. *The Care of the Self*. Vol. 3 of *The History of Sexuality*. Trans. Robert Hurley. New York: Vintage, 1988.

———. *The History of Sexuality: An Introduction*. Vol. 1 of *The History of Sexuality*. Trans. Robert Hurley. New York: Vintage, 1988.

———. *The Use of Pleasure*. Vol. 2 of *The History of Sexuality*. Trans. Robert Hurley. New York: Vintage, 1990.

———. *Discipline and Punish: The Birth of the Prison*. Trans. Alan Sheridan. New York: Vintage, 1995.

Foulks, Beverley. "Living Karma: The Religious Practices of Ouyi Zhixu (1599–1655)." PhD diss., Harvard University, 2009.

Frauwallner, E. *The Earliest Vinaya and the Beginnings of Buddhist Literature*. Trans. from the German by L. Petech. Rome: Italian Institute for the Middle and Far East (Is.M.E.O.), 1956.

Freedman, Maurice. *The Study of Chinese Society*. Ed. William Skinner. Stanford, CA: Stanford University Press, 1979.

Freiberger, Oliver. *Asceticism and Its Critics: Historical Accounts and Comparative Perspectives*. Oxford: Oxford University Press, 2006.

Fujita, Tadashi 藤田忠. "Koudai usai ni tsuite no kōsatsu" 漢代雩祭についての考察. *Kokushikandaigakubungakujinbungakkaikiyō* 国士舘大学文学部人文学会紀要 21 (1988): 83–99.

Fukino, Yasushi 吹野安. "Chūgoku kodai shiu kō" 中国古代止雨考. *Kokugakuin zasshi* 国学院雑誌 82 (10) (1981): 1–14.

Furth, Charlotte. "Androgynous Males and Deficient Females: Biology and Gender Boundaries in Sixteenth- and Seventeenth-Century China." *LIC* 9 (2) (December 1988): 1–31.

———. "Patriarch's Legacy: Household Instructions and the Transmission of Orthodox Values." In *Orthodoxy in Late Imperial China*, ed. Kwang-Jing Liu, 187–211. Berkeley: University of California Press, 1990.

———. *A Flourishing Yin: Gender in China's Medical History, 960–1665*. Berkeley: University of California Press, 1999.

———. "Blood, Body, and Gender: Medical Images of the Female Condition in China, 1600–1850." In *Chinese Femininities, Chinese Masculinities: A Reader*, ed. Susan Brownell and Jeffrey N. Wasserstrom, 291–314. Berkeley: University of California Press, 2002.

Gager, John G. "Body-Symbols and Social Reality: Resurrection, Incarnation, and Asceticism in Early Christianity." *Religion* 12 (1982): 345–63.

Gearhart, Suzanne. *The Open Boundary of History and Fiction: A Critical Approach to the French Enlightenment*. Princeton, NJ: Princeton University Press, 1984.

Gentz, Joachim. "Dong Zhongshu." In *The Encyclopedia of Religion*, 2nd ed., vol. 4, ed. in chief Lindsay Jones, 2418–19. Detroit: Macmillan Reference USA, 2005.

Gernet, Jacques. "Les suicides par le feu chez bouddhistes chinois de Ve au Xe siècle." *Mélanges publiés par l'Institut des Hautes Études Chinoises* 2 (1960): 527–58.

Gerritsen, Anne. "From Demon to Deity: Kang Wang in Thirteenth-Century Jizhou and Beyond." *TP* 90 (1–3) (2004): 1–31.

Girard, René. *Violence and the Sacred*. Trans. Patrick Gregory. Baltimore: Johns Hopkins University Press, 1977.

Godley, Michael R. "The End of the Queue: Hair as Symbol in Chinese History." *East Asian History* 8 (December 1994): 53–72.

Goodrich, L. Carrington, ed., and Chaoying Fang, associate ed. *Dictionary of Ming Biography, 1368–1644*. New York: Columbia University Press, 1976.

Goossaert, Vincent. "Starved of Resources: Clerical Hunger and Enclosures in Nineteenth-Century China." *HJAS* 62 (1) (2002): 77–133.

Graf, Fritz. "Violence." In *Encyclopedia of Religion*, ed. Lindsay Jones et al., 9595–9600. Detroit: Macmillan Reference USA, 2005.

Graff, David A. "Meritorious Cannibal: Chang Hsün's Defense of Sui-Yang and the Exaltation of Loyalty in an Age of Rebellion." *AM* (3rd ser.) 8, part 1 (1995), 1–16.

Graham, A. C. *Disputers of the Tao: Philosophical Argument in Ancient China*. La Salle, IL: Open Court, 1989.

Granet, Marcel. *Chinese Civilization*. London: Kegan Paul, Trench, Trübner, 1930.

Gray, David B. "Eating the Heart of the Brahmin: Representations of Alterity and the Formation of Identity in Tantric Buddhist Discourse." *HR* 45 (1) (August 2005): 45–69.

Greenbaum, Jamie. *Chen Jiru (1558–1639): The Background to Development and Subsequent Uses of Literary Personae*. Leiden: Brill, 2007.

Groner, Paul. "The Fan-Wang Ching and Monastic Discipline in Japanese Tendai: A Study of Annen's Futsū jubosatsukai kōshaku." In *Chinese Buddhist Apocrypha*, ed. Robert E. Buswell Jr., 251–89. Honolulu: University of Hawaii, 1990.

Groot, J. J. M. de. *La code du Mahâyâna en Chine: Son influence sur la vie monacale et sur le monde laïque*. Bilingual ed. Amsterdam: 1893.

———. *The Religious System of China: Its Ancient Forms, Evolution, History, and Present Aspect, Manners, Custom and Social Institutions Connected Therewith*. 6 vols. Taipei: Ch'eng Wen, 1976.

Guo, Qitao. *Exorcism and Money: The Symbolic World of the Five-Fury Spirits in Late Imperial China*. Berkeley: Institute of East Asian Studies, University of California–Berkeley, Center for Chinese Studies, 2003.

Haar, Barend J. ter. *The White Lotus Teachings in Chinese Religious History*. Leiden: Brill, 1992.

———. "Rethinking 'Violence' in Chinese Culture." In *The Meanings of Violence: A Cross-Cultural Perspective*, ed. Göran Aijmer and Jon Abbink, 123–40. Oxford: Berg, 2000.

———. "Violence in Chinese Culture." In *The Blackwell Companion to Religion and Violence*, ed. Andrew R. Murphy, 249–62. Oxford: Wiley, 2011.

Habito, Ruben L. F. "Bodily Reading of the Lotus Sūtra." In *Readings of the Lotus Sūtra*, ed. Stephen Teiser and Jacqueline Stone, 186–208. New York: Columbia University Press, 2009.

Handlin, Joanna F. *Action in Late Ming Thought: The Reorientation of Lü K'un and Other Scholar-Officials*. Berkeley: University of California Press, 1983.

———. "Lü Kun's New Audience: The Influence of Women's Literacy on Sixteenth-Century Thought." In *Women in Chinese Society*, ed. Margery Wolf and Roxanne Witke, 13–38. Stanford, CA: Stanford University Press, 1975.

Hao, Chunwen 郝春文. *Tang houqi wudai Songchu Dunhuang sengni de shehui shenghuo* 唐后期五代宋初敦煌僧尼的社會生活 (*The Social Life of Buddhist Monks and Nuns in Dunhuang during the Late Tang, Five Dynasties, and the Early Song*). Beijing: Zhongguo shehui kexue chubanshe, 1998.

Harper, Donald. *Early Chinese Medical Literature: The Mawangdui Medical Manuscripts*. London,: Kegan Paul International, 1998.

———. "Iatromancy, Diagnosis, and Prognosis in Early Chinese Medicine." In *Innovation in Chinese Medicine*, ed. Elisabeth Hsu, 99–120. Cambridge: Cambridge University Press, 2001.

Harpham, Geoffrey Galt. *The Ascetic Imperative in Culture and Criticism*. Chicago: University of Chicago Press, 1987.

Harrell, C. Stevan. "When a Ghost Becomes a God." In *Religion and Ritual in Chinese Society*, ed. Arthur Wolf, 193–206. Stanford: Stanford University Press, 1974.

Hasebe, Yūkei 長谷部幽蹊. *Minshin bukkyō kyōdanshi kenkyū* 明清佛教教團史研究. Kyoto: Dohosha Shuppan, 1993.

Hauf, Kandice. "'Goodness Unbound': Wang Yang-Ming and the Redrawing of the Boundary of Confucianism." In *Imagining Boundaries: Changing Confucian Doctrines, Texts, and Hermeneutics*, ed. Kai-wing Chow, On-cho Ng, and John B. Henderson, 121–46. Albany: State University of New York Press, 1999.

Hayashi, Minao 林巳奈夫. "Chūgoku kodai no ibutu ni arawasarete 'Ki' no zushōteki hyōgen 中國古代の遺物に表はされて「氣」の圖像的表現" (Ancient Chinese Figural Representations of "Qi" 氣). Tōhō gakuhō 東方學報 61 (March 1989): 1–93.

He, Shengdi 贺圣迪. "Daojiao fengyu shu" 道教风雨术. *Shijie zongjiao yanjiu* 世界宗教研究 2 (1991): 49–57.

Hegel, Robert. *Reading Illustrated Fiction in Late Imperial China*. Stanford, CA: Stanford University Press, 1998.

Heijdra, Martin. "The Socio-Economic Development of Rural China during the Ming." In *The Cambridge History of China*, vol. 8, *The Ming Dynasty, 1368–1644*, part 2, ed. Frederick W. Mote and Denis Twitchett, 417–578. Cambridge: Cambridge University Press, 1998.

Heinrich, Busch. "The Tung-lin Shu-yüan and Its Political and Philosophical Significance." *Monumenta Serica* 14 (1949–1955): 1–163.

Hida, Romi 肥田路美. "Hen to un: Daikōzu hensōzu ni okeru imi to kinō wo megutte 変と雲–大構図変相図における意味と機能をめぐって" (The Meaning and Function of Clouds in Bianxiang). Waseda daigagu daigakuin bungaku kenkyūka kiyō 早稲田大学大学院文学研究科紀要 (Bulletin of the Graduate Division of Literature of Waseda University) 3 (45) (1999): 123–37.

Ho, Ping-ti. *Studies on the Population of China, 1368–1953*. Cambridge, MA: Harvard University Press, 1959.

Ho, Virgil Kit-yiu. "Butchering Fish and Executing Criminals: Public Executions and the Meaning of Violence in Late Imperial and Modern China." In *The Meanings of*

Violence: A Cross-Cultural Perspective, ed. Göran Aijmer and Jon Abbink, 141–60. Oxford: Berg, 2000.

Holcombe, Charles. "The Exemplar State: Ideology, Self-Cultivation, and Power in Fourth-Century China." *HJAS* 49 (1) (June 1989): 93–139.

Horner, Isaline Blew (1896–1981). *The Book of the Discipline*. London: Published for the Pali Text Society by Luzac, 1949–1966.

Howard, Angela Falco. *Summit of Treasures: Buddhist Cave Art of Dazu, China*. Trumbull, CT: Weatherhill, 2001.

Howard-Johnston, James and Paul Antony Hayward, ed., *The Cult of Saints in Late Antiquity and the Middle Ages: Essays on the Contribution of Peter Brown*. Oxford: Oxford University Press, 1999.

Hsieh, Yu-wei. "Filial Piety and Chinese Society." In *The Chinese Mind: Essentials of Chinese Philosophy and Culture*, ed. Charles A. Moore, 174–83. Honolulu: University of Hawaii Press, 1967.

Hsu, Dau-lin. "Crime and Cosmic Order: On the Religious and Philosophical Bases of Chinese Law," *HJAS* 30 (1970): 111–25.

Hsu, Pi-Ching. *Beyond Eroticism: A Historian's Reading of Humor in Feng Menglong's* Child's Folly. Lanham, MD: University Press of America, 2006.

Hsu, Sung-peng. *A Buddhist Leader in Ming China*. University Park: Pennsylvania State University Press, 1979.

Hu, Bingzhang 胡炳章. "Cong bianshi dao jilong" 从鞭石到祭龙. *Zhongnan minzu xueyuan xuebao* 中南民族学院学报 2 (1997): 43–45.

Huang, Lin 黃霖, and Han Tongwen 韓同文. *Zhongguo lidai xiaoshuo lunzhu xuan* 中國歷代小說論著選 (*A Collection of Prefaces from Chinese Fiction through the Ages*). Vol. 1. Nanchang: Jiangxi renmin chubanshe, 1982.

Huang, Martin W. *Desire and Fictional Narrative in Late Imperial China*. Cambridge, MA: Harvard University Press, 2001.

Huang, Ray. *Taxation and Governmental Finance in Sixteenth-Century Ming China*. London: Cambridge University Press, 1974.

———. *1587, a Year of No Significance: The Ming Dynasty in Decline*. New Haven, CT: Yale University Press, 1981.

———. "The Lung-ch'ing and Wanli Reigns, 1567–1620." In *The Cambridge History of China*, vol. 7, part 1, ed. Denis Twitchett and Frederick W. Mote, 511–84. Cambridge: Cambridge University Press, 1988.

Hucker, Charles O. *A Dictionary of Official Titles in Imperial China*. Stanford, CA: Stanford University Press, 1985.

Hui Seng. *Buddha Speaks the Brahma Net Sutra: The Ten Major and Forty-Eight Minor Bodhisattva Precepts*. Ukiah: Sino-American Buddhist Association, 1982.

Hurvitz, Leon, trans. *Scripture of the Lotus Blossom of the Fine Dharma*. New York: Columbia University Press, 1976.

Hymes, Robert. *Way and Byway: Taoism, Local Religion, and Models of Divinity in Sung and Modern China*. Berkeley: University of California Press, 2002.

Idema, Wilt. *Personal Salvation and Filial Piety: Two Precious Scroll Narratives of Guanyin and Her Acolyte*. Honolulu: University of Hawaii Press, 2008.

Ikeda, Suetoshi 池田末利. "Jōdai Shina no seiu girei nit suite." 上代支那の請雨儀礼, *Shūkyō kenkyū* 宗教研究 133 (1952): 63–66.

Ikezawa, Masaru 池澤優. "The Philosophy of Filial Piety in Ancient China." PhD diss., University of British Columbia, 1994.

Itano, Chōhachi 板野長八. *Jukyō seiritsushi no kenkyū* 儒教成立史の研究. Tokyo: Iwanami Shoten, 1995.

Itō, Seiji 伊藤清司. "Chūgoku kodai no sangaku kami saishi" 中國古代の山岳神祭. In *Ine fune matsuri: Matsumoto Nobuhiro Sensei tsuitō ronbunshū* 稲·舟·祭: 松本信廣先生追悼論文集, ed. Ine Fune Matsuri Kankō Sewanin稲·舟·祭刊行世話人, 387–408. Tokyo: Rokkō Shuppan, 1982.

Ivanhoe, Philip J. *Confucian Moral Self Cultivation*. New York: Lang, 1993.

Iyanaga, Nobumi 彌永信美. "Daikokuten 大黒天." In *Hōbōgirin*, ed. Adrien Maisonneuve and Jean Maisonneuve, vol. 7, 839–920. Tokyo: Maison Franco-Japonaise, 1994.

———. "Dākinī et l'Empereur—Mystique bouddhique de la royauté dans le Japon medieval." In "Reconfiguring Cultural Semantics: The Construction of Japanese Identity," ed. Fabio Rambelli and Patrizia Violi, special issue, *Versus* (Quaderni di studi semiotici) 83/84 (May–December 1999): 41–111.

Izushi, Yoshihiko 出石誠彦. *Shina shinwa densetsu no kenkyū* 支那神話傳說の研究. Tokyo: Chūō Kōronsha, 1973.

Jan, Yün-hua. "Buddhist Self-Immolation in Medieval China." *HR* 4 (1965): 243–65.

———. "The Chinese Understanding and Assimilation of Karma Doctrine." In *Karma and Rebirth: Post-Classical Developments*, ed. Ronald W. Neufeldt, 145–68. Albany: State University of New York Press, 1986.

Jay, Jennifer W. "Another Side of Chinese Eunuch History: Castration, Marriage, Adoption, and Burial." *Canadian Journal of History* 28 (3) (December 1993): 460–78.

Jiang, Anning. *The Water God's Temple of the Guangsheng Monastery: Cosmic Function of Art, Ritual, and Theater*. Leiden: Brill, 2002.

Johnson, David, ed. *Ritual Opera, Operatic Ritual: "Mu-lien Rescues His Mother" in Chinese Popular Culture*. Papers from the International Workshop on the Mu-lien Operas, with an additional contribution on the woman Huang legend by Beata Grant. Berkeley: University of California: Distributed by IEAS Publications, 1989.

———, Andrew J. Nathan, and Evelyn S. Rawski. *Popular Culture in Late Imperial China*. Berkeley: University of California Press, 1985.

Juergensmeyer, Mark. *Terror in the Mind of God*. Berkeley: University of California Press, 2000.

Kaelber, Walter O. "*Tapas*, Birth, and Spiritual Rebirth in the Veda." *HR* 15 (1976): 343–86.

———. "*Tapas* and Purification in Early Hinduism." *Numen* 26, fasc. 2 (December 1979): 192–214.

Kaji, Nobuyuki 加地伸行. "Confucianism, the Forgotten Religion." *Japan Quarterly* 38 (1) (1991): 57–62.

———. *Jukyō to wa nani ka* 儒教とは何か? Tokyo: Chuō kōronsha, 1990.

Kao, Karl S.Y. "*Bao* and *Baoying*: Narrative Causality and External Motivations in Chinese Fiction." In *Chinese Literary Essays* 11 (December 1989): 115–38.

Katz, Paul R. *Demon Hordes and Burning Boats: The Cult of Marshal Wen in Late Imperial Chekiang*. Albany: State University of New York Press, 1995.

Keightley, David N. "Shamanism, Death, and the Ancestors: Religious Mediation in Neolithic and Shang China (ca. 5000–1000 B.C.)." *Asiatische Studien/Études Asiatiques* 52 (3) (1998): 763–831.

Kelsay, John. *Arguing the Just War in Islam*. Cambridge, MA: Harvard University Press, 2007.

Kieschnick, John. *The Eminent Monk: Buddhist Ideals in Medieval Chinese Hagiography*. Honolulu: University of Hawaii Press, 1997.

———. "Blood Writing in Chinese Buddhism." *JIABS* 23 (2) (2000): 177–94.

Knapp, Keith Nathaniel. "*Se* 色." In *RoutledgeCurzon Encyclopedia of Confucianism*, ed. Yao Xinzhong, 533–34. London: RoutledgeCurzon, 2003.

———. *Selfless Offspring: Filial Children and Social Order in Medieval China*. Honolulu: University of Hawaii Press, 2005.

Ko, Dorothy. *Teachers of the Inner Chambers: Women and Culture in Seventeenth-Century China*. Stanford, CA: Stanford University Press, 1994.

———. *Cinderella's Sisters: A Revisionist History of Footbinding*. Berkeley: University of California Press, 2005.Stanford, CA

Kōno, Ryōsen 河野亮仙. "Minami Indo no seiuhō" 南インドの請雨法. *Mikkyō zuzō* 密教図像 7 (1990): 46–56.

Kutcher, Norman A. *Mourning in Late Imperial China: Filial Piety and the State*. New York: Cambridge University Press, 1999.

Kuwabara Jitsuzō 桑原隲蔵 (1870–1931). "Shina jinkan ni okeru shokujin niku no fūshū 支那人間に於ける食人肉の風習." *Kuwabara Jitsuzō zenshū* 桑原隲藏全集, ed. Miyazaki Ichisada 宮崎市定 et al. 6 vols. Vol. 2: 153–205. Tokyo: Iwanami Shoten, 1968–1969.

———. "Shina no kōdō, koto ni hōritsujō yori kantaru Shina no kōdō 支那の孝道殊に法律上より観たる支那の孝道." *Kuwabara Jitsuzō zenshū* 桑原隲藏全集, ed. Miyazaki Ichisada 宮崎市定 et al. 6 vols. Vol. 3: 9–92. Tokyo: Iwanami Shoten, 1968–1969.

———. *Tōyō bunmei shiron* 東洋文明史論. Tokyo: Heibonsha, 1988.

Lai, Whalen. "Looking for Mr. Ho Po: Unmasking the River God of Ancient China." *HR* 29 (1990): 335–50.

Lamotte, Étienne. Trans. from the French by Sara Webb-Boin under the supervision of Jean Dantinne. *History of Indian Buddhism: From the Origins to the Śaka Era*. Louvain-la-Neuve: Institut Orientaliste, Université de Louvain, 1988.

Laqueur, Thomas. *Making Sex: Body and Gender from the Greeks to Freud*. Cambridge, MA: Harvard University Press, 1990.

Late Imperial China. "Symposium on Poetry and Women's Culture in Late Imperial China." *LIC* 13 (1) (June 1992). 1–172.

Lau, D. C. *The Analects (Lun yu)/Confucius*. Harmondsworth: Penguin, 1979.

———. *Mencius*. Rev. ed. New York: Penguin, 2001.

Lee, Cheuk Yin. "Emperor Chengzu and Imperial Filial Piety of the Ming Dynasty." In *Filial Piety in Chinese Thought and History*, ed. Alan K. L. Chan and Sor-hoon Tan, 141–53. London: RoutledgeCurzon, 2004.

Legge, James. *The Sacred Books of China: The Texts of Confucianism*. Part 4, *The Li Ki*. *The Sacred Books of the East*, vols. 27–28. Oxford: Clarendon, 1879–1885.

———. *The Sacred Books of China: The Texts of Confucianism*. Part 1, *The Hsiâo King*. *The Sacred Books of the East*, vol. 5. New York: Scribner, 1899.

———. *The Ch'un Ts'ew, with The Tso chuen*. In *The Chinese Classics*, vol. 5. Taipei: Chin-hsüeh shu-chu, 1969.

———. Trans. *A Record of Buddhistic Kingdoms: Being an Account by the Chinese Monk Fâ-Hien of His Travels in India and Ceylon (A.D. 399—414) in Search of the Buddhist Books of Discipline*. San Francisco: Chinese Materials Center, 1975.

Lei, Daphne P. "The Blood-Stained Text in Translation: Tattooing, Bodily Writing, and Performance of Chinese Virtue." *Anthropological Quarterly* 82 (1) (2009): 99–128.

Leung, Angela Ki Che. "Elementary Education in the Lower Yangtze Region in the Seventeenth and Eighteenth Centuries." In *Education and Society in Late Imperial China, 1600–1900*, ed. Benjamin A. Elman and Alexander Woodside, 381–416. Berkeley: University of California Press, 1994.

———. "Women Practicing Medicine in Premodern China." In *Chinese Women in the Imperial Past: New Perspectives*, ed. Harriet T. Zurndorfer, 101–34. Leiden: Brill, 1999.

Lévi, Jean. "The Body: The Daoists' Coat of Arms." In *Fragments for a History of the Human Body*, ed. Michel Feher, with Ramona Naddaff and Nadia Tazi, 105–26. New York: Urzone, 1989.

Lévy-Bruhl, Lucien. *Primitive Mentality*. Trans. Lilian A. Clare. Boston: Beacon, 1966.

Lewis, Mark Edward. *Sanctioned Violence in Early China*. Albany: State University of New York Press, 1990.

———. *Writing and Authority in Early China*. Albany: State University of New York Press, 1999.

———. *The Construction of Space in Early China*. Albany: State University of New York Press, 2006.

Li, Guangxin 李光信. "*Shanxi tongzhi* zhong de shanchuan chongbai" 山西通志中的山川崇拜. *Shihuo banyue kan* 食貨半月刊 4 (3) (1936): 127–39.

Li, Jianmin 李建民. "Zhongguo gudai 'jinfang' kaolun" 中國古代"禁方"考論. *BIHP* 歷史語言研究所集刊 68 (1) (1997): 117–66.

Li, Zhongfu 李中馥. "Liancai haoju 憐才豪舉." In *Yuan Li erzai* 原李耳載. In *Shuoku* 說庫, comp. Wang Wenru 王文濡. Shanghai, 1915; repr. Hangzhou: Zhejiang guji, 1986.

Li, Zhuoran 李焯然. "Lun Donglin dangzheng yu Wanming zhengzhi 論東林黨爭與晚明政治." *BMQS* 明清史集刊 1 (1) (1985): 63–76.

Lian, Ruizhi 連瑞枝. "Qian Qianyi de Fojiao shengya yu linian" 錢謙益的佛教生涯與理念. *Zonghua Foxue xuebao* 中華佛學學報 7 (1994): 317–70.

Liang, Fang-chung. *The Single Whip Method (I-T'iao-Pien Fa) of Taxation in China*. Trans. Wang Yü-ch'uan. Cambridge, MA: Harvard University Press, 1956.

Liang, Qichao 梁啓超 (1873–1929). *Intellectual Trends in the Ch'ing Period* (Qingtai xueshuo gailun 情代學説概論). Trans. with intro. and notes by Immanuel C. Y. Hsü. Foreword by Benjamin I. Schwartz. Cambridge, MA: Harvard University Press, 1959.

Liao, Tengye 廖藤葉. *Zhongguo mengxi yanjiu* 中國夢戲研究. Taipei: Xuesi chubanshe, 2000.

Liao Zhaoheng 廖肇亨. "Xuelang Hong'an chutan: Jianti Dongjing Neige wenku suocang 'Guxianglu' 雪浪洪恩初探: 兼題東京内閣文庫所藏"谷響錄." *Hanxue yanjiu* 漢學研究 14 (2) (December 1996): 35–57.

Lifshitz, Felice. "Beyond Positivism and Genre: 'Hagiographical' Texts as Historical Narrative." *Viator* 25 (1994): 95–113.

Lin, Fushi 林富士. *Guhun yu guixiong de shijie: Bei Taiwan de ligui xinyang* 孤魂與鬼雄的世界: 北臺灣的厲鬼信仰. Taipei: Daoxiang chubanshe, 1995.

———. "Religious Taoism and Dreams: An Analysis of the Dream-Data Collected in the Yün-Chi Ch'i-Ch'ien." *Cahier d'Extrême-Asie* 8 (1995): 95–112.

Lin, Yin 林尹. *Zhouli jinzhu jinyi* 周禮今註今譯. Taipei: Taiwan shangwu yinshuguan, 1972.

Lincoln, Bruce. "Conflict." In *Critical Terms for Religious Studies*, ed. Mark C. Taylor, 55–69. Chicago: University of Chicago, 1998.

Liu, Hui 劉煇, and Yang Yang 揚揚, eds. *"Jin Ping Mei" zhi mi* 金瓶梅之謎. Beijing: Shumu wenxian chubanshe, 1989.

Liu, Ts'un-yan. "Taoist Self-Cultivation in Ming Thought." In *Self and Society in Ming Thought*, ed. William Theodore de Bary, 291–330. New York: Columbia University Press, 1970.

Liu, Xicheng 刘锡诚 et al. *Zhongguo xiangzheng cidian* 中國象征辭典. Tianjin: Tianjin jiaoyu chubanshe, 1991.

Liu, Yangdong 劉仰東. "Jindai zhongguo shehui zaihuang zhong de shen chongbai xianxiang" 近代中國社會災荒中的神崇拜現象. *Xueshu luntan* 學術論壇 2 (2001): 22–26.

Liu, Yuanru 劉苑如. *Shenti, xingbie, jieji: Liuchao zhiguai de changyi lunshu yu xiaoshuo meixue* 身體·性別·階級: 六朝志怪的常異論述與小說美學 (Body, Gender, and Class: The Commonalities and Differences in Fictional Art in Zhiguan Literature of the Six Dynasties). Taipei: Zhongyang yanjiuyuan Zhongguo wenzhe yanjiusuo faxing, 2002.

Liu, Zhixiong 劉志雄, and Yang Jingrong 陽靜榮. *Long yu Zhongguo wenhua* 龍與中國文化. Beijing: Renmin chubanshe, 1996.

Loewe, Michael. *Chinese Ideas of Life and Death: Faith, Myth, and Reason in the Han Period (202 BC–AD 220)*. London: Allen and Unwin, 1982.

———. "The Cult of the Dragon and the Invocation for Rain." In *Chinese Ideas about Nature and Society*, ed. Charles Le Banc and Susan Blader, 195–213. Hong Kong: Hong Kong University Press, 1987.

Long, Xianzhao 龙显昭. "Wuji chanshi yu Chushan Zhaoqi shiji kaosuo 无际禅师与楚山绍琦史迹考索" (An Historical Examination of Chan Master Wuji and Chushan Zhaoqi). 西南民族大学学报 *Xinan minzu daxue xuebao* (*Journal of Southwest University for Nationalities*) 2 (2006): 91–95.

Lu, Guanzhou. "Taizhou xuepai huasu yanjiu 泰州學派化俗研究." PhD diss., Zhongshan Daxue 中山大學, 2004.

Lu, Hanchao. "Arrested Development: Cotton and Cotton Markets in Shanghai, 1350–1843." *MC* 18 (4) (October 1992): 468–99.

Lü, Miaw-fen 呂妙芬. "晚明《孝經》論述的宗教性意涵：虞淳熙的孝論及其文化脈絡" (Religious Dimensions of Filial Piety Developed during the Late Ming: Yu Chunxi's Interpretation of the *Xiaojing* and Its Cultural Context). *Bulletin of the Institute of Modern History Academia Sinica* 48 (June 2005): 1–46.

———. "Zuowei yishixing wenben di Xiaojing: Ming-Qing renshi Xiaojing shijian di gean yanjiu 做為儀式性文本的《孝經》：明清士人《孝經》實踐的個案研究." Paper presented at the 2006 meeting of the American Academy of Religion, Washington, DC (Nov. 18–21, 2006): 1–26.

Lu, Weijing. *True to Her Words: The Faithful Maiden Cult in Late Imperial China*. Stanford, CA: Stanford University Press, 2008.

Luo, Xiwen. *Compendium of Materia Medica* (*Bencao gangmu*). 6 vols. Beijing: Foreign Languages Press, 2003.

Magnin, Paul. *La vie et l'œuvre de Huisi (515–577): Les origines de la secte bouddhique chinoise du Tiantai*. Paris: École Française d'Extrême-Orient, 1979.

Mair, Victor. *Painting and Performance: Chinese Recitation and Its Indian Genesis*. Honolulu: University of Hawaii Press, 1988.

Mann, Susan. "Widows in the Kinship, Class, and Community Structures of Qing Dynasty China." *JAS* 46 (1) (February 1987): 37–56.

———. "'Fuxue' (Women's Learning) by Zhang Xuecheng (1738–1801): China's First History of Women's Culture." *LIC* 13 (1) (1992): 40–62.

Mao, Wenfang 毛文芳. "Wanming 'Kuangchan' tanlun 晚明「狂禪」探論." *HXYJ* 漢學研究 19 (2) (2001): 171–200.

Marks, Robert B. "'It Never Used to Snow': Climatic Variability and Harvest Yields in Late-Imperial South China, 1650–1850." In *Sediments of Time: Environment and Society in Chinese History*, ed. Mark Elvin and Liu Ts'ui-jung, 411–46. Cambridge: Cambridge University Press, 1998.

Marmé, Michael. "Population and Possibility in Ming Suzhou: A Quantified Model." *MS* 12 (Spring 1981): 29–64.

Mauss, Marcel. *Sociology and Psychology: Essays*. Trans. Ben Brewster. London: Routledge and Kegan Paul, 1979.

Menegon, Eugenio. "Child Bodies, Blessed Bodies: The Contest between Christian Virginity and Confucian Chastity." *Nan Nü: Men, Women and Gender in Early and Imperial China* (Leiden) 6 (2) (2004): 177–240.

Meskill, John, trans. *Ch'oe Pu's Diary: A Record of Drifting across the Sea*. Tucson: University of Arizona Press for the Association for Asian Studies, 1965.

Meyer, Birgit, and Peter Pels. *Magic and Modernity: Interfaces of Revelation and Concealment*. Stanford, CA: Stanford University Press, 2003.

Michihata, Ryōshū 道端良秀. *Bukkyō to jukkyō rinri: Chūgoku bukkyō ni okeru kō no mondai* 仏教と儒教倫理: 中国仏教における孝の問題. Kyoto: Heirakuji shoten, 1968.

———. *Chūgoku Bukkyō to Jukyō rinri kō to no kōshō* 中国仏教と儒教倫理孝との交涉. Vol. 9, 83–101. Tokyo: Shoen, 1985.

———. "Chūgoku Bukkyō to shokuninniku no mondai 中國佛教と食人肉の問題" (Chinese Buddhism and the Problem of Eating Human Flesh). In *Jikaku Daishi kenkyū* 慈覺大師研究, ed. Fukui Kōjun 福井康順, 391–404. Tokyo: Association of the Tendai Sect for Buddhist Studies, 1964; rept., Tokyo: Waseda Daigaku Shuppanbu, 1980.

Miyakawa, Hisayuki 宮川尚志. *Rokuchō shūkyōshi* 六朝宗教史. Tokyo: Kokusho Kankōkai, 1974.

Mizoguchi Yūzō 溝口雄三. *Chūgoku zen kindai shisō no kussetsu to tenkai* 中国前近代思想の屈折と展開. Tokyo: Tōkyō Daigaku Shuppankai, 1980.

McLaren, Anne E. "Constructing New Reading Publics in Late Ming China." In *Printing and Book Culture in Late Imperial China*, ed. Cynthia J. Brokaw and Kai-wing Chow, 152–83. Berkeley: University of California Press, 2005.

Mollier, Christine. *Buddhism and Taoism Face to Face: Scripture, Ritual, and Iconographic Exchange in Medieval China*. Honolulu: University of Hawaii Press, 2008.

Mori, Yasutarō 森安太郎. "Hebo Pingyi" 河伯馮夷. *Kyōtō Joshi Daigaku jinbun ronsō* 京都女子大學人文論叢 10 (1964): 14–23.

Mote, Fredrick W. *Intellectual Foundations of China*. New York: Knopf, 1989.

Mou, Sherry J. "Writing Virtues with Their Bodies: Rereading the Two Tang Histories' Biographies of Women." In *Presence and Presentation: Women in the Chinese Literati Tradition*, ed. Sherry J. Mou, 109–47. New York: St. Martin's Press, 1999.

Mowry, Hua-yuan Li. "Ch'ing-shih and Feng Meng-lung." PhD diss., University of California–Berkeley, 1976.

Muller, Charles. "The Yogācāra Two Hindrances and Their Reinterpretations in East Asia." *JIABS* 27 (2004): 207–35.

Müller, Markus. "Interview with René Girard." *Anthropoetics: Electronic Journal of Generative Anthropology* 2 (1) (June 1996). http://www.anthropoetics.ucla.edu/AP0201/interv.htm (accessed March 28, 2007).

Munakata, Kiyohiko. *Sacred Mountains in Chinese Art*. Urbana: University of Illinois Press, 1991.

Nakayama, Shigeru, and Nathan Sivin. *Chinese Science: Explorations of an Ancient Tradition*. Cambridge, MA: MIT Press, 1973.

Naquin, Susan. "The Baoming Temple: Religion and the Throne in Ming and Qing China." *HJAS* 48 (1) (1988): 131–88.

———. *Shantung Rebellion: The Wang Lun Uprising of 1774*. New Haven, CT: Yale University Press, 1981.

———, and Chün-fang Yü. *Pilgrims and Sacred Sites in China*. Berkeley: University of California Press, 1992.

Narumiya, Kazō 成宮嘉造. "Chūgoku kodai no u ni tsuite" 中国古代の雩について. *Birin ronshū* 美林論集 5 (1978): 1–14.

Nattier, Jan. *Once upon a Future Time: Studies in a Buddhist Prophecy of Decline*. Berkeley: Asian Humanities Press, 1991.

Needham, Joseph, with the research assistance of Wang Ling. *Science and Civilisation in China*. Vol. 2, *History of Scientific Thought*. Cambridge: Cambridge University Press, 1956.

———. *Science and Civilisation in China*. Vol. 5, *Chemistry and Chemical Technology*. Cambridge: Cambridge University Press, 1979–1983.

———. *Science and Civilisation in China*. Vol. 6, *Biology and Biological Technology*, part 6, *Medicine*. Cambridge: Cambridge University Press, 1986.

Nell, Victor. *Lost in a Book: The Psychology of Reading for Pleasure*. New Haven, CT: Yale University Press, 1988.

Ngai, MayYing Mary. "From Entertainment to Enlightenment: A Study on a Cross-Cultural Religious Board Game with Emphasis on the Table of Buddha Selection Designed by Ouyi Zhixu of the Late Ming Dynasty." PhD diss.. University of British Columbia, 2011.

Ngo, Van Xuyet. *Divination, magie, et politique dans la Chine ancienne: Essai*. Paris: Presses universitaires de France, 1976

Nie, Qin 聶欽. *Taishan daoli ji* 泰山道里記 [*An Itinerary of Mount Tai*]. Taipei: Yiwen yinshuguan, 1968.

O'Connor, Stanley J. "Metallurgy and Immortality at Caṇḍi Sukuh, Central Java." *Indonesia* 39 (April 1985): 52–70.

Ohnuma, Reiko. "The Gift of the Body and the Gift of the Dharma." *HR* 37 (4) (1998): 323–59.

———. *Head, Eyes, Flesh, and Blood: Giving Away the Body in Indian Buddhist Literature*. New York: Columbia University Press, 2007.

Okada Takehiko 冈田武彥. *Ō Yōmei to Minmatsu no jugaku* 王陽明と明末の儒學. Tokyo: Kōmeisha, 1970.

Ong, Robert K. *The Interpretation of Dreams in Ancient China*. Bochum: Brockmeyer, 1985.

Ortner, Sherry. "Is Female to Male as Nature Is to Culture?" In *Woman, Culture, and Society*, ed. Michelle Zimbalist Rosaldo and Louise Lamphere, 67–87. Stanford, CA: Stanford University Press, 1974.

Overmyer, Daniel L. *Folk Buddhist Religion: Dissenting Sects in Late Traditional China*. Cambridge, MA: Harvard University Press, 1976.

———. *Precious Volumes: An Introduction to Chinese Sectarian Scriptures from the Sixteenth and Seventeenth Centuries*. Cambridge, MA: Harvard University Press, 1999.

Paderni, Paola. "Between Constraints and Opportunities: Widows, Witches, and Shrews in Eighteenth-Century China." In *Chinese Women in the Imperial Past: New Perspectives*, ed. Harriet T. Zurndorfer, 258–85. Leiden: Brill, 1999.

Perkins, Dwight H., with the assistance of Yeh-chien Wang, Kuo-ying Wang Hsiao, and Fung-ming Su. *Agricultural Development in China, 1368–1968*. Chicago: Aldine, 1969.

Peters, Larry G., and D. Price-Williams. "Towards an Experimental Analysis of Shamanism." *American Ethnologist* 7 (3) (1980): 397–418.

Peterson, Willard. *Bitter Gourd: Fang I-Chih and the Impetus for Intellectual Change*. New Haven, CT: Yale University Press, 1979.

———. "Confucian Learning in Late Ming Thought." In *The Cambridge History of China*, vol. 8, *The Ming Dynasty*, part 2, ed. Denis Twitchett and John K. Fairbank, 708–88. Cambridge: Cambridge University Press, 1998.

———. "The Life of Ku Yen-wu (1613–1682)." *HJAS* 28 (1968): 114–56; 29 (1968): 201–47.

Plaks, Andrew. "After the Fall: *Hsing-shih yin-yüan chuan* and the Seventeenth-Century Chinese Novel." *HJAS* 45 (2) (1985): 543–80.

———. *The Four Masterworks of the Ming Novel: Ssu ta ch'i-shu*. Princeton, NJ: Princeton University Press, 1987.

Pomeranz, Kenneth. "Water to Iron, Widows to Warlords: The Handan Rain Shrine in Modern Chinese History." *LIC* 12 (1) (1991): 62–99.

Porkert, Manfred. *The Theoretical Foundations of Chinese Medicine: Systems of Correspondence*. Cambridge, MA: MIT Press, 1974.

Porter, Roy. *Greatest Benefit to Mankind: A Medical History of Humanity*. New York: Norton, 1998.

Queen, Sarah A. *From Chronicle to Canon: The Hermeneutics of the Spring and Autumn, according to Tung Chung-shu*. Cambridge: Cambridge University Press, 1996.

Qiu, Zhonglin 邱仲麟. "Buxiao zhi xiao—Tang yilai gegu laioqin xianxiang di shehiushi chutan" 不孝之孝—唐以來割股療親現象的社會史初探 (A Sociohistorical Study of the Phenomenon of "Slicing the Flesh to Heal Parents" from the Tang Dynasty to the Modern Era). *Xin shixue* 新學史 6 (1) (1995): 49–94.

Raphals, Lisa. "Reflections on Filiality, Nature, and Nurture." In *Filial Piety in Chinese Thought and History*, ed. Alan K. L. Chan and Sor-hoon Tan, 215–25. London: RoutledgeCurzon, 2004.

———. *Sharing the Light: Representations of Women and Virtue in Early China.* New York: State University of New York, 1998.

Rawski, Evelyn Sakakida. *Agricultural Change and the Peasant Economy of South China.* Cambridge, MA: Harvard University Press, 1972.

———. *Education and Popular Literacy in Ch'ing China.* Ann Arbor: University of Michigan Press, 1979.

Raz, Gil. "Blood Rites and Pure Covenants: Lineage Construction in Early Daoist Ritual and Narrative." Paper presented at the American Academy of Religion, San Antonio, November 20–23, 2004.

Reischauer, Edwin O., ed. *Ennin's Diary: The Record of a Pilgrimage to China in Search of the Law.* New York: Ronald, 1955.

Rennie, Bryan, and Philip L. Tite. *Religion, Terror and Violence: Religious Studies Perspectives.* New York: Routledge, 2008.

Richey, Jeffrey L. "Ascetics and Aesthetics in the *Analects*." *Numen* 47 (2000): 161–74.

Riley, Jo. *Chinese Theatre and the Actor in Performance.* Cambridge: Cambridge University Press, 1997.

Robbins, Jill. "Sacrifice." In *Critical Terms for Religious Studies*, ed. Mark C. Taylor, 289–90. Chicago: University of Chicago Press, 1998.

Rosemont, Henry Jr., and Roger T. Ames. *The Chinese Classic of Family Reverence: A Philosophical Translation of the Xiaojing.* Honolulu: University of Hawaii Press, 2009.

Rosenlee, Li-Hsiang Lisa. *Confucianism and Women: A Philosophical Interpretation.* Albany: State University of New York Press, 2006.

Rousselle, Aline. *Porneia: On Desire and the Body in Antiquity.* Trans. Felicia Pheasant. Oxford: Blackwell, 1988.

Ruppert, Brian O. "Buddhist Rainmaking in Early Japan: The Dragon King and the Ritual Careers of Esoteric Monks." *HR* 42 (2) (November 2002): 143–74.

Sangren, P. Steven. "Female Gender in Chinese Religious Symbols: Kuan Yin, Ma Tsu, and the 'Eternal Mother.'" *Signs* 9 (1), *Women and Religion* (Autumn 1983): 4–25.

Santangelo, Paolo. *Sentimental Education in Chinese History: An Interdisciplinary Textual Research on Ming and Qing Sources.* Leiden: Brill, 2003.

Sawada, Mizuho 澤田瑞穂. *Hōkan no kenkyū* 寶卷の研究. Tokyo: Kokusho Kankōkai, 1975.

———. *Zōho hōkan no kenkyū* 增補寶卷の研究. Tokyo: Kokusho Kankōkai, 1975.

Scarry, Elaine. *The Body in Pain: The Making and Unmaking of the World.* New York: Oxford University Press, 1985.

Schafer, Edward. *The Divine Woman: Dragon Ladies and Rain Maidens in T'ang Literature.* Berkeley: University of California Press, 1973.

———. "Ritual Exposure in Ancient China." *HJAS* 14 (1/2) (June 1951): 130–84.

Schipper, Kristofer. "The Taoist Body." *HR* 17 (3/4) (February–May 1978): 355–86.

———. "Vernacular and Classical Ritual in Taoism." *JAS* 45 (1) (November 1985): 21–57.

Schopen, Gregory. *Buddhist Monks and Business Matters: Still More Papers on Monastic Buddhism in India*. Honolulu: University of Hawaii, 2004.

———. "Vinaya." In *Encyclopedia of Buddhism*, ed. Robert E. Buswell Jr., 885–89. New York: Macmillan, 2004.

———. *Figments and Fragments of Mahayana Buddhism in India: More Collected Papers*. Honolulu: University of Hawaii, 2005.

Seaman, Gary. "The Sexual Politics of Karmic Retribution." In *The Anthropology of Taiwanese Society*, ed. Emily Ahern and Hill Gates, 381–96. Stanford, CA: Stanford University Press, 1981.

Shahar, Meir, and Robert P. Weller. *Unruly Gods: Divinity and Society in China*. Honolulu: University of Hawaii Press, 1996.

Sharf, Robert. *Coming to Terms with Chinese Buddhism: A Reading of the Treasure Store Treatise*. Honolulu: University of Hawaii Press, 2002.

———. "The Scripture in Forty-Two Sections." In *Religions of China in Practice*, ed. Donald S. Lopez Jr., 360–71. Princeton, NJ: Princeton University Press, 1996.

Shaw, Teresa M. *The Burden of the Flesh: Fasting and Sexuality in Early Christianity*. Minneapolis: Fortress, 1998.

Shigeta, Atsushi 重田徳 (1930–73). "The Origins and Structure of Gentry Rule." In *State and Society in China: Japanese Perspectives on Ming-Qing Social and Economic History*, ed. Linda Grove and Christian Daniels, 335–85. Tokyo: University of Tokyo Press, 1984.

Shirakawa, Shizuka 白川靜 (1910–2006), trans. Kaji Nobuyuki 加地伸行 and Fan Yuejiao 范月嬌. *Zhongguo gudai wenhua* 中國古代文化 (Ancient Chinese Culture). Taipei: Wenjin chubanshe, 1983.

Sieber, Patricia. "Turning Lethal Slander into Generative Instruction: Laws, Ledgers, and Changing Taxonomies of Fictional Production in Late Imperial China." In *The Magnitude of Ming: Command, Allotment, and Fate in Chinese Culture*, ed. Christopher Lupke, 205–24. Honolulu: University of Hawaii Press, 2005.

Sivin, Nathan. *Chinese Alchemy: Preliminary Studies*. Cambridge, MA: Harvard University Press, 1968.

———. *Traditional Medicine in Contemporary China: A Partial Translation of Revised Outline of Chinese Medicine (1972): With an Introductory Study on Change in Present-Day and Early Medicine*. Ann Arbor: Center for Chinese Studies, University of Michigan, 1987.

Smith, Joanna Handlin. *The Art of Doing Good: Charity in Late Ming China*. Berkeley: University of California Press, 2009.

Smith, Jonathan Z. *Imagining Religion: From Babylon to Jonestown*. Chicago: University of Chicago, 1982.

———. "Religion, Religions, Religious." In *Critical Terms for Religious Studies*, ed. Mark Taylor, 269–84. Chicago: University of Chicago Press, 1998.

Smith, Richard J. *Fathoming the Cosmos and Ordering the World: The Yijing (I ching, or Classic of Changes) and Its Evolution in China*. Charlottesville: University of Virginia Press, 2008.

———. *Fortune-Tellers and Philosophers: Divination in Traditional Chinese Society.* Boulder: Westview, 1991.

Snyder-Reinke, Jeffrey. *Dry Spells: State Rainmaking and Local Governance in Late Imperial China.* Cambridge, MA: Published by the Harvard University Asia Center: Distributed by Harvard University Press, 2009.

Sommer, Deborah. "*Xing* 刑." In *RoutledgeCurzon Encyclopedia of Confucianism*, ed. Yao Xinzhong, 694–95. London: RoutledgeCurzon, 2003.

Sommer, Matthew H. *Sex, Law, and Society in Late Imperial China.* Stanford, CA: Stanford University Press, 2000.

———. "Dangerous Males, Vulnerable Males, and Polluted Males: The Regulation of Masculinity in Qing Dynasty Law." In *Chinese Femininities, Chinese Masculinities: A Reader*, ed. Susan Brownell and Jeffrey N. Wasserstrom, 67–88. Berkeley: University of California Press, 2002.

Spence, Jonathan. *The Death of Woman Wang.* New York: Viking, 1978.

Qiu, Xigui. "On the Burning of Human Victims and the Fashioning of Clay Dragons in order to Seek Rain as Seen in the Shang Dynasty Oracle-Bone Inscriptions," trans. K. Fowler. *Early China* 9/10 (1983–1985): 290–306.

Stein, Rolf A. "Avalokiteśvara/Kouan-yin, un exemple de transformation d'un dieu en déese." *Cahiers d'Extrême-Asie* 2 (1986): 17–77.

Sterk, Darryl Cameron. "Chan Grove Remarks on Poetry by Wang Shizhen: A Discussion and Translation." Master's thesis, University of Toronto, 2002.

Stevenson, Daniel B. "Tales of the Lotus Sūtra." In *Buddhism in Practice*, ed. Donald S. Lopez, 427–51. Princeton, NJ: Princeton University Press, 1995.

———. "Nanyue Huisi (515–577): Recollections, Works, and Motifs." In *The Meaning of the Lotus Sūtra's Course of Ease and Bliss*, ed. Daniel B. Stevenson and Hiroshi Kanno, 3–182. Tokyo: Meiwa, 2006.

Strickmann, Michel. *Chinese Magical Medicine.* Stanford, CA: Stanford University Press, 2002.

———. "Dreamwork of Psycho-Sinologists: Doctors, Taoists, Monks." In *Psycho-Sinology: The Universe of Dreams in Chinese Culture*, ed. Carolyn T. Brown, 25–46. Washington, DC: Asia Program, Woodrow Wilson International Center for Scholars; Lanham, MD: Distributed by arrangement with UPA, 1988.

Sutton, Donald. "Consuming Counterrevolution: The Ritual and Culture of Cannibalism in Wuxuan, Guangxi, China, May to July 1968." *Comparative Studies in Society and History* 37 (1) (January 1995): 136–72.

———. "From Credulity to Scorn: Confucians Confront the Spirit Mediums in Late Imperial China." *LIC* 21 (2) (December 2000): 1–39.

———. *Steps of Perfection: Exorcistic Performers and Chinese Religion in Twentieth-Century Taiwan.* Cambridge, MA: Harvard University Asia Center: Distributed by Harvard University Press, 2003.

———. "Prefect Feng and the Yangzhou Drought of 1490: A Ming Social Crisis and the Rewards of Sincerity." *Minsu quyi* 民俗曲藝 143 (3) (June 2004): 19–47.

Swanson, Paul L. "Chih-I's Interpretation of *Jñeyāvaraṇa*: An Application of the Three-Fold Truth Concept." In *Annual Memoirs of the Otani University Shin Buddhist Comprehensive Research Institute*. Vol. 1, 51–72. Kyoto: Ōtani Daigaku Shinshū Sōgō Kenkyūjo, 1983.

Szonyi, Michael. "The Illusion of Standardizing the Gods: The Cult of the Five Emperors in Late Imperial China." *JAS* 56 (1) (February 1997): 113–35.

———. "The Virgin and the Chinese State: The Cult of Wang Yulan and the Politics of Local Identity on Jinmen (Quemoy)." *JRS* 19 (1) (2005): 87–98.

Tanaka, Masatoshi. "Popular Uprisings, Rent Resistance, and Bondservant Rebellions in the Late Ming." In *State and Society in China: Japanese Perspectives on Ming-Qing Social and Economic History*, ed. Linda Grove and Christian Daniels, 79–100. Tokyo: University of Tokyo Press, 1989.

T'ang, Chün-I. "The Development of the Concept of Moral Mind from Wang Yang-ming to Wang Chi." In *Self and Society in Ming Thought*, ed. William T. de Bary, 93–119. New York: Columbia University Press, 1970.

Tao, Siyan 陶思炎. "Qiyu saoqing zhitan" 祈雨掃晴摭談. *Nongye kaogu* 農業考古 3 (1995): 242–47.

Taylor, Rodney L. "The Centered Self: Religious Autobiography in the Neo-Confucian Tradition." *HR* 17 (3/4) (February–June 1978): 266–84.

Taylor, Romeyn. "Official and Popular Religion and the Political Organization of Chinese Society in the Ming." In *Orthodoxy in Late Imperial China*, ed. Kwang-Ching Liu, 126–57. Berkeley: University of California Press, 1990.

Teiser, Stephen F. *The Ghost Festival in Medieval China*. Princeton, NJ: Princeton University Press, 1988.

———. "The Ritual behind the Opera: A Fragmentary Ethnography of the Ghost Festival, A.D. 400–1900." In *Ritual Opera, Operatic Ritual*, ed. David Johnson, 191–223. Berkeley: University of California: Distributed by IEAS, 1989.

———. *The Scripture on the Ten Kings and the Making of Purgatory in Medieval Chinese Buddhism*. Honolulu: University of Hawaii Press, 1994.

———. "The Spirits of Chinese Religion." In *Religions of China in Practice*, ed. Donald S. Lopez Jr., 3–37. Princeton, NJ: Princeton University Press, 1996.

———. *Reinventing the Wheel: Paintings of Rebirth in Medieval Buddhist Temples*. Seattle: University of Washington Press, 2006.

Teng, Zhanneng 腾占能. "Cixi de longwang miao ji qiuyu huodong" 慈溪的龍王及求雨活動. *Zhongguo minjian wenhua* 中國民間文化 5 (1992): 69–79.

Theiss, Janet M. "Dealing with Disgrace: The Negotiation of Female Virtue in Eighteenth-Century China." PhD diss., University of California–Berkeley, 1998.

———. *Disgraceful Matters: The Politics of Chastity in Eighteenth-Century China*. Berkeley: University of California Press, 2004.

Thompson, Laurence G. *Chinese Religion: An Introduction*, 5th ed. Belmont, CA: Wadsworth, 1996.

T'ien, Ju-K'ang. *Male Anxiety and Female Chastity: A Comparative Study of Chinese Ethical Values in Ming-Ch'ing Times*. Leiden: Brill, 1988.

Tong, Chee-Kiong. *Chinese Death Rituals in Singapore*. London: RoutledgeCurzon, 2004.

Topley, Marjorie. "Marriage Resistance in Rural Kwangtung." In *Women in Chinese Society*, ed. Margery Wolf and Roxanne Witke, 67–88. Stanford, CA: Stanford University Press, 1975.

Tsai, Shih-shan Henry. *The Eunuchs in the Ming Dynasty*. New York: State University of New York Press, 1996.

Tu, Wei-ming. "Pain and Suffering in Confucian Self-Cultivation." *Philosophy East and West* 34 (4) (October 1984): 379–88.

Turner, Victor. *The Forest of Symbols: Aspects of Ndembu Ritual*. Ithaca, NY: Cornell University Press, 1967.

———. *The Drums of Affliction: A Study of Religious Processes among the Ndembu of Zambia*. Oxford: Clarendon; London: International African Institute, 1968.

———. *From Ritual to Theatre: The Human Seriousness of Play*. New York: Performing Arts Journal Publications, 1982.

———. *The Ritual Process: Structure and Anti-Structure*. New York: de Gruyter, 1995.

Twitchett, Denis, and Frederick W. Mote, eds. *The Cambridge History of China*, vol. 8, *The Ming Dynasty, 1368–1644*. Cambridge: Cambridge University Press, 1998.

Valantasis, Richard. "Constructions of Power in Asceticism." *JAAR* 63 (1995): 775–821.

Van der Loon, Piet. "Les origines rituelles du théâtre chinois." *Journal Asiatique* 265 (1977): 141–168.

Van Gennep, Arnold. *The Rites of Passage*. Trans. Nicole Belmont. Chicago: University of Chicago Press, 1960.

Van Gulik, R. H. *Erotic Colour Prints of the Ming Period: With an Essay on Chinese Sex Life from the Han to the Ch'ing Dynasty, B.C. 206–A.D. 1644*. Leiden: Brill, 2004.

Vitiello, Giovanni. "The Forgotten Tears of the Lord of Longyang: Late Ming Stories of Male Prostitution and Connoisseurship." In *Linked Faiths: Essays on Chinese Religions and Traditional Culture in Honour of Kristofer Schipper*, ed. Jan A. M. De Meyer and Peter M. Engelfriet, 227–47. Leiden: Brill, 2000.

Von Glahn, Richard. "Municipal Reform and Urban Social Conflict." *JAS* 50 (2) (May 1991): 280–307.

Wakeman, Frederick, Jr. "Price of Autonomy: Intellectuals in Ming and Ch'ing Politics." *Daedalus* 101 (Spring 1972): 35–70.

Waley, Arthur. "Notes on Chinese Alchemy (Supplementary to Johnson's 'A Study of Chinese Alchemy')." *BSOS* 6 (1) (1930): 1–24.

———. *The Nine Songs: A Study of Shamanism in Ancient China*. London: Allen and Unwin, 1955.

Waley-Cohen, Joanna. *The Culture of War in China: Empire and the Military under the Qing Dynasty*. London: Tauris, 2006.

Waltner, Ann. "Widows and Remarriage in Ming and Early Qing China." In *Women in China: Current Directions in Historical Scholarship*, ed. Richard W. Guisso and Stanley Johannesen, 129–46. Youngstown, NY: Philo, 1981.

———. "Visionary and Bureaucrat in the Late Ming: T'an-yang-tzu and Wang Shih-chen." *LIC* 8 (1) (1987): 105–33.

———. "Learning from a Woman: Ming Literati Responses to Tanyangzi." *International Journal of Social Education* 6 (1) (1991): 42–59.

Wang, Bomin 王伯敏. *Zhongguo banhua shi* 中國版畫史. Shanghai: Shanghai renmin meishu chubanshe, 1961.

Wang, David Der-wei, and Shang Wei. *Dynastic Crisis and Cultural Innovation from the Late Ming to Late Qing and Beyond*. Cambridge, MA: Harvard University Press, 2005.

Wang, Lanyin 王蘭蔭. "Mingdai zhi xiangyue yu minzhong jiaoyu 明代之鄉約與民衆教育." *Shida yuekan* 師大月刊 21 (1935): 103–22.

Wang, Richard. "The Cult of Qing: Romanticism in the Late Ming Period and the Novel *Jiao Hong Ji*." *MS* 33 (August 1994): 12–55.

Wang, Xiaolian 王孝廉. "Huanghe zhi shui—Heshen de yuanxiang ji xinyang chuancheng" 黃河之水—河神的原像及信仰傳承. *Hanxue yanjiu* 漢學研究 8 (1) (1990): 347–62.

Wang, Yuji 王育濟. *Tianli yu renyu* 天理與人欲. Ji'nan: Qi Lu shushe, 1992.

Watanabe, Shinichirō 渡部信一朗. "Kōkyō no seiritsu to sono haikei 孝經の成立とその背景." *Shirin* 69 (1) (1986): 53–86.

Watson, Burton. *The Lotus Sutra*. New York: Columbia University Press, 1993.

———. *The Tso chuan: Selections from China's Oldest Narrative History*. New York: Columbia University Press, 1989.

Welch, Holmes. *The Practice of Chinese Buddhism*. Cambridge, MA: Harvard University Press, 1967.

Weller, Robert P., and Peter K. Bol. "From Heaven-and-Earth to Nature: Concepts of the Environment and Their Influence on Policy Implementation." In *Confucianism and Ecology: The Interrelation of Heaven, Earth, and Humans*, ed. Mary Evelyn Tucker and John Berthrong, 313–41. Cambridge, MA: Distributed by Harvard University Press for the Harvard University Center for the Study of World Religions, 1998.

Wen, Chongyi 文崇一. "*Jiuge* zhong Hebo zhi yanjiu" 九歌中河伯之研究. *Zhongyang yanjiuyuan Minzuxue yanjiusuo jikan* 中央研究院民族學研究所集刊 9 (1960): 139–62.

Werner, Edward T. C. (1864–1954). *A Dictionary of Chinese Mythology*. Shanghai: Kelly and Walsh, 1932.

White, Douglas Alan. "Interpretations of the Central Concept of the *I-Ching* during the Han, Sung, and Ming Dynasties." PhD diss.. Harvard University, 1976.

Whitfield, Roderick. *The Art of Central Asia: The Stein Collection in the British Museum*. 3 vols. Tokyo: Kodansha International in co-operation with the Trustees of the British Museum, 1985.

Widmer, Ellen. "The Epistolary World of Female Talent in Seventeenth-Century China." *LIC* 10 (2) (December 1989): 1–43.

Wiens, Mi Chü. "Cotton Textile Production and Rural Social Transformation in Early Modern China." *JICSCUHK* 7 (2) (1974): 515–35.

———. "Socioeconomic Change during the Ming Dynasty in Kiangnan Area." PhD diss., Harvard University, 1973.

Williams, Raymond. *Marxism and Literature*. Oxford: Oxford University Press, 1977.

Wilson, Liz. "Ascetic Practices." In *The Encyclopedia of Buddhism*, ed. Robert E. Buswell Jr., 32–34. New York: Macmillan USA, 2004.

Wimbush, Vincent L., and Richard Valantasis, eds. *Asceticism*. New York: Oxford University Press, 1995.

Wolf, Arthur P. "Gods, Ghosts, and Ancestors." In *Religion and Ritual in Chinese Society*, ed. Arthur P. Wolf, 131–82. Stanford, CA: Stanford University Press, 1974.

Wolf, Margery. *Women and the Family in Rural Taiwan*. Stanford, CA: Stanford University Press, 1972.

Wright, Arthur Frederick. "Fo-t'u-teng: A Biography." *HJAS* 11 (3/4) (December 1948): 321–71.

———. "Buddhism and Chinese Culture: Phases of Interaction." *JAS* 17 (1) (November 1957): 17–42.

Wu, Jiang. *Enlightenment in Dispute: The Reinvention of Chan Buddhism in Seventeenth-Century China*. Oxford: Oxford University Press, 2008.

Wu, Pei-yi. "Self-Examination and Confession of Sins in Traditional China." *HJAS* 39 (1979): 5–38.

Wu, Wenzhang 吳文璋. *Wushi chuantong he rujia de shenceng jiegou* 巫師傳统和儒家的深層結構. Gaoxiong: Fuwen tushu chubanshe, 2001.

Wu, Yenna. *Ameliorative Satire and the Seventeenth-Century Chinese Novel, Xingshi yinyuan zhuan: Marriage as Retribution, Awakening the World*. Lewiston, NY: Mellen, 1999.

———. "Moral Ambivalence in the Portrayal of *Gegu* in Late Imperial Chinese Literature." In *Ming Qing wenhua xinlun* 明清文化新論, ed. Wang Chengmian 王成勉, 247–74. Taipei: Wenjin chubanshe, 2000.

Wu, Yi-li. "The Bamboo Grove Monastery and Popular Gynecology in Qing China." *LIC* 21 (1) (June 2000): 41–76.

Xiao, Gongquan (Hsiao, Kung-chüan) (b. 1897). *Rural China: Imperial Control in the Nineteenth Century*. Seattle: University of Washington Press, 1960.

Xu, Shuofang 徐朔方. "Tang Xianzu nianpu" 湯顯祖年譜. In *Xu Shuofang ji* 徐朔方集. Hangzhou: Zhejiang guji, 1995.

Yamamoto, Kosho. *The Mahayana Mahaparinirvana-Sutra: A Complete Translation from the Classical Chinese Language*. 3 vol. Ube, Japan: Karinbunko, 1973–1975.

Yang, C. K. *Religion in Chinese Society: Study of Contemporary Social Functions of Religion and Some of Their Historical Factors*. Berkeley: University of California Press, 1961.

Yu, Anthony C. "'Rest, Rest, Perturbed Spirit!' Ghosts in Traditional Chinese Prose Fiction." *HJAS* 47 (2) (December 1987): 397–434.

Yü, Chün-fang. *Kuan-yin: The Chinese Transformation of Avalokiteśvara*. New York: Columbia University Press, 2001.

———. *The Renewal of Buddhism in China: Chu-hung and the Late Ming Synthesis*. New York: Columbia University Press, 1981.

Yu, Kuang-hong. "Making a Malefactor a Benefactor: Ghost Worship in Taiwan." *Bulletin of the Institute of Ethnology* 70 (Autumn 1990): 39–77.Yuan, Li 苑利. "Huabei diqu qiyu huodong zhong hanba yu zhan hanba yishi" 華北地區祈雨活動中旱魃與斬旱魃儀式. *Sixiang zhanxian* 思想戰線 27 (3) (2001): 116–17.

Zamperini, Paola. "Eros and Suicide in Late Imperial Chinese Fiction." In *Passionate Women: Female Suicide in Late Imperial China*, ed. Paul S. Ropp, Paola Zamperini, and Harriet T. Zurndorfer, 77–104. Leiden: Brill, 2001.

Zeitlin, Judith T. *Historian of the Strange: Pu Songling and the Chinese Classical Tale*. Stanford, CA: Stanford University Press, 1993.

———. "Embodying the Disembodied: Representations of Ghost and the Feminine." In *Writing Women in Late Imperial China*, ed. Ellen Widmer and Kang-I Sun Chang, 242–63. Stanford, CA: Stanford University Press, 1997.

———. "The Life and Death of the Image: Ghosts and Female Portraits in Sixteenth- and Seventeenth-Century Literature." In *Body and Face in Chinese Visual Culture*, ed. Wu Hung and Katherine R. Tsiang, 229–56. Cambridge, MA: Harvard University Asia Center: Distributed by Harvard University Press, 2005.

———. *The Phantom Heroine: Ghosts and Gender in Seventeenth-Century Chinese Literature*. Honolulu: University of Hawaii Press, 2007.

Zhang, Guangqian, trans. *The Peony Pavilion*. Beijing: Foreign Language Press, 2001.

Zhang, Jing 張敬. *Lienü zhuan jinzhu jinyi* 列女傳今註今譯. Taipei: Taiwan shangwu yinshuguan, 1994.

Zhang, Shengyan 張聖嚴. *Minmatsu Chūgoku Bukkyō no kenkyū: toku ni Chigyoku o chūshin to shite* 明末中國佛教の研究: 特に智旭を中心として. Tokyo: Sankibo Busshorin, 1975.

———. *Mingmo fojiao yanjiu* 明末佛教研究. Taipei: Dongchu chu ban she, 1987.

Zhang, Xiumin 張秀民. *Zhongguo yinshua shi* 中國印刷史. Shanghai: Shanghai renming chubanshe, 1989.

Zheng, Peikai 鄭培凱. *Tang Xianzu yu Wanming wenhua* 湯顯祖與晚明文化. Taipei: Yunchen wenhua shiye gufen youxian gongsi, 1995.

Zheng, Run 鄭閏. *Jin Ping Mei he Tu Long* 金瓶梅和屠龍. Shanghai: Xielin chubanshe, 1994.

Zhong, Zhaopeng 鍾肇鵬. *Chunqiu fanlu jiaoshi* 春秋繁露校釋. Shijiazhuang: Hebei renmin chubanshe, 2005.

Zhou, Zhiyuan 周致元. "Mingdai Junchen daoyu de zongjiao chanshi" 明代君臣祷雨的宗教阐释. *Anhui daxue xuebao* 安徽大学学报 26 (1) (January 2002): 22–27.

Zou, Yuanjiang 鄒元江. *Tang Xianzu xinlun* 湯顯祖新論. Taipei: Guojia chubanshe, 2005.

Zhougong jiemeng daquan quanshu 周公解夢大全全書. http://toptech.ira.org.tw/dream/05.htm. Accessed Dec. 2, 2011.

Zürcher, Erik. *The Buddhist Conquest of China: The Spread and Adaptation of Buddhism in Early Medieval China*, 3rd ed. Leiden: Brill, 2007.

Index

Page numbers in italics refer to illustrations.

www.ingramcontent.com/pod-product-compliance
Ingram Content Group UK Ltd.
Pitfield, Milton Keynes, MK11 3LW, UK
UKHW021135160926
475595UK00020B/68